CU01454959

UNIVERSITY
of
EXETER
PRESS

University of Exeter Press has pleasure in sending for review

THE BIG SHOW: British Cinema Culture in the Great War 1914-1918
Michael Hammond

Publication date: 10 March 2006
Hardback £45.00/US$85.00   ISBN 0 85989 758 3

A copy of your review would be appreciated

*All UEP titles are available in the USA and Canada through our
North American distributor, The David Brown Book Company,
PO Box 511, Oakville, CT 06779, USA*
phone *800 791 9354 or 860 945 9329* ***fax*** *860 945 9468*
email *david.brown.bk.co@snet.net*
website *www.oxbowbooks.com*

**University of Exeter Press
Reed Hall, Streatham Drive, Exeter EX4 4QR, UK
Telephone +44 (0)1392 263066   Fax +44 (0)1392 263064
uepsales@ex.ac.uk
www.exeterpress.co.uk**

THE BIG SHOW

In writing the definitive account of film exhibition and reception in Britain in the years 1914 to 1918, Michael Hammond shows how the British film industry and British audiences responded to the traumatic effects of the Great War.

The author contends that the War's most significant effect was to expedite the cultural acceptance of cinema into the fabric of British social life. As a result, by 1918, cinema's function had shifted from public service educator to therapeutic pastime, and film-going had emerged as the predominant leisure form in Britain.

Drawing on the cinema culture of Southampton, an important gateway port to the battlefields of Europe, Hammond presents a series of case studies. These allow him to analyse the impact of the depiction of war on audiences, and to assess the cinema's role in managing the traumas and stresses of war on the home front.

Through a consideration of the films, the audience, the industry and the various regulating and censoring bodies, the book explores the impact of the Great War on the newly established cinema culture. It also studies the contribution of the new medium to the public's perception of the War.

Michael Hammond is lecturer in Film in the Department of English at the University of Southampton. He has written extensively on the reception of early cinema in Britain, including a contribution to *Young and Innocent? The Cinema in Britain, 1896–1930*, edited by Andrew Higson (University of Exeter Press, 2002).

Exeter Studies in Film History
General Editors: Richard Maltby and Steve Neale

Exeter Studies in Film History, published in association with the Bill Douglas Centre for the History of Cinema and Popular Culture, is devoted to publishing the best new scholarship on the cultural, technical and aesthetic history of cinema. The aims of the series are to reconsider established orthodoxies and to revise our understanding of cinema's past by shedding light on neglected areas in film history.

University of Exeter Press also publishes the celebrated five-volume series looking at the early years of English cinema, *The Beginnings of the Cinema in England*, by John Barnes.

THE BIG SHOW

British Cinema Culture in the Great War
1914–1918

Michael Hammond

UNIVERSITY
of
EXETER
PRESS

First published in 2006 by
University of Exeter Press
Reed Hall, Streatham Drive
Exeter EX4 4QR
UK
www.exeterpress.co.uk

British Library Cataloguing in Publication Data
A catalogue record for this book is available
from the British Library.

ISBN 0 85989 758 3

Typeset in Adobe Caslon
by JCS Publishing Services

Printed in Great Britain
by Antony Rowe, Chippenham

Contents

Illustrations

Acknowledgements

There are a lot of people to thank. I would first like to thank series editor Richard Maltby for his generosity, patience and for having a quiet confidence in my ability to bring this to completion. Thanks also to Simon Baker whose patience and support in bringing this to publication was essential. Martin Pumphrey and Roberta Pearson both offered invaluable guidance and were always ready to discuss this book with enthusiasm and insight. I want especially to thank Nicholas Hiley whose insight, unfailing interest and support for the project made it possible. Jon Burrows was an immense help in shaping this book. I would also like to thank my colleague and friend Linda Ruth Williams who read and commented on most of this; if there is a good idea or an elegant phrase in here, then it was probably put in at her suggestion. A note of thanks to Andrew Higson whose support and advice was a very valuable source of encouragement. Much of the methodology was discussed in the reading group on reception that was held jointly between the University of Southampton and Southampton Institute; thanks to you all. Cora Kaplan and John McGavin, as heads of the English Department at the University of Southampton, were immensely supportive and encouraging, particularly in the gaining of the research leave required to complete this. I am grateful to Lawrence Napper, Jane Bryan, Jim Cook, David Glover, Sujala Singh, Caroline Blinder and Lucy Hartley who each read some of this and offered helpful comments. Pam Cook, Tim Bergfelder, Lucy Mazdon and Denise Göktürk were especially supportive, offering suggestions and reading drafts of sections. Stephen Bending deserves a special mention for helping me with the illustrations. I would also like to thank Anne Massey for her generous support for this project while I was at Southampton Institute. Thanks are due to my undergraduate and postgraduate students at Southampton Institute and at Southampton University for their enthusiasm for the research projects on British local cinemas I assigned them. I would like to thank all on the organising committee for the annual Silent British Cinema conference held at Nottingham's Broadway Cinema, particularly Laraine Porter and Christine Gledhill. I would like to thank Bryony Dixon and Neil Brand at the NFTVA archive for their consistent support and enthusiasm for this project. A special note of thanks goes to Scott Curtis, now at Northwestern University, who was at the time at the Margaret Herrick Library and found the exhibitors' letters in the Selig Collection for me. I would also like to thank Steven Grace and Joanne Smith at the Southampton Library and Local Archive for sharing their knowledge of the collections and of local history. I owe David Robinson my gratitude for taking time to share some of his collection of Chaplin material. Thanks go to Peter Kramer whose suggestions and comments were incisive and challenging. Peter Stanfield has been a great help in discussing the arguments and the ideas contained here. I would also like to thank Mark Kermode for his support and friendship during the writing of this book. I want to thank Charles Barr for suggesting that I follow my interest in the Great War and British Cinema when I was his MA student at UEA. I must also thank Chris Poole for his knowledge of the popular songs of the period and his ability to sing them.

Parts of this book have appeared as articles in the following journals or collections. A version of chapter 3 appeared as 'Anonymity and Recognition in the British Local Roll of Honour Films (1914–1917)', in *Scope: An Online Film Journal*, Institute of Film Studies, University of Nottingham, available at http://www.nottingham.ac.uk/~aazwww/films/journal/index.htm, December 2000. A version of chapter 5 appeared as "A Soul Stirring Appeal to Every Briton": The Reception of The Birth of a Nation in Britain (1915–1916)', in *Film History*, vol. 11, no. 3, 1999. Finally, a version of chapter 6 appeared as "A Great American Sensation": Thomas Ince's Civilization at the Palladium, Southampton, 1917', in Melvyn Stokes and Richard Maltby, eds, *Hollywood Abroad: Audiences and Cultural Exchange*, (London: BFI, 2004).

A project like this requires a lot of time in archives often far away. I want to thank Katherine Moy for her unselfish hospitality for the five years that I was researching this. Being able to relax after a hard day at the archives in London was a blessing. Betty Bradshaw's generosity with her home and her memories of cinema-going in York helped to give an otherwise unattainable perspective. I also want to thank Frank Simes in Los Angeles for his hospitality and good company, and Betty Lou and Kelly Hammond for putting up with us in San Diego and for sending me video collections of the early Chaplin films.

ACKNOWLEDGEMENTS

I want to thank Sarah Hammond and Alex Hammond who have been a constant source of joy throughout. I suppose the first time I really thought about this subject was when I was introduced to the poets of the Great War. The long route it took to get from there to British cinema audiences and reception is only interesting to me but there is one person who travelled with me. She managed to stay interested and supportive while having two children and a career of her own. She read this whole thing in many different forms and discussed it with me as if she was writing it herself. I owe to her anything good that comes to me: this book is for Mary Hammond.

Introduction

. . . I would dawdle to the brickyard up beyond High Street, 'Prince's Clay-'ole', a stagnant pool among half-quarried wastes, and tie a pebble to the corners of an old handkerchief, swing it high and watch the parachute miraculously waft a loved and fearless girl over the perilous clay cliffs and skeleton-strewn ravines. There, one day in the afternoon sun, I crouched by the lagoon, its shallows ensludged with broken bottles, old boots and dead cats; as other children would have fished for tiddlers, I retrieved from the vile water a wodge of old Hip posters which had been pasted up every week for a year. I scraped off one limp strip after another. *A Daughter of the Gods* Annette Kellerman, *The Beast* George Walsh, *The Birth of a Nation*, The Six Floradora Dancers, *Flame of the Yukon* Dorothy Dalton . . . Carefully I toiled, squatting on the slimy stones and clawing after romance with in my nostrils the smell of decay. Love can go no further.

Emlyn Williams, from *George—An Early Autobiography*, 1961.[1]

[The film business] lives by catering for and reflecting the popular mood, and these moods have been profoundly affected by the war. There has been a change in the type of film demanded by audiences. Films which in pre-war days were thought interesting and amusing are no longer welcome; the tendency is to favour films which would provide distraction from the stress of war conditions. The quiet film, the placid story, does not appeal at the moment to people whose nerves are jangled and strained by worry and loss. They seek distraction with an avidity and a feverishness which is quite natural but not normal. In considering the types of films which find most favour at the present moment, this qualifying factor of abnormal conditions must be born in mind.

Mr F.R. Goodwin, (Chairman of the Cinematograph Exhibitors' Association (London Branch) written testimony given to the Cinema Commission of Inquiry instituted by the National Council of Public Morals, 1917.[2]

These two accounts, separated by almost half a century, offer differing impressions of the impact of cinema in Britain during the Great War.[3] One is an internalised memory of the effect of cinema on one boy's imagination, while the other gives an external account of the effect of a devastating war on British cinema audiences and, therefore, on the industry. To be sure, George Emlyn Williams's passage is nostalgic. Written in 1961, the memory has been elaborated and embroidered as memories are. But if we could imagine his ornate prose as a frame for his memory then that gilt and somewhat gaudy object would not have been out of place hanging in the 'old Hip' or any of the foyers in a high-street cinema during the Great War. Williams's romantic imagery helps to introduce the effect of cinema culture by capturing something of the ephemeral nature of the encounter between the heroic, passionate images passing across the cinema screen and the pungent realities of everyday life. The adventure of the fearless girl and the parachute, the exotic image of a lagoon, contrasts with the industrial and organic detritus of a brickyard in a small Welsh town. The encrusted posters packed together make a whole lump of evenings of entertainment, emblems of an evaporated commodity that, taken together, mean only cinema experience in the abstract. But as each limp strip of paper falls away, one night's memory arises, an image appears through the brown water and mud, specific and unique. This contrast between the individual experience and the clump of repeated visits known as the 'cinema habit' presents us with a metaphor for a dynamic that makes up the unknown (and unknowable) end of the spectrum of cinema culture occupied by the audience. The audiences who disappeared into their own private worlds when the lights went up exist now only in the skeletal remains of past performances, the advertised programmes in newspapers, the songsheets, the memories of those who wrote them down and the films that have survived. Like flesh that has long since fallen from old bones, the audiences made those performances complete.

Although referring to a childhood memory that dates from 1916, Williams's account of the individual effect of the cinema on his childhood and his imagination gives no sense of the impact that the Great War was having on his community. F.R. Goodwin, on the other hand, could not stress the impact of the war strongly enough. By January 1917, when he presented his statement to the cinema commission's inquiry into the effects of cinema on British social life, the patrons of the cinema were not in a normal state of mind; for Goodwin, the impact of the Great War is 'profound' and the cinema is offering a palliative. What is striking about

Goodwin's comment is that he explicitly connected the content of the films themselves with the internal mood of the audience of the time. Moreover. in his construction of the audience, the war was creating an unusual environment, an admission that ran counter to the fact that in the first stages of the war the industry's catchphrase had been 'business as usual'. Goodwin foregrounded the war in his opening statement in order to argue for the positive effects cinema had had on the community during those years. These ranged from the analgesic and the artistically uplifting to the socially responsible. Later in his statement Goodwin pointed to the profound changes that the cinema itself had undergone as an art form. The move from the short two- to five-minute film of the first decade of the century had given way to the 'magnificence and costliness' of films such as *The Birth of a Nation, Cabiria* and *Quo Vadis*. He drew the commission's attention to the positive social effects of this new form of leisure; this had created not only a new audience who were '. . . not in the habit of attending any other places of amusement' but 'provided a centre of social intercourse for thousands who previously spent their evenings drifting about the streets . . .'.[4] His account combined the films, the audiences and the cinema theatre as a social space under one heading, 'the cinema'.

Goodwin and Williams offer two insights into the culture of cinema in Britain that are counterpoised and help to introduce the aim of this book. Williams's memory provides an insight, if anecdotal, into the role cinema played on his active inner life and imagination as a young boy as he responds to the exotic imagery of the cinema. His amnesis regarding the impact of the war reminds us of the continuities of history; cinema was a part of a continuum of entertainment culture and everyday life. Goodwin, on the other hand, gives a compassionate yet externalised account of the impact of the war on the British public and the cinema's role as a welcome distraction. His account hinges on a contemporary shared understanding of the historical moment as a watershed, a break from the past. Cinema here heralds a modern antidote to the terrors of the modern age. Yet both provide a glimpse, however refracted through romanticisation or through the rhetoric of an industry striving for social respectability, of the experience of cinema audiences in Britain during the Great War.

The experiences of audiences expressed by Williams and Goodwin prompt two questions at the centre of this book: how did the Great War affect the development of cinema as a cultural and social entity in Britain, and how might audiences have made sense of the films they saw? These two questions are interlinked. The impact of the war on the British exhibition industry was reflected, as Goodwin points out, in audience preferences; in turn those preferences were the constant concern not only of exhibitors such as Goodwin but also of the other elements in what I term 'cinema culture'. By this I mean a realm of discursive exchange in which film industry producers (both British and international), distributors, exhibitors and subsidiary media such as the fan and trade press as well as the national and local press participate. This definition of cinema culture also includes the official regulating institutions of national and local government and the efforts of 'unofficial' censuring bodies such as reformers and political advocates. It is through the concerns and address of these sectors of cinema culture that it is possible to see how audiences were encouraged to make sense of the films they saw and in turn how 'the cinema', in Goodwin's inclusive meaning, was seen to be affecting audiences . These traces, these records of the way audiences were conceptualised and thought about are the evidence on which this book is based.

Cinema Culture

My use of the term cinema culture draws upon and extends Andrew Higson's concept of a national film culture. Arguing that a study of a national cinema should move beyond the level of production, he highlights three areas of inquiry:

> the range of films in circulation within a nation state; . . . the range of sociologically specific audiences . . . and how these audiences use these films in particular exhibition circumstances; . . . the range of and relation between discourses about film circulating within that cultural and social formation, and their relative accessibility to different audiences . . .[5]

He is pointing to the necessity of recognising the experience of cinema-going as an essential part of a more complete film history. That experience includes not only the films but the surrounding forms and artefacts that make up a cinema culture. These include the information pertaining to cinema in newspapers, such as reviews and advertising, the fan magazines, the cinema auditoria and the various manifestations of censorship and regulation that occur at the local, national and international levels.

I have chosen the term 'cinema culture' rather than 'film culture' in order to emphasise the cultural space of cinema and cinema-going. The three areas Andrew Higson outlines offer a starting point for this study. First, the films that were circulated and distributed in Britain across the four years of the war were predominantly US productions. This period is a crucial moment in the rise to the dominant position that US mainstream films hold in Britain up to the present day. A production-based study of a national cinema would necessarily elide the fact that a large percentage of films viewed by British audiences were from the USA. The benefits of a locally based study are borne out in the second area of 'sociologically specific' audiences and the way in which those audiences used these films. For this reason my analysis of British cinema culture during the war is informed by a specific local focus on cinema culture in the port town of Southampton. This both affords a comparative reference point with other areas in Britain, and allows a focus on the local space as a site of convergence of the international and national practices and discourses associated with cinema. It further allows, through reference to other local areas in England, Scotland, Ireland and Wales, a reasonable account of cinema culture in Britain that does not simply assume that the major cities such as London stand in for the nation, nor that 'England' stands in for 'Britain'. Finally, Higson alludes to the discursive practices inherent within a film culture. Here he focuses on the discourses *about* film, but I shall extend this to include cinema culture as a discursive practice, a place where discourses beyond those associated with cinema are expressed. A salient example is the way in which the front was imagined through the films and the intertextual forms that surrounded them. Cinema culture was a site of the expression of this 'homefront imagination'.

The Changes Wrought by War

Three arguments inform this book throughout: that there was a shift in the industry and more generally towards a more heterogeneous perception of the cinema audience; that the changes in the perception of the war—the 'homefront imagination'—in cinema culture were a part of the dynamic of the discourse of cinema as education or entertainment, and ultimately positioned the social function of cinemas as primarily a site of entertainment rather than information; and finally that the study of the reception/exhibition aspect of British cinema culture must include US films in order to afford a more complete picture of the attempts by cultural institutions to shape audience interpretations and experience at that time. The role of US films is central to this study as this is the moment when the Hollywood industry achieved dominance in the British market.

As a means of demonstrating the changes that took place in cinema culture and illustrating the prevailing attitudes toward cinema's social function during the war years, the book is organised around four areas; local exhibition, the 'homefront imagination' in cinematic depictions of the front, the role of the prestige feature or 'superfilm', and finally the place of comedy in the transforming conceptions of the social function of cinema across the war years .The role played by the exhibitor and the local community in the shaping of cinema culture is the subject of the first two chapters. Here the war provided an opportunity for cinema managers to practise what Leslie Midkiff DeBauche has termed 'practical patriotism'.[6] This refers to the responses of exhibitors who saw the war as an opportunity to aid their attempts to validate the role of cinema in the local community. By shaping their advertising strategies and house management policies to instigate patriotic benefits and programmes that raised the profile of the cinema in the local community, exhibitors contributed to the long-term acceptance of cinema as a socially legitimate form of leisure. These first two chapters concentrate on the cinema culture of Southampton, but the role of the exhibitor informs the book as a whole.

The second area is the 'homefront imagination', or the conception of the front by the industry, the government and the local community, and cinema's role as a place both for the public display of patriotism and as an educational medium for the war effort. Chapter 3 demonstrates that exhibitors had incorporated patriotic programmes such as the local Roll of Honour films from the outset of the war as a means of attracting audiences and as a way of participating in the 'national cause'. As the war dragged on, the national concept of the Roll of Honour changed from a celebration of patriotic endeavour, as it was in the early months of the war, to a memorialising process. In response exhibitors altered their use of these films and, on the whole, had deleted them from their programmes by 1917. Cinema's role as an educational tool for the war effort is outlined in chapter 4. This chapter shows how the War Office Cinematograph Committee chose to release its feature-length actuality *Battle of the Somme* (1916) commercially, combining a profit motive with the industry's desire

6

to promote the educational, and therefore socially legitimate, properties of the medium.

A third area is the discourse of cinema as an art form and the methods by which distributors and exhibitors attempted at times to redirect the meanings of foreign (often US) films for a British audience within a discourse of 'uplift'. This is exemplified in the cases of D.W. Griffith's *The Birth of a Nation* (1915) in chapter 5 and Thomas Ince's *Civilization* (1917) in chapter 6, where promoters attempted to extrapolate a relevant war message from the films' depiction of the effects of war on families.

While both the official war films and the prestige productions like *The Birth of a Nation* were initially popular, the most reliable element of the cinema programme was the comedy short. The role that comedy films played in establishing the cinema as a place where the burdens of everyday life could be relieved for an hour or two is the subject of the final two chapters. The transformative language employed by cinema managers drew from already existing practices in the wider entertainment culture of sport, variety and music hall. Chapter 7 concentrates on the Chaplin phenomenon and traces the use of his films by local exhibitors to ensure a competitive edge over other local cinemas. Chaplin's reception in Britain suggests that while comedy had provoked images of the cinema audience as vulgar, it increasingly came to be seen as having a cross-class appeal through its association with rejuvenation in wartime and through its status among moralists as a more acceptable alternative to 'lurid' society melodramas and crime films. Chapter 8 illustrates these changes by contrasting the melodramatic representation of the front in D.W. Griffith's *Hearts of the World*, partially financed by the War Office, with the comic representation of the trenches in Chaplin's *Shoulder Arms*. The final chapter outlines the comparative success and reception of Chaplin's *Shoulder Arms* and indicates that war-weary audiences, and cinema managers, were more receptive to Chaplin's comic depiction of the front than the tragic reminder of loss in *Hearts of the World*.

Historical Reception

As the book is concerned with exhibition and reception contexts during the Great War, the structure utilises case studies of specific films and film stars as a basis for illustrating general tendencies and trends prevalent at the time. My specific method for this centres around the concept of historical reception studies as outlined by Janet Staiger.[7] The work of reception studies in Staiger's model is to study the 'event of interpretation'. In this she recognises that meanings circulate through the processes of interpretation and that those processes are contingent upon discursive formations that are in turn shaped by historical forces. Cinema culture, including local exhibition examples, is the evidence base for this study. Exhibition strategies at the local level, distribution practices, their interrelationship with the production companies' recommended advertising and the response of regulating bodies such as local councils offer concrete examples of interpretations that seek to direct meaning and encourage audience comprehension. This evidence necessarily requires interpretive work, as it is an exploration of the dynamics of interpretation and their historicisation; in that sense it is subject to the pitfalls of unavoidable subjectivity. However, by asking how audiences were encouraged to engage with the films they saw through the practices of the nascent cinema culture in Southampton specifically and then, comparatively, in Britain, I have attempted to ground those interpretations through using specific case studies and through a process of triangulating the evidence sources. These are: the film text, the intertexts (i.e. reviews, advertisements, newspaper articles), and the historical and cultural forces relevant to the varied circulations, constructions and productions of meanings surrounding the act of cinema-going.

I am aware that the very breadth of the terms 'cultural and historical forces' requires some qualification. The third 'issue' in Andrew Higson's call for an expansion of the concept of film culture provides a starting point. Recognising 'the range of and relation between discourses about film circulating within that cultural and social formation, and their relative accessibility to different audiences', makes it possible to place some limitations on the historical and cultural forces through a focus on 'discourses *about* film'.[8] Specifically, these limitations are productive in that they highlight the industry and those areas of public discourse where debates about film were taking place. This study will, of course, pay significant attention to such discursive practices. However, film is a representational medium through which other discursive practices are expressed and enacted. The period of the Great War simply provides a high-profile example of how cinema sits within a larger set of forms of cultural expression; in this case the discourses associated with total, modern war permeate the film texts and their intertexts. Since reception studies seek 'to understand textual interpretations as they are produced historically',[9] these will necessarily fall beyond the realm of the discourse *about* film to include discourses that the film texts articulate or invoke.

Tropes of Reception

The analysis of reviews and advertising in Staiger's model is primarily concerned with the intertexts, or artefacts of cinema culture that surround the film text. With a few exceptions where contemporary references to film texts are non-existent, I have tried to limit my analysis of the reception of films by using contemporary accounts of the films themselves. These are most abundant in high-profile films such as *The Birth of a Nation*, and in the summaries of films in the trade press. The use of metaphor and references to other media in these accounts have offered a means of determining different types of discourse prompted by the subject matter as well as the form of specific films. Here I borrow the term 'tropes of reception' from Yuri Tsivian. Tsivian is concerned with the way in which early cinema was encountered and written about by the 'educated Russian public', a phenomenon that he terms 'cultural reception'. His concept of a 'trope of reception' is contingent upon the role of intertexts in the act of interpretation. When some Russian critics, writers or novelists encountered the new technology of cinema Tsivian notes that the emphasis was upon the unrealistic nature of the images. The interpretive dynamic, Tsivian suggests, is one of relating these new images to already existing 'tropes' from other forms, often literary: for him '. . . early film reception worked by putting new life into old literary clichés'.[10] He argues that the frame of reference for comprehending these images, for making sense of them, was also drawn from other fictional texts. Like the layers of the posters in Emlyn Williams's memory, each previous text builds upon a lexicon of *probable* interpretive frames.

The use of tropes from literary, theatrical, and cultural forms informs the reception of films. One example will suffice here. The reception of the film *Battle of the Somme* (1916) was marked by the possibility that it offered to its audiences of seeing or recognising on screen someone they knew. The film's intertitles were careful to indicate which regiment was being shown, and local Southampton press accounts of the film's initial reception referred to people recognising their son or brother or father. These factors suggest two levels of expectation. The first is that audiences had been attracted to moving pictures since the earliest days of travelling exhibition by the possibility of seeing themselves on screen. On a second, more elusive level, recognition as a narrative device was prevalent in melodramas and fiction at this time. Such a recognition scene exists in D.W. Griffith's *The Birth of a Nation*. As the Little Colonel lies wounded in a Northern hospital he recognises Elsie Stoneman as the woman whose picture he has held with him throughout the war. In addition, the advertising for *The Birth of a Nation* emphasised a different kind of recognition as it encouraged audiences to 'see a nation reborn as England will be when this war is over'. There are also numerous examples of such tropes in novels like *East Lynne*, theatrical productions such as *Trilby* and of course in films like Chaplin's *The Vagabond* (1916).[11] With *Battle of the Somme* the trope of reception offered is one of recognition, which draws on or indicates a narrative trope that existed across a number of popular fictional forms.

Interpretive Frames

Audiences were also encouraged to make sense of the films they saw through external, often regulatory forces such as local councils and also through reform groups such as the National Council of Public Morals.[12] These types of 'interpretive communities' existed across regional/national and local levels and it is here that the rationale for utilising a local focus on the work unfolds most forcefully. Perhaps the most powerful form of official control over cinemas came with the Cinematograph Act of 1909 that required cinema proprietors to acquire a licence issued by local councils. Ostensibly this was to ensure that safety procedures were adhered to, but the Act was used to regulate the content of the types of films and posters exhibited as well as enforcing Sunday closing in those districts. For example, the Gaiety was a large purpose-built cinema located on the High Street in Southampton. Southampton Council threatened to revoke the cinema's licence because of the objectionable nature of posters that the manager Arthur Pickup had exhibited in the front of the cinema. In determining the propriety of the posters, the council was acting as an official, or authorised, interpreting body. Here is a case where local authorised interpretation was derived from what Annette Kuhn has termed 'legal moralism'.[13]

Other types of interpretive communities that were not invested with official authority but held significant influence locally included the local branch of the National Education League, local school boards, library committees, trade union organisations, the local branch of the Women's

Political and Social Union, and church groups such as the non-conformist Congregationalist Church, or the St Augustine's Church Council.[14] While some of these groups had relatively little direct impact on specific interpretations, they represent manifestations of probable interpretations; through their articulation of discursive positions on specific issues relating to film content they offer identifiable interpretive frames.

Transnational Reception

The fact that the period 1914–18 is part of a larger transitional period in British cinema culture (1911–20), which saw a steady increase in the number of US films on British screens with a commensurate decrease in other foreign films (the percentage of British films for this period actually slightly increases), requires consideration of transnational reception. In their study of the reception of the Vitagraph Quality films in the USA Urrichio and Pearson are concerned with:

> the Film Industry's desire to ally itself with dominant social formations in creating consensual values. The reception of the films might be interpreted in terms of appeals to the assimilationist and upwardly mobile tendencies of the workers and immigrants alleged to have constituted the bulk of the nickelodeon audience.[15]

In a cinema culture where the majority of the films screened are US-based it is crucial to expand or modify their model. What happens when these desires to 'ally' with 'dominant formations' cross the Atlantic? What kinds of differences are there in the dominant social formations in Britain as opposed to the USA? As I will show in chapter 5, these differences are apparent in the case of *The Birth of a Nation* and are actually inscribed, primarily at the levels of production and distribution, where the advertising campaign for the film was tailored specifically for a British audience. 'Assimilation' here is expressed through the 'redirected' interpretations of the reviews and the advertising that encouraged class and national unity through struggle. It draws parallels with 'England' and the USA through the struggle of a nation at war.

There is a need here to state that this book will not include a detailed discussion of the dominant social formations in the USA at this period of time. The significance of the address of the distributors lies in the redirections for a British audience. That said, in order to account for the address of US films it is necessary to reference those forces as they relate to the reception of the films in Britain. The local level provides the point where international and national strategies of address converge with those of the local exhibitor. The geographic relationship of cinemas to communities, combined with the list of programmes and advertising practices that each cinema produced, provides evidence of how they targeted their audience. In turn these exhibition sites negotiate in various ways with the distribution/production agents, with local and national policy and with authorised and 'non-authorised' interpretive communities. Viewed from the side of exhibition this allows a plausible means by which to delineate the formative struggles within cinema culture in Britain, including its transnational relationships—increasingly with US companies—and with forces exerted not only nationally but also internationally. In short, US texts are manifestations of discourses endemic to the USA and the effect of their importation into British cinema culture is a central and necessary concern of this book. The assimilationist intent of *The Birth of a Nation* provides an example that emphasises the way in which the advertising of a US-produced film attempted to redirect the meaning in order to appear relevant to a British market. It also shows, through its exclusionary practice of charging high prices and exhibiting only in the 'finest theatres', an expression of 'high art' discourse. In this regard the mode of address is implicit and readable in the combination of publicity, the pricing and the film text itself.

Horizons of Expectations

Neither historical reception studies nor an exploration of dominant/non-dominant discourses, however, can fully account for interpretive frames that are predicated on the social act of cinema-going or the expectations associated with certain genres. The traditions of cinema-going were a part of an already existing entertainment culture where elements ranging from performance traditions to house management techniques were important to the overall experience, particularly to audience expectations, and therefore the interpretive act. Chaplin's reception in Britain is an illuminating example that is the subject of chapter 7. As an established sketch comedian his popularity in Britain pre-dated his film career and, although he became more widely known as a film star, his early career drew upon techniques and personas familiar to music hall audiences. While Chaplin clearly reached a new audience through the cinema, his star persona circulated not only through fan magazines but was also picked up through the well-established music hall traditions of star circulation, which extended beyond the stage to be incorporated into forms of street culture ranging from children's skipping rhymes to soldiers' songs. Cinema audiences and managers for stars like Chaplin reproduced the dialogic relationship between star and audience that was endemic to music hall and variety. Chaplin imitation contests are only one example of the number of ways, common in variety and music hall, in which managers drew on publicity stunts. British comedian Fred Evans made a habit of travelling with his films; performing live between them capitalised on this relationship. His films' use of intertitles and his direct address to the camera is understandable when seen as being within this dialogic tradition.[16]

These kinds of interrelationships between performers, managers and their audiences help to extend the concept of interpretive frames beyond the boundaries of intertexts to include the social act of cinema-going. At the end of his landmark study of the local area of Lexington, Kentucky, Gregory Waller points out that Staiger's model is 'basically dependent on what has been written about particular films, in other words, on movie reviews and film criticism'. He argues that this approach, dependent as it is upon a model of 'dominant and marginalised interpretive strategies' does not account for what Miriam Hansen has called 'the public dimension of cinematic reception'.[17] Her concept of the public dimension is predicated on a public sphere in transition from the 'relatively autonomous' working-class world of the nickelodeon to the heterogeneous arena of consumer culture, represented by the larger more prestigious picture palaces and the rise of the feature film.[18] Similar transitions in the public sphere had been taking place in Britain since the late nineteenth century. One effective means of charting this shift is the change that took place in the music hall industry in the period from 1880 to 1914, most significantly with the larger music hall syndicates moving towards attracting a middle-class audience. Cinema managers were well aware of the importance of interacting with the community and, since many had come from showmanship backgrounds, they were able to draw on their experiences. After 1914 they were forced to contend with significant demographic shifts brought about by mobilisation and the gearing up of industry for war production. These shifts resulted in the creation of new audiences, particularly soldiers and women workers, and need to be seen as particularly important for high-street cinemas and picture palaces built before the war, which faced stiff local competition. Managers found it necessary to adopt programming strategies that reflected these shifts and in the process anticipated, and attempted to shape, audience expectations. It is through the traces of these strategies that it is possible to determine to a reasonable extent the nature of audience expectations. The war's impact on these factors needs to be taken into account in order to understand the increasing dominance of Hollywood products beyond an economic determinist model.

The focus on the local area of Southampton contributes to this understanding because it provides the 'public dimension' by outlining the developments in the local exhibition sector and its relationship to local institutions. This study differs from Waller's, primarily through its concentration on a comparatively short period of time, 1914–18, rather than providing—as Waller does with Lexington—a detailed study of Southampton's commercial entertainment across the four decades of cinema before sound. The purpose of this local vantage point is to provide a basis for comparison with other cities and local areas in Britain. The fact is that the history of British cinema in this period has received considerably less attention than has US cinema history of the same time. Through its basis in exhibition and reception in Southampton, this book will help to rectify that neglect and contribute to the study of British cinema culture by recognising the international range of films that actual audiences saw.

In summary, this book addresses the question of how audiences were *encouraged* to make sense of the films they saw by focusing on the exhibition sector of the industry and on the wider evidence offered by the artefacts of the cinema culture of the time. This approach allows the consideration of forms of address that originate at the level of production and distribution and also includes the other forms of address that have a bearing on the experience of the film event, such as the advertising and the in-house work of the local exhibitor. It also considers those traditions of management and audience expectation that were derived from the wider entertainment culture. In other words, through its focus on local exhibition, this book tries to determine the way audiences were thought about, not only in the way they may respond to particular films, but also in the way they might expect to use the physical space of the cinema. In doing this I hope to illuminate the details and mechanics of cinema culture in Britain in the Great War, to offer a more multifaceted understanding of the impact of the war on this new form of leisure, and in turn highlight the social function of cinema in the everyday life of its audiences. While it may not be possible to account, as Emlyn Williams does, for the internal effect that cinema culture at this time had on individual memories and imagination, it may be possible, through evidence like the testimony of F.R. Goodwin, to come to some better understanding of the texture of experience of those audiences.

1

Local Tracks
Exhibition Culture in Southampton

When war in Europe broke out in August 1914, Southampton had fourteen cinemas and by the end of the year a further two had opened for business. Apart from one, all of these cinemas were still operating at the end of the war in November 1918. The relatively new form had made significant inroads into the established entertainment culture of the town from the first screenings at the Philharmonic Hall on the High Street in 1897. In line with a nationwide trend there was considerable investment in cinemas in the years 1912–14.[1] These speculative enterprises were undertaken by local businessmen like Percy Vincent Bowyer, whose main interest was in property speculation, and William Dalton Buck, a local builder in the adjacent township of Shirley. William Buck constructed the Atherley, the first purpose-built cinema in the Southampton area in 1912. He managed the cinema himself with his wife leading the orchestra. By contrast, Percy Bowyer was typical of the kind of investment interest that fuelled the national boom in cinema-building. His family were well known in political and business circles: his brother Henry had until recently been Mayor of Southampton and Bowyer himself was an alderman on the town council. He had a number of business interests and property investments, including four cinemas by the autumn of 1914. The first of these was the Carlton, which opened in January 1914 at the northern edge of the retail district in the town. In March 1914 Bowyer bought the Shirley Electric from the Jury Imperial Pictures Company who were divesting their exhibition holdings and in the same month applied for a cinema licence for the newly built Scala on Cobden Bridge in Bitterne. In June he applied for a licence for another new cinema, the Northam Picturedrome, which opened in September 1914.

While William Buck owned and operated his concern, Bowyer, in his role as managing director, brought in showmen, like George Elliot, from outside the town to run his businesses. To attract audiences cinema managers drew upon existing traditions of showmanship that were tailored to specific markets, depending on the cinema's location. Southampton's status as a commercial port meant a considerable turnover of travellers and businessmen, consequently cinemas, like the Alexandra and the Gaiety, located on or near the High Street in the centre of the city depended on passing trade. The cinemas outside the centre, such as the Atherley in Shirley, the Palladium in the middle-class suburb of Portswood and the Picturedrome in the working-class area of Northam, worked to appeal to their local area through programming and house management strategies designed to maintain audiences and encourage the 'cinema habit'.

Between August and December 1914 business practices in both cases shifted dramatically as Southampton changed from a commercial to a military port and became the primary embarkation point for the British forces. Managers and owners also engaged with the complexities of official and unofficial regulation, national and international pressures within the changing production and distribution sectors, and the unpredictability of the changes brought about by the first few months of the Great War. These included temporary but significant local unemployment resulting from the August 1914 closure of the port's commercial activities, the town's main form of industry. This situation was soon alleviated, however, by the influx of troops and related industries. Nevertheless, just as the confidence in cinema as an investment was at its height, the situation of the first months of the war cast an air of uncertainty that did not bode well for entertainment of any kind.

This dramatic shift in economic infrastructure makes Southampton somewhat atypical as few towns and cities experienced the impact of economic and social change on the scale that Southampton did during the first few months of the war. Yet the impact of these changes was, to a greater or lesser degree, eventually felt by every major town and city in the United Kingdom. Southampton's position as the point of primary embarkation and return for troops and the wounded was unique, but in other ways it had similarities with other British cities. For example, the significant number of local men serving at the front was on a par with that of other areas of the country. While Southampton did not share the concentrated loss of local men in the same way that, say, Accrington did in 1916, the overall percentage of dead and wounded local men paralleled most towns in Britain. The position of Southampton as a provincial town makes it comparable with most of the cities and towns outside the larger urban centres of London, Birmingham or Glasgow. Southampton's position for this study then operates as an indicative area of inquiry. The purpose of this chapter is to map out Southampton cinema culture, to bring to life the nature of the challenges faced by cinema owners and managers, highlight the strategies they used to meet those challenges and in the process trace the means by which they understood audience behaviour. This microcosm of Southampton will provide a basis from which to consider cinema exhibition and reception at this time in Britain generally.

'Packed Houses' and 'Beaming Managers': The Local Entertainment Scene

On Easter Monday, 13 April 1914, 'our young man', a journalist for the Southampton amusements paper *What's On in Southampton*, took a trip around the amusements of Southampton in order to see 'thoroughly for himself how Southamptonites disported themselves' on this Bank Holiday.[2] He began in the early morning with a visit to the 'various boat excursions' by the docks, which were 'well patronised'. He fought off the temptation to take one himself and 'miss seeing anything else' and instead stopped off at the office for petty cash to finance his day of leisure reporting. He noticed that the pubs were 'quieter than on an ordinary day, but all the bosses seemed cheerful knowing they would make up for the morning slackness when the boys and girls returned from their various outings'. Still, there was activity in 'two little rendezvous where the little room with the piano going' was doing 'packed business'. These were the Baker's Arms and the Evening Star, both owned by the same host, 'Walter', who 'wore a beaming smile'. The pianos were played by local musicians, featuring a repertoire of traditional tunes as well as popular songs that could be heard at the two large music halls, the Palace or the Hippodrome, or available at one of a number of music shops on or near the High Street, like H.P. Hodges, (where it was also possible to book seats for the Grand Theatre or for some of the High Street cinemas).

The journalist took his lunch at Scullard's, a restaurant and hotel on the top part of the High Street above the old city wall 'bar gate' called 'Above Bar', and then made his way to the Common, a mile north of Southampton city centre. The Common had been a public park since 1844 and at 365 acres was the largest park within the city boundaries at that time. Its centrality for residents of Southampton and adjacent villages and towns made it a popular place for travelling shows and public gatherings. 'Our man' found it to be 'the point of attraction for the afternoon' and 'simply one seething mass of humanity and all the "fun of the fair" ...' He noted that the most popular entertainment was 'the Brothers Beckett's boxing booth', where patrons could watch their friends go a couple of rounds with a professional. Here the phrase 'all tastes were catered for' was used, a standard euphemism for popular entertainment at the time, as distinct from educational or 'cultural' events.

Moving back to the city he found that the parks in the centre were filled with children and their parents, and games of cricket and rounders were the order of the day. After a refreshing cup of tea 'our man' stopped in at the 'various halls and palaces'. The two music halls, the Palace and the Hippodrome, were located on or near the High Street while the Grand Theatre, which brought the latest plays from the West End and Drury Lane, was nearby, just off Above Bar Street. This particular week the Grand was featuring a return visit of *The Whip* (Cecil Raleigh and Henry Hamilton), which had first appeared at Drury Lane on 9 September 1909.

The first stop for 'our man', however, was a cinema, the Alexandra, on Above Bar Street. The 'Alex' had been converted from a concert hall, the Philharmonic Hall, in 1911. The Walturdaw Ltd Co., a London-based film distribution company, had bought the Philharmonic in 1909. They did not undertake the conversion, however, but sold it to the Southampton Picture Palace Ltd, a local firm that renovated and renamed it the Alexandra Picture Theatre. This was the most prestigious addition to their cinema-building enterprise. The already successful Southampton Picture Palace (just off the High Street on East Street) had been converted from a Baptist chapel and opened in May of that same year. At the time of its conversion the Alexandra was the most 'modern and luxurious' in the city, offering roomy plush 'tip-up seats' and conveniently located next to the popular Scullard's Hotel.

As with much of the journalism of *What's On* the description of the conditions at the Alexandra is glowing as the reporter notes that the crowds were waiting to get in all evening.[3] He then found the same standing-room conditions at the Hippodrome and the Palace. He moved north up the High Street, past the newly unveiled monument to the engineers of the *Titanic* in East Park, to the Carlton. The Carlton was located in the upmarket shopping district of London Road and adjacent to Regency-period Carlton Crescent, a well-to-do residential area.[4] The

Carlton cinema was 'packed to suffocation' this particular day and the feature of the programme was *In Mid Atlantic*: 'a drama of the sea'.

The journalist was then faced with a choice as to which direction to take in order to cover fully the possibilities for amusement. The two most significant communities for this were Portswood and Shirley. They lay on either side of the Common, directly north of the High Street. On the western side was Shirley, with a population of 8,651 people, most of whom were clerks or worked as stewards in the liner trade. There were three cinemas there: the Atherley, owned and operated by William Buck, Percy Bowyer's Shirley Electric and the Regent, proprietor William Foster Christmas. On the eastern side was the distinctly middle-class ward of Portswood, population 8,298, bordered to the north by the village of Highfield, where the new building for the university was being built. Located on Portswood Road, the main shopping district for this affluent area, was the Palladium, on its opening in 1913 deemed 'the prettiest picture palace south of London'.[5] Rather than visit either of these districts 'our man' decided to phone the Palladium in Portswood and the 'various houses in Shirley' to hear that they were all 'packed out, thanks for enquiring'.

Covering his assignment by phone in this way allowed the reporter to turn back towards the city centre, where he stopped by the Grand and saw for himself that they were doing a brisk business with the staged production of *The Whip* and its ever-popular rendition of the spectacular train wreck.[6] He then moved on to the cinema houses towards the bottom of the High Street to report that the Kingsland's manager had 'a smile as broad as his shirt front' due to the full house. At the Southampton Picture Palace—just far enough from its new sister cinema the Alexandra, it was hoped, to maximise its share of audiences without directly competing—he caught the eye of Percy Lambert the manager 'over the heads of the struggling crowd' and noted his satisfaction with the day's business.

Finally, his day came to an end with a visit to the Queen's Restaurant at the Royal Pier, which he found 'full of patrons enjoying the excellent music' and particularly enjoyed the addition of the 'cello to the 'little orchestra'. Also on the pier itself was one of the concerts regularly given by the Band of the 11th Hussars, accompanying the famous tenor Frederic Lake. The refreshment room on the pier had recently been refurbished and 'our man' predicted a record summer season for the venue. He ended his report:

Now in conclusion, *re* Southampton generally, why don't the council boom the town as a holiday centre (not of course seaside resort). Knowing thoroughly as we do the kingdom inside out, we cannot call to mind any place with such facilities for interesting excursions, both marine and inland, and apart from these, the unsurpassed historical associations.[7]

Biased as his excursion across Southampton is, the journey nevertheless gives a remarkably clear indication of the accessibility of amusements in the city on the eve of the Great War. The confidence of the local entrepreneurs in the new industry was exemplified by the number of cinemas and the increasing investment in picture palaces with five new fixed-site cinemas opening in 1914, three of them prior to the onset of the war in August. Nevertheless, much of this confidence was based on the value of the building and the property itself that offset the risk of the cinema venture. An example of such risk-spreading is evident in the case of the Shirley Cinema, the sale of which was reported in the regular column on regional cinemas in *The Bioscope* on 2 July 1914:

An important local business deal has been completed during the past week, Mr. John Lewis having disposed of his interest in the Shirley Cinema together with the Shirley Hotel and the Shirley Bowling Green, Mr. William Foster Christmas, representing the Christmas Bros., of the Edinburgh Hotel. The cinema was originally the assembly rooms attached to the hotel, and was converted about eight months ago. The venture was very successful and the hall can boast of a regular set of patrons. Mr. Lewis intends taking a six month's [sic] rest, and will be heard of in the picture world again.[8]

Here is a case of local hoteliers investing in a cinema yet the multipurpose use of the building as part of the hotel gave a sense of security should the cinema craze prove to be temporary.

The size of the cinemas in Southampton at this time ranged between 600 and 1,200 seats and in order to maximise audiences and revenue most house management strategies encouraged multiple use. Consequently managers used words such as 'intimate' or 'cosy elegance' in their advertising. The Carlton, located as it was in the affluent shopping district, provided a tea room, as did the Winchester Picture Theatre to the north of Southampton. These were places that stressed the social utility of the space as part of the cinema-going experience. The Kingsland Picture Theatre was located in the town's busiest market square where much of the overseas produce reached the local populace. This was a central meeting point in the town and this cinema was characterised as a 'popular rendezvous', a stopping-off point for rest and refreshment in the same manner as a hotel or public house. The Northam Picturedrome, recognising its main clientele as working class, encouraged the benefits of the cinema experience at Christmas when it was time for the 'jaded and worn out worker to visit the warm and cosy Picturedrome . . . where there is a special extra holiday programme that at once cheers one up and makes them forget their worries and their troubles for a few hours'.[9]

This kind of product differentiation and target marketing was the result of the considerable competition that existed between local exhibitors in Britain generally. Southampton provides a clear example of the results of the expansion and increase in venues where there was fierce competition at every level for the exhibitor, from securing the most desirable films to providing the kind of environment that would encourage the cinema habit. At the close of 1914, with sixteen cinemas open and each playing three programmes a week, the town was 'well catered for'. This also meant that in order to fulfil the image of 'packed houses' managers had to fill 7,000 seats per day. With the population at 119,000 this meant that potentially fifty per cent of the town's population would have to attend at least once a week in order to keep the cinemas running at a profit. The picture painted of a bustling Easter Monday by the *What's On* reporter was anomalous. A comment a month earlier on the national craze for cinema-building in the fan magazine *Pictures and the Picturegoer* tells a different story:

> Every week we hear of new picture theatres just opening or building or about to be built, and unless there be a builder's strike or some sort of stoppage we shall have more tip-up seats than people to sit on them even if we all become picture-goers. Surely in some districts at least a reasonable limit is being exceeded in this mania for 'running up.' We want enough houses to go round, of course, but in some of these newest palaces (each one is better than the last) nothing is wanted except an audience—apparently a secondary matter at the time of building . . .[10]

This story made tangible the fears expressed by local exhibitors in Southampton the previous December when the Works Committee of the Southampton Council received a letter from Frank Bromley, the manager of the Kingsland Cinema. Bromley drew the council's attention to the

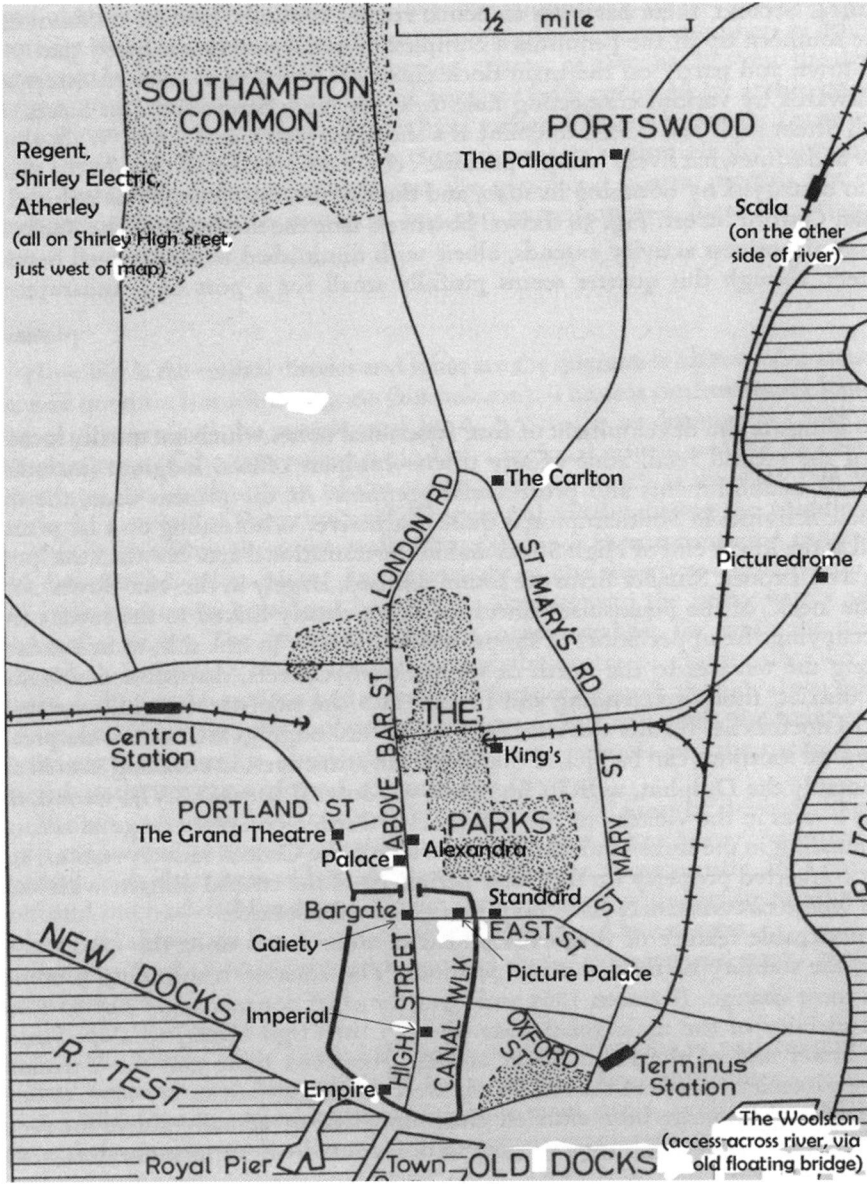

½ mile

SOUTHAMPTON COMMON

PORTSWOOD

The Palladium

Regent,
Shirley Electric,
Atherley
(all on Shirley High Sreet,
just west of map)

Scala
(on the other
side of river)

LONDON RD

The Carlton

ST MARY'S RD

Picturedrome

ABOVE BAR ST

Central
Station

THE

King's

ST MARY ST

PORTLAND ST
The Grand Theatre

PARKS

Alexandra

Palace

Bargate

Standard

Gaiety

EAST ST

Picture Palace

NEW DOCKS

Imperial

HIGH STREET

CANAL WLK

OXFORD ST

R. TEST

Empire

Terminus
Station

The Woolston
(access across river, via
old floating bridge)

Royal Pier

Town

OLD DOCKS

R. ITC

1.1   Southampton map, showing the locations of cinemas and the two music halls, the Palace and the Empire, 1914–18.

large number of entertainment venues being granted licences. His letter was 'on behalf of the existing entertainment caterers asking that a deputation be received by committee to consider the position of the present caterers and the advisability of any further licenses being granted for new or proposed houses of entertainment in Southampton'. The council resolved that they were not prepared to receive a deputation on the matter.[11] This indicated two important factors: the first being that the council was committed to expansion and development and the second that the entertainment and leisure business community were anticipating, and perhaps experiencing, market saturation and seeking official regulation. The council's 'hands-off' attitude had often benefited exhibitors, particularly on the continuing question of Sunday opening, yet this situation placed the cinema managers in the unusual position of arguing for intervention. The onset of the war in August 1914 gave the exhibitors the regulation they had wanted by virtue of the fact that confidence in the future of the exhibition business faltered and in many cases the building plans for larger picture palaces were suspended or abandoned altogether.

'Uncertainty': August 1914

As the summer of 1914 commenced there was every indication that the cinema boom had peaked with the market close to saturation. Summer was a slow time of year for exhibitors and many used this time to cut back on expenditure on overheads, such as advertising, relying instead on front-of-house posters and programme information leaflets. The summer of 1914 was particularly warm and not conducive to sitting in a darkened cinema. The description of the cinema attendance both in the local press and in *The Bioscope* during the months of June and July were upbeat but often qualifying clauses suggested that the summer months were a period to get through with a minimum of loss in the accounts. The review of the Edison talking pictures that were shown at the Alexandra on the High Street indicated that a novelty was necessary to draw patrons into the cinema in the summer: 'The speaking pictures were a great success and were of sufficient novelty to pack the house at every performance despite the weather.'[12] Readers of *What's On in Southampton* were reminded of the Carlton's warmth in the winter and '. . . owing to its system of ventilation every cupful of fresh air is secured with the object of making the place bearable [during] this hot weather . . .'.[13] The national trade press often discussed the problem of summer exhibition and offered solutions, for example, though its policy of reporting the programmes and practices of exhibitors region-by-region in each weekly issue. In the summer of 1914 *The Bioscope* offered information on how cinemas were gearing up for the summer months. The Shirley Cinema, 'a comfortable little hall' was 'fitted with a double roof and electric fans have been installed in each corner of the hall'. It was noted that the Portswood Palladium's manager Mr Urquhart had told the reporter that the owners, Messrs Sydney Bacon and H.J. Hood, '. . . placed a contract for the installation of a multibladed electric fan'. The Scala, apparently without the advantage of cooling fans, inaugurated special prices on Sundays that were 1d cheaper than weekday admission charges.

In spite of the positive rhetoric in the press the complexion of exhibition by August 1914 was one of tense uncertainty, with managers hoping for better business when the weather became cooler and the regularity of the working week became re-established. Unfortunately, the outbreak of the war in the first week of August put paid to any thoughts of business as usual. This was further complicated by the fact that in the first months of the war the port's regular business was seriously curtailed and there was widespread unemployment. This situation prompted the postponement of the building of the town's largest, most prestigious cinema. In July *The Bioscope* had announced the confirmation of plans for 'a new picture theatre on a very elaborate scale', designed by the well-known theatre design firm Messrs Frank Matcham and Co. The cinema was to be on Above Bar Street adjacent to and surrounded by the parks on two sides '. . . and in illustration of the modernity and completeness of the design for the new hall, it may be mentioned that there will be a roof tea garden overlooking the Parks'.[14] This cinema, the Picture House, was built after the war and opened in 1920. Similar plans were postponed across the country and in the metropolis. In Bloomsbury in London the construction of a 1,000-seat luxury hall was postponed and did not open until 1921.[15]

The uncertainty was general across the regions, in spite of *The Bioscope* correspondent's attempt to gloss over the situation. The report from Sunderland and Wearside noted that despite managers 'showing a very brave face' the outlook was 'by no means good'.[16] In Southampton, however, the crisis situation was soon alleviated as the wartime industries of munitions and shipping became established. As early as the second week of August *The Bioscope* held Southampton up as 'an example [of] a town more directly affected by the war than many other centres', but which was not experiencing the kind of drop in audiences generally feared, in spite of the 'diversion of its shipping services'. This was a reference to the government's temporary closing of the harbour and loss of local jobs. Such survival was due to Southampton's status as the main embarkation point for the military. (As a result, by the end of the war 8,149,685 British, Colonial and American troops had passed through and had been billeted in camps on the Common.) This centrality to the war effort kept Southampton cinema culture afloat as the effects of the conflict resonated across the economic and social infrastructure of the community.

If their worst fears did not materialise, exhibitors still faced the fact that the additions to the number of cinemas had increased the competition. This meant that there were more 'tip-up seats' to fill than the previous year. Although, as Nicholas Hiley has shown, there was a steady increase in attendances up to early 1917 nationwide, these increases did not mean full houses.[17] The increase in attendance also hides the significant shifts in markets and social formations that were a consequence of the mobilisation of the military and labour required by the war effort. Women had taken an active role in the city services and the private industries and Southampton was not unique in this respect. Further, as well as being the primary embarkation point for the military, Southampton was also the main port of entry into the country for refugees and prisoners of war. More poignantly it was also the port of entry for returning wounded with 1,117,125 passing through Netley Hospital and the various clearing stations dotted around the outskirts of the city.[18] From the outset the war's pageantry, and its consequences, were evident in Southampton. In the next four years exhibitors would attempt to take account of these shifts as they strove to maximise and maintain audiences.

Local Competition and the Open Market

Exhibitors in each local area were in stiff competition for films as well as audiences. The films were the central part of the programme and a highly visible way of differentiating the experience of each specific cinema. This competition for films was primarily a result of the 'open market system' of booking at the time and the number of film theatres situated in close proximity throughout British towns and cities. With sixteen cinemas and a population of 119,039 the conditions for exhibitors in Southampton were typical.[19] The open market system was the norm, where 'producers sold their films to as many theatres as they could'.[20] This had a number of consequences for local exhibitors. The most sought-after films would often be rented to cinemas in the same districts (hence the use of the term 'exclusive' in amusement papers such as *What's On* indicates that that cinema is the only one in town showing that particular film[21]). The 'shelf-life' of a film was about ninety days, which resulted, as Kristin Thompson has shown, in a pressing requirement for new films as well as a surplus of imported films that were not taken up. The rapid turnover of films created a need for cinema exhibitors to get the product as quickly as possible, and before their local competitors, as the potential audience for films would rapidly dissipate.[22] The Palace music hall, for example, devoted its entire Sunday evening programme to the screening of films that it consistently advertised as 'an excellent programme of FIRST TIME SCREENED pictures'.[23] Exhibitors regularly advertised their success in getting the latest films and managers were often praised for their ability to do so.

Exhibitors obtained their films primarily through rental exchanges that bought copies from production companies. In 1914 few companies had exclusive deals with one rental company, but the whole complexion of film distribution would change over the four years of the war. There were approximately 100 exchanges serving 4,000 theatres with cinema licences. The exhibitors would often work with the same rental exchange but would also go to companies where they could obtain exclusives ahead of their local competitors. While the British market was, in terms of population, smaller than the US, as a result of the rapid consumption of films through the high concentration of outlets in cities and towns and the higher proportion of major first-, second- and third-run cinemas '. . . nearly as many titles would be sold there [in Britain] as in the USA'.[24] Because of this the renters were forced to overcompensate by buying more copies of films than they were realistically able to rent. In short, the exchanges were at the mercy of the supply of the producers and the demand of the exhibitors. Through a desire to stabilise the product and ensure profit, both the exhibitors and the producers, US and British, were to move towards an exclusive distribution system that ultimately resulted in bringing about 'modifications in the British distribution system in the second half of the teens, with manufacturers beginning to rent direct on an exclusive first-run basis by district'.[25]

In addition to the competition for films, exhibitors throughout the war presented their venues as offering a 'rendezvous point', as an accessible public space, although with varying address to different 'classes' of clientele. The environment of the picture theatre was an important means of product differentiation in the face of the number of venues with which each exhibitor had to compete. The 'hot-house' effect of social upheaval brought about by the war gave rise to exhibitors' engagement with new audiences and new social formations that required them not only to draw on existing traditions of showmanship and 'house hospitality' but also to reshape those traditions. In this respect the demographic upheaval recalls the conditions for immigrant audiences in the USA, as described by Miriam Hansen, where 'the cinema offered an horizon that made it possible to negotiate the historical experience of displacement in a new social form'.[26] As exhibitors strove to compete effectively by differentiating the experience of their particular hall through decor, attentive service and 'the value of the show as a live performance over the projection of the film as uniform product', they made possible the 'structural conditions for locally specific, collective formations of reception'.[27] New audience formations were represented by women taking over jobs previously held by men, soldiers on their way to and from the front and, increasingly, middle-class audiences brought in by news films of the war and the spectacular super-films like *The Birth of a Nation*. The evidence of exhibitors' attempts to respond to these shifts traces the transformation in the dominant, official and unofficial, conception of the social function of cinema. These significant social changes in Britain coincided with the US film industry's growing dominance in overseas markets. Nevertheless, these changes were not fully anticipated by Hollywood, initially caught unprepared for the changes brought about by the outbreak of war. Still, Hansen's assertion that the 'American "culture industry" emerges as the hegemonic model for ... mass cultural production and reception in European countries and elsewhere' is compelling. The conditions of reception in towns like Southampton parallel similar conditions in the USA, conditions that, in Britain, were caused and intensified by the effects of the war.

The attractions of the house as an environment of leisure and entertainment and—within certain limitations—the choice of particular films were under the specific control of the exhibitor, in contrast to the ways that the films themselves were becoming increasingly standardised formally at the level of production. The exhibitor as 'showman' was a considerable factor in a particular cinema's 'identity' as it was presented to the public through local press publications such as *What's On*; this expressed itself in the cinema's decor, its front-of-house management, the live music and often in live acts. Exhibitors distinguished between a regular clientele and 'passing trade' and their advertising strategies and overall presentation differed depending upon which audience they sought to attract. What follows is a closer examination of the strategies employed by the Palace music hall and by George Elliot, who managed two of Bowyer's theatres, the Northam Picturedrome in 1914–15 and the Carlton from 1915 to the end of the war. Both the Palace and Elliot utilised the existing showman traditions of publicity and programming as they tried to cope with significant changes in the production/distribution practices, the demographic shifts brought on by the war, and the changes in the way the cinema was perceived by official, and unofficial, public institutions.

Sunday Evening at the Palace

The Palace music hall on Above Bar Street had been showing films as part of its Sunday concert series since 1909. This practice had gradually turned into showing mainly films on Sunday with a few acts between reels. The Palace's policy of first-run films worked effectively between the exhibitor's demand and the exchanges' ability to supply. The booking policy of virtually all the cinemas in Britain by 1914 worked around three programme changes a week: on Mondays, Thursdays and Sundays. The most sought-after films would be in highest demand by cinemas for either the Monday–Wednesday slot or the Thursday–Saturday slot. Few cinema managers were interested in having a potentially popular programme for Sunday only. This was often a variable evening at best.[28] In this case the Palace was able to secure first-run programmes partly because it was able to acquire the films at a time in the week where there was much less competition. Perhaps most important, however, was the fact that the Palace was a part of the MacNaughten Variety circuit run by Frank MacNaughten. Previously known as Gordon's Palace of Varieties, it was renamed the Palace when MacNaughten took it over in 1905. In 1909 MacNaughten made an exclusive arrangement with the Gaumont Company, which he maintained throughout the war.[29] This arrangement and others with distributors such as the Western Import Company, which distributed Keystone comedies, allowed the MacNaughten circuit (which covered most of the provincial regions of England and Wales and some of the most important halls in London, such as Sadler's Wells and the Bow Palace) to offer renters and, in the case of Gaumont, producers the

29

advantage of securing Sunday exhibition outlets on a national scale. As a result, throughout the war the Palace was able to secure first-run films and often the most desirable ones, such as Charlie Chaplin or Mary Pickford films.

In a speech delivered in December 1907 at the Burnley Palace in Warrington Frank MacNaughten stated that he called his halls 'Palaces' and 'Hippodromes' in order 'to draw a distinction between the old "music hall" of the past, frequented by men only, and the new vaudeville entertainment of the present day, to be patronised by women and children'. The Palace provides an important insight into the permeable nature of cinema's 'respectability' and the important relationship between moving pictures as a technology of entertainment and burgeoning art form and the 'status' of the premises in which they appeared. The 'move to respectability', which was a goal of the comparatively new cinema industry, had its antecedent in the music hall's move towards 'revue-style sophistication', which featured sketches and dramatic episodes, the construction of large 'palaces' with ranked-price seating, culminating with the stamp of approval of the Royal Command Performance initiated in 1912.[30] The status of the music halls in the local hierarchy of respectability in Southampton is reflected in the way that *What's On* characterised the role of the entertainment industry in Southampton during the war and the need for the local populace to patronise it.

> There is no doubt that we [Southampton] have too many places of entertainment, if we include the outskirts, which even at the busiest times it is almost impossible to fill. Residents should not forget that the oldest and principal places are the Grand Theatre, Palace and Hippodrome. Then we come to the town picture palaces 'The Alexandra' 'The Southampton Picture Palace' 'Empire', 'The Standard' and the latest 'Kingsland'. All of these places employ a large number of residents . . .[31]

The listing of the Palace and the Hippodrome, along with the Grand Theatre gives an indication of the level of respectability that music halls had achieved by 1914. Frank MacNaughten's statement seven years earlier articulated this elevated status in terms of 'family entertainment'. MacNaughten's circuit, along with Sir Edward Moss' Empire circuit and Sir Oswald Stoll's Tours offered a consistent standardised fare that catered for an audience of some diversity. The price of seating at the Palace for Sunday evenings began at 1s for stalls (1/3 if booked) 6d for circle (9d if booked), 6d for pit stalls (not bookable) and 2d for the gallery. It is the drop from 6d to 2d that is directly competitive with the cinemas if the prices are compared with those at the Gaiety, further down the High Street, which were 1s, 9d, 6d and 3d. The fact that prices for seats were comparable with the prices charged at cinema theatres suggests that, on the High Street at least, the competitive edge for the music hall was the added benefit of the brand of 'quality' associated with the MacNaughten name. The programmes not only included first-run films but also a section of the house orchestra and live performances by the Palace 'star' comics. At the beginning of the war in August 1914 the Palace featured the first screening in Southampton of the Selig serial *The Adventures of Kathlyn*, along with the patriotic *Men of the Moment*, which featured 'scenes of all the various units of the Army, guns of all kinds, flying machines, and various ships of the Fleet, famous generals and admirals, Lord "Bobs", and concluding with Earl Kitchener at Southampton . . .'.[32] This film, reviewed a week later, 'naturally aroused the patriotic feelings of the audience to a pitch of the greatest enthusiasm, showing as it did all our bluejackets and soldiers at work, views of all our Colonial troops and the portraits of public men who are playing a great part in the present European crisis'.[33] The association of first-run features and shorts with the latest war news provided by the Gaumont Graphic and patriotic films and performances signalled the Palace as a place of distinctive entertainment.

The Palace's advertising policies are an example of how audiences were targeted, and in turn conceptualised by both cinemas and music halls. Advisory articles on cinema advertising in trade journals and publications often pointed out the need to recognise different types of audience. In *The Bioscope* in June 1915 an article entitled 'Dressing the Window' appeared as part of a regular 'Talks to Managers' column. Techniques of arranging the front-of-house decor, the display of posters and programme information were discussed as having three objects: '. . . (1) to attract attention to the theatre; (2) to attract attention to the particular entertainment offered by the theatre; and (3) to bring the public inside'. However, the methods recommended needed to be modified to the particular circumstances: 'A floating clientele needs attracting in a different way from a regular clientele, and a high class from a low class public'.[34] These distinctions were carried over into the way the advertisements that appeared in the local press were designed. The Palace, located on the High Street, Above Bar, where 'passing trade' was significant, pitched its advertising accordingly. As well as advertising all of their films as 'first time screened' phrases such as 'first class' and 'first rate' often appear. While this is not necessarily specific to the Palace a fruitful contrast of 'address' is evident in the Northam Picturedrome's advertising strategies that were aimed primarily at the residents of Northam.

The Northam Picturedrome

Northam was a working-class district to the east of the city centre on a bend in the River Itchen. The area had benefited from the boom in the shipping industry in the first decade of the century and had expanded in terms of support industry and manufacturing and housing. The 1911 census records that 11,597 people lived there. Surrounded by water on three sides, it was sectioned off from the rest of the city by the rail track that ran north and south. With only one point of access to the centre of the city, the Northam Bridge, the Northam Picturedrome had little competition from the other areas. The Picturedrome was situated on the corner of Northam Street and Clarence Street directly across from St Augustine's Church. It was the fourth cinema of the local cinema circuit owned by Percy Bowyer. Bowyer's family had been a fixture in local government since the 1890s and his brother Henry had twice been the Mayor of Southampton, and had initiated the Titanic Distress Relief Fund. Bowyer, along with the rest of his family, had a history of land and property speculation and ownership. This relationship between private interests and involvement in local government probably explains why Southampton never adopted Sunday-closing for entertainments. It may also explain why Frank Bromley's deputation in 1913 failed to secure a limitation on new entertainment ventures in the town. In fact, while Bromley's deputation was being received, Bowyer was already committed to the opening of the Picturedrome and the acquisition of the Carlton. Bowyer's position as alderman on the council certainly wielded some influence, although he did not sit on the Works Committee that awarded cinema licences.

In the spring of 1914, while construction of the Picturedrome was underway, the Works Committee received a letter from the St Augustine's Church Council and a copy of a resolution that asked that the Picturedrome be denied the right to open on Sunday '. . . as the premises are opposite the Church, and such exhibitions would tend seriously to interfere with divine worship'. The council's response was 'That the

Church Council be informed of the conditions attached to Sunday Exhibitions'. [35] *The Bioscope* applauded the Works Committee's decision, that they had not '. . . allowed themselves to be influenced by narrow views'.

Bowyer is also reported in *The Bioscope* as having control of the booking procedures for all four of the cinemas, 'Mr. P.V. Bowyer is determined to keep the halls under his control in the forefront of local picture theatres.' [36] His control of programming, however, was soon delegated to his managers. The Picturedrome was opened in September 1914 but did not start to advertise its programme in *What's On* until November. The decision to advertise beyond the boundaries of the local community was probably taken by the new manager, George Elliot, whose arrival was announced in *What's On* in November. Elliot's background was as a showman and the announcement, which he no doubt composed, gave a detailed biography:

> For the past sixteen years Mr. Elliot has piloted the London Lyceum and Aldwych theatrical productions on tour of the principal cities and towns of Great Britain during the winter months and in the more congenial summer weather his energies have been confined to the managerial duties of circus and show life, having been engaged with 'Lord' John Sanger's circus and other shows 'on the road'. [37]

Elliot seems to have been a particularly astute manager and throughout the nine months of his management of the Picturedrome he placed advertisements and commentary in *What's On* that clearly targeted the local populace of Northam. Recognising his constituency as a potentially 'regular clientele' he appealed to the working-class audience through emphasising the atmosphere of the theatre. He attempted to assuage the concern and potential disruption of the St Augustine's Church Council by instigating Sunday evening concerts and courting the child audience through Saturday matinees at 3p.m. He also began to promote his projectionist, William Brimble. In an article, typical of the *What's On* style, the author gives an account of a 'perchance' stop at the Picturedrome:

> Passing along the Northam Road the other evening; and having a couple of hours to share [sic]; the writer popped into the Northam Picturedrome and settled down snugly in the luxurious easy chair, to witness the programme. I was immediately struck with the clearness and steadiness of the pictures and the sharpness of focus, and what

> pleased one most, was the quickness in which the change of pictures
> were made, doing away with the tedious waiting so often experienced
> at picture halls . . .[38]

By stressing the cosy atmosphere and the quality of the image Elliot made use of his significant experience as a showman to emphasise the quality of the theatre and often, in the *What's On* coverage, this emphasis took precedence over the actual film programme.

Elliot also utilised 'star comics' in the manner of music hall, as the Palace did. In his autobiography, Emlyn Williams recalls the kind of acts these were and where they came in the programme in a similar size cinema, the Hippodrome in Flint, North Wales. Following a description of the excitement of a Pearl White serial he is disappointed by 'the Variety sandwiched between the films':

> I was left cold by the comics in front of a painted Chester street with
> the local references—'ee, Ah wuz courtin' t'oother day oop Wepre
> Drive'—to shrieks of local laughter. But I feasted on the occasional
> troupes: The Eight Bing Babies, in their dazzling new Song and
> Dance Scene 'Babes in Toyland', were ladies of seventeen dressed as
> flaxen haired toddlers in tiny frills over biscuit coloured tights,
> holding parasols and tap-dancing in graceful time to the tinny piano.
> . . . After the final number—high kicks in rhythm with the spinning
> parasols, 'There's a Girl . . . for Every Solejah!'— . . .'[39]

'Left cold', perhaps, but Williams's account of the 'shrieks of laughter' suggests he was in a minority, a distinction he is happy to make. But Elliot was attempting to set up a business with a regular clientele. He was 'leaving no stone unturned', in the parlance of the time, to bring audiences in. In addition to the Sunday evening concerts and within weeks of taking the cinema over he held special shows for the war effort. He entertained Belgian soldiers with cigarettes and chocolate and 'Though some of the Belgians were seriously wounded they seemed to enjoy thoroughly the programme and the reception they received'. On Intercession Day, 2 January 1915, he gave the cinema over to the vicar of Northam, the Rev. Percival Scott, for a special service on Sunday, instead of the regular concert programme. In February an advertisement ran that heralded

> . . . the capital programme . . . [which] . . . made the tired and jaded
> workers merry and bright and just fit for the next day's work, thus a

little pleasure now and then is welcomed by the wisest men and during the war crisis an evening's amusement at the Northam Picturedrome decidedly acts as a sure rest cure to the worried worker.[40]

Each of these strategies was an exercise in attempting to embed the cinema into the area as an integral part of the local culture and, through the advertisements, addressed a local, working-class audience.

In February of 1915 Elliot began showing the Selig serial, the *Adventures of Kathlyn*. This had been screened at the Palace beginning in the middle of August 1914. The Palace advertisement at the time stated that 'no one should fail to witness the masterpiece of the cinematograph' and hastened to point out that 'Each of the Kathlyn episodes are complete in themselves'.[41] Five months later the Picturedrome ran the following advertisement which stands out from the type of advertising other houses in Southampton were using:

'Oh I say, Maude, where would you like to go tonight, shall we go for a walk on the common?' 'No Charlie, it's too cold tonight, take me to the Northam Picturedrome where its warm and cosy, and we are sure to see some extra good pictures.' This conversation is frequently overheard, and judging by the continued excellent business at the above hall, it is quite evident that there is more than one who knows where the comfort is.

For the week commencing Feb. 15, Selig's serial wild animal series will be introduced with part one, 'The Unwelcome Throne' shows Kathlyn in a remarkable series of incidents and exciting adventures among the wild animals and war-like tribes, and cannot fail to please the most exacting taste, and no doubt picture-goers will eagerly await the following parts which will be shown week by week.[42]

The series featured Kathlyn Williams as Kathlyn Hare, the daughter of a collector of wild animals (Col. Hare) who has been captured by Prince Umballah, ruler of Allaha, a small principality in East India. Kathlyn travels with her sister to Allaha and the serial is concerned with the many adventures she undergoes while trying to rescue her father. In the advertisement the use of the scenario of the couple is highlighted over the actual description of the serial. The environment is meant to attract in conjunction with the film. This combination differs from the Palace in its emphasis on the young courting couple and the comfort of the theatre. Also the serial itself is advertised as a series of attractions where, through the open ending of each episode, the lack of closure was seen as a selling point. Conversely, the Palace's emphasis was on 'each episode complete in itself'. In the case of the Palace this may reflect a concern that serials were not value for money in the minds of patrons. In a letter to E.H. Montague, the head of Selig's London office, A.S. Strom, manager of the Balsall Heath Picturedrome in Birmingham wrote of the *Adventures of Kathlyn*:

> The above [*Kathlyn*] is undoubtedly to draw particularly to the ladies and the disappointment of the sudden changes are audibly expressed. One patron while booking to see part three asked if that was the finish but when the worker told him there were ten more parts he nearly collapsed. In the worker's opinion [the cinema attendant] it is good but too long.[43]

The properties of the serial format were highlighted in *The Bioscope*'s discussion of the serial film and *Kathlyn* in particular. In this article the serial film was seen as having a double appeal and 'includes both the longest and the shortest plays on record'. Based on 'sound artistic principles' the serial picture had helped to 'substantiate the justness of the parallel which has often been drawn between the cinematograph drama and the novel' and was linked to the serial story and predicted to 'occupy an equally prominent and lasting place in public favour'. The article went on to highlight the many spectacular attractions of the 'adventure', including the wild animals that 'no important Selig film would be really complete without'. This was balanced by an emphasis on narrative structure that stressed, as the Palace advertisement did: 'Each part . . . is a distinct story complete in itself, but no doubt the author, with the ingenuity common to all serial writers, will hint just enough at sensations to come to whet the appetite of his audiences for the following instalments'.[44] The Palace and the Picturedrome emphasised the different properties of the serial identified by *The Bioscope*. The Palace was concerned with assuaging the impression of a 'partial' product while the Picturedrome focused on the spectacular attractions.

This background and Elliot's strategy of using serial films to build an audience brings into relief the intention behind the Picturedrome's advert for the *Adventures of Kathlyn*. For the exhibitor, serials, if successful, were a way of ensuring an audience loyalty to their cinema as well as securing, for the run of the serial at least, a consistent and popular product. So in both directions, maximising audiences and gaining consistent access to product from producers and distributors, the serials provided some stability. But the serials seemed more suited to 'provincial halls'. *The Bioscope*, which found the serials particularly suited to the regular clientele that made up the majority of the provincial cinemas, saw disadvantages for the house that catered to a floating clientele:

> For one thing the audience becomes accustomed both to the events leading up to the particular story and to the characters, and learns to look for the next instalment with the same zest as the regular readers of the latest feuilleton. With the 'continuous' hall it is a somewhat different proposition. Regular patrons are, perhaps, in the minority [with] the greater part of the audience being obviously drawn from passers-by. To them of course the serial does not appeal in anything like the manner it does to the regular patron; and though, happily, each part of the film serial is generally distinct and complete in itself, nevertheless, the story must, to some extent, run throughout the film, and one can hardly be expected to take the same interest in either story or character if neither is conclusive.[45]

The Palace as a music hall, and placed as it was on the High Street, was dependent on the passing trade to a greater degree than the Picturedrome was. Indeed the Palace seems to have dropped the *Kathlyn* series after two episodes. This may have been instigated by a 'railway disturbance' in the last two weeks of August 1914, caused by the influx of military trains into Southampton, but it is more likely that the serial was not proving popular. This is anomalous in light of the fact that the *Kathlyn* series was considerably popular throughout Britain, but it does indicate that different programming strategies anticipated and attracted different audiences. The Palace did, however, return to the serial format in 1916 when it ran Lucille Love in *The Broken Coin*. By this time the audience constituency had shifted to include a larger percentage of young women who had replaced men in clerical positions and had taken up work in nearby factories. A more specific and convincing example of the use of serials to attract the new female audience was that of the Regent in Shirley, which was located near three factories associated with war work where women replaced the predominantly male workforce to a significant degree. In the same week that Elliot had the *Adventures of Kathlyn*, manager William F. Christmas had experienced successful houses with his first serial the Thanhouser production of *The Million Dollar Mystery* (1914).

In addition to providing insights into the use of intertexts the Northam
Picturedrome advertisement presents an amusing yet significant reference
to the use that audiences were encouraged to make of cinemas as a space.
The conversation between Maude and Charlie played out in the
advertisement points to the advantages of the Picturedrome as a place of
comfort. Through analysis of attendance figures and contemporary
accounts of audiences, Nicholas Hiley's work on British cinema audiences
at this time has shown that the cinema offered, apart from the film itself,
other attractions such as the chance to 'meet friends, sit in their favourite
seats, and to enjoy the sensation of being in an audience whilst others
hoped to find the darkness and privacy which they could not enjoy at
home'.[46] The advertisement for the Picturedrome provides a clue, then, to
the type of audience the cinema was addressing. The Common, as we
have seen, was a favourite place for local festivals, fairs and open-air
concerts in the summer. The courting habits of the local populace referred
to in the advertisement suggest that it was also a favoured place for
couples to gain some privacy. The public recognition of courting extended
to the city's advertisement for the uses of its parks. The *Southampton
Annual* of 1902 stated that, as well as spaces for cricketing and football,
there were 'sequestered nooks where young love may babble its dreams
undisturbed and build castles in its Spain which may or may not ever find
inhabitants'.[47] The Common as a place of privacy, however, had other
drawbacks apart from the cold during the winter months: it was over a
mile's walk from the Northam area. Policing the Common was a regular
feature in the chief constable's annual report to the Southampton Watch
Committee. In March 1914 it seemed that the complaints of indecency
on the Common had increased to thirteen from nine the previous year.[48]
While this primarily pertains to women walking unaccompanied, the
advantage of a warm, albeit somewhat dark cinema, with a friendly and
watchful manager and staff offers, as the advertisement indicates, a more
appropriate courting venue. Clearly, by attempting to appeal to courting
couples the Picturedrome offers a safe space as well as a comfortable one.
This concern with darkness and the potential for 'indecency' was the
source of criticism from moral guardians, and much of the 1917 National
Council of Public Morals Cinema Commission's report was taken up
with it. The 'safety' of the darkness in the picture theatre offered the
possibility of relative privacy as well. The chairman of the London branch
of the Cinematograph Exhibitors' Association stated in defence of these
criticisms: 'When investigation is made it is usually found that alleged

misconduct is nothing more than the privileged manifestation of affection between the sexes.'[49]

The Picturedrome, a 500-seat hall, offered the most competitive prices in town with seat prices at 6d, 4d, 3d and 2d. While it may be that the majority of its patrons were from the Northam area, there are compelling reasons to assume that there was a need to draw from the wider population of Southampton, not the least of which was the rising unemployment in the shipping industries at this time and the loss of income represented by men joining the services. The fact that Elliot advertised so extensively in *What's On*, a city-wide publication, suggests that his intention was to widen the cinema's constituency beyond the boundaries of Northam. The newly renovated areas of Simmel Street on the west side of the city behind the High Street and the consistently transient population of workers and sailors associated with the shipping and liner industry provides evidence of a wider 'working-class' constituency.

Nonetheless, at the beginning of the Great War the Picturedrome was almost as large as the High Street cinemas like the Gaiety, which had 800 seats, or the Kingsland Picture Theatre, which had 600. The size of the Picturedrome and Elliot's marketing strategies raise a question of mobility and transport. The range of choice available to cinema-goers at any given time would depend partly upon the accessibility of the cinema in relation to the demographic profile of a particular community and their leisure habits. While the Picturedrome in Northam was convenient for local residents, the High Street was less than a half-mile walk and was also connected by tram. Eight of the sixteen cinemas in the Southampton area were located on or near Above Bar Street with two more, the Palladium in Portswood, near the affluent area of Highfield, and the Scala in St Denys to the north, between half a mile and a mile away. Most of these cinemas were priced competitively during the war with seats ranging from 2d to 6d (although this increased in 1916 with the imposition of the entertainments tax). The advantage of the Picturedrome for a Northam couple was that the price of a tram ride was not included in the night out. It suggests that the address to courting couples was due to that group's willingness to travel farther with a long walk being a pleasurable and cheap part of the evening. The reference to the Common read in this way appeals to a wider group than the Northam community because the Common was at least a mile and a half away and was used by the whole of the city. Later, after Elliot and Brimble had moved to the Carlton on London Road, the management was taken over by Jack Mathers from County Armagh in (Northern) Ireland. The policy of associating the personality of the manager with the hall was continued and was probably a plan agreed with managing director Bowyer. Mathers also had a show business background, having been initially an actor with the Jayson and Montgomery stock company associated with the Alhambra Theatre in Belfast. He had then moved into 'advance work' with theatres and circuses, a similar background to Elliot's. He continued the strategies put into play by Elliot for the next year. Towards the middle of 1917 the Northam's placement of advertisements became more perfunctory and sparse and simply announced the programme with little emphasis on the qualities of the house itself. This was due to the change in management and directorship as Bowyer sold the last of his interest in the group of cinemas he had built up. It is also, though, an indication of the stabilisation of a regular clientele. Oral histories and the continued presence of the Picturedrome (it later became the Queen's and then the Roxy before its closure in 1934) suggest that the Picturedrome's ultimate identity and that of later incarnations was in fact as a typical neighbourhood local cinema.

Mr Elliot Moves to the Carlton

While the Northam was turning a profit Bowyer's other cinemas had not fared so well during the first months of the war. Bowyer responded and reduced his risk by selling his interest in three out the four cinemas in his circuit: the Carlton, the Shirley Electric and the Scala. In each of these cases the cinema licence was transferred, although it is likely that Bowyer and the investment trustees maintained ownership of the property. The Carlton was leased to Mr C.A. Brown, whose first step was to take over from Samuel Apperly as manager. *What's On in Southampton* reported that Apperly was to '. . . have a benefit here on Monday, Dec. 21, where he hopes to see many friends'.[50] While George Elliot was getting his policy underway at the Northam Picturedrome, Apperly was holding a benefit for his own leaving, a tradition which gave friends and patrons a chance to show their goodwill. Unlike Elliot, Apperly was well known to the community. His abilities as a swimmer were well publicised in the local press as he regularly swam the Solent from Southampton to the Isle of Wight. Benefits, or 'bens', were a strong tradition in the music halls 'at which proceeds would be given to a particular member, associate or servant of the Company'.[51] The example of Apperly's benefit shows a simultaneous 'inward and outward' appeal of the hall and illustrates the influence of music hall proprietorship practices on cinema houses at this time. Outward, in terms of the appeal to a 'higher class' audience by 'booming' the quality of the house furnishings and accommodation and of course the quality of the films and the musical accompaniment. Inward in terms of an appeal to the local business that knew Samuel Apperly as a part of the community through his exhibition swims across the Solent and his work as a swimming instructor. In the usual case of benefits the normal prices were raised and the proceeds given to the beneficiary. In the case of Apperly the proceeds were to benefit him as he left the cinema exhibition business.

C.A. Brown's interest in the Carlton was short-lived, however, and the business was bought by George Elliot and Wilfred Brimble. As a contrast to the well-known local figure of Apperly, Elliot and Brimble were professional showmen whose expertise and success at the Picuredrome had given them the confidence to go into part-ownership of the Carlton in June 1915. The previous week *What's On* had announced the change in management. Elliot and Brimble's strategy was to reinvigorate the business by recognising and appealing to the local clientele as they had at the Picturedrome. The Carlton on London Road was in reach of the passing trade experienced by the High Street houses and at the same time was placed in a predominantly middle-class retail district. The demographic shifts that occurred in Southampton during the first year of the war tended to favour the larger High Street halls while the smaller houses, such as the Imperial on Orchard Place, which closed in 1915, suffered the most. Elliot and Brimble's management of the Northam Picturedrome was an exception.

Elliot's strategy to raise the profile of the cinema began with an event, much like a benefit, which accompanied his taking over of the hall. The issue of *What's On* for the week ending 26 June devoted a column to Elliot's arrival:

> Monday June 14, will be long remembered as a red letter day, when the Carlton Picture House opened under the management of Messrs. Elliot and Brimble. Destiny evidently does not mean that the above house should be a failure; and judging from the representative and appreciative audience the tide has turned and the traditions of The Carlton altered from failure to success.[52]

The tradition of the music hall manager as the 'last word' in liberality is evident in the way in which *What's On* presented Elliot and Brimble as 'having a hearty send-off from the jovial and merry host of the Northam Inn, Charlie, and a few of his friends, whose presence certainly added to the gaiety of the evening'.[53] Connecting the tradition of the music hall manager with the older antecedent of the publican, this intimation of 'liberality' not only recommended the house as a place of comfort and quality but also broadened the appeal of the house by accentuating the social value of the manager. Peter Bailey has shown that the public indulgence of luxury and an impression of 'fulsome provision' was part of the presentation of the music hall manager as the 'host of a great feast while simultaneously charging for it'.[54]

In the absence of the provision of alcoholic refreshment, the cinema manager's equivalent to this liberal plenitude was the comfort and decor of the hall and the emphasis on the cinema as a place to take non-alcoholic refreshment in similar surroundings to that of a tea room or a restaurant such as Scullard's. At the Winchester Picture Palace Captain Fletcher opened his tea rooms for refreshment regardless of whether the patrons were there to attend the pictures. During the early months of the war Fletcher opened the rooms to soldiers and supplied them with letter-writing materials and a quiet space in which they could write letters home. Fletcher was later able to negotiate a Sunday opening policy with the strict Winchester Council by gaining the support of the commanding officer, Col. Lord Hardinge. A significant factor here was the general understanding that the cinema would 'provide something ... fairly healthy to the minds of the men' and keep them out of the pubs.[55] Utilising the image of liberality in this way Elliot spoke to the opening-night audience and announced that 'he would leave them to select their own pictures and follow up any suggestions that they liked to make for their amusement and comfort'.[56] He was acting within the traditions of house management, which pre-date the cinema but appealed to patrons of the time. The construction of the cinema space as a socially respectable aspect of the community required dependence on these traditions as the 'fulsome' manager was also the responsible manager on whom the exhibition industry would depend, particularly during the war when the scrutinising gaze of moral authorities, such as the National Council of Public Morals—and to some extent governmental agencies—became actively concerned with the social and psychological effects of cinema on people in general and on children specifically.

The ability of Elliot to provide his patrons with their most desired product was based on his assumption of audience preference. In a fashion similar to his approach to publicity at the Picturedrome he sought to expand his constituency. *What's On* reported on 10 July that he gave sweets to children at Saturday matinees and compared his inspirational management to the story where Robert the Bruce noticed a spider's web, a fable of perseverance and tenacity. He made changes to the front of house that were lauded by *What's On* as they reported that the 'smart attendants see to the patrons as they arrive and conduct them into the comfortable seats'.[57] He soon secured a week-long run of the Moss Empire Ltd London production of *The Midnight Wedding* and advertised it as a 'stirring and romantic military drama, teeming with thrilling scenes and incidents'. The performance was hampered by the breakdown of the cooling fans, which prompted Elliot and *What's On* to announce that the fans 'will be completely fixed and in working order for the coming week [and] will make The Carlton one of the coolest halls in the country'.[58]

The summer of 1915 was, in one respect, a good one for business as it was the months in which the Chaplin craze in Britain was fully established. If the serial was a form that helped Elliot build his clientele at the Picturedrome, Chaplin was the centrepiece in his bid to attract audiences to the Carlton. His ability to move quickly in this direction is exemplified in the coverage in *What's On* of 24 July, where he announced that 'Lovers of Charlie Chaplin will also find their favourite comedian appearing in humorous scenes'.[59] For the rest of the summer Chaplin comedies featured on the programme without the specific titles being

1.2   The Carlton, during Elliot's tenure, from *What's On in Southampton*, week ending 2 October 1915. Note the Chaplin cut-outs on the left and right with the programme board in the centre.

mentioned. (Elliot's front of house featured two life-size Chaplin cut-outs.) Elliot also continued to attempt to attract child audiences by charging 1d and 2d at Saturday matinees.

In a clever combination of attempting to attract children and raising the profile of the cinema as an educational venue, Elliot and Brimble took advantage of an opportunity to further integrate their cinema into the community. The children of the Gladstone Club were rained out of their sports day so Messrs Elliot and Brimble showed three hours of pictures: 'The scholars marched to the Carlton just before two o'clock and many of the adult members accompanied the children. The Carlton was crowded . . . [and] . . . the audience voted it . . . the best entertainment they had ever had.'[60]

By September Elliot was clearly attempting to woo a more 'high-class' audience by emphasising his commitment to exclusive pictures that 'ensure one of originality, freshness of subjects and something far ahead of the old system of cheap films and clap trap style, which will not do for high class audiences'. Chaplin films were a standing feature at this point, which indicates that his films were advertised as a cut above the run-of-the-mill comedy. The emphasis on Elliot and Brimble as a manager and technician who would spare no expense continued in the press through their announcement that Elliot was now 'personally' booking his films direct from the film production companies. This was at the point in early February 1915 when Essanay announced that they would only deal directly with exhibitors, with the Hepworth Company following suit in June.[61] Elliot's publicised commitment to the exclusive system was probably driven by the desire to publicise the theatre as 'exclusive' in terms of its own taste; status thereby incorporating the high-class environment of the hall with 'high-class' product (in October he opened a separate entrance to the luxuriant reserved seats in the balcony). Further coinciding as it does with Essanay's announcement, this enabled Elliot to present himself as a forward-thinking manager, guaranteeing a steady flow of new Chaplin films.

Elliot courted the favour of the community through his use of charity and free shows for wounded soldiers. Every Tuesday was set aside for these programmes. An indication of the elaborate nature of the bill is provided in the account of the 5 October 1915 show. As well as showing the full-length British feature *Harbour Lights* and the usual Chaplins, there was 'excellent singing' by Mrs Moody who sang, 'Somewhere a Voice is Calling', 'The Little Grey Home in the West' and 'Mother Machree', accompanied by Miss Chick 'a clever pianist'. Significantly, the songs were recent hits apart from 'Somewhere a Voice is Calling' which was a 'sacred song'. In addition to the unique combination of live performance and films: 'Several ladies gave their services and looked after the soldiers' comfort, (while) . . . Mrs. Moody . . . generously gave every soldier a nice cigar'.[62]

In the same manner as his strategy of providing the local church committees with space for services on Sunday at the Picturedrome, Elliot announced in the 2 October 1915 edition of *What's On* that he would close his cinema on Sundays, '. . . an wholly altruistic and earnest motive in consideration and for the betterment of the staff and all concerned'.[63] As a counter measure to this he instigated a continuous programme, from 6p.m. to 10.30p.m. with matinees on Wednesdays and Saturdays that began at 2.30p.m. The change to continuous programming suggests that the clientele were more fluid and of the 'passing trade' variety. This is supported by the location of the Carlton, just at the top of the High Street and in a well-to-do shopping district next to Wynton's furniture store, Brown's haircutting salon and a chiropodist that featured electric massage. Elliot's clientele, while they were passing trade in the sense that they did not ritually attend at specific times or day of the week, were regular in that they patronised the shops: hence the value of a continuous programme that accommodated that type of clientele.

The shift in programming policy also allowed longer opening times in the week. The Sunday-opening policy in Southampton was along the same lines as other places in the country that allowed Sunday opening. The cinemas were not allowed to open before 7.45p.m. and were under constant scrutiny by Watch Committees and unofficial groups such as church committees to ensure that programmes appropriate for Sunday were shown.[64] The elaborate musical accompaniment and the use of a number of uniformed attendants in order to maintain the image that Elliot strove for may well have been prohibitively expensive for the few hours of opening on Sunday. The change of policy in October, three months into his proprietorship, also suggests that the preferences of the clientele in this part of the town were such that attendances would not warrant the expense that Sunday opening incurred. The decision to close for the 'benefit' of the staff—while implying a sacrifice on the part of Elliot—had, in the larger strategy towards respectability, a cultural currency that, for Elliot, gave the added attraction of minimising risk on Sunday evening performances.

Elliot and Brimble are an example of how cinema managers, with backgrounds as showmen, actively courted particular clientele in a way that was based on 'producing' their audiences through advertising strategy, cinema decor, house management and special events. The desired effect was to give the impression of a hall that was within the predominant taste parameters of the local area. The choice here of making the house distinct from other houses was to pitch the advertising towards the exclusive, 'high-class' audience. The entertainment of troops and returning wounded, as well as charity benefits for particular causes, were ways in which cinema exhibitors like Elliot were able to position their houses as respectable places for friends and families to attend. The war conditions were incorporated into the creation of house identities and cinema owners utilised the connection with the war as an endorsement of their legitimacy. This utilisation of the image of the house prompted, productively for Elliot and Brimble, their quick response to production trends such as serials, Chaplin comedies and exclusive features. Exhibitors with such a close relationship to their audiences looked to distribution and production companies for guidance and advice but maintained an ability to shape at least partially their reception through their assumptions and negotiations with the taste preferences of their audience.

In November 1916 the Carlton began to push its exclusives policy and explicitly connected the 'exclusive' nature of their films with their audience: '. . . the attractions arranged for the week commencing Monday, Nov. 6, prove that the management . . . are determined to be in the front rank by introducing only first class exclusive features, and their efforts have been rewarded by continuous crowded houses and representative social audiences'.[65] In late 1917 Brimble and Elliot dissolved their association. The Carlton continued to be managed by Elliot, however, under the same set of policies of providing high-class films in a friendly environment. His charity work for soldiers continued throughout the rest of the war. His style of management of cinemas in Southampton is marked by an innovative approach for the period of the war and illuminates the significant shifts that the exhibition sector underwent at this time. His example provides an insight into the development of local cinema culture in Southampton and, by extension, to that of other areas in Britain at this time. He also represents an example of a 'road not taken'. Cinema management publications and the regular columns in the trade press, such as *The Bioscope's* 'The Manager's Bureau', give the impression that the style of 'liberality and conviviality', the publicised sense of ownership, was the preferred method. The emphasis on variety was clearly standard practice, which in some sense made necessary the identification of the cinema with a personality. As the exclusive system began to take hold, and the star system became more firmly established, audiences with a choice such as that offered in Southampton would make choices based on films rather than the house. In the next chapter I explore the programming and marketing strategies of the Gaiety, a themed cinema on the High Street. This cinema provided an environment that offered comfort but an experience of exotic surroundings that complemented the thrills and excitement of the most popular films. This emphasis on the spectating experience rather than manager's personality and liberality anticipated the post-war exhibition strategies of the super cinemas.

2

The Crisis of Total War and New Audiences

When taking a larger national perspective on the health of cinema attendances and the growth of cinema palaces across the war years it is easy to assume that the transition from peacetime to war was simply a matter of 'business as usual'. However, the paradox is that developments within local cinema scenes were swift, with middle-class investors such as the type represented by Bowyer reducing risk as managements and proprietorships changed hands regularly. The uncertainty that characterised the period from August 1914 to the spring of 1915 persisted against a mercurial set of changes in potential audiences as concentrations of soldiers were moved into and out of areas, as staple industries were halted and as women began to replace men in factories and the war industry generally. Three overarching themes that converged with the outbreak of the war emerged: increased competition for audiences, an emphasis on the theatre space as at least equal to the film, and increased competition for films in particular for US products. The highly competitive condition in Southampton was echoed in other towns and cities. In August in the northern town of Sunderland the colliery industry was virtually halted and the always-present scrutiny of authorites became nakedly apparent. *The Bioscope* reporter noted:

> ... the outlook locally is by no means good for some of the establishments . . . stringent economics are being instituted, and more than one place has already decided to close whilst I hear authoritatively that several in the neighbouring colliery villages are also to follow suit. The police authorities are already counselling certain of the managers of halls in the colliery districts to at once cease their Sunday Shows. Vaudeville is also being extensively dropped. One manager in the town was, I may mention, quite surprised the other morning to receive a visit from a 'gentleman in khaki' who inspected the hall and intimated that the Authorities might commandeer it.[1]

In fact these dire predictions were not fully realised. Nevertheless, the changes in audience make-up presented significant challenges to exhibitors and their investors. As George Elliot did, many exhibitors met this with tried and true exhibition strategies that drew upon house management traditions of music hall, emphasising the liberality and good citizenship of the manager. This type of management was best suited to building regular clientele; the transient nature of audiences, particularly in areas that were most affected by the demographic shifts of the war, required innovations that departed from the presentation of the convivial manager.

All of this took place against the background of the shift from the 'open market' of film booking, where managers had a degree of control, to the 'exclusives' method that favoured the production companies and was eventually to result in the advance block-booking policies of the 1920s. Managers such as George Elliot were quick to take advantage of the prevailing patriotic climate and worked to incorporate their houses into the local community by holding charity benefits for war aid and providing special concessions and programmes for soldiers and refugees. In this way managers at the local level were able to use the 'timeliness' of the war to strengthen their case for a positive, and recognised, social function of cinema.

The example of Arthur Pickup, manager of the new Gaiety in Southampton, presents a different approach to cinema management. This chapter will explore how Pickup met the challenges of a transient demographic by highlighting the Gaiety's 'cosmopolitan and imperial image' through an architecture and decor that called up exotic images of empire and a name that mimicked the progressive image of London's West End. Its name, the Gaiety, was taken from the popular London theatre, known for its musical comedy and for its 'Gaiety Girls'.[2] Here I will trace the patterns of address constituted by the film programme, the front-of-house advertising, particularly in the form of posters and the decor and architecture of the cinema itself and how they reflect the unpredictable shifts in audience make-up as they occurred through the first two years of the war.

A Tradition of Public Service

During the first few months of the war its effect on Southampton cinema attendance attracted national trade interest. Using the town as an example that was more extreme than most, in October 1914 *The Bioscope* expressed a concern that the enlistment of young men would create a gap in the regular clientele of cinemas. Characterising Southampton as a town with a high concentration of cinemas and 'having supplied many more men for the country's needs than any other town of its size in the Kingdom . . .', the journalist for *The Bioscope* set the scene to announce the unique success story of the newly opened Gaiety cinema on the High Street.[3] There was indeed a concern that cinemas would suffer during the war and, as we have seen, a number of building projects planned for new picture palaces were either shelved or cancelled altogether. The Gaiety was already well beyond the point of no return in its construction by August 1914 and the proprietors proceeded with plans for opening. As manager, Arthur Pickup had planned a clear strategy for attracting audiences. There was a grand opening by the sheriff of the town, Councillor G. Etheridge, and in attendance were a number of dignitaries from the town council. Mr D.L. Elkin, as spokesman for the proprietors, expressed their hope to 'establish a tradition of public service which would always be maintained by the management'. He went on to point out that 'The ideal of the founders was to provide, not only a place of amusement and entertainment, but to contribute something towards the educational life of the town'. The sheriff, in his address to the crowd gathered for the opening, concurred and congratulated the architect and builders 'on having provided such a handsome building, remarking that it would have an educational value'.[4]

The local press, copy supplied by Mr Pickup, reported the opening of the Gaiety as an addition to the 'growing list' of places of amusement in Southampton and that it would particularly strive to provide 'first time screened' films. In contrast to the expressed concern of *The Bioscope* that the male population was dwindling due to enlistment, Pickup distinctly pitched his cinema towards the 'businessman': 'Centrally situated in the High Street the businessman, besides the leisured classes, will occasionally adjourn to find temporary relaxation from the worry and bustle of his daily calling, as the performances will be continuous from 2pm till 10.45'.[5] The contrast in the local advertising and the national trade press over perceived audiences is revealing. Pickup's strategy for audiences was no doubt devised prior to the outbreak of hostilities. His reconsideration of that strategy, which was almost immediate, is instructive in terms of how the exhibitors coped with the changing demographics brought about by the war. This needs to be understood in terms not only of the perception of audiences by exhibitors but also of the ways in which the cultural boundaries of taste and propriety were negotiated. Pickup was forced to change his strategy to the extent that he found his audience to be primarily women and directed his programming and advertising strategies accordingly. At the same time he never outwardly relinquished the 'educational, moral and patriotic mission of the theatre'.[6]

Elkin announced the basis of this mission at the opening where the proceeds were donated to the Mayor's fund 'for the relief of local distress'. Mayor Henry Bowyer had set up this fund for the relief of the distressed dependants of the crew of *Titanic*. Like Elliot, the directors and the manager of the Gaiety were keen to bolster the image of their cinema as providing a positive contribution to the cultural and moral health of the community, and the choice of contributing to the Mayor's Fund, and not the war effort, was a gesture towards the inhabitants of Southampton specifically and across classes.

At both the Picturedrome and the Carlton, George Elliot's attempts to construct an image of liberality and conviviality through benefits for soldiers and the war effort generally were clearly derived from traditions associated with the 'showmanship' of music hall management. By contrast, Arthur Pickup's strategies looked forward to a kind of *cinema* management style that placed less emphasis on his own personality and instead foregrounded the features and exclusives set within the exotic luxury of the hall itself. Crucial to the difference in style was that Pickup began to develop programming that was dominated by feature films of 'highly coloured' melodramas, or 'pathetics', often with controversial subject matter as their themes. While much of the actual programme was indistinguishable from that of the Carlton, or the luxury suburban cinema, the Palladium in Portswood, the emphasis in the press, and in the front-of-house display, was on this type of pictures. These publicity practices resulted in a complex set of negotiations with the council, officially, and with the unofficial, yet authorised, interpretive communities of the town. In turn these negotiations were reflections of national concerns about the cinema as a public space that were to mark the debates about the social and moral function of the cinema throughout the war.

On that opening day the sheriff's emphasis on the architecture of the building itself set the tone for the local image of the Gaiety by declaring it as having 'educational value'. This remark was prompted by the Gaiety's 'oriental' style of architecture. The description of the decor of the Gaiety in *The Bioscope* is worth quoting at length:

... In design Oriental, it is architecturally one of the features of the Southampton High Street. The hall, which is both spacious and loft, is reached through a large vestibule, and no expense has been spared to make it as comfortable as possible, all the latest improvements have been installed. For instance, electric footlights enable one to take a seat without stumbling over the feet of those who are already seated. The seats themselves are, of course, of the tip-up variety, and are upholstered in red, the remainder of the scheme of decoration being carried out in oak and pale blue. Hand painted panels on the wall add to the charming effect, everything being most pleasing to the eye. A fine wide stone staircase leads to the balcony, outside which is a spacious landing for smoking. A first rate orchestra of six instruments has been engaged under the personal direction of Mr. Ernest Verdi, and there is no doubt that the hall is destined to enjoy a widespread popularity.[7]

Mentions in the national trade press such as this highlight the wider trend towards the ornate palace and the use of themes. The oriental theme has antecedents in theatrical architecture and with the origins of cinema. The Egyptian Hall in Piccadilly, London is the clearest example of the connections between oriental themes and the cinema. Antonia Lant has made a provocative connection between Egyptian themes and their associations with exoticism, death and reanimation, the sensual, the voyeuristic and the cinema: 'The configuring of Egypt with the cinema expressed cinema's twin realist and fantastic character'.[8] The continuing fascination with the 'orient', and Egypt in particular, in the British imperial imagination at the end of the nineteenth century was one avenue in a discursive paradigm that simultaneously allowed the depiction of eroticism within a framework of education and, at times, the aesthetics associated with high art. D.W. Griffith's Babylon scenes in *Intolerance* (US, 1916) are, perhaps, the most well-known example of this.[9] Lant puts it more succinctly: 'By mining the pharaonic archive, the disturbing potential of the cinema to produce pornography through extremely realistic representations of the human body could be diffused, safely channelled, into a distant yet compelling culture, claimed through the imperialism of Egyptology'.[10] The fact that the Gaiety's exterior incorporated a mosque theme merely replaces Egypt for another 'distant yet compelling culture'. The building itself, then, functioned as a means of negotiating desire through the associations with eroticism and the 'oriental' on the one hand and educational 'uplift' on the other.

The Gaiety's architecture was such a significant feature of the hall's identity that a press block accompanied all of the advertising in *What's On* until the 1920s. The block was a detailed sketch of the exterior of the building depicting the twin mosque towers with two smaller mosque towers in between. This engraving also depicted a crowd of well-dressed adults queuing around the block. This visualisation of an ideal audience, consisting of stylishly dressed adults and couples, lends an air of 'modern sophistication' that is distinct from the 'family rendezvous' of the Carlton, or the communal cosiness of the Northam Picturedrome. Added to the exoticism of the architecture was the choice of films. Arthur Pickup's advertising strategy suggests that he was committed to the feature. His commitment is evident, not so much in the actual programme, however, for the Gaiety's was a continuous programme from the outset. Instead of simply playing features at set times he advertised them exclusively, highlighting the upcoming features and briefly mentioning a full programme. Only exceptional shorter-length subjects were mentioned in his advertising. For example, Chaplin's short films were often named but never headlined as they were with other cinemas such as the Carlton or the Southampton Picture Palace.

Cosmopolitan Associations

The Gaiety's namesake was the West End theatre that specialised in musical comedy from the late 1890s up to the war. The Gaiety Theatre in London was well known throughout the country for musical comedies such as *The Gaiety Girl* and *The Shop Girl*. These comedies reflected the steady increase of women in the workplace and celebrated this phenomenon through what Peter Bailey has called 'the rhetoric of the girl'. Setting the plays in workspaces like department stores enabled the writers to exploit 'a locus of everyday life that was already theatricalised'. The department store was also a space where the shop girl could instantly become a consumer and in turn, of course, was consumed and put on display. This was extended to include leisure spaces such as seaside resorts or parks or fairgrounds, spaces that facilitated romantic encounters. The 'rhetoric of the girl' in these romantic comedies characterised the woman as 'naughty but nice' and worked to simultaneously 'sensationalise and contain sexual expression in a manageable form'.[11] These plays contained an element of reflexivity that featured a working woman involved in a romantic relationship with a wealthy man or a man of higher class status.

Bailey has suggested that the audience for these plays were from a wide class constituency. His evidence for this lies in the 'wide media exposure' and their popularity throughout 'the provinces'. The genre sparked fan followings for female stars such as Mabel Russell and Ada Reeves, a media infrastructure and tradition that pre-dated and then co-existed with the star personas of Mary Pickford, Kathlyn Williams or British star Alma Taylor.

These plays made their way round Southampton theatres such as the Grand and the Eastleigh Variety Theatre and were well known to audiences. The Gaiety's name then held 'cosmopolitan' associations that distinguished it from the neighbourhood cinemas. Similar development in the USA emphasised the urban experience of theatre and movie-going as 'the industry standard'. Kathryn Fuller has suggested that the small-town cinema was inadequate for 'consumer-culture-driven fantasies' in terms of decor and film presentation and yet those fantasies were preserved by fan magazines.[12] It is clear that a similar phenomenon was at work in smaller towns in Britain; the place of London in the cultural imagination of the modern urban experience was central, and the type of spectacle associated with consumption and modern women was a particular feature of West End musical comedies.[13] Yet Southampton's status as a port, the influx of troops and the increased number of women in the labour force created a distinctively urban environment. The Gaiety's location on the High Street, although at the edge of the shopping district, reinforced the cosmopolitan image of the cinema. By naming the theatre the Gaiety the proprietors were drawing on an existing urban fantasy that, in tandem with the decor and the films, promised a particular modern experience that was distinct from the 'cosy' image that Elliot had developed with the Carlton and the Northam Picturedrome.

The Programme: 'Intense and Realistic Dramas'

While the cosmopolitan image of the Gaiety's name made reference to the musical comedy of London's West End, the films themselves were less light-hearted. The programming strategy of the first few weeks at the Gaiety is revealing. It was characterised by its emphasis on features that were either a 'pathetic' melodrama, or a war subject, normally a drama but also a place for the longer actualities. A third feature of the programme was the Official War Pictures that played there from its opening to the end of the war. The opening feature was the British and Colonial Company's feature directed by Maurice Elvy entitled *The Loss of the Birkenhead* (1914). Pickup had secured this as an exclusive and gave it its first Southampton screening. In line with the patriotic trend of exhibitors he advertised the film as able to 'arouse not merely their [Britons'] interest and enthusiasm, but their national pride'.[14]

In the following week Arthur Pickup screened *Dealers in Human Lives*, 'a white slave traffic exposure': a film on white slave traffic had particular local resonance and, while tangential to the issue of exhibition strategy, it is worth a brief mention here. The Criminal Law Amendment Bill of 1912 had been dubbed the 'White Slave Traffic Bill' and passed in December of that year. Lucy Bland has recorded how W.T. Stead, the editor of the *Pall Mall Gazette* in the late 1880s, had been influential in the passing of the original Act of 1885, which had 'outlawed brothel keeping and the procurement of women', through publishing articles entitled 'The Maiden Tribute of Babylon'. Stead had died in the *Titanic* disaster and, as Bland notes, Stead's reputation was invoked in order to gain support for the bill. 'For when Stead drowned in the Titanic disaster in April 1912, it was proposed that the Bill should stand as memorial to his memory . . .'.[15] Southampton's relationship to the *Titanic* disaster is of relevance here as a link between national and local identity: in the popular press the town had stood in for the nation as a site of mourning. Significant also was its status as a port for emigration.[16] The international nature of the white slave trade had been a crucial part of the panic as it fed into fears about abduction of English women by foreigners, often identified as Jews. Bland points out that this construction of foreign, and Jewishness, as other added to 'the old anxiety over the dangers of urban life [which] took not simply a racial and class form, but a gendered one too, as young women moved into cities to take up new occupations, with new freedoms, away from the traditional networks of support and control'.[17]

The Gaiety, in its position to the north of East Street just below the Bargate, was, in 1914, at the edge of the retail zone. Below East Street was the older part of the High Street that mainly consisted of maritime business offices. Running parallel to the High Street and connecting with East Street was Canal Walk. This street, joining the docks to the town, had become something of a 'sailors' paradise'.[18] The police strength dedicated to this area was three times that of the outlying areas of Portswood and Shirley.[19] This area was where Southampton's status as a port town was most visible. With its considerable number of lodgings for sailors and the transient population it resembled those sexually dangerous settings in the white slave narratives prevalent on stage and screen in 1913–15.

White slave narratives were crucial to the development of cinema, not only in terms of the stylistic elements of the feature (the diegesis) and the development of industry policy towards censorship, but also in terms of their impact on the production of audiences.[20] These films were at the same time a challenge to the industry's bid for social respectability. The high profile of the white slave scare in Britain tempts a certain equivalence with the reception of white slave films in the USA. Films that had caused the most concern were those showing the activities of criminals. However, exhibitors in Britain were consistently pointing out that criminal activity in the US films rarely if ever went unpunished. The debates about film censorship in the USA helped to reinforce the British industry's arguments for acceptance of US films in Britain. During the interviews undertaken by the National Council of Public Morals in 1917, which resulted in a comprehensive report, Mr John D. Tippett expressed the sentiments that the industry as a whole, both producers and exhibitors, utilised to ensure social acceptance:

> No manufacturer in his senses would invest money in a picture which was indecent or immoral. As a matter of fact such pictures to-day cannot be said to exist. But the real crux of censorship in my opinion, lies in discriminating as to the effect a picture will have upon all kinds of audiences, old and young, and whether methods of presentation employed are such as not to offend the canons of good taste, nor to present life from such an angle as to glorify crime or wrong-doing and to make probity ridiculous. *Of course we must not be debarred from presenting a powerful story, or facing sex problems of vital import to the future of our race, but it is certain that all this can be done with propriety, decency and proper dignity.*[21] [my italics]

In the last phrase Tippett articulates the industry's argument for the screening of controversial subject matter that Arthur Pickup had used in his advertising for *Dealers in Human Lives*. As a 'white slave exposure' the film is advertised as educational. Placed so close to the opening of the Gaiety, Pickup's strategy in exhibiting a white slave film is trying out product in search of an audience. He advertises the cinema as a place where a businessman can spend a spare hour and indeed its position across the street from the Westminster bank and in the busiest business district of the city supports that. But, as Shelly Stamp Lindsey has suggested, in the USA the white slave films were attracting female audiences but '. . . not on the virtuous grounds which the exhibitors purported to uphold but through sensationalism and titillation'.[22] None of the audience figures for this film at the Gaiety survive and it is difficult to determine with any degree of factual accuracy the kind of audience that attended the Gaiety on that second week of its opening. There is one scant account of the audience response to the film in *The Bioscope*. The article had been praising the ability of the hall to attract patrons when most of the men had enlisted and then praised the management: 'It is tribute to the wise discrimination of the management in booking to the taste of the public that such success has been achieved. The exclusives screened by Mr. Pickup last week were both intense and realistic dramas—"Dealers in Human Lives" and "Locked in Death".'[23] The article went on to describe the upcoming feature *The Slave of the Poppy* as 'ruthlessly exposing' the horrors of the opium traffic.

The focus on 'intense and realistic dramas' was to become a hallmark of the Gaiety in the next year. Combined with the decor of the hall the experience of a white slave film or an exposé of the opium trade was an incitement to desire at a number of ideological levels in terms of gender, race and the colonial gaze. Such desire was ostensibly governed by the rationale of educational value. Significantly, the film shown after *Dealers in Human Lives* was a war drama, a subject that has as its appeal a different, but I believe, related mobilisation of desire, which—to rephrase Michel Foucault—'. . . intensified [the audience's] awareness of [the war and death] as constant danger, and this in turn created a further incentive to talk about it'.[24] Foucault is referring to the curiosity incited by the social interdiction on talking about sex, a mechanism at work in the white slave films but it is a dynamic as easily applied to the unknowable, and similarly 'unspoken' nature of events at the front.

The next week's film was 'of great topical interest, *The Eye of the Government* throwing a lurid light on the spy system, and the following week's first feature was the London Film Company's production of George du Maurier's *Trilby*, as played by Sir Herbert Beerbohm Tree and a leading London company'.[25] *Trilby* was a well-known play and had been the subject of a number of revivals on the stage since its opening on Drury Lane in 1893. Its status as a literary and stage success was underpinned, in the Gaiety's publicity, by the emphasis on the virtuosity of Sir Herbert Tree's performance:

It was only after considerable persuasion that Sir Herbert Tree, undoubtedly England's greatest actor, consented to be filmed and he appears, of course, in his original character of 'Svengali.' Sir Herbert is afforded the opportunity of showing to perfection what a past master he is in the art of facial expression.[26]

Attitudes towards the cinematic portrayal of novels and plays varied, as exemplified by the testimony to the National Council of Public Morals of Miss Margery Fox, a representative of the Head Mistresses' Association. In reference to being questioned about the difference in treating subjects of 'sexual passions', she replied that 'The thing is treated on the legitimate stage in a different manner from the way it is treated on the cinema'. She was then asked if she thought the cinema was incapable of dealing 'modestly and honestly with such questions as sexual passion on the film . . . as . . . if they were spoken on the stage?' She agreed.[27] The impact of the visual without a regulating discourse afforded by the spoken language left the images open to 'unhealthy' interpretation. Fox is speaking from a critical tradition that drew clear distinctions between the virtue of the content of the fiction and the treatment, or execution of it. Writing about *Trilby* in *The Speaker* in 1893, critic and academic Arthur Quiller-Couch outlined his reasons for disliking hypnotism in fiction. In a striking pre-echo of concerns about the damaging effects of the cinema for children he writes:

> . . . the terror of these hypnotic stories resembles that of a child in a dark room. . . . the hypnotiser in these stories is always the villain of the piece. For the same or similar reasons, the subject is always a person worthy of our sympathy, and is usually a woman. Let us suppose it to be a good and beautiful woman—for she is the commonest victim. The author gives us to understand that by hypnotism this good and beautiful woman is for a while completely in the power of a man who is *ex-hypothesi* a beast, and who *ex-hypothesi* can make her commit any excesses that his beastliness may suggest. Obviously we are removed outside the moral order altogether; and in its place we are presented with a state of things in which innocence, honesty, love, and the rest are entirely at the disposal and under the rule of malevolent brutality; the result, as presented to us, being qualified only by such tact as the author should choose to display. That Mr du Maurier has displayed great tact is extremely creditable . . . But it does not alter the fact that a form of fiction which leaves us at the mercy of an author's tact is a very dangerous form in a world which contains so few Du Mauriers.[28]

Hypnosis in itself takes the reader beyond the boundaries of the moral order. The careful hand of du Maurier contains the explosive nature of the material through tact, or things left unspoken. The story of an innocent and beautiful woman, brought under the power of the Jewish villain Svengali and ultimately destroyed by him is ameliorated in the novel by the emphasis on her virtuous suitor Little Billie and his two trustworthy friends, Sandy and the Laird. In fact, the novel remains with these characters' viewpoints as Trilby—lost to them and under the spell of Svengali—has become the toast of the highest circles in Europe through her singing voice. At what is to be his crowning achievement Svengali arranges Trilby's London debut, attended by Little Billie, the Laird and Sandy. Just as the concert begins Svengali has a heart attack and dies. Trilby collapses on stage and after a long death scene ultimately dies from the sight of a portrait of the dead Svengali gazing out at her. The love between her and Little Billie is made doubly impossible through her 'contamination' by Svengali. The tale shares thematic similarities with the white slave narratives, young girls caught up in the social evils abounding in the city, rendered helpless and submissive, usually by ethnic 'others'.

Quiller-Couch's objection to the hypnotic in fiction anticipates the fear of the hypnotic influence of the cinema. The Hon. and Rev. Dr E. Lyttleton, headmaster at Eton, stated at the Cinema Commission, 'A large number of people come out of the cinema shows in a state of a coma'.[29] Interestingly, by focusing on Tree's portrayal through facial expression, the Gaiety's press release and the general publicity for the film, fed into the discourse of fear surrounding sensational film dramas and the effects of the pictures on the innocent, that is, women and children.

As Shelley Stamp Lindsey has shown for women audiences in New York, the forbidden nature of the subject matter was precisely the aspect of the films that attracted young female audiences. The circulation of these narratives coincides with the increase of young women into Southampton in the spring and summer months of 1915.[30] In the first part of May 1915, the Variety Theatre in Eastleigh, a few miles north of Southampton, staged a production of *The White Slaves of London*, 'a story of young girls who are led away by the gaiety and life of a big city'.[31] In the last week of May 1915 the Variety staged *Trilby* with Wilson Benge as Svengali and Sadie Smith as Trilby, and the Grand staged the play *The White Slave Girl*, which 'shows the perils which beset young girls who have to work for their living in the great cities or even in the country. It deals strongly and yet carefully with this delicate subject.'[32]

'Tragic Women' and 'Coloured Monstrosities': The Poster Problem

In the summer of 1915 male workers who had enlisted were being replaced by women. By September of that same year the most visible manifestation of this were the women tram conductors. There were a number of munitions factories in Southampton that were extensive employers of women, such as the Government Rolling Mills at Woolston, the Redbridge Schultz Factory and the Oakley Road Factory in Shirley, the Gun Cotton Factory in Millbrook, near Shirley, and the Reliance Works at the Floating Bridge in Northam. Apart from Millbrook, each of these areas had local cinema theatres, the Woolston Picture Theatre, the three cinemas on Shirley High Street and the Picturedrome in Northam. However, by the summer of 1915 women were already being used to replace men as clerks in banks, offices and in the postal services. Many of these jobs were centred on or near the High Street of the town. In this regard the men who had held these jobs in peacetime and in the first year of the war were the 'businessmen' that Arthur Pickup referred to in his advertisements for the Gaiety.

The Gaiety's gambit to equate the sensational with the educational became transparent in the summer of 1915. While in the first few weeks of opening the Gaiety had been presented as a place where '. . . in dreary winter days no two hours can be more profitably spent',[33] or as a culturally enlightening experience where the 'pictures are accompanied by an orchestra who have a capacity for playing high class music with real art', throughout the winter and spring of 1915 the advertisements for the Gaiety began to focus on the sensational elements of the features.[34] In February the film *Ghurka's Revenge* was advertised as 'Showing how a German forces his unwelcome attentions on a Ghurka's wife, who finally has the satisfaction of avenging her death'. The advertisements also began to employ the use of sensationalist language. In April the film *1914* by 'Rita' (a pseudonym for the popular writer Eliza Margaret Jane Gollan) was advertised as a 'War drama palpitating with excitement'. In the first week of May the programme advertised Elisabeth Risden in *Florence Nightingale*, a film which 'stirs the utmost depths of your heart' and *Woman*, an Italian film which featured the 'Tango of Death'. The story was of a 'princess forced by scandal to dance the Tango of Death on a music hall stage'.[35] In the last week of June the theme of white slavery returned in *Honour Thy Mother*, with 'vividly realistic scenes in life's underworld'. In July the adventure film *The Little Chauffeur*—advertised as an 'Intensely dramatic story of a girl's escapade'—was accompanied by *Nana of the Moulin Rouge*. The advertisement for *Nana* included a quote ostensibly from an intertitle: 'In a blind rage I drew my revolver . . .'. *Two Women* was advertised as 'throbbing with human interest and passionate excitement'.[36] Two weeks later the programme for Monday, Tuesday and Wednesday featured *The Evil Men Do*, which was 'vibrating with heart stirring problems of passionate emotion', and *Her Martyrdom*, in which 'villainy and blackmail reward a woman's sacrifice', and the second half of the week featured *The Child*, an 'Intensely dramatic story of life's underworld'.[37]

The balance between the 'sensational and the educational' was precarious, however. During the summer, at the same time that this distinct trend in the Gaiety's advertising was hitting its stride, the cinema's use of front-of-house advertising came under official scrutiny. The Southampton City Council Minutes records that on 26 July 1915 it was brought to the attention of the Works Committee that a poster advertising a film was found to be objectionable. Subsequent letters throughout the next two months show that the Works Committee, which was responsible for awarding licences, threatened the proprietor E.S. Edgar with non-renewal of the licence. Letters from Edgar and the Kinematograph Trading Company were presented to the Works Committee, but the committee had resolved, 'the advertising material is still objectionable, and ask that an undertaking be given to improve the same'. At the next meeting the committee was presented with letters from Edgar and the advertising contractors, S.H. Benson Ltd, who wrote of their 'intention to introduce such modifications in the general tone and character of the advertisements, as would, in their opinion be . . . calculated to meet the requirements of the Committee'.[38] The exact nature of the poster and film is not recorded and unfortunately the City Archive has not kept the letters and supporting material for the minutes. Nonetheless, there were two films that the Gaiety screened during the week of 10 July 1915 where advertising may have been the cause of consternation. They were *The World's Desire*, starring Lillian Braithwaite, and *Her Nameless Child*, starring Elisabeth Risden. Both films' advertising hints at two of the twenty-two grounds for which films had been cut, which the British Board of Film Censors had published in its annual report of 1914. These were 'indelicate sexual situations' and 'scenes suggestive of immorality'.[39] These two films in themselves were probably not the subjects of the concern, as Braithwaite was a well-respected British stage actress while Risden was already an established British film star. It was more likely the sensationalist tone of the advertising that drew the attention of the council.

Posters were a potential problem for all cinema exhibitors at this time due to the already established censorship system for poster hoardings overseen by the Billposters Association. The jurisdiction of this body did not, however, include the front of the picture palace, which was a privately owned space. This was where the exhibitor was most likely to utilise the expensive publicity material that accompanied the films. The

2.1   Gaiety advertisement in *What's On in Southampton*, week ending 16 August 1916, around the time of the poster problem.

production companies made this material available to exhibitors at extra cost. Nevertheless, letters to the Selig Company from British exhibitors during the war period show that many were keen to have high-quality colour posters of popular stars hanging in frames in their hall. Most of the posters advertising particular films featured artists' renditions of scenes, and it was these that attracted the attention and reproach of many moral guardians. During the interviews undertaken by the Cinema Commission for the National Council of Public Morals there was an exchange between Mr C.W. Crook, President of the National Union of Teachers and Mr F.R. Goodwin, Chairman of the London Branch of the Cinematograph Exhibitors' Association that gives an indication of the perceived transgressions posters such as these potentially represented:

> [*Mr Crook:*] Has your body ever considered, not the nature of the film itself, but the nature of the advertisement of the film?
> [*Mr Goodwin:*] Yes
> [*Mr C.:*] Does the censor touch these?
> [*Mr G.:*] No.
> [*Mr C.:*] Who does?
> [*Mr G.:*] The Billposters Association. They are an extremely powerful organisation and well-organised body, and no bill can go on to the hoardings unless it is sanctioned by them. We welcome that.
> *Here the Chairman of the Committee, The Bishop of Birmingham, intervened:* The Bill Posters Association has no authority as to the bill which is on the private house, I mean on the actual cinema palace itself.
> [*Mr C.:*] That is what I am aiming at.
> [*Mr G.:*] We are in accord with the Billposters Association, and there is only one thing left for us to do, and that is for us to control the posters which are put on to our own members' front halls.
> [*Mr C.:*] I mean these coloured monstrosities, those shady pictures where the revolver is very prominent and the woman always looking very tragic?
> [*Mr G.:*] Do you ever see such posters?
> [*Mr C.:*] Yes, the other day.
> [*Mr G.:*] Then the Billposters are not looking after their work. The tendency of these posters now is only to illustrate the star of the performance. The posters of this year are nearly always a photograph of the leading lady or the leading gentleman. They are getting so well known that their photographs are used.
> [*Mr C.:*] I mean those coloured posters of perhaps one incident in the drama which is highly coloured.[40]

The whole exchange is revealing in terms of what, for Mr Crook, constitutes propriety. In this case the imaginings of the poster artist, the use of the term colour in both the sense of the bright pigment as well as the 'passionate', or sensationalist treatment of the scene are the signalling factors. Quiller-Couch's concerns about the representations of hypnotised young women committing excesses are restated in these concerns about the posters. The sensationalist aspect that caused the greatest concern were those of women in peril or women in gestures or poses that were excessive. The extent to which the excessive gesture was associated with the cinema is exemplified in a cartoon from the 'London Opinion' that ran in *What's On* in June 1917, depicting a scene in a local grocery shop. In the centre of the frame is a well-dressed woman on one knee with the other leg extended, in a pose of plea with her hand held out over the counter towards a recalcitrant grocer. The assistants are looking on in horror. The caption was 'No! This is not a scene from the latest Film Tragedy, but merely a respectable young housewife asking for a pound of sugar at the local stores!' The humour has an edge in that the conditions of rationing have reduced a respectable woman to the excessive behaviour of a film actress, which is extraordinary and unseemly.

The object of posters was to catch the eye of passing trade and entice customers to enter the cinema. While poster advertising was one of the chief means of announcing programmes, its function was primarily limited to the front of house. In terms of reaching the wider community, newspaper advertising provided the most effective means for the exhibitor to disseminate information about the programme. Advice about the use of posters generally focused on the 'tasteful' and 'artistic' quality and presentation within the lobby. Epes Winthrop Sargent noted, 'As a general thing the picture theatre lobbies are overdressed. The arch is framed in lurid lithographs, the space is blocked by smaller sheets and there are houses where patrons have to actually stoop to enter because the top display drops so low.' His recommendation was, if possible, to employ a poster artist to tailor the type of posters needed for the cinema and to hang them tastefully. 'The aim of the exhibitor should be to suggest the dramatic theatre rather than the side show and this means a sparing use of paper in the lobby.'[41] An article-length advertisement for the posters accompanying the exclusive detective film *The Amazing Mr. Fellman* lays out the appeal of the poster in terms of spectacle and narrative:

> The tones and colours employed are such as to compel attention either night or day ... The exhibitor has here some of the most

2.2 *The White Slave Traffic*: example of the type of poster considered unacceptable by the Billposters Censorship Committee.

telling features, and a veritable introduction to the various characters in the play, which is bound to arouse anticipation . . . There is a definite 'punch' in each, yet they are served up in a style which cannot offend the most capricious of critics . . .[42]

The relationship of the front-of-house poster to the film did not simply function to provide a glimpse into the film. The uses of 'lurid colour' and excessive pose or gesture were attractions in themselves. Their position outside of the cinema, on hoardings, while regulated, offered pleasures beyond those of the film. Emlyn Williams's memory of the attraction of these posters gives a sense of the vicarious pleasure they offered when there was no money for admission:

> Non picture evenings, I would take sad pleasure in hanging around the Hip, watching people straggle in, their faces should have been aglow, then looking up at 'the pipe', which ran up the side of the building to emit urgent pants of steam throughout the performance. It must have been to do with exhaust (heating?) but to me the endless chug-chug spoke of adventure, and grief, and gaiety. . . . Friday was set aside for a long walk . . . my quest was not for birds' nests or even shop windows, but hoardings, so as to drink my fill of the new poster: a graphic scene, in colour, from one of next week's episodes. Some Fridays held more promise than others: once, on the corner of the Central Hotel, Shotton, I found Marie Walcamp staring horror-struck at water from which emerged a giant octopus with one tentacle round her ankle; another time I came upon Ruth Roland, bound and gagged, hanging upside down from a ten-storied pagoda next to the Congregational Church, Services 10.30 and 6.0 All Welcome.[43]

Williams's memory exemplifies the permeable boundary between the public space and the private sphere of imagination and desire. The juxtaposition of the sacred space of the Congregational Church and the imperilled female body 'bound and gagged' was undoubtedly an irresistible device to Williams writing in the post-Freudian 1950s. But the residue of the cinema experience held in the spectacular representations of the poster remains. Annette Kuhn has suggested that the cinema audience in Britain at this time was to an extent 'discursively constructed around a series of fears . . .'.[44] Within the regulating discourses of bodies such as the National Council for Public Morals the prevailing assumption was of the cinema as a proletarian public sphere. Moreover, this audience was seen to be predominantly women and children. The Cinema Commission report reflects these assumptions in its concern with the effects of the cinema, physically, socially and emotionally, on this perceived audience. Further, the nature of the space inside the cinema was contested in profound ways. The experience of the cinema takes place in a discursively liminal space between public and private. The poster, in its position as an invitation to that space and articulated in terms of visual representation and with the purpose of solicitation, occupies a gateway, a site of negotiation between the public and private spheres. The emphasis on the star personality in Goodwin's exchange with Crook is an articulation of the exhibitors' strategy of positioning the cinema space along the lines of the legitimate theatre, and in the process attempts to refocus the attention (of the social regulators as well as the spectator) onto the personality of the actor. By conceding that the poster to which Crook refers is problematic, Goodwin, as spokesman for the London Branch of the Cinematograph Exhibitors' Association aligns the association with the moral imperatives of the committee. While he recognises that the posters most likely to offend were those that depicted excessive scenes within the fiction (the climax of the narrative where 'thrills' are visually represented), he attempts to distance the majority of the trade by attributing the particular poster Crook refers to as uncharacteristic of the general practice.

Yet the depictions of dramatic moments, spectacularly staged, were directly addressing the private pleasures the cinema offered. These posters represented a gateway, not only between the public space of the street/ outside and the private space of the auditorium/inside, but it was also a window into filmic moments that spoke to the private world of the viewer. They were a popular part of cinema culture and the uses of scenes from the film were certainly representative, as they are today, of the most appealing moments in the fiction. The posters that accompanied *The Amazing Mr. Fellman* depicted a significant moment in an illicit card game, a couple in an embrace and two 'rogues' fighting, with their 'moll' in between trying to separate them.[45] In a moment of some degree of tension during the interviews with Mr Goodwin, his frustration with the inability of the panel to be specific about the offending posters surfaces:

> *The Right Reverend Monsignor Brown:* I live almost opposite a cinema, and I have an opportunity of seeing the picture palace people. I also have an opportunity of seeing the bills which are posted up outside. I have seen one this morning of a girl in a certain kind of dress, and round about are quite a number of heads floating in the air, and nearly all are engaged in looking up at this girl's feet. It is called 'The Cup of' something.

> *Mr Goodwin:* It is so nice to get something definite. I would propose, if you would allow me, to have a copy of this poster sent to you— (*hear, hear*)—because there are such different aspects of these things.

For Crook and Monsignor Brown, the offensive nature of the posters lay, predictably, in the representation of women in (morally and/or physically) dangerous situations. This is borne out in the findings of the National Council of Public Morals Cinema Commission on the issue of posters and sensationalism. One of the recommendations was that censorship of films be extended to include posters, the prevailing reason given that there were a large number of children attending the cinema. They also found that 'apart from "sex" and "crime" films, an injurious effect is produced on young minds by the excessive sensationalism and frightfulness of the some of the films shown ...'.[46] Although the discourses that surrounded the cinema as a public sphere were articulated in the first study of the social phenomenon of cinema in Britain in 1916, when the main work of the commission took place, there are strong indicators one year earlier of the dynamics at play, in Southampton Council's interchange with the Gaiety. The poster policy was at issue and, given the context of the sensationalist language of the newspaper advertisements in relation to the way other cinemas on the High Street and in the suburbs were advertising. it is not surprising that the Gaiety was singled out for pushing the boundaries.

The Gaiety's advertising was toned down to an extent but the cinema had succeeded in the first year in establishing a clear identity. Through the combination of the architecture and the décor, and by emphasising the exclusives on the film programme, Arthur Pickup was able to anticipate and attract audiences in Southampton and establish a regular clientele. Through these marketing and programming strategies the Gaiety experience differentiated itself by aiming to attract young working women, particularly those who had newly acquired disposable income through work made available by the enlistment and conscription of men. Throughout the war the programme was in reality as varied as the programmes of the Alexandra or the Carlton, but nevertheless two kinds of films consistently appeared there throughout the war: the 'society' and 'crime' film and the official war pictures. This specific address to a female audience lay in the marketing strategies at the local level. Guaranteed attractions such as Chaplin and comedy were a part of the programme but the Gaiety rarely signalled it in their advertising beyond the phrase 'as well as our first class programme'.

In the shift from peace to war the complexion of Southampton's cinema culture changed significantly as it engaged with official and unofficial regulation, national and international pressures within the changing production and distribution sectors and shifting audience constituencies. From an examination of the advertising, architecture and the programming of three cinemas in Southampton a number of points can be made that lay the groundwork for a deeper understanding of the cinema culture and exhibition in Britain during the Great War. Firstly, the close proximity of cinemas created a competitive environment for audiences. The audiences for each cinema varied depending upon their location and that variance was evident in the presentation strategies of managers. The competition with music halls was beyond simply differentiating the experience and at times the cinemas and the music hall competed for the same 'new audience'. Related to this was the influence of music hall traditions of house management. Cinema managers such as Elliot employed the techniques learned in the management of small theatres, circuses and music halls to ensure social acceptance within the community. Benefits for soldiers, refugees and even the continuing relief of the relatives of the *Titanic* disaster were undertaken by all of the cinemas in order to achieve this social respectability. In this regard one of the effects of the war was to aid the relative acceptance of cinema as part of the landscape of leisure and entertainment.

The establishment of so many new cinemas set against the precarious economic climate that accompanied the onset of the war raises the question of how films were used as a means by which those businesses established themselves. Without a doubt, the serials, the 'sex' and 'crime' films and the comedies of Charlie Chaplin were instrumental in securing regular clientele. Yet the official war films and newsreels afforded the exhibitor a consistent high-interest subject that had the added attraction of appealing to the middle-class audience. The combination of the up-to-date information provided by these films and the opportunities for patriotic special events almost immediately thrust the cinema house to the forefront of the local entertainment culture as the site of information about the war and in turn as the centre of the visual rendering of the front in the national imagination. Having established the conditions for the reception of these films, in terms of the way in which cinema managers addressed their audiences through their programming strategies and house management styles, it is now possible to explore in more detail the role cinema played in shaping the 'homefront imagination'.

3

Anonymity and Recognition
The Roll of Honour Films

In September 1914 Messrs Bacon and Hood, proprietors of the Palladium in Portswood, rented premises on Southampton High Street in order to set up a 'cinema rifle range'. Images of German soldiers were thrown on a reversible steel screen . . . and the public was 'invited to get their own in against the Germans!'[1] Obviously, the methods of taking advantage of the war to increase business for exhibitors were numerous. Throughout the war exhibitors employed a variety of techniques, from special admission prices and shows for outgoing and returning troops, the wounded and refugees, patriotic decor and participation in recruiting drives, to the shaping of programmes with a war subject and the screening of the latest war news. Henry Hibbert, managing director of Hibbert's Pictures Limited, a circuit of picture theatres in Bradford, wrote to *The Bioscope* in September 1914 to suggest that the war had provided the opportunity to develop the argument for Sunday opening. He suggested 'giving 25 per cent of the gross takings [from all Sunday performances] to the Prince of Wales War Fund, or distributing to the fund that is being subscribed for by each local authority'.[2] He saw that 'it would help foster a spirit of patriotism, and would serve as a means to an end'. He urged that this would have the 'desired effect' of achieving Sunday-opening permanently throughout the country in the future. These types of practical patriotism continued throughout the war and formed a significant plank in the Cinema Exhibitors' Association's (CEA) argument for the relaxation of restrictions during the testimonies of the National Council of Public Morals 1917 report. As late as October 1918, in the run up to the December national election, an egalitarian rhetoric was employed by *The Bioscope* in an article subtitled 'Equality of treatment for all Classes of Amusement'.[3] It argued that the Lighting and Heating Order of earlier that year had come close to disadvantaging cinema exhibitors in its twenty-five per cent reduction of electricity for all places of entertainment. This was feasible for the theatre and music halls but the cinema projectors would not be able to operate adequately with such a cut. The CEA had succeeded in gaining exemption partly on the grounds that people who were not burning fuel in their homes because they were at the cinema would save more energy. Further, they argued that the cinema was the best means of getting information to the largest number of people. 'Patriotism is to-day imperative; let it be writ large as one of our attributes.'[4]

As we have seen, the practice of practical patriotism by Southampton exhibitors worked to integrate their halls into the community. As these exhibitors drew on the traditions of showmanship and theatre management they also strove to emphasise the special qualities of the cinema by programming newsreels and, from 1915 onwards, official war films. Cinema's role, they argued, was not only as a house of entertainment contributing to the war effort through benefits and charity shows, but through regular screening of the latest war pictures and official war films such as *Battle of the Somme* (1916) it was an effective means of educating the populace about the events of the war at the front. While film footage of the troops at the front was meant to educate and inform the population it often did this within an appeal to local audiences. Troops marching away and returning had been popular subjects for locally produced films in the Boer War and this continued to be the case throughout the years of the Great War. As did all local films or 'topicals' as they were called, these films invoked a form of visual engagement that emphasised recognition as the films depicted the soldiers marching past the camera.[5] The official war films drew on these traditions, often showing soldiers identified by regiment. While this was meant to provide a morale-boosting link between the front and home these images were juxtaposed with images of death and destruction that also gave rise to questions about the suitability of these images in a public space.

The variety programme meant that the experience of cinema audiences at this time was of a combination of not only fiction films but national news events as well as the visual representation of the local space. Important events in the local community were often filmed and then screened for audiences by cinema managers. For example, in June 1914 the managers of the Portswood Palladium, the same group who erected the cinema rifle range two months later, secured the rights to the filming of the Southampton Tudor Pageant that took place at the Deanery grounds and screened it for their patrons.[6] Local interest films such as

71

these placed alongside the newsreels of national and international news linked the space to those events. More specifically, the local news film worked as part of managers' overall strategy of supporting the war effort with depictions of soldiers departing or at drill, or pictures of recruitment centres and the queues outside all serving to knit the local into the national. A striking example of the combination of the local news film and the cinema space as performing the social function of patriotic morale boosting occurred in the locally produced Roll of Honour films and slide shows that were shown throughout Britain. These films were the cinematic expression of the common newspaper practice of publishing photographs and listing the names of local men who were serving. Later this practice shifted to include those who had been wounded, reported missing or killed. The phenomenon of the Roll of Honour films provides an insight into the social function of cinema in local areas and suggests modes of engagement that depended on the public performance of patriotic response. Significantly, these films were generally discontinued as the war moved into its third year. This suggests that these films provoked a more private response: one that was not given, nor allowed, public expression and which was a reminder of the mounting human cost of the war. This chapter explores the function of these locally produced Roll of Honour films as a strategy of practical patriotism and as a local example of the tensions between the public recognition they offered and the private anxieties they engendered.

A Modern Memory

There are six examples of Roll of Honour films held at the Imperial War Museum and the National Film and Television Archive in London.[7] These are locally produced films of photographs of men who had been killed, wounded or taken prisoner or who were still serving at the front. They were produced in varying quality. Some were quickly made on a rostrum with a rough black background with handwritten nameplates the only form of identification. Others were produced with more care, the borders flat against a deep black background and the names printed with information about their deaths, wounds or predicaments. Some cut the figure out of the photograph and placed them on a black background, the edges softened to give the image an eternal spiritual quality. In each case these films stressed the relationship between the cinema exhibitor and the local community that practical patriotism worked to achieve.[8] They publicly acknowledged the role of the community in the war effort and the cinema theatre provided the public space for the recognition of the individual sacrifice of its members.

3.1   From Will Onda's *Preston and District 'Roll of Honour', Sixth Series.*

An example of these films from the town of Milnrow in Lancashire appeared in *The Long Summer* (1996) a Channel Four documentary series about British culture between the two world wars. This Milnrow film opens the first of a six-part series and is meant to be a powerful evocation of a nation in mourning. It stands as an indicator of the prevalence of bereavement at this time. The narrator, Alan Bennett, explains that it was produced and exhibited by the manager of the Empire Cinema. Here the photographs, paradoxically still images projected by an animating machine, arrest for a brief moment the momentum of modernity. They are a visual pause prior to the frenetic pace of the jazz age. Their poses suggest a wide-eyed innocence and vitality lost, frozen in the pre-moment of their entry into eternity. The backgrounds look back to a nineteenth-century mode of pictorial representation, of landscapes and props that suggest, in these faded images, the worn cloth on the furniture in stately houses, the musty smell of flat scenery in an abandoned theatre. At the start of the twenty-first century they represent a memory of the war as tragedy and these young faces are its victims. The pictures, or portraits, are shown with a reverent commentary, 'The years of the long summer would be dominated by the memory of men like these' and are accompanied by the funereal chords of a brass band. In the representational harness of the documentary these men have already never

73

existed. Their moment, and the film's original purpose, is erased. They exist only to represent the bereavement of a nation.

When they were screened for audiences at the time, however, these films were meant to represent fulfilment of duty and glorious sacrifice. They were screened with patriotic musical accompaniment and were greeted with applause. The *Durham County Advertiser* reported in January 1916 that the Globe Cinema had shown Roll of Honour images as part of the programme: 'As various photographs were projected on the screen and recognised by the audience, they were greeted with enthusiastic applause'.[9] This indicates a socially recognised performative response, one that exhibitors understood and saw as part of including their establishment in the war effort. From the perspective of the early twenty-first century this response to the films provides evidence that helps towards an understanding of the developing sense of the war as national tragedy. The cost of the war and its consequences dawned slowly and the role cinema played in the unfolding knowledge of the nature of the front in the homefront imagination was played out on the local as well as the national level.[10]

The Roll of Honour films were the cinematic expression of a common practice of local and national newspapers that depicted the photographs and listed the names of those local men who were serving. As with the local press these served to weave the local space into the national narrative of the war effort. Locally produced Roll of Honour films functioned overtly as a strategy of practical patriotism but they are also evidence of the tensions between public recognition and the private fears of anonymous obliteration in the homefront imagination. There are then two broad questions that arise from these films. The first and most accessible is, how were audiences encouraged to respond to these films and to make sense of them? The second is, how might these films give a deeper indication of the changing perceptions of audiences as the war dragged on? I want to approach these questions through three interconnected areas of investigation, their performative and aesthetic antecedents, the expectations audiences brought to them and, finally, the undercurrent of loss and anonymity that existed alongside their more public patriotic significance. The films themselves arose out of the traditions of the local actuality film, newsreels, slideshows, the aesthetics of Victorian portrait photography and from the use of portraits in newspapers and magazines. In the first section I will explore those antecedents. In the second section I will suggest that these films worked through a reception trope of recognition. By this I mean that recognition was an expectation that accompanied these films. This operated on two levels of meaning: the predominant public recognition central to the ennobling of local soldiers and their sacrifice and, as the war progressed, the more subdued function of the private identification of individuals. The last section seeks to explain why these films were rarely, if ever, part of cinema programmes after 1917 as they increasingly depicted the human cost of the war in a public entertainment space.

Antecedents

The Local Film on the Programme

The Roll of Honour films fitted into the programme as part of the exhibition of local scenes for local audiences. In 1914 local films were a regular programme feature.[11] Between 1897 and 1913 firms such as Mitchell and Kenyon had built their business on this type of film.[12] Initially screened in travelling shows, these films continued to have a place on the picture palace programme. Exhibitors such as Hood and Bacon in Southampton tended to hire production firms but others, like Will Onda in the Lancashire town of Preston, had their own filmmaking equipment and would film local events and screen them for their audiences. Onda had a large network of cinemas throughout the north-east and produced not only the local scenic films but also larger budget short fiction features and comedy sketches up until the 1940s. *Festive Crowd Scenes* (1914), a local 'topical', featured crowded streets and a number of boys waving at the camera. It is possible to follow some of the same faces as they swirl around, sometimes on each other's shoulders, at other times rushing towards the camera. The attraction of these films was to recognise oneself or friends and acquaintances. The gesturing and moving towards the camera in the films has its mirror image in the viewer who works to make sense of the films. The local viewer knows the space of the city and the faces of some of the participants and can attach stories to go with those spaces and the familiar faces. The reading of the local town space through cinematic mediation requires an investigation of familiarity, a placing of oneself into the text. On a less abstract level, we know that from the late 1890s showmen and travelling exhibitors had been reaping the rewards of attracting audiences with the possibility of seeing themselves in a local film. This is a very different mode of reception to that associated with the classical spectator. The classical style that characterised the rise of the feature film prompted the classical

75

reception mode where the fictional space is maintained by the dictates of the narrative. Peter Krämer and Ine Van Dooren have argued that this mode could be disrupted by direct address to camera and used to 'create heightened dramatic effects and/or to explicate the film's message, often for propagandistic purposes, so as to influence the audience's attitudes and behaviour with respect to the war effort'. Within the factual film they argue that direct address was often used for propaganda purposes but that it was just as likely that direct address held no more specific intent than to interpolate the audience with 'An offer they could not refuse: I want YOU to look at THIS.'[13] The local films functioned in this manner. The familiarity of the local space re-presented on the same screen where the most exotic scenes and places appeared created an uncanny effect, a familiar space and/or face in a different frame.

Films of the street were not the only type of local subject the exhibitors would film. During the war favourite subjects were the parade of new recruits through the city, special occasions such as royal visits, dedication ceremonies and sporting events. In contrast to *Festive Crowd Scenes*, one local film *Recruits* (1915) depicted the 1st Surrey Volunteer Training Corps going through their drills on a field in Croydon. The camera slowly pans across orderly, well-dressed, crowds who have turned out to watch the local men. There is a festive air to the event that looks to be a genteel picnic on a summer's day but unlike *Festive Crowd Scenes* the camera and the crowd are restrained. The frantic rush to and around the camera is replaced by the symmetrical lines of the marching men and these are echoed by the spectators, who stand in a similar rank posing as if for a still camera. Movements are reserved for straightening the clothes of the children. Occasionally someone ventures a grin or laughs as they look at the camera. Slow panning shots provide close-ups of recruits with their families after the drill is over.

The pose, the slow panning movement, the *mise-en-scène* of the park in which the drill takes place all work to include the viewer in the proceedings. At the same time their appeal also lies in their contrast to the national and global images that accompanied them on the film programme. The slow panning allows time for recognition of familiar faces and locations set against the abstract recognition of world leaders, royalty, film stars or exotic locations of the other films on the programme. The drill in the setting of the park is a military display against fields; an idealistic reconstruction of the battlefield within the iconography of military pageant and a marked contrast to the devastated buildings and scarred scenery of the front, which by 1915 characterised much of the newsreel footage of the war. The park presents a pastoral background for the relief of everyday existence in factories and in town and city centres for which they were designed. Perhaps more abstractly the collection of families posing with relatives in uniforms recalls the separation of families from their loved ones already at the front. These local films, and the Roll of Honour films particularly, depended upon a pattern of looking that suspended the tension between the placement of the local community within the public narrative of the nation and the displacement and disruption to those communities that made up the texture of individual, private experience during the war.

Portraits of Heroes

In the seventh series of Will Onda's Preston and District Roll of Honour films (1915) each photograph was accompanied by brief narrative information. For example, the photograph of Private Rampling is reported as 'Wounded on June 16th in the arm and back', while the next is of Corporal F.W. Holmes: 'The first soldier to gain the VC and the French Legion of Honour'. These explanatory titles worked to celebrate and ennoble the local man in his role as ordinary soldier. The pose and background of the Roll of Honour films worked within the formal codes of nineteenth-century portraiture. The photographer's studio props of ornate chairs and painted backgrounds drew on the portrait tradition of associating the personality with property and the sign of authorship. Will Onda's tenth series of films depicted two photographs signed by local photographer A. Winter of Preston. The first is a full-length portrait of 2nd Lieutenant W.A. Davies, killed, and the second is a bust, surrounded by fog, of 2nd Lieutenant Norbert Craven, wounded. In the case of the second the treatment of the photograph serves to aestheticise the soldier, to place a mist of infinity around the bust to raise his image beyond the quotidian.

Similarly magazines that featured 'celebrities' imbued the photograph with an aesthetic of distinctiveness.[14] Their address worked to bridge the distance between the reader and the 'important person'. These photographs, placed in magazines meant for a new middle class, worked to democratise the images. The readers were brought into a 'close though formal relationship' with celebrities not only through the pose and the photographic reproduction, which in themselves functioned to distance the reader, but also by the text, which took the form of a personalising narrative. This 'condescension' effect worked to bring the reader into the *private* life of the celebrity. In an article in the *Pall Mall Magazine*, January–April 1901, entitled 'Victoria the Well Beloved', accompanied by engravings of the queen at various stages of her life, Sir Herbert E. Maxwell, MP wrote an accompanying narrative. Recounting a number of stories of the queen's kindness and clarity of thought, the article balanced a familiar tone with due reverence. One story told of how she instigated the award of war medals to soldiers of the rank:

> It pained the Queen ... to see the breasts of Princes and Ministers, who perhaps had never seen a shot fired in earnest, glittering with stars and orders, while the men who had offered their lives and endured wounds and hardships in the service of their country were undistinguished from the latest recruit. So in 1848 the Queen bestowed medals upon all the old soldiers, of whatever rank, who had served in their country's wars; and such has remained the rule ever since.[15]

The case for her greatness is made through her natural attributes of sensitivity and a sense of justice through a glimpse into her private thoughts. By contrast the Roll of Honour films worked along this transforming dynamic but with the reverse effect, formalising and distancing a close relationship.

Striking in that reversal was the films' use of portraiture codes that were clearly within the conventions of presenting a public image. Unable to utilise extensive text, the films depended upon audience recognition of individuals, and the more detailed narratives available in the local press and word of mouth. The Rolls of Honour in newspapers ennobled the local soldier by stressing their *public* life. An example is that of 2nd Lieutenant Major W. Booth [sic.], 'whose death is reported in action, [and who] was a very prominent member of the Yorkshire eleven for five seasons. Although a fine punishing batsman when set his chief claim to fame will rest on what he accomplished with the ball.'[16] While Booth was undoubtedly a commissioned officer and the narrative of his qualities at cricket provided a metaphorical testament to his bravery commensurate with his class status, similar treatment was also given to non-commissioned officers and men of the rank. Private Ragless of Southampton had appeared in the local newspaper's Roll of Honour as missing the previous week and received three paragraphs of biography on the report of his death on the Somme, focusing on his service record and his training for the Royal Engineers prior to the outbreak of the war.[17]

The Roll of Honour films, unable to provide such detailed information, achieved this ascension effect through the quality of the image, the pose and their appearance in the public space of the cinema.

The Roll of Honour films worked for exhibitors in two ways. First, as a form of practical patriotism, they worked within the industry's general, if largely uncoordinated, strategy of establishing respectability and thereby expanding audiences. For example, Will Onda's Prince's Theatre was a high-street cinema with ranked seating for over 1,000. The Roll of Honour films were only a part of his commitment to practical patriotism. In April 1915 he followed the lead of exhibitors all over the country and showed an actuality 'illustrating fighting in the Vosges. Its scenes made a deep impression on the mind as to the great war and some of its problems . . .'.[18] Actualities depicting the fighting at the front were having the effect of bringing sectors of the community, particularly the middle class, into the cinema. This trend would continue throughout the war.

Secondly, the Roll of Honour films functioned to ennoble the local soldiers in the same way that the magazines worked to democratise celebrities. Onda followed the war actualities with a pageant of the new local regiment: 'Mr. Onda created much local interest with his exclusive production of Preston "Pals" Company of the Loyal North Lancashire Regiment at drill and play. These local features can never be made too much of, and it is really surprising that more of them are not produced.'[19] Pals regiments were devised by the War Minister Lord Derby to take advantage of local solidarity and were themselves a form of the recognition of the local community's commitment, and later sacrifice, to the war effort. While generally seen as a working-class movement the Pals, like the Roll of Honour films, signalled the democratisation of duty and honour and raised the local recruit to heroic status.

From Active Service to Memory

The use of the ennobling conventions of the portrait made the transition from celebration of duty to memorialising sacrifice very easy. The Roll of Honour portraits, in spite of the patriotic fervour, were memorials to the sacrifice of the local community.[20] By 1916 the Roll of Honour practice in all areas of public life had taken on a resonance of loss and had begun to acquire its more sombre meaning. Following the release of the official film *Battle of the Somme* in September 1916 a series of magazines entitled *Sir Douglas Haig's Great Push*, in eight fortnightly parts (they were actually extended as the battle dragged on to make up at least thirteen parts), were published by Hutchinson and Company of London 'by arrangement with the War Office'. They sold for 8d, which was almost three times that of the cheapest price of admission to the cinema. On the inside of the cover page of the fifth instalment was an announcement entitled the Roll of Honour 'now being compiled by The Marquis de Ruvigny', author and editor of *The Blood Royalty of Britain* and *The Titled Nobility of Europe*. The marquis was now turning his considerable skill to the collation of an illustrated biographical record of all 'officers, non-commissioned officers and men of his majesty's forces who are killed or die on active service'. No one providing information would be charged and no fee would be accepted. The intention was to include a large number of portraits of officers and men but 'with over 100,000 dead for the first year, it is clearly impossible to undertake that one will be given in every case'. The form at the bottom of the page stated 'Please send me a form so that I may give you particulars concerning ——— who was killed on active service'. It was intended to include 'a biographical sketch of their career, extracts from letters of Commanding Officers or Comrades relating to the action in which the Officer or Man fell, or to the particular circumstances of his death'.

The language of this announcement is significant for its rhetoric of reverence and transcendence. The photographs are referred to as portraits, the aestheticised image was to be accompanied by a biographical narrative, an act of bringing to life in the memory of those who have been left behind, a penance for a debt that could never be repaid. The Marquis de Ruvigny's announcement denotes a change in the nature of Rolls of Honour. By 1915 the films' function of celebrating the ordinary soldiers had shifted to one of commemoration. By locating them within their community, these films became a precession of the community's loss.

Precisely how the Roll of Honour films were exhibited is difficult to ascertain as very little information exists about their screening conditions. What is known is that they were shown in the manner that slides of military leaders such as Kitchener were and accompanied by patriotic music. In fact many theatres used slides rather than film.[21] There are some indications of the kind of music that may have accompanied them through what is known about the music for the official war films. *The Bioscope* columnist for music, J. Morton Hutcheson, printed the recommendations he had supplied to William Jury, the booking director for the trade screenings of *Battle of the Somme* in August 1916 and for *The*

VOLUME I. with about 7,000 biographies and names of those who fell between 1914–1915, NOW READY, PRICE £2 2 0

IMPORTANT.

THE GREAT NATIONAL TRIBUTE.

The ROLL OF HONOUR

AN ILLUSTRATED BIOGRAPHICAL RECORD OF **ALL**
OFFICERS, NON-COMMISSIONED OFFICERS AND MEN
OF HIS MAJESTY'S FORCES WHO ARE KILLED OR
DIE ON ACTIVE SERVICE

NOW BEING COMPILED BY

THE MARQUIS DE RUVIGNY

Author and Editor of "The Blood Royal of Britain," "The Titled Nobility of Europe," and other works.

THE debt which the Empire owes to those who have laid down their lives in the present War must, from the very nature of things, for ever remain unpaid.

There is, however, a universal desire to keep them in remembrance, and to ensure that their names and their glorious deeds shall not be forgotten.

For this purpose, "THE ROLL OF HONOUR" is now being prepared, to place on permanent record the name of every Officer, Non-Commissioned Officer and Man of His Majesty's Forces on land or sea who is killed in action, who dies of wounds, or whose death is otherwise caused in the present War.

It may here be briefly stated that it is proposed to give, whenever obtainable, the full name, place and date of birth, parentage, biographical sketch of career, and date and place of death, with extracts from letters of Commanding Officers or Comrades relating to the action in which the Officer or Man fell, or to the particular circumstances of his death.

Many a deed of heroism is covered by the bare announcement of a name in the daily long roll of casualties. To collect and record these is the purpose of the "ROLL OF HONOUR." The names of children will also be included, so that in the years to come they may themselves read, or teach their children to read, of the glorious way their fathers died; of those individual acts of bravery that are the chief redeeming feature of war.

Much valuable help is being given by the Authorities, by the Regiments, by Public Institutions, and the Heads of Schools, and the Publishers appeal with confidence to those who have read relatives to assist them in the task they have undertaken by sending at once to the Editor the necessary particulars, extracts, from letters, etc.

The Editor and Publishers wish it to be distinctly understood that the insertion of any name is not in any way dependent upon the payment of any fee or of subscription to the book, and that no fee will be accepted for the insertion of any name.

A large number of portraits of Officers and Men will be included. With over 100,000 dead for the first year, it is clearly impossible to undertake that one will be given in every case, but when a portrait is supplied the Publishers will do their best to include it, and in the case of one supplied by a Subscriber, where there is no copyright fee, they guarantee that it will be reproduced.

SEND FOR A FORM to fill in particulars of your relation or friend who has been killed on active service. There is no charge, and his biography ought to be included. Unless you write probably only his name will given.

To THE STANDARD ART BOOK CO. LTD.,

Publishers of "THE ROLL OF HONOUR,"

30-32, LUDGATE HILL, E.C.

EDITORIAL OFFICES:—
MARQUIS DE RUVIGNY,
"The Roll of Honour",
14-15, Hanover Chambers,
Buckingham St., Adelphi, W.C.

Please send me a form so that I may give you particulars concerning ....

...who was killed on active service.

Name ....

Address ....

PRINTED AT THE CHAPEL RIVER PRESS, KINGSTON-ON-THAMES.

3.2 An early indication that the Roll of Honour had begun to shift from a list of the serving to a list of the dead. This first appeared in the 22 November 1916 edition of *Sir Douglas Haig's Great Push*, part 5 of a fortnightly magazine reporting on the Battle of the Somme, making extensive use of photographs from the film.

Battle of the Ancre and the Advance of the Tanks in January 1917. For *Battle of the Somme*, which depicted actual footage of the dead and the wounded, Hutcheson warned:

> Musical directors should, if and where at all possible, 'rehearse' the accompaniment *before* showing it to the public, and also that they—musicians especially—must realise the seriousness and awfulness of the scenes depicted most realistically, and even where the scenes are showing the brighter side of events in The Great Push the 'accompaniment' *must* not be too bright. We don't want to hear 'Sunshine of your Smile' played in any part of this film. The pictures themselves will impress the public . . . and the "accompaniment" must be treated with all respect and seriousness, having regard to the tragic situations depicted.[22]

Hutcheson often wrote disparagingly about the widely varying types of music in the cinemas generally and the purpose of the column was to offer guidance. He complained about the kind of music played in cinemas but here his recommendations are directed at the treatment of the music. These selections were meant to be played with reverence and solemnity.[23] Thus it cannot be ruled out that any of the Roll of Honour films were accompanied by sombre music. Most likely in the early months the music drew on the patriotic pageantry of music halls and theatres and was primarily military marches, but it is likely that this changed—in treatment if not in selection—with any of these films exhibited after 1916, as casualty lists grew.

Portraits of soldiers were a popular way of personalising postcards. Travelling photographers often frequented training centres and areas of troop concentration and made postcard-sized portraits for the soldiers to send home. The exhibitors who made these films obtained the photographs from parents, friends or even the soldiers themselves in much the same way as the marquis or the local newspapers: by appealing for them through posters and handbills advertising the programme. The local portrait films worked in tandem, if not intentionally, with those in the local press. The audiences for these films had available the narratives of the soldiers through the newspaper prior to seeing them on the screen. The columns that provided the information were often run a few days after the announcement of the fate of local men serving. In the *Southern Daily Echo* these biographies were run in the column 'Topics of the Hour'. The dynamic between the biographical notes and the portrait elevates the local personality to the status of hero and the inclusion of men from all ranks worked towards a conception of community that subsumed class distinctions. This inclusive form of address at the local level placed the local community within the context of the national narrative of the war; a serial narrative with an open ending. The films were also inclusive intralocally in that they engaged or located the viewer/reader within the local community through encouraging an effect of empathy and recognition. While there were precedents for these types of subjects in magazines and in the local scene film, these films remain unique from those antecedents in significant ways. They were funereal, they depicted the cost of the war and, however mediated by the music, by the portrait/ biography format or by the pleasure of recognition inherent in the local scene film, this sombre nature had the effect of counting the cost to the community.

Public or Private?

The 4th Loyal Lancasters Roll of Honour film shown in Preston in July 1915 shared a bill with Chaplin's *A Gentleman of a Nerve*. Audiences expected variety and viewing habits were shaped by the continuous programme where they tended to come and go at various points. Will Onda's film received special attention in the Preston press in the same way that his pageant of the 'Pals' regiment had. However, this is the only instance where Onda 'boomed' these films. This example of a shift or, more accurately, a response by an exhibitor to shifting reception contexts, is evidence of an engagement with his audiences' 'social horizon of understanding'. Here Miriam Hansen's assertion that this horizon is 'not a homogeneous storage of intertextual knowledge but a contested field of multiple positions and conflicting interests' helps to account for the public/private split that characterises the reception of these films. The cinema during this period was a relatively new social space of entertainment and created conflicting perceptions and debates about its social function; it was also a point in time when the cinema converged with other social and cultural formations that required particular delineations between the public and private spheres. As Hansen puts it '. . . the question is which discourses of experience will be articulated in public and which remain private . . .'.[24] The Roll of Honour films' placement between the serials, short comedies and features set up a diverse set of texts that, in conjunction with a 'discursive organisation of experience'—here associated with nation/community, identity/

anonymity, alienation and loss—resonate across each other.[25] The dominant discourse of patriotism was the primary public language of the homefront imagination, yet private anxieties that accompanied this as an 'undercurrent' were made up of significant concerns: anonymity, loss and disappearance, the shock and trauma of the loved one returned, or the apparent rearrangement of class and gender boundaries both at the front and at home. These were all the subjects of the films that surrounded the Roll of Honour films on the programme and within cinema culture of the period; it is to these resonances that I now turn.

Recognition and Audience Expectations

In the Will Onda 4th Loyal Lancasters Roll of Honour film there is a photograph of a group of soldiers who were wounded at Aisles. Beneath the caption in brackets is the phrase 'you may be able to recognise them'. The Roll of Honour films call attention to the different meanings of the term 'recognition'. As we have seen, the portraits in conjunction with the biographical information constituted a trope of social recognition. Elevating the individual to heroic stature, they functioned in the same way as the uniform and medals of honour in that they bestowed a culturally recognised social status. The means by which these images were acquired, given to the press/exhibitor by family or friends, suggests a private desire to express publicly the recognition of their service, sacrifice and loss.

A second, more discreet type of recognition is subservient to this public recognition. This is the literal recognition of faces and individuals. The caption 'you may be able to recognise them' presents this more private dimension as a possible pleasure. Pathé made this personal recognition the centre of their advertising campaign for the *Pathé Gazette* in 1915. Entitled 'Pathé Types', these appeared in *Pictures and the Picturegoer* in the autumn of 1915. The first 'type' was 'the munition worker', a drawing of a young woman in a fashionable work smock and cap, with the caption 'Oh yes, I always enjoy the Pathé Gazette. You see, it shows us pictures of our workshops and the girls just as they are. Besides I've seen Bert several times with his regiment . . .'.[26] The following week the second type, 'The Wounded Tommy', appeared, depicted with arm in a sling: 'I dunno about danger, but those Pathé Gazette chaps that take the pictures were in the thick of it. It's really grand to sit down and see the scenes that you've been in . . .'.[27] The pleasure in these films was directed at personal, private expectation and couched within the interpolative form of direct address. YOU might expect to recognise someone, or even yourself, in these films.

Yuri Tsivian, in his book on the cultural reception of early Russian cinema, argues that in this early period the cinematic image was perceived in ways that are lost to presentday viewers. In encountering this new medium Russian commentators drew on existing forms of representation and mapped those onto the new moving images. Writing about a

3.3 'Pathé Types': recognition was one of the attractions of the war actualities.

response to the Lumières' train coming into a station, Tsivian quotes Vladimir Stasov: '. . . it gets bigger and bigger and you think its going to run you over, just like in Anna Karenina—it's incredible'. Tsivian adds, 'real fun has been replaced by literary fun'. For Tsivian this relationship is reciprocal; while the real is replaced by the literary so the moving image breathes life into literary cliché.[28] The attachment of literary frames, of course, can easily be extended to a range of interpretive frames available to cinema audiences at the time. These frames of reference make up a 'mediascape' that includes cinema culture, 'popular' and 'literary' fiction and theatre. These can be construed as an *identifiable* part of an individual's horizon of experience. In order to contain a potentially endless range of references in trying to map an interpretive frame, I have selected texts that contain similar scenarios involving recognition known to be familiar to audiences at the time. Following Tsivian I assume tropes of reception are echoes or mirror images of tropes within texts and that the act of 'matching' them in these texts is central to their intelligibility if not to their pleasure. There are two themes I would like to draw out of these implied pleasures of recognising, and of being recognised. The first concerns the way that intertextual frames of reference form a mode of reception, in this case the reception trope of recognition. The second is the action of investigative looking that an expectation of recognition incites.

Recognition Scenes

The Roll of Honour films required a reception trope of recognition, a trope that resonates with the recognition scenes prevalent in popular film and theatrical productions of the day. Three examples, Chaplin's *The Vagabond*, the British film *The Man Who Came Back*, and a contemporary account of a single response to the stage melodrama *East Lynne*, testify to the ubiquity of recognition scenes in contemporary entertainment culture. Charles Chaplin's move from the 'vulgar' Keystone comedies to more 'respectable' work entailed the incorporation of pathos in his slapstick comedies. In the 1916 Mutual film *The Vagabond* Charlie rescues an orphan woman/child (Edna Purviance) from a brutal Gypsy family. In the middle of the comic rescue there is a fade to a rich woman in her parlour who pulls from her embroidery box a portrait of a little girl. The trope is familiar enough to signal that the girl in the picture is the woman Charlie is rescuing. An artist who is roving the countryside for inspiration sees the woman after she has escaped from the Gypsies and paints her portrait. Her long-lost mother happens into the gallery where he is showing his work and recognises the woman as her daughter. She is led to the daughter by the artist and Charlie is left on his own, until the newly united daughter realises that she really loves him and they all ride off in the mother's car together.

The Man Who Came Back (1915) begins with Harold March, the son of a wealthy merchant, faking his own death so that he might join up in the ranks. His father and his aristocratic stepmother read of his death in the newspaper. His stepbrother George is an officer who has just received his orders to take his regiment to the front. Harold has changed his name to John Learning and has been in the thick of the fighting since the beginning. Returning to the British lines as the only survivor from his company, he meets George. He begs his stepbrother to follow him with some men to take a German artillery post. George, who does not recognise him, as indeed he would not recognise any enlisted man, takes his time following. Our hero goes ahead and takes the guns out single handed. Just before his stepbrother arrives with reinforcements a shell explosion knocks him out. George is given credit for silencing the German gun while kindly Belgians take Harold/John in. Returning to England disguised as a Belgian refugee, Harold/John goes to his home. On his return to the estate he is recognised by his old servant who tells him that a celebration dinner is being held for his stepbrother who has won the VC for silencing the German gun. The next shot shows Harold and the servant peering through the window at the celebration dinner. Looking up from her plate his sweetheart sees him through the window and recognises him. Slipping outside she stands with the servant and Harold and pleads with Harold to tell the truth. After a significant amount of hand wringing Harold looks at the camera and the accompanying title reads: 'No dear they must never know the truth, if they did, those men who have just vowed to serve their King and Country, would think it all a mockery, and go back on their words.'

Melodramas such as *East Lynne* (a novel by Mrs Henry Wood, various versions in play form) work for their effect of tears through tropes of recognition/misrecognition. Lady Isabel, due to the dastardly deception of Francis Levinson, has been reduced to raising her own son by disguising herself as his nanny, Madame Vaux. She never reveals herself to her son, even on his deathbed. When Little Willie dies, she utters the immortal line 'Willie, my child—he is dead, dead and never called me Mother!' In 1916 the *Bristol Observer* ran the following story that offers an insight into audience familiarity with, and their response to, this type of scene. The article was titled 'The Emotion of An Ex-Convict':

> It was in a Leeds Theatre that the writer found himself one evening seated next to a man who had more than once done duty as a convict in His Majesty's Gaol. Forgery and Swindling had been brought to a fine art by this person but he still posed as a 'gentleman' when at liberty. On this occasion the play was the inimitable *East Lynne* and it may seem strange, but it is perfectly true, that when the death bed scene with Little Willie and Madame Vaux took place, this man had big tears rolling down his cheeks, and was sobbing like a child! He turned to the writer and said: 'Pardon me, sir. I don't know how this scene affects you but it always makes me cry like a kid!' I nodded that I understood. He didn't know he was recognised by me, but I felt there must be a tender spot somewhere in such a convict to cause such a result.[29]

In each example the recognition scene is the emotional centre of the narrative. In *East Lynne* the power of the scene rests on the fact that Lady Isabel never tells her son of her true identity. It is this depiction of her impossible choice that prompts the tears of the ex-convict. The journalist in turn is enlightened through the power of the trope to the true nature of the ex-convict. The turn to pathos (and Chaplin's move toward respectability) in *The Vagabond* depends on a recognition scene and, as in the Roll of Honour portraits, the recognition is of a loved one who has been lost, her salvation dependent upon the investigating gaze of the mother. In *The Man Who Came Back*, Harold Marsh/John Learning is positioned in the same space in the homefront imagination as the men in the Roll of Honour films. He can never be known but by a few and is therefore able to traverse class boundaries and oddly acknowledge the irresponsibility of the upper class while at the same time covering it up. What marks this film is the scene when the father and the stepmother read of his death in the papers. This re-enacts the terrible moment of recognition that accompanied the arrival of the telegram for officers' families and letters for enlisted men. The film then generates through a fantasy of loss of identity a re-establishment of the family, if only for the audience. He still exists but is carrying out his duties to his country under another guise.

The Investigating Gaze

Recognition was also one of the attractions of the official war films. An attraction akin to the searching for a familiar face in a crowd at a football match, these films, as seen with the *Pathé Gazette*, were talked about as offering the possibility of seeing someone you knew. The reception trope of recognition here exists in the same way that the Roll of Honour films work. They require a narrative to be placed alongside the images. The *Battle of the Somme* film encouraged a double engagement, as a citizen of the nation and as a viewer with a personal interest. To prepare the viewer each regiment was identified in a title prior to the image. Like the *Recruits* film, the official war films and particularly the *Battle of the Somme* used the slow pan to provide close-ups of faces. This concentration on the visage, this appeal to private recognition, encourages a searching engagement with the films.

The etiology of the act of reading faces in public and in photographs has been the subject of a number of critical histories. Richard Sennett, for example, in charting the rise of the 'personality' from the eighteenth century, has centred his ideas on shifts in public concepts of the nature of appearance. He suggests that the personality had, by the nineteenth century, replaced the Enlightenment concept of natural character, resulting in a situation where 'appearances made in the world are not veils but guides to the authentic self of the wearer'.[30] Reading faces became a popular obsession with the publication of physiognomy books in the mid-nineteenth century. Jennifer Green-Lewis has suggested that the availability of the photographic image 'validated and authorised ... certain kinds of readership ... [and] ensured the practice of reading faces would become widespread'.[31] These physiognomy books featured photographs of criminals and the insane accompanied by narratives that aided the practice of reading the face. This constructed a mode of reception that assumed that the photograph, as scientific recording device, would unveil the mind. Following from the dynamic relationship between the narrative and the portrait a similar reception mode is referenced in the investigative gaze of the mother in *The Vagabond*. She identifies her now grown daughter through her shamrock-shaped birthmark. Her gaze simultaneously matches and socially validates both the tramp's and the artist's recognition of her daughter's innate beauty. Most crucially, this trope of recognition is imbedded in a narrative of anonymity/identity and loss/recovery; therein it contains a resonance with the type of visual engagement assumed and encouraged by the Roll of Honour films.

The local personality is the object of the investigating gaze in the Roll of Honour films. The investigating look is drawn into high relief when compared with the experience of viewing these films outside the local context. A stranger would read a meaning of sacrifice and patriotism but these would be general, undifferentiated readings. The inquisitive, but detached, gaze here may be left to speculate or perhaps invest the faces of these soldiers with an image of the 'angelic invalid' or search for a spiritual sign of doomed youth. In this regard they most match the viewing practices of the physiognomy books that turned on difference. Photographs of the insane or the criminal 'promoted the inferiority and otherness of their subjects'.[32] In the Roll of Honour films the images were invested with an otherness in the sense that the men they depicted were dead, wounded or made different by their experience. This difference was mediated through a dominant public discourse of noble sacrifice and yet within a local context with local knowledges, which attached individual identities, ran the undercurrent of private loss.

The sub rosa dynamics present in the Roll of Honour photographs and films are brought poignantly to the fore in the case of Sir Oliver Lodge. Lodge was well known before the war for his work in 'psychical research' in Britain and the USA. His interest lay primarily in bringing scientific methods to explaining psychic phenomena. His son Raymond was killed at the front in 1915, prompting the publication in 1916 of *Raymond or Life and Death*, which was a treatise on the existence of a spiritual world and the probability of communication with it. The book is organised much like a prepared court case with evidence meticulously laid out. One of the pieces of evidence that Raymond was communicating through spiritual mediums hinged on the existence of a photograph. The medium mentioned a photograph Raymond had told her about but one which had been unknown to Lodge and his wife as it had been taken at the front three weeks before he had been killed. The photograph was broadly described by the medium and then a few months later it was were found. While much of the account is taken up with Lodge trying to prove his case, a significant part is concerned with a reading of the photograph. There were three photographs of Raymond sitting amongst a group of officers. Two of these photographs depict Raymond sitting uneasily as a soldier behind him has rested his hand on his shoulder. Putting the three photographs together Lodge attempts to read the thoughts into his son's face. The photograph showed:

... some one's [sic] hand sitting on Raymond's shoulders and Raymond's head leaning a little on one side, as if rather annoyed. In another the hand had been removed, being supported by the owner's stick; and in that one Raymond's head is upright. This corresponds to his uncertainty (in his 'discussions' with the medium after his death) as to whether he was actually taken with the man leaning on him or not. In the third, however, the sitting officer's leg rests against Raymond's shoulder as he squats in front, and the slant of the head and slight look of annoyance has returned.[33]

Lodge's use of the photograph as evidence of the hereafter is also evidence of his desire to see the static images move, to re-animate. The comparison of the three photos is a cinematic re-animation. The re-animation does not simply stop at the movement of Raymond but the reading reawakens his thoughts, his appearance indicating his personality, as does the actual existence of the photographs.

The importance that Lodge attaches to the recognition of his son's personality is paramount in his treatise on the existence of the afterlife. He predicates his case on establishing in the reader an empathy for his son Raymond. The first part of the book contains the letters from Raymond to his family and friends in order to impart 'The life lived and the spirit shown by any number of youths, fully engaged in civil occupations, who joined for service when the war broke out and went to the Front'. The object was to 'engender a friendly feeling towards the writer of the letters, so that whatever more has to be said in the sequel may not have the inevitable dullness of details concerning an entire stranger'. As a memorial to his son, the book strives not only to establish that 'communication across the gulf is possible' but to iterate his son's actual existence in this life, to counterpose the anonymity intrinsic to military service, death at the front and finally to that obliteration of identity in the spirit world. His sense of duty was driven by 'the amount of premature and unnatural bereavement at the present time'; his strategy of making his son's identity known to the reader was a gesture of defiance to his anonymous obliteration.[34]

Lodge's method was that of the 'rational scientist' and in this sense he followed the methods of the Spiritualist movement with which he was associated. In his use of photography he was also part of a conception of the realism of the photographic image as testimonial. While he stops short of spirit photography, its afterimage remains. In this respect the static images of the Roll of Honour films, representing as they do noble sacrifice *and* the counter-current of nameless loss, perform a similar function. They provide a public testament but also signal private anxieties.

Anonymity and Audience Anxieties

Still Life and Moving Pictures

Lodge, in his desperate wish to reanimate his son through photographs, was not only bringing to the foreground unspoken private anxieties, grief and fear, he was also raising the spectre of primal fears associated with the cinema and photography specifically and modern technologies generally. The official war film *Battle of the Somme* provided an example of re-animated soldiers in a faked attack that was undoubtedly the main attraction of the film. By late 1917 it had circulated throughout the country and the depiction of these soldiers going over the top had taken on the texture of ghosts. Yet from the outset the cinematic image had been associated with the spirit world. Maxim Gorky's famous response to the Lumières' first showings as 'This is not life but the shadow of life' is but one association of cinema with a necropolis. That association was also accompanied by an unease that at times became fear. In his account of the cultural reception of early cinema in Russia, Yuri Tsivian points to the centrality of the Symbolist sensibility that dominated Russian literary culture. Many Russian critics absorbed the new technology through the language of Symbolism. Gorky's association of the cinema image with the land of the dead gives evidence to the anxiety provoked by the uncanny black-and-white world.[35] One of the aspects of this anxiety was the fear of seeing one's own image. He quotes Olga Votskoya's memoirs of Alexei Tolstoi's visit to the cinema for a film in which he appeared. After watching himself for a few minutes he left saying, 'I don't know why but I feel frightened'.[36] Although Tsivian uses these quotes to argue that the perception of the moving image was not always as universal or 'stable' as it has become, it is clear that the transition to a viewer comfortable with images on the screen, from a cinema of attractions to a cinema of absorption, has never been complete.[37]

Earlier associations between projected images and fears in viewers were evident in the slide shows and phantasmagoria throughout the nineteenth century. Phantasmagoria often used themes of raising the dead or the depiction of departed loved ones. Terry Castle has argued that the phantasmagoria has shifted in meaning to become a metaphor for the 'spectralization or ghostifying of mental space'.[38] Given this older continuum of visual engagement and the cinema's associations with the showmanship of the carnival, the series of static images in the Roll of Honour films take on the qualities of apparitions.

Through their stasis, these images were marked out as distinct from the rest of the programme, whether it was live acts or moving pictures. The paradox of these static images projected by a moving picture machine can be imagined to have had the effect of freezing these men in time and space in a defiance of the forward temporal movement suggested by the parade of moving soldiers and munitions in the official war films. In this there is encoded a desperation, a placing of the ideal, and still, portrait across the moving images of the soldiers in the official war films. The ideal is represented in the pose. Most of the men are looking straight into the camera but some are posed looking off camera and up, inspired by, and bathed in, a divine light. The settings contain either a background of indeterminate colour and texture that suggest infinity or they are idyllic. In some the picturesque countryside is hinted at, while the classical pedestals connote a timelessness. The one backdrop scenery in the Milnrow films that refers to battle has an early nineteenth-century cannon in a grassy field, a stark contrast to the chalky, churned up greys of the fields in the newsreels and official war films, where at times the men disappear, swallowed up by the vast sweeping long shots, or simply because they too are the same colour as the land. They disappear as individuals into uniform columns meant to be an impressive display of the modern army. The Roll of Honour films replace for a brief moment this modern crowd of soldiers in two ways, by their static eternal pose, and through their identifiability, their recognisability. Both qualities incorporate the local position within the national narrative while countering the primary anxiety of anonymous absorption within that narrative.

The Hidden Necropolis in the Homefront Imagination

In peacetime the fear of anonymous death had been associated with paupers, bodies unclaimed by family or friends. These bodies often ended up truly obliterated in dissection laboratories of medical schools. Further, the threat of anonymous death throughout the nineteenth century had been associated with fears of crowded urban conurbations and social transience. Joanna Bourke has argued that the war had the effect of extending this indignity to the corpse on the battlefield and thereby creating a necessity for differentiating the experience. 'The allure of a clean death was pervasive. The vision of death during war—painful, humiliating, ugly—intensified the urge for its immaculate counterpart.'[39] The traditional nineteenth-century funereal rituals that signified a 'clean death' marked out class distinctions and social or community recognition. Yet the war created bereavement on a massive scale and as the bodies remained in graves at the front these traditions were largely inadequate. Adrian Gregory has remarked of parental grief:

> Their affective state was miserable, a combination of the worst of Victorian sense of grief and modern sense of loss, but without access to the defensive strategies of either period, extravagant public mourning or 'denial of death' ... the needs of wartime morale prevented the former, yet the latter, the long term internalisation of processes in the mores of mourning, would not be effective for at least a generation.[40]

The shift in the traditions of remembrance of the dead were largely predicated on ameliorating anonymity and culminated at the end of the war in the burial of the Unknown Warrior on Remembrance Day 1920. The cinema's role in this bereavement was similarly caught between traditions and processes. The local Roll of Honour films seem to be one clear example of the changing role of the cinema theatre in the community. The potential for public mourning was contained through the accepted attitude of maintaining morale. The highly codified public displays of mourning of the Victorian and immediate pre-war period were not on the whole desirable; more subdued forms of public mourning were adopted.[41] Social codes around grief and mourning changed significantly as casualties mounted. Since the Roll of Honour films required public expression of support it is not surprising that the few accounts of responses report applause and enthusiasm. A more accurate indicator of the kind of tensions these films may have presented for audiences, and in turn for exhibitors, is the fact that after 1917 instances of these films or slides on the programme are sparse.

The Roll of Honour films are evidence of an alternative experience that hinges on their over-determined theme of identity. The undercurrent of anxiety around anonymity was not allowed expression in public forms of ritual but had ready access to expression through fictional texts. Raymond Williams, in his unfinished work on the politics of modernism, outlined five literary themes that existed in pre-modern art forms and '... in certain conditions led to actual and radical changes of form'.[42] All of these themes were formed in response to the rise of the metropolis and three were overtly driven by anxieties of loss and anonymity: depictions of crowds of strangers, isolation and loneliness, and a sense of impenetrability. Williams offers these themes as structuring agents in the development of modernism. They are useful here in that they were also predominant themes in the films of the period. Chaplin's use of pathos incorporated these themes, as did melodramas depicting the dangers for women in the 'dark city' such as Ideal Films' *Alone in London* (1915), starring Florence Turner. Perhaps more telling is the enacting of the dangers of anonymity and disappearance in the city enacted by Harold/John in *The Man Who Came Back*. He fakes his own death by attaching a suicide note to an anonymous body found in the Thames, leaving an unanswered question, utterly repressed by the film, about the identity of the corpse he found.

The association of the experience of modernity with the city is axiomatic, but those anxieties of anonymity have their parallel in those that constituted a significant part the homefront imagination. The official war films echo this image of modernity in their depiction of the war effort as industrialised mass production, the plenitude of shells, ships and tanks, the isolation of separation from home, of the anonymity of the endless identically dressed soldiers and, of course, the chance, the danger, of disappearance. The Roll of Honour films worked to hold at bay these images of the front as dangerous. The front as feared in the homefront imagination in terms of the chaos of imminent impersonal death and injury, is an imagining that is more easily associated with the city than the rural adventure of the fox-hunt. The Roll of Honour films, through their poses and painted backgrounds, along with the newspaper biographies that told of their subjects' achievements at home and of their bravery at the front, served to hide those imaginings and at the same time are their strongest evidence. The war's actual unseen necropolis, of course, escaped the representational powers of the cinema. Wilfred Owen wrote in a letter to his sister: 'I have not seen any dead, I have done worse. In the dank air I have perceived it and in the darkness, felt. Those "Somme Pictures" are the laughing stock of the army, like the trenches on exhibition in Kensington.'[43]

Finally, the Roll of Honour films call up another form of exhibition associated with anonymity and disappearance. In George du Maurier's novel, *Trilby*, the Paris morgue is an attraction, an exercise in sensational voyeurism, and a threat. Sandy and the Laird often walk through the streets of Paris as artists and *flâneurs* who seek inspiration and frequently visit the morgue as part of the routine of their long wanderings. Vanessa Schwartz has observed that the morgue was a municipal institution primarily there to serve as 'a depository for the anonymous dead', the function being to place corpses in public view in hope of an identification.[44] This was recognised as a kind of public theatre. Svengali threatens Trilby with this fate of anonymous death. 'And people of all sorts, strangers, will stare at you through the big plate glass window . . .'.[45] The fear and threat of dying anonymously, which is so evident here, lies just under the surface of the Roll of Honour films. This was present as early as the first weeks of the war. In September 1914 photographs found on dead soldiers were published by the *Daily Sketch*, offering another example of the anxiety present in the homefront imagination.[46] In a reverse of the spectacle of the morgue, it is the traces of the individual as father or brother or husband represented by photographic evidence that are presented in the search for identity, rather than the body, the corpse.

At the beginning of the war the Roll of Honour films functioned to provide a distinction for the local audience. They referenced the older function of the colourful uniform of the soldier, to be recognised in the crowd—a man in uniform. They combined the private with the public, opposed anonymity with identity, and wrote the local into the narrative of the nation. At the end of Will Onda's tenth series of the 4th Loyal Lancashires Roll of Honour (1915) there was the title 'more to come'. This perpetuity, the seemingly endless procession of the dead, with time, worked to an effect that was less inspirational. Onda exhibited his last Roll of Honour films in 1915. By 1917 exhibitors moved by 'practical patriotism' to keep up morale were responding to their audiences' stated desires—they were not attracted to war films. By the end of the war the cinema's role had become more clearly defined as a modern space for entertainment and news.

The first and most successful of the official war films, *Battle of the Somme*, capitalised on audiences' desire to see moving pictures of the events at the front. It appealed to audiences through its depiction of 'real fighting' and its official nature, through its validation by the War Office. In this respect it succeeded in attracting a wider section of the populace than normally attended the cinema. It also depended upon the same socially accepted modes of reception and response that the Roll of Honour films did. Like those, *Battle of the Somme*, through its depiction of named regiments and through the use of panning shots of troops, attempted to appeal to audiences by ennobling the enlisted soldier and naming them in terms of locality. Yet it also depicted the dead and the dying. In doing so the film gave rise to national public debate that brought to the surface the anxieties that Roll of Honour films had hinted at and—publicly at least—contained. It also significantly shaped the way that exhibitors, and the industry, shaped their arguments for the social function of the cinema.

4

Education or Entertainment?
Public and Private Interpretations of *Battle of the Somme*

> The tragic fear and pity may be aroused by the Spectacle; but they may also be aroused by the very structure and incidents of the play—which is the better way and shows the better poet
>
> Aristotle, *Poetics*[1]

> Above all I am not concerned with Poetry.
> My subject is War, and the pity of War.
> The Poetry is in the pity.
>
> Wilfred Owen, 'Preface'[2]

At the beginning of 1915 there were signs that war news had saturated the public press. *The Bioscope* reported that there was a 'growing opinion that the public is being given quite enough, if not too much, war topics . . .'. Audiences who went to the cinema were looking for 'relaxation and encouragement in its daily tasks' and would not have found that in the proliferation of fictional war dramas in last months of 1914. As with the Roll of Honour films there was a concern about the private anguish that these might bring to the mind of '. . . many of the audience who have given a father, a son, a relative, or friend to the forces [or] who have perhaps lost a loved one in those many deadly battles . . .'.[3] Already the industry was aware of the distinctions between public performance of patriotic response and the private anxieties around loss and anonymity that characterised the reception of the Roll of Honour films. The complaint concerning war dramas centred on the growing understanding of the war as a grim reality rather than a setting for adventure. However, the cinema's function as a place for getting up-to-date information and actual pictures of the front did not diminish. High street cinemas in Southampton such as the Gaiety and Alexandra as well as the suburban cinemas of William Buck's Atherley and Hood and Bacon's Palladium ran actuality war footage in the form of newsreels. After December 1915 these included the official war films such as *Battle of the Somme* (1916) and *The Battle of the Ancre and the Advance of the Tanks* (1917). *Battle of the Somme*, arguably one of the most popular films of the war, was the high-water mark in the tide of enthusiasm for war actualities. For that reason, and for the fact that this film has played a significant role in the image of the Great War in modern cinematic memory, its reception offers an insight into the general impact of war actualities on audiences and on the industry itself at the time.

This chapter explores the various forms of address implicit in the film and its advertising as they were intended by both the exhibitors and the War Office with specific examples of the film's reception. It is an example of where the strategies of the War Office and the industry converged and it highlights the public debate about the cinema's function as a form of entertainment and/or education. Further, the film's structure and mode of address was an engagement with the developing classical mode of representation. Much of its shape owes something to the feature fiction film, both in terms of the decision by Charles Urban of Wellington House to give the film a narrative structure, and in the choice to exhibit the film in cinemas as a special event. The special event status constituted a highly visible form of practical patriotism for exhibitors and the topical nature of the film attracted new audiences to the cinema. However, the result of these intentions at the level of production created tensions between public and private modes of reception that were the result of the film's depictions of death and dying, a spectacle that aroused pity and fear, and the form of narration that attempted to contain them.

A Figment of Imagination?

The film images that we have of the First World War—the explosion of the mine at the Hawthorne redoubt, the over-the-top sequence and the haunting image of the exhausted British soldier moving through the trench toward the camera with a mortally wounded soldier on his back— are in large measure images drawn from the official war film *Battle of the Somme*. Since the 1960s these images have been used in television documentaries and tributes on Remembrance Day to reinforce the perception of a war of 'Lions led by Donkeys', of useless slaughter and the turning point of the century: the true dawning of modernity. These impressions are the legacy of a cultural memory that is the culmination and convergence of a range of popular, literary and academic discursive practices that position the First World War within the larger narrative of the twentieth century. 'Pointlessness' and 'futility' are bywords in these representations. In fact, much of the scholarship that surrounds *Battle of the Somme* also adheres to this axiom. When Stephen Badsey argued in 1983 that the film was a missed opportunity for a powerful propaganda message he argued from the point of view that the film was unable to represent the tragedy of the affair and that the film lacked an overall sense of the battle and its consequences. His praise for the film as a 'haunting masterpiece' is centred in the abiding modern memory of the war as tragic.[4] In another commitment to the theory of traumatic watersheds Modris Eksteins points to the war as the moment of modernity in which 'Reality, a sense of proportion and reason . . . were the major casualties of the war. The war became a figment of imagination . . .'. He focuses on the staged sequence of the attack as the point that cancels out the verity, the truth value, of the rest of the film.[5] In both of these accounts the film is evaluated, and then condemned for its inability to convey the truth. In Eksteins' case the condemnation lies in the film's role in the creation of the war as a 'figment of imagination'. Eksteins is pointing towards an imagined construction of the war by the news media and the propaganda machines that was the work of 'all the belligerents'.[6] There is an implicit dismissal of the means by which these constructions were negotiated by audiences and readers. In that sense Eksteins's figment is a one-way street. This chapter continues with the more complete conception of a homefront imagination that includes not only textual and intertextual address but also modes of reception as the primary elements in the production, exhibition and reception of *Battle of the Somme*.

That the 'figment of imagination' could be a more fruitful subject of analysis is hinted at by Nicholas Reeves, who maintains that the film offered a unique experience for contemporary audiences that contrasted with the widely circulating 'dishonest, unrealistic, mendacious images of the war. In posters, in cartoons, in speeches, in newspaper stories, the war was characterised as a titanic but exhilarating struggle between good and evil . . .'.[7] He concentrates on the film's understated and 'dispassionate' production values as qualities that stood out and signalled a strong sense of 'realism'. Careful to point out that this film also marked the apex of the popularity of the official war films with cinema audiences, he points to 'the fact that, at the time of its initial screening, this one film did give its audience a sense that they had seen the true face of modern war'. He makes the important point that the contemporary audience was persuaded on two levels; that these were authentic representations of conditions at the front and that '. . . the official, factual film was indeed an appropriate medium in which to visualise the nature of the battle front'. Reeves's careful reminder that the film needs to be understood on the terms of contemporary audiences raises three issues. The first is the contemporary assumption of the authenticity of photographic representations of reality and, moreover, the moving photographic image. Secondly, confidence in the medium of film to represent reality was an important element in arguing the industry's case for social acceptability. Finally, it was those other circulating texts and intertexts, those 'dishonest' images, which Reeves pronounces as offering the crucial contrasting element, that allowed the film its quality of authenticity and informed audience expectations.

In 1916 these images of the front were intended by the War Office and the producers of the film to be inspirational through the presentation of a factual account of the soldiers' experience at the front. Further, the film's reception by the press was, with few exceptions, extremely positive. In fact *Battle of the Somme* (1916) was one of Britain's most popular non-fiction films of the period 1914–18, comparable to D.W. Griffith's *The Birth of a Nation* (1915), which was released generally throughout Britain within the same month. Yet to ascribe the word popular to the film's reception is inadequate if only in the sense that the term has an equivalence to entertainment. This was not the case. The film contained disturbing footage of the dead and wounded and particularly the over-the-top sequences that showed men falling. Press reviews and advertising for the film focused on the enlightening properties of this footage, appealing to the public's sense of duty. There was a tension between the attraction of real action footage and the educative properties of experiencing first hand what the boys at the front were going through. The contrast, between the informative enlightening properties of the images and the entertainment value of 'real battle scenes', was evident throughout the film's initial exhibition and reception. My purpose here is to examine these elements of production and reception and cast them against a background of available historical knowledges to lend some depth to the understanding of the way in which this non-fiction British film captured the interest, curiosity and fascination of British audiences.

The War Office and the Trade: An Aesthetic of Authenticity

The research that has been done on the official British film propaganda of the First World War shows that the industry and the government saw the importance of film propaganda for providing information to a mass audience about the war from often, but not always, different perspectives and positions.[8] Exhibitors were concerned with maximising audiences, while the popularity of the cinema attracted the attention of the War Office as a means of informing the public about the progress of the war. Over the course of the years 1915–18 the War Office Cinematograph Committee (WOCC) shifted their production strategy to accommodate audience preferences. This shift in the WOCC's approach to the use of film footage from the front was a shift from its treatment as spectacle, mainly short sections of film in the style of the newsreel, to a sense that narrative form or 'story interest' was essential in providing the footage with a cohesive 'plot', and would therefore prove more popular with a mass audience. This is evident in the move from the expository style of *Britain Prepared* (December 1915) through an attention to linking shots with a narrative structure in *Battle of the Somme* (August 1916), to the fictional narrative film *Hearts of the World* (1918). While this seems a neat construction of a trajectory from 'attractions' to narrative it is complicated by a number of factors: the difference between the way cinema audiences were perceived by the industry and the War Office, the ultimate goals that determined the position and policy of both sectors—i.e. profit, overseas markets and propaganda 'value'—the way in which the War Office viewed the film industry generally and the War Office's and the trade's perception of the way audiences imagined the war itself.

The fact that this shift takes place across the years in which the classical style of narrative filmmaking was becoming the dominant form requires that propaganda filmmaking in Britain can be seen in the context of the development of cinema as a whole. The rise of the classical narration system is characterised by the development of narrative clarity within the filmic text and the subsequent removal of non-filmic elements such as the lecturer, the use of on-site performers and eventually the elimination of live sound altogether. Through this system of narrative integration the audience is brought into the diegesis through alternating mechanisms of identification and separation. These mechanisms are seen to have developed partly through the industry's need to develop 'strategies of narration and address to reach the widest possible audience'.[9] Therefore the subject configured in the classical paradigm is addressed as unified and homogeneous. This system of representation and address has also been seen in the context of the rise of consumer culture, particularly in the United States where, as Miriam Hansen has noted, 'Consumerism, offering "the image of a homogenous population pursuing the same goals" not only became the ticket to full American citizenship, but fundamentally affected the relation of public and private spheres ...'.[10] These strategies of textual and industrial organisation are further seen as contributing to the production of a silent, gazing viewer that had the effect of 'policing' the behaviour of the film-going audience through pleasure. Hansen has gone on to argue that these strategies should not be seen as completely successful, that the desire to create a more stable mode of spectatorship was not smooth and uniform, and that this unequal development left 'traces of resistance in the films themselves'.[11] From a different perspective and one that focuses on the British cinema auditorium, Nicholas Hiley has pointed out that textual strategies did not in themselves have a marked effect on audience behaviour at least until the 1920s. Other factors, from seating policy, pricing arrangements, the entertainments tax of 1916 and the rise of picture palaces, combined to force 'new habits of spectatorship' for the post-war period. British production companies were 'hoping to encourage the working class audience to abandon its communal habits in favour of the middle class virtues of individual spectatorship and concentrated attention'[12]

It is essential then to look at the official propaganda films of the First World War in Britain against this background of an industry coming to terms with rationalisation of production and distribution and the concurrent developments in exhibition and textual practices. While *Battle of the Somme* owed more to the tradition of actuality and the industrial process film, its feature length and its attempt to narrate the events of the first few days of the battle followed the exhibition format of a prestige, exclusive fiction film. These strategies, which were designed to appeal to a mass audience, to encourage a 'homogeneous population', to pursue the same goals (the war effort), would be the common ground on which the cinema industry in Britain and the War Office could unite. This concurrence is illustrated by a report to Arthur Balfour, First Lord of the Admiralty in August 1915 by Charles Masterman and Sir Gilbert Parker of Wellington House. Lord Balfour wrote:

> They said that the most successful weapon which Germany had used for moulding the opinion of neutral countries was the kinomatograph. This reached the intelligence of the least intelligent:

> it required no reading: it touched on no controversial topics: it threw
> no strain upon the spectator's powers of realisation.[13]

It is no small irony, then, that the industry, marked by the need to maximise profit and the War Office's somewhat reluctant intention to take advantage of this rising form of mass entertainment as a means of providing information to a wider audience, found their interests intersecting. In short, the cinema-going public in Britain and abroad became an important 'market' for the propaganda effort while the official films of the front were potentially 'good box office' for exhibitors.

The history of the relationship between the trade and the War Office is characterised by these differences and similarities but it was not always as clear-cut as I have just outlined. For example, the reluctance of the War Office to allow filming on the front for the first year of the war was more to do with military suspicion of the press generally on the part of the official propagandists like Charles Masterman, rather than any scepticism about the informative value of film. Indeed, it was Masterman and the other officials who argued, along with the trade, for the need for filming at the front. The War Office was also interested in financial gain and had much to learn from the trade on the effective distribution of their films. As the initial ban on filming at the front was relaxed the question of the appropriate form for official filmmaking became an issue. Nicholas Reeves has suggested, 'All those who argued the case for official film propaganda saw the factual film as the only form such propaganda should take'.[14] The format of the newsreel was well established by 1914 and newsreel companies such as Pathé's Animated Gazette, Warwick Bioscope Chronicle and Gaumont Graphic had been sending back footage from Belgium and other areas where they had been allowed to film. Geoffrey Malins, cameraman for many official war films, including *Battle of the Somme*, had previously worked for Gaumont in Belgium. The newsreel format provided the precedent and model for an aesthetic of 'authenticity' that marks the initial form these films took. Nicholas Hiley explains:

> When covering an event the aim of the cameraman was to obtain his
> minute or so of film in the most economic manner, and this discipline
> demanded a standard approach. The event would be photographed in
> two or three shots, which could be assembled with the minimum of
> editing into a short sequence able to stand on its own after the
> introductory title. Unusual camera angles and compositions were

considered confusing and worthless and material not included in the newsreel was wasted. An event was broken down into standard images which were at once recognisable to the audience.[15]

This realist aesthetic was developed out of pragmatics of 'getting the shot', further determined by the cumbersome equipment and a common sense notion of what kind of shots constituted or signified the truth. Since newsreel wings of most film companies were not particularly profitable, the need to be aware of expense also limited the way cameramen could cover events.[16]

By 1914 the newsreels had become a small but popular part of the cinema programme. This generally consisted of a fifty-minute main feature, two short dramas, a serial and/or two comedies. With the outbreak of war, footage from the front was very much in demand. Increasingly, however, there was a general dissatisfaction from the public with the content of the films. By the time the official war filming began in December 1915 the 'topical' subjects were no longer in favour and one trade correspondent stated that 'the public are tired of seeing pictures without any story interest'.[17] Nevertheless, this kind of filmmaking persisted. In Southampton war topicals were shown as part of the overall cinema programme at the Alexandra and the Palladium while throughout the war the Gaiety in Southampton advertised the 'Latest War Pictures' as part of a 'brilliant programme of exciting and humorous incidents'.

'Viewed as a Drama . . .': The Front through a Dramatic Frame

The image of the war in the imagination of the public, as the government and the trade perceived it, had implications for the form the films from the front took. These perceptions were based on images of war from the 'death and glory' style of war artist reporting in the late nineteenth century and also from popular literature and pre-war cinema. Indeed, D.W. Griffith's later Bioscope films such as the 1912 films *A Feud in the Kentucky Hills*, *The Massacre*, and *The Informer* are evidence of a style of cutting from panoramic overviews to close-ups of the participants during battle scenes that duplicate the 'death and glory' aesthetic and that prefigure those in *The Birth of a Nation*. British-made fiction films such as *The Man Who Came Back* (1915) also featured representations of the front that focused on individual heroics. These depictions of heroics and drama on the battlefield work towards a visual aesthetic of war that by 1916 was well known to cinema audiences. The war artist/reporter and cameraman

Frederic Villier's recourse to dramatic reconstruction in his account of filming a battle during the Sudan campaign of 1898 is revealing. The cinema equipment he was using during the battle of Omdurman failed him and he had to return to his sketchbook where his only comfort was '... that from [his] vantage point [he] saw many things ... that no camera of [his] kind could have registered'.[18] Malins himself gave an account of his intentions in filming *The Battle of the Ancre and the Advance of the Tanks* in the autumn of 1916: 'I tried to introduce the horrors, joys, sorrows and romance of the war'.[19] Newspaper accounts of the battles often utilised a lexicon of imagery that effaced the mechanised nature of the war and focused on heroism. In the *Yorkshire Evening Press*, 17 October 1916, a story ran that illustrates this process:

> So the fight went on during the night. 'Our men', I was assured by an officer who was present, 'actually enjoyed the thing, it was an infantryman's fight. The Germans could not shell us and we had only to get the better of the Boche with rifle and bayonet. Our fellows were singing and laughing as they went off. Of course comrades dropped, but they did not mind that. It was a straight fight, man against man, and we were the best at the game'.[20]

The emphasis on action and hand-to-hand fighting has more than a hint of the frustration with indiscriminate shelling and a static battlefront, the implication being that this is an unfair, unsportsmanlike and 'German' way to conduct warfare. This in itself indicates an acknowledgement of the reader's awareness of the nature of the experience at the front. The problems associated with bringing the official war films in line with these expectations of heroic action are best illustrated in the statement made by Griffith that 'viewed as a drama, the war is in some ways disappointing'.[21] Griffith's battle scenes in *The Birth of a Nation* and later *Hearts of the World* are sweeping and full of movement, in stark contrast to the stasis of the western front by 1916.

The reality of war footage did not live up to these expectations for a number of reasons. The use of smokeless explosives was virtually invisible on film, the nature of warfare waged across great expanses and limitations of lens technology and film stock—not to mention the danger of the enterprise—created little opportunity to film the kind of heroic struggles that were circulating in the press. There was no visual field of combat in a kind of warfare where to be visible was tantamount to being killed. *Battle of the Somme* was released in August 1916 against this background of public expectation of the spectacle of heroic charges and an unrepresentable reality.

The decision to produce feature-length films was sparked by the footage shot by Geoffrey Malins and J.B. Macdowell on the first day of the Somme offensive. Nicholas Reeves has noted that 'as early as May 1916 both the military authorities in France and the propagandists at Wellington House were convinced of the need for a larger, more ambitious form of factual film. The problem was to find the right kind of material out of which to construct it.'[22] The need for films of feature length had also been a concern of Charles Urban of Wellington House, but there was some resistance from the trade to give over a whole performance time to footage that was proving less and less popular with audiences. The Somme pictures provided a counter to these worries in that the narrative structure of the battle had been widely circulated in the press reports of the 'advance', which aided narrative comprehension. The already well-known structure of the battle provided fairly strict parameters within which Urban could work to achieve a sense of realism and veracity. Further, if the over-the-top sequences were faked, as is generally believed, then the attack was seen by Urban the editor, and by Malins the cameraman,[23] as central to ensure clarity and that audience interest was maintained.

With the editing completed and the film passed by the War Office, the screening for the trade took place on 10 August 1916 at the Scala Theatre in London. The response was very positive. The film was hired out in the manner of an exclusive fictional feature, rather than sold through the open market system and was treated with the kind of advance publicity organised for *The Birth of a Nation* a few weeks later, although on a smaller scale. Having a clearly structured, and successful, feature-length official war film helped to attract large audiences to official films for the rest of the year and the better part of 1917. It also solved another concern for the War Office and the Foreign Office: it set the precedent of making their film central to the cinema programme and not simply a short addition. In June 1916 Lord Derby had voiced concern about showing official films on the same programme with 'Charlie Chaplin and similar films . . . I think it is rightly felt . . . that the Army ought not to be sandwiched in such a fashion . . .'. and Miles Lampson, the Foreign Office film propaganda expert, stated 'I always thought these film people were the scum of the earth'. He regretted that war films were not profitable and that 'what does pay is Charlie Chaplin and similar trash to which the public flock unceasingly'.[24] While this perception of the trade and cinema audiences may not suggest that the official films were made for a particular audience, it does indicate that these films were intended to be viewed with reverence and as unmediated truth and therefore too worthy to be placed alongside cheap amusements. A discourse of uplift is evident in the idea that these films, in telling the 'real' story, would enlighten and encourage the 'common' cinema-goer through the catharsis of encountering the reality of the war effort. These hopes for transcendence through the experience of seeing the war 'as it really is', also sit comfortably in an industry that is aspiring to a 'better class' of customer.

The Big Push: A Narrative Structure

Battle of the Somme's intertitles divide the film into five parts but its narrative actually obeys a 'three act structure'. The first depicts the build-up to the attack on 1 July 1916, the second the attack itself, which includes staged footage of the men going over-the-top. The third and final section has scenes of the wounded being carried in, prisoners being brought back, the dead collected and buried and it ends on an upbeat scene of the Worcesters waving and 'continuing the advance'. Much of the footage is of the kind that would have been included in the topicals: a display of weaponry, the marching of troops to the front and troops resting, each group identified by regiment. This visual arrangement was coupled with the audience's familiarity with the 'big push' from newspaper accounts and letters home, to produce an identifiable narrative.[25] Charles Urban stated that it was important to '. . . arrange all future films "to tell a story, working to a climax" instead of simply joining up the various episodes irrespective of sequence of happenings or relative connection of various incidents shown by the negatives'.[26] The climax of the film is the staged attack that had probably been shot because attempts to film the actual advance had not been successful, and in order to enhance the realism and to narrativise the battle by lending pace and a sense of time and space. This is noted in the *Southern Daily Echo* in advertisements that announced the forthcoming screenings of the film at the Alexandra and Palladium cinemas. The Alexandra announced the film as showing 'Actual Fighting' and quoted the London press: 'Nothing more stirring than the sight of the infantry rushing over the parapet to the attack' (*The Times*); 'Pictures extraordinarily realistic' (*Morning Post*); 'Riveted the attention of an invited audience' (*Daily Mail*). The

Palladium advertised the film as: 'The official record of the great advance. Photographs of the actual fighting. An intimate and vivid survey of the most glorious deeds performed by the British Empire Troops.'[27]

These advertisements reveal two important assumptions by the producers and exhibitors: firstly, they demonstrate general awareness of the larger narrative of the great advance amongst the cinema-going audience; secondly, they show that it was to be a special event unique to the cinema and of interest to a wider public than its usual patrons. As for the first, *Battle of the Somme* depended upon audience familiarity with the events of the front for its effect. The film was given a general release two months after the first assault. The actual battle was still going on when the film was first screened throughout the country and would continue until November. Casualty lists of the first weeks had been published throughout July and August and, although these may actually have been incomplete the cost, in terms of dead and wounded, was recognised generally as having been heavy. Throughout the month of July newspapers had been reporting the 'big push' so that the newspaper-reading populace knew the structure of the battle (at least of the first few days): the bombardment, the attack and the aftermath. Concurrent with these mediated representations of the battle was the war's impact on everyday life, from the experience of personal loss to the visible evidence of its effects in the public sphere. That visibility was particularly pronounced in Southampton. A story entitled 'Dramatic Scene at Southampton Docks', which appeared in the *Southern Daily Echo* on 7 July, a week after the devastating first day of the battle of the Somme, gives an indication. It recounts the passing of two trains, one full of troops headed for the front, the other of wounded returning.

> The writer watched them from an office window overhead and could plainly see in the faces of the untried troops their eager interest, their profound respect of their comrades who had been tried. An assured pride, an easy fearlessness of the man who has proved himself in the very teeth of death, this was marked in the faces of the wounded, but no man spoke a word . . .[28]

The reporter went on to recount that the silence was broken by an officer from the wounded train shouting 'Are we downhearted', and answered with a resounding 'No!' This tense moment was relieved by the '. . . music of the roar which rose now from the cabined hundreds of both trains [that] was something to penetrate the vitals of a Briton'. This story emphasised the necessity of the public face of patriotism but at the same time allowed the expression, however muted, of the visible evidence of the war's consequences. The private anxiety of the moment, the silence, is both expressed and contained by the soldiers' public patriotic response. These knowledges and the narrative structures that attempted to contain them had been widely circulated by the time of the film's release. They offer a template for the reception of the film in that they reveal one aspect of a discursive mechanism that was utilised by the exhibitors to justify the exhibition of film footage of the wounded and the dead.

The Industrial Process of War: A Special Event

The special event status of the film was implied in its local Southampton premiere at the ornate High Street cinema the Alexandra and at the Palladium in the affluent suburb of Portswood. *Battle of the Somme* was the first of the feature-length official war films and its simultaneous release pattern of 100 prints across the country in the first week of September dictated that it was first shown at prestige cinemas in the main cities and towns. In its subsequent runs it appeared at smaller houses throughout the autumn of 1916 and the spring of 1917. The regional release was the subject of an intense build up of pre-publicity. The Palladium and the Alexandra 'boomed' the film as a coming attraction two weeks prior to its screening. The technique was one of 'roadshowing' that had been used to such a great effect in the success of *The Birth of a Nation*, which had been touring the country since the previous April. The difference was that *Battle of the Somme* was shown in cinemas rather than theatres, a decision that reflects the War Office's concern to reach the widest possible audience. An indication of the confluence of special event status with prestige venue was given as a testimony to the National Council of Public Moral's inquiry into the cinema at the time of the release of *The Battle of the Ancre and the Advance of the Tanks* (1917), the follow up to *Battle of the Somme*. Miss Margery Fox, representing the Head Mistresses' Association, was answering questions from the Bishop of Birmingham:

> *Bishop of Birmingham:* Have you seen the picture of the Tanks?
> *Miss Margery Fox:* No; I only go to the bad cinemas, those I think are going to be bad.[29]

However unique the exhibition strategies were, the style of *Battle of the Somme* belongs to the already existing genre of the 'educational' film. While the film depends for its intelligibility on audience foreknowledge and awareness of the events of the war, like many educational films of the period its structure hinges on the depiction of a process. Primarily associated with industrial process films, this method of narrative followed the production of an object through the series of tasks necessary to its creation. *Battle of the Somme* contains such a set of processes, often showing the complete process between each title. Made up of sixty-three titles, the film devotes considerable space to showing a set of processes that celebrate the efficiency of the military and the medical services. For example intertitle eight reads: 'Along the entire front munitions "dumps" are receiving vast supplies of shells: Thanks to the British Munitions Workers'. There then follow three shots depicting the process of unloading shells from trucks. The first is a panning shot of the munitions dump, the second is a parade of trucks pulling into the dump and the third depicts the men unloading the trucks. The next section shows the movement of spent shells from the battery and new shells to them. Intertitle nine reads: 'Hidden batteries were pounding the German trenches for five days before the attack. Refilling limbers with 18 pounder shells after "dumping" the cases.' This consists of five shots that first depict the hidden batteries (the first image of the battle front) while the next four shots depict men loading shell cases into horsedrawn limbers. This process format was repeated in part 1 of Hutchinson and Company's magazine series *Sir Douglas Haig's Great Push: The Battle of the Somme*. The photographs were taken primarily from the film and the captions that accompany the photographs from this sequence elaborated on the process, describing in detail the action of loading the limbers.[30] One caption under the image of a motorcycle and truck entering the dump, which comes from shot two of sequence eight, points to the thrift and efficiency of the process: 'A transport wagon coming up to where the limbers are, and bringing from the base hundreds of shells. Notice the empty cartridges lying about: all are taken back, refilled, and freshly charged ready to be used again in the guns.'[31]

The 'industrial process' format figured significantly in debates about the educational value of film generally. Even Margery Fox, who was loath to admit any value to cinema at all, admitted that there was potential in this genre. Mr A.P. Graves, MA, chairman of the Representative Managers of the London City Council Elementary Schools and a member of the Cinema Commission, asked Miss Fox if 'A lesson might

Here you see one of our men lifting a box containing shells off the transport wagon.—

—No sooner is one box lifted from the wagon than another man comes forward—

—and takes another box,—

—and this goes on until the wagon is emptied and a line made of the boxes of ammunition ready to fill the limbers.

UNLOADING BOXES OF SHELLS FROM TRANSPORT WAGONS.

4.1 A set of four photographs depicting the 'process' of battle, taken from the film and reprinted in *Sir Douglas Haig's Great Push*, part 1, p. 22.

be given illustrating a certain process, and this lesson might wind up with a cinematographic summary of the process, which, say, might be lumbering?' She replied, 'I should always want it safeguarded so that the child did not go too often'.[32] This genre of film was common to the experience of most cinema-goers and particularly to those middle-class audiences whose visits to the cinema were infrequent but who attended lectures and educational screenings at public halls. In fact, the commission reported in its findings that the educational value of films was reflected in essays that schoolchildren had written when asked to describe useful information they had acquired at the pictures. These included: 'Facts of geography, history, literature, natural science, industrial processes, social life, and current events detailed in great variety'.[33] Each of these subjects, apart from perhaps natural science, accurately describes the parameters of the educational content of the official war films; so much so that the findings of the commission singled out the official war films' educational value as 'undeniable'.[34]

Educational films were a problem for exhibitors, however. The educational value of cinema was a strong plank in the industry's negotiations with official governmental bodies and unofficial interest groups, but the drawbacks for audiences expecting an evening's entertainment were considerable. The commission concluded that the cinema's social function was primarily a venue of amusement and recreation. This of course coincided with the industry's desires. The educational film's lack of success was recognised by the commission as indicative of the insufficient general knowledge of the cinema-going public 'to form that connection between previous experience and the subject matter of the film which is so essential to vivid interest'.[35] Further, and repeating Lord Derby's concerns, it recognised that the atmosphere of the cinema was:

> ... highly antagonistic to their favourable reception and to their educational value. A film, however beautiful, of the life-history of a plant or insect sandwiched between a Charlie Chaplin film and a thrilling episode of the *Exploits of Elaine* has little chance of survival. The interest—if it ever had been aroused—is soon switched off, and a feeling of boredom results. To be effective in such surrounding the film must have interests other than purely educational.[36]

'... Not a Holiday Picture ...': Uplift and Spectacle

While *Battle of the Somme* shares the didactic format of the educational industrial process film, it was not hindered by a lack of public interest. The representation of the industrial process of war included graphic and spectacular depictions of its results. As noted, the film showed an attack sequence and depictions of the wounded and the dead. Apart from the broader debates this engenders for theorists and historians to which I will return at the end of this chapter, the War Office's construction of the cinema audience as uneducated illustrates anxieties as to whether the film would impart education about the grave struggle or offer spectacular entertainment. Reports of the film's reception around the country highlight the contradiction between advertising real action as an 'attraction' and arguments for the enlightening and informative power of the footage. In Manchester the correspondent for the 'Northern Section' of the *Kinematograph Weekly* reported on 7 September 1916: 'Much discussion has arisen as to whether its realism is not too pronounced, but all agree that the useful purpose is to bring home to those who live in peace whilst their brothers and husbands are fighting the horrors of warfare'.[37] Implicit in this report is the desire to see action (along with the attendant glorious sacrifice) and the need to interpret the films as uplifting, in short a tension between entertainment and transcendence. This is borne out in the following week in a report in *Kinematograph Weekly* on 'Holiday Audiences and the Somme':

> A Holiday audience differs to some extent from a city audience, for the former, who are bent on having a good time, do not hesitate to show their warm approval of the fare submitted when it pleases them ... In Southport where the film was shown last week, and at Blackpool ... 'The Battle of the Somme' had been witnessed by an almost complete absence of outward demonstration. Yet it was plain to see the audiences were visibly and uncomfortably impressed ... [it] is not a holiday picture but it is one which holiday makers should certainly see, despite the disturbing effect it is likely to produce upon some of those who are enjoying themselves in the sun ... whilst their comrades are engaged in a deadly struggle on our Ally's soil[38]

Both accounts stress the duty to keep the war effort in mind, particularly in the context of entertainment and leisure. The resolution of the contradiction between uplift and amusement or entertainment lay in the conceptualising of the spectacle as education and information.

Tom Gunning has suggested that the World Expositions of the late nineteenth century provided a new space where spectacle was intended to be both educational and entertaining and that it may be that, however much these films were meant to address an elite, they may have provided a 'basis for international and cross-class experience' for the cinema.[39] He argues that these spaces performed the ideological function of presenting an image of the 'world-wide power of capitalism' and raised the 'commodity form of entertainment to a new technical perfection'.[40] *Battle of the Somme* and many of the official films depended on such a perception of spectacle as education and entertainment. The cinema became a site of the imagined landscape of the war where modernity was celebrated through the increasingly technical perfection of the cinematic apparatus itself, combined with the heroics of the camera operators and the evidence of industrial efficiency through the spectacle of mass-produced ordinance and destruction. The cinema also became, like the exposition, a space that collapses the immensity of its subject within boundaries. The boundaries of the exhibition hall hold the spectacle and history of the world and in a similar fashion the official war films attempt to contain the enormity of the war within spectacle and increasingly, as we have seen, narrative.

'They See their Own Flesh and Blood . . .': Private Recognitions

As mentioned in the previous chapter, a striking element of the official films, and *Battle of the Somme* particularly, is the inclusion of regiments and the address to specific regions of the country. For example in the 2 September edition of the *Southern Daily Echo* a regular column entitled 'Topics of the Hour', which consisted of short obituaries mainly of local officers, contained the announcement that 'In the Official Pictures of the Battle of the Somme, which are to be shown at Southampton next week, a certain unit, containing many local men may be identified. When it was shown at Bournemouth many people were able to recognise Lieutenant D.S. Godfrey, the well known musical director.'[41] In fact this element of personal address was highlighted in the initial trade reviews after the 10 August screening with phrases such as: 'At times one almost imagined one recognised the face of a friend . . .' or '. . . it is as a human document that it will make its strongest . . . appeal to the people. They see their own flesh and blood, these soldiers who march before them, there are thousands of faces, each of which will be recognised by someone!'[42] This form of address to a heterogeneous audience warrants some consideration. As in films such as *Recruits* the slow camera-pans across the faces of the soldiers afford the possibility of recognition. The direct address of the soldiers resting in the sunken road may speak to us today as a testament of doomed youth but for the contemporary audience these shots provide the chance of finding the face of someone they knew. It is at once particular and general. It is inclusive and yet exclusive. It is an attraction predicated on possibility rather than shock or astonishment and it acknowledges the spectator's position in a real space, the cinema. While privileging the realism of the image, it acknowledges the gap in space and time between the spectator and their friend or loved one. The fact that this mode of address does not conform completely to one of attraction or narrative integration indicates the contradictory position that this film, and the official films generally, occupy in the history of cinema and spectatorship.

Giuliana Bruno has noted that for the Italian popular theatrical form *sceneggiata*, which first appeared during the First World War, there was an accepted form of response understood and performed by audiences:

> The *sceneggiata's* mode of reception does not belong to the atomization and privatization of forms of spectatorship. The popular body interacts in the spectacle ... As a figuration the genre (sceneggiata) continues the mode of spectatorship typical of popular spectacles, where people come in groups, and crowds act collectively, providing an alternative model to the isolated, privatised film-going experience.[43]

What mode of reception did the audiences for *Battle of the Somme* adopt? The advertisement of the film foregrounds the 'spectacle' and 'thrill' of realism, which implies a robust, patriotic *performance* of response by the audience. Previous official war films and the format of the newsreel, as we have seen, formed the expectation of what war footage would reveal. The reports of the war throughout the local and national press were also cues for expectation and understanding. Further, the significance of the casualty lists to a local population for determining probable audience expectations of what would be shown and how to respond appropriately is crucial and demands attention. For example, the Hampshire regiment suffered significant casualties on the first day of the advance. The regimental history records: 'The 1st Hampshires indeed had had their worst experience of the war, comparable to the 2nd Battalion's ordeal at Cape Helles on Aug. 6, 1915 ... July 1st, 1916 had cost them eleven officers and 310 men killed and missing, 15 officers and 250 men wounded.'[44]

The War Office's procedures for notification of casualties to families is complicated by the categorisation of 'wounded', 'killed' or 'missing' and these total figures may not have been known, although it is certainly the case that the fate of the officers, through the *Southern Daily Echo* column 'Topics of the Hour', was continually unfolding. The story of Lieutenant Colonel Laurence Palk 'who fell at the head of the Hampshires in the heavy fighting of July 2nd' was run in the 11 July edition of the *Southern Daily Echo*. The regimental history records: 'Colonel Palk's loss was deeply regretted. A tower of strength from Le Cateau onwards, where his coolness and calm had been an inspiration to many who were enduring their "baptism of fire"'. In the 31 July edition of the *Echo* an article appeared, entitled 'Hampshires in the Thick of it—73 Killed and 362 Wounded', reproducing the casualty list issued by the War Office. Ten per cent of those killed came from Southampton. The relatives of these men may not constitute a significant part of the potential cinema audience, but if those who knew the men and/or their families, those who had relatives and friends serving on the western front and those who had friends or relatives listed as missing are taken into account, then it is safe to assume that a significant number of people affected in this way would have an interest in seeing the film. This background, the pre-knowledge of the events at the front through the popular media and any personal understanding through letters home all offer probable contexts for the reception of the film. Nicholas Reeves has documented the responses of audiences as predominantly one of silence and respect, much like that of the Blackpool holiday audience. In some cases he found evidence that audiences had cheered during the lighter marching scenes, a phenomenon common to the slide shows of military leaders and to the Roll of Honour films.

4.2   A still from the film showing the Hampshire Regiment 'moving up to the attack', reprinted in *Sir Douglas Haig's Great Push*, part 1, p. 31.

These contexts for the film's reception highlight the tension between the awareness of personal loss, the desire to see real battle scenes and the patriotic sense of duty. The education/entertainment dilemma is reproduced at the site of reception, the public space of the cinema auditorium. While the example of the Blackpool holiday audience may be evidence of the didactic tone of an industry anxious to celebrate the cinema space as informative and educational, it is also an indicator of how the film sits as a unique viewing experience for the audience of the time. What was the appropriate response to these images of the living and the dead? The auditorium was certainly a place where much more than viewing took place and the 'cinema habit' constituted as much active behaviour as it did silent viewing.[45]

Central to the consideration of audience response to the film is the background of the shifting social responses to death across the four years of the war. In his reception study of Armistice Day Adrian Gregory usefully draws a distinction between bereavement, grief and mourning:

> Bereavement refers to the objective situation of someone who has experienced the loss of someone significant to them through death. Grief is the emotional response to that loss. It includes psychological and somatic reactions. Mourning refers to acts expressive of grief. Mourning is shaped by the customs of a given social or cultural group, which create expectations of correct behaviour for one bereaved.[46]

He points out that grief as understood here is primarily a psychological state, while mourning 'has been the realm of anthropologists'. Driven by models that 'stress the social construction of personality and personal psychology',[47] more recent work in this area challenges these demarcations. Here the function of the 'cultural activity' of mourning is to mediate '. . . between social structure, which varies from society to society, and the psychological imperatives (distancing from the corpse, release from affective bonds, coming to terms with separation) which are universal'.[48] When mourning cultures of different societies are compared, such mediation creates differences not only in the cultural activity but also in the emotional effect. In short, attitudes to death in different cultures indicate that individuals *feel* grief differently. Such difference in feeling across cultures may also change in the same culture at different periods. Gregory points to two contrasting factors that make the First World War unique in the history of changing attitudes to death. The first, as noted in relation to the Roll of Honour films, was the social interdiction of public displays of mourning, while the second lay in the psychological effects of falling infant mortality rates, which had eroded 'the emotional defences that had reconciled previous generations to the loss of children'.[49] The memorialisation of the war dead after 1918 was in part the public response to these shifts in the effect of traumatic loss. Citing Kubler-Ross's study *Living with Death and Dying*, Gregory points to the two steps to coping with sudden death, or the phase of 'acceptance'. The first is being able to cope with memories by visualising the deceased. The second step is to 'overcome the inevitable guilt' by constructing a story that 'makes sense of the death and finds some good in the event'.[50] He argues that both of these were the work of the memorialisation process.

The factors that Gregory lays out as characteristic of the war period, where bereaved individuals are caught between the inability to mourn publicly and the—arguably historically unprecedented—blow of the unexpected death of a child, a 'modern denial of death', provide an important context for the reception of cinema generally at this period. As with the Roll of Honour films this historically specific emotional state underlies the reception of *Battle of the Somme* to the extent that, within the accounts of its reception, the textual address and the circulating intertexts, it threatens to break through to the surface. *The Film Renter*, a trade paper for exhibitors in the north of England, exemplifies a barely contained tension in the first two sentences of this paragraph from its review of the film:

> There is no doubt that scenes showing German dead, and several of our own boys in the position they have fallen, will make many people who have relatives 'out there' feel the lump rise in their throats. But what a different sensation thrills you when you see the boys returning after grappling with death. Instead of being set, tense and grim they could not appear more cheerful if they had been returning from a football match.[51]

In this brief paragraph the mechanics of Kubler-Ross's steps to the 'acceptance phase' are played out. The recognition of the body is followed by a story that gives the death meaning. Crucially, the address in the first sentence refers to those directly affected in the third person, ascribing them to the realm of (an)other. The dramatic shift to the first person for the description of the thrill works hard to offset the impact of the depiction of corpses by enveloping the living figures in smiles and a masculine tradition of home: the football match. The result of these 'steps' played out in public, spectacularised in the cinema space, ultimately excluded private resolution through a public mourning.

The film itself presents the visualisation of the corpses within a narrative of process. The shots of the dead being buried come after the shots of the wounded in the dressing station and the depiction of captured prisoners. The most extensive shots of the dead are introduced by intertitle fifty: 'The Manchester's pet dog fell with his master charging Danzig Alley'. This nine-shot sequence takes up forty seconds of the ninety-second segment and is a considerably long segment in a film where the average shot length is sixteen seconds and the average length of segments between intertitles is sixty seconds. The first shot shows the corpse of the dog in the foreground and in the background lies the soldier amongst blades of grass blowing elegaically in the wind. This is then followed by five shots of bodies lying where they fell. The remaining four shots depict the burial parties gathering the British dead and covering them with dirt. The logic of the sequence is the process of the burial detail. In most of the accounts of the film's reception these scenes were encountered with silence.[52]

Because the film offered a unique type of experience, a chance for a 'real' glimpse at the war, the audiences expected to respond with patriotic applause (as many did), with astonishment at the spectacle of real battle and finally with reverence at the depiction of death. The patriotic response is a public response where, as in the *sceneggiata*, people acted collectively. Yet, as in the Roll of Honour films, the extensive number of those with relatives in the service or those suffering bereavement indicates a mode of reception of a private nature and one that exists within the liminal boundary between public and private as well as that between historically specific traditions of mourning. The mode of reception for the film was, for these reasons, incoherent, or at least hybrid, and it is not surprising that the more familiar modes of film reception that accompanied the cinema programme would be activated.

Melodrama and comedy were modes of reception that activated audience response and were the pervasive forms of fiction films shown on the screens of Britain at this time. Published accounts of the screenings of *Battle of the Somme* are examples of 'reflective, responsive or interventionist' forms of cultural reception that, in striving to make the film legible, drew upon an interpretive frame recognisable as an echo of tropes within fictional texts, in this case melodrama. Peter Brooks notes that the function of melodrama in the novels of Balzac and James was:

> ... to offer a complete set of theatrical signs, words and gestures, corresponding to heightened meanings. It was thus a complete convention in the interpretation of life as inhabited by significant forms. Its theatricality constitutes the substratum of Balzac's and James' art: referring us to 'life' by way of the theatrical medium— through the reader's and the characters' own consciousness of their heightened enactments—they postulate significant form, read out meaning from the indifferences of reality. To state it bluntly (to overstate it): they could not have written their novels as direct interpretations of reality; they needed the model of reality made significant and interpretable furnished by theatricality, and particularly ... melodrama.[53]

The 'melodramatic imagination' functions to make legible a conflicting, chaotic world through the construction of a Manichaean universe, of personalised forces of evil and good. Its project, Brooks suggests, may be to reorder an otherwise illegible world. James Douglas's description of the film in *The Star* of 25 August 1916 shows traces of this melodramatic field of interpretation when he refers to the 'demented German prisoners, [and] the kindly British soldiers showering cigarettes upon their captives'. He constructs the British soldiers as an idealized masculinity while the Germans are 'demented' and pathetic, they are vanquished villains.

Melodrama is also a drama of recognition. The film's textual address emphasises recognition that echoes the recognitions and misrecognitions of melodramatic scenarios, as Mary Ann Doane writes:

> The 'events' that crowd each other within melodrama often have to do with meetings and recognitions that are mistimed or barely in time: just-missed arrivals or departures, recognitions that occur 'too late', last minute rescues, blockages of communication that could have been avoided. Hence Franco Moretti claims that the pathos of melodrama, its moving effect, is generated by a 'rhetoric of the too late'.[54]

Commentators encountering the images of identifiable individuals consistently refer to the temporal gap between them and the events on the screen. The recognition trope in these films emphasises this gap and is imbued with a 'rhetoric of the too late'. Writing to *The Times*, 'Orbatus' stated: 'I have lost a son in battle, and I have seen the Somme films twice. I am going to see them again. I want to know what was the life, and the life-in-death, that our dear ones endured, and to be with them again in their great adventure.'[55]

Orbatus articulates the unbearable consequences of the too late and at the same time the near-hysteria of repetition, of reliving the traumatic moment. As in melodrama the loss of a loved one at the front defied the logic of a rational universe, the consequences exceeded any transgression imaginable. Seen in this light, the following responses to the film are significant. Mr W. Jefferson Woods, manager of the Broadway Cinema in Hammersmith, had refused to screen it and showed a slide instead which stated: 'WE ARE NOT SHOWING THE BATTLE OF THE SOMME. THIS IS A PLACE OF AMUSEMENT, NOT A CHAMBER OF HORRORS'. In a conversation with a reporter from the *Evening Standard*, Mr Wood defended his decision: 'I don't think it is suitable for those who have lost relatives. I think it is harrowing and distressing . . . I was at a trade view . . . and one man gave a shriek and said, "Let me out. I feel so bad. I have just lost a brother'".[56] In the same district as the Broadway, the Blue Halls screened the film. Their proprietor told the *Evening Standard* 'One boy recognised his brother in the picture, an officer: "Look, look," he cried, "that's my brother'".[57]

Here is the inclusive/exclusive character of the address where the unaffected viewer imagines while the affected viewer remembers. The recognition that brings tears in melodrama is not a specific reference to a personal tragedy as it is in these accounts. The effect that is brought into play in melodrama is one of empathy and response to the excessive consequences of minor and often unintentional transgressions, or the unexpected act of fate or divine intervention. Audiences familiar with this mode have recourse to this interpretive mechanism in connecting, recognising and empathising with the soldiers depicted in the factual films as well as with fiction film and theatre.

While this mode of reception characterised the public responses to the film the private experiences of those directly bereaved indicates a different register. Nicholas Reeves in his analysis of the reception of *Battle of the Somme* draws attention to Lloyd George's secretary Frances Stevenson's diary. She had recently lost her brother in the war and she recorded her response to the film:

> . . . There were pictures of men mortally wounded being carried out of the communication trenches, with the look of agony on their faces. It reminded me of what Paul's [her brother's] last hours were: I have often tried to imagine myself what he went through, but now I know: and I shall never forget. It was like going through a tragedy. I felt something of what the Greeks must have felt when they went in their crowds to witness those grand old plays—to be purged in their minds through pity and terror.[58]

The reference to Greek tragedy is a striving for the purifying Aristotelian notions of tragedy. The desire is for illumination and transcendence, to be reconciled to a higher sacred order. Her personal narrative intertwines with the public narrative of the film that in turn is written across the broader open-ended narrative of the battle and the war itself. Frances Stevenson's recognition of her brother's ordeal is not contingent on her actually seeing him but on recognising and empathising with his plight and resigning him to his destiny. A more public expression, given the interdiction of mourning or outward expression of excruciation, necessarily depended upon a melodramatic imagining where virtue, however oppressed and threatened by evil, ultimately triumphs.

'Entertainment which Wounds the Heart'

The transitional quality of *Battle of the Somme* sits, as I have argued, between the tradition of newsreels and their dependence on display and spectacle and narrative integration. The narrative structure of the film coincided with and built upon audience foreknowledge of events while the shots of soldiers, identified by regiment, provided the possibility of personal recognitions. Significantly, its reception shows evidence of deeper ambiguities surrounding the social construction of death and mourning rituals and the public display of patriotic response.

In its depictions of 'real battle scenes' the film was unique; it showed men being shot, and it depicted the dead, a quality that the later official films lacked.[59] This characteristic made the official war film the central feature of the programme and for the next year the official films were good box office. Geoffrey Klingsporn, in tracing the Timothy O'Sullivan *Harvest of Death* photograph of the dead at Gettysburg through American war photography and films, has argued that a 'common justification' for the distribution of these types of images is that they inspire a pacifist response in all those who encounter them. He also points out that the depiction of the dead incites fascination. 'The fascination derives not from some human impulse to gaze upon misfortune but from war photography's triple reality: death is "the blank horror and reality of war," war the reality of history and photography the "Reality Itself"'.[60] It is clear that the depiction of death was an attraction in *Battle of the Somme* and that the ideological justification worked, as we have seen, through similar strategies that utilised the indexable qualities of photographic representation. The self-evident 'truth' effect characterised the debates around its value as education and its potential for prurience as entertainment. Undoubtedly this film constructed a vision of the war, the purpose of which was, in the words of Geoffrey Malins—the photographer responsible—'that the millions of people at home would gain their only first hand knowledge of what was happening at the front'.[61]

In this remark and in the choice of shots, the industrial process genre to which it belongs, the faked attack sequence, the identification strategies between the intertitles and the slow pans, the wounded and the dead and the cheering Tommies directly addressing the camera after a hard day's work, we find both an assumption and a *construction* of the contemporary audience. But there are also traces in the reception of this film that indicate that the overt rhetoric of the film, pacifist only in that the road to peace was to continue the fight, produced other readings. It is here that *Battle of the Somme* differs, at least in its contemporary reception, from that of *The Harvest of Death* photographs. Instead of 'satisfying the public's appetite for vicarious war'[62] these responses indicate a complexity where the gap between home and the front, the image and the cinema spectator is made manifest. Frances Stevenson's private response alone testifies to the conflict between the personal recognition address, emphatically built into the film, and the depiction of corpses. The Dean of Durham, H. Hensley Henson's objections to these images gives further evidence to their potential effect when a significant number of the audience has such personal investment: 'I beg leave respectfully to enter a protest against an entertainment which wounds the heart and violates the very sanctities of bereavement'.[63]

One cannot escape the temptation to read the Dean of Durham's comment as ironic. His objections were clearly within a discourse of taste and propriety, that these films 'violate' sanctity. Given that all of the feature-length official war films took as their controlling form the 'industrial process' film, one detects a Ruskinesque objection to mass production, and a puritanical dissent to pleasurable consumption underlying this sensitivity. Yet particular problems do arise when traditions of the celebration of modernity through spectacle are drawn upon to represent the subject matter of the official films. The depictions of actual death, the 'production line' for destruction and the open-ended nature of the films offer a self-reflexive representation of the artifice and inadequacy of the project. They recall Daniel Pick's characterisation of the idea of war as a machine as having two 'contradictory permutations of cultural representation'. The first is the depiction of war 'under the sway of the logic of technology, science and planning'. This contains its own 'friction': that of the reality of its practical impossibility. 'This insistence endures in the present century and is often anchored in the "moral" of the Somme.' The second representation is '. . . nightmarish: War is no longer the stable object of representation, but the threat of a more drastic foreclosure of meaning'.[64] In this sense *Battle of the Somme* is a modern film, not a deception, as Ecksteins would have it, but through the power of its images it is a critique of its form. Its reception indicates that it was broadly received on two levels; a public patriotic response and a private response of anxiety, loss and grief. The interaction between the film in the head of the spectator and the film on the screen in this instance allowed for individual response within the public domain of the cinema. Latent in the text itself, images of the making of war in the style of an industrial process film provoked most published responses to strive to contain that fundamental contradiction within the language of patriotism and glorious sacrifice. Others, such as the Dean of Durham and cinema manager Jeffrey W. Woods, disavowed the contradiction and put in its place objections to the propriety of such a public display.

The official films' shape and development were the result of the industry's and the government's competing and sometimes concurring perceptions of the audience. That perception of the audience proved accurate in August/September 1916. There is no doubt that the predominant nature of the public response to the film was overwhelmingly positive, but the impact of the film's subjective, private address probably explains the fact that the public tired of the feature-length official war films by the end of 1917. Wilfred Owen's insistence on the power of the effect: 'the poetry is in the pity', resonated across private emotional states that outlasted the Aristotelian preference for structure. The battle, and the war, had not ended in September 1916 and as its effects became more widely known the film's mode of private address became more pronounced.

Perhaps the strongest evidence of this powerful undercurrent in the reception of *Battle of the Somme* and the Roll of Honour films lies in the attempts made after the war, through memorialisation, to make sense of the loss. In 1925 the *Russell's Handbook of Southampton* described in the following terms the cenotaph, designed by Robert Lutyens, and used as a model for the national cenotaph in London:

> ... the inscription is permanent, and with age the names will show more prominently ... The pylon is surmounted by a cenotaph supported North and South by Lions and East and West by the Arms of Southampton. On the Cenotaph is placed a recumbent effigy of a fighting man, it is placed high up so that the face is not seen, thus allowing the imagination of every Mother the representation of her lost Son.[65]

For exhibitors, however, *Battle of the Somme* was probably the strongest example of practical patriotism of the war. For a brief period after the exhibition of this film cinema-going became a part of the war effort, a patriotic duty. On the day the film was released in a column entitled 'A Real War Film', the *Southern Daily Echo* stated: 'It shows war as war is, in all its real reality, on the white curtain of the picture theatre, but it is *good medicine* for those who stay at home' (my italics).[66] In keeping with the dictates of practical patriotism, Southampton exhibitors worked to take advantage of the film's success, as did local exhibitors throughout Britain. *Battle of the Somme* was followed in subsequent weeks with the French official war film *The Defence of Verdun* and the French version of the *Battle of the Somme*, both at the Alexandra in the city centre. These films, however, made up a part of the programme and were 'sandwiched' (in fulfilment of Lord Derby's fears) with Charlie Chaplin in a 'Rollicking 2 Part Comedy *His Trysting Place*' and *The Criminal*, a 'Broadway Star Feature'.

While there is no clear evidence that middle-class cinema attendance increased due to *Battle of the Somme* the film's role in the industry's strategy for respectability was significant. 1916 was a watershed year for audience attendance, mainly because of the entertainments tax that took effect in May. Nicholas Hiley has shown that 1916 was a peak attendance year for British cinemas generally, reaching figures of 2.2 tickets per household per week in late 1916. Following that the figures steadily decline until 1922. Hiley argues that much of this decline is the result of fewer ticket sales among the working class.[67] If he is correct the evidence suggests that middle-class attendance did not increase, or if it did it was not enough to replace the falling attendance figures of working-class audiences. Yet by 1916 the feature was a permanent fixture on cinema programmes and it marked the super-film debate amongst exhibitors. At the centre of this was D.W. Griffith's film *The Birth of a Nation. Battle of the Somme*'s example of education and entertainment as an advertising strategy was reproduced in Southampton in the exhibition of *The Birth of a Nation* six weeks later. The film opened on 30 October. not at a cinema, but at the Grand Theatre in keeping with Griffith's demand that his film only be shown in 'the highest class theatres and at prices charged for the best theatrical attractions'.[68] Such prestige rhetoric was the primary focus of advertising for cinemas such as the Palladium and the Alexandra. The discourse of uplift, the mechanisms of exclusion through signalling the 'high-class' nature of the production and exhibition can be read as being targeted at a 'respectable' middle-class audience. However, the next two chapters will consider these form of address, as they are manifested in the 'appeals' of the advertisements for *The Birth of a Nation* and Thomas

Ince's *Civilization* (1916). By contending that these should be seen as prescriptions for audience behaviour and response through appeals to a sense of 'duty' and 'pride', the advertising indicates an attempt to expand audiences rather than exclude a working-class audience. The overwhelming popularity of *Battle of the Somme* and *The Birth of a Nation* shows that these films were not simply attended by a middle-class audience and this needs to be seen in the larger perspective of the relationship between local exhibitors, the shifting terrain of distribution, and the increasingly powerful impact of the practices of the US film industry. Griffith's *The Birth of a Nation*, its advertising and the roadshow technique of exhibition provides a salient example of a strategy, the aim of which was to integrate a heterogeneous audience under a rubric of good taste and transcendence through entertainment and education.

Artful and Instructive

Respectability and *The Birth of a Nation*

Wrapping up the significant events of 1915 for the exhibition trade at the beginning of 1916 the *Kinematograph Year Book* published an article written by D.W. Griffith in which he outlined the significance of the 'big' film for the future of film as an art.

> We are wise, in my opinion, to develop to their utmost all such points of superiority of our medium, for thereby we shall the sooner secure the recognition of kinematography as a distinct art in itself which is so eminently necessary if the future of the cinema theatre is to be the successful and glorious art we all hope and believe.

In the same issue an article appeared by British director and producer Percy Nash, who also had been stage manager to Sir Herbert Beerbohm Tree and Sir Henry Irving. Entitled 'Some Thoughts on Film Producing', the article recounted his enlightenment about the stringent requirements for making quality films that met audience expectations. 'I have come to the conclusion that the public looks for and expects more reality and correctness of detail in the smallest moving picture than the greatest stage production ever placed before them.'[1] By comparing the cinema to the theatre both Griffith and Nash were articulating an argument about the respectability of the cinema that the trade had been developing throughout the previous decade.

October 1915 had seen the exclusive exhibition in London of Griffith's *The Birth of a Nation*, which by January 1916 had achieved a kind of mythical status amongst audiences and exhibitors. The film was expected to continue its exclusive London run for some time. From mentions in the House of Commons to vociferous debates amongst the exhibition trade about the exclusive release of such 'super-films' in theatres and not cinemas, Griffith's film had created not only talk but also a palpable sense of achievement for the industry as a whole. Hence Griffith's and Nash's emphasis that the properties cinema possessed were beyond that of the theatre. Cinema's ability to convey realism anchored their arguments for cinema's educative powers. The war and the subject of war in both accounts, was central to these claims. Nash recalled being offered a chance to produce a successful Drury Lane production for the screen where he was offered the use of the scenery and an airship, which prompted him to remark '. . . how little . . . the theatrical mind realises that the requirements of the pictures is *reality* not *make believe*'.[2] Griffith claimed that his film '. . . does not profess to be a sermon, but if, incidentally, it does something to show the real character of 'glorious war' it will, I think, have served at least one useful purpose'.[3]

Griffith's statement hints at audience responses when confronted with the cinematic depiction of the realities of warfare. Nash's comment is less grandiose and is content with the cinema's capabilities of realistic depiction of scenes. As we saw in the last chapter, footage of the events at the front in *Battle of the Somme* proved an attraction to audiences who did not frequent the cinema. After almost a year of piecemeal footage these audiences were moved by the curiosity of seeing depictions of the front in the way that Nash was celebrating, the real machinery and soldiers on the actual field of battle. Griffith takes the argument further by emphasising an emotional realism that is achieved through cinema's capacity for actuality combined with dramatic scenarios. In seeming anticipation of the declining interest in the actuality footage of *Battle of the Somme* and the later official war films Griffith emphasised cinema's capacity to generate sympathy as an enlightening property.

> The man in the street, who does not read history, or, at best, cannot be expected to read with the student's imagination, may have some sort of mental image of those events, but there is one medium, and one medium only, which can place them before him with all the impressiveness of actuality. A stage production may do something to make them more real, but it is the motion picture screen alone which can reconstruct them on the same scale in which they occur and place the twentieth century observer in the position to appreciate and sympathise with the viewpoint of the actual actors.[4]

Griffith did not state it, but by emphasising the experience of appreciation and sympathy he was referring to the developing cinematic properties of his own style of staging, acting and editing. Consciously or not, he was also drawing on a position in British public intellectual debates that held that altruism and selflessness were essential in the construction of a society where, as Stefan Collini has suggested, '. . . morality was "a statement of the conditions of social vitality". . .'. Collini points to the role played in this debate by 'imaginative literature' first in stimulating sympathy, and also as a controlling argument for the value of the study of literature.[5] Griffith's argument for cinema's educative power through its ability to generate sympathy in the spectator fits easily into these existing debates.

In the same discursive vein these words, written by Cecil Chesterton in 'An Explanation' in the Scala film theatre programme, accompanied the London premier of *The Birth of a Nation* on 27 September 1915.

> I think I should not be far wrong if I said that most Englishmen, if asked for their impression of the struggle between North and South, would answer that it was about slavery, which the North attacked and the South defended, and then ended with the emancipation of the slaves. Short as this summary is every phrase of it contains an error.[6]

Following a special screening of the film on the afternoon of 27 September, the critic for the *Pall Mall Gazette* wrote: 'most people would define the cause of the American Civil War as a struggle for the abolition of slavery. The conception is, however, inaccurate and misleading, and the drama at the Scala throws a new light upon this darkest chapter of American history.'[7] These remarks bear the traces of Griffth's and Nash's claims for the enlightening power of cinema as art and at the same time initiate a set of interpretations that were offered as a guide for British audiences as they encountered Griffith's spectacle. Chesterton points to the need for such guidance in the first paragraph of his 'explanation' of the 'second phase' of the war (i.e. Reconstruction) that 'is at once one of the most romantic and one of the most instructive episodes in history, [with which] very few Englishmen are at all familiar'. He acknowledges the 'misapprehensions' of his assumed audience and initiates a process of redirecting meanings that characterised the film's initial run during the years 1915–16 in Britain. Such reshaping of interpretations was engaged in most forcefully by the critical press and in the advertising strategies for the regional distribution of the film.

'A Soul Stirring Appeal to Every Briton'

Not surprisingly, these redirections of historical understanding do not differ substantially from the dominant discourse that characterised the reception of the film in the United States. This interpretation of the history of the American Civil War and Reconstruction was one that W.E.B. Du Bois had characterised as 'a structural amnesia'.[8] What does seem to mark out the popular reception of *The Birth of a Nation* in Britain as different—what is missing—is a dissenting voice, a counter-argument. There were no well-publicised debates or objections to the film's racist representations, no attempts to censor or ban the film at local exhibitions and no public disturbances such as those that accompanied the film in the United States. Criticisms of the film lay mainly in the nature of the kind expressed by the critic in the theatrical trade journal *The Era*:

> The second Act is perhaps marred by the mass of horribly realistic details, showing how the negroes [sic] vilely misused their newly given freedom. One or two of the scenes left one cold with horror and unless those pieces of realism help to bring about the day of the human brotherhood that Mr. Griffith represents in a rather poor epilogue, we cannot see that they serve any purpose . . . and think some of the scenes might well be deleted.[9]

Here, rather than questioning Griffith's representation of history, the criticism is based on 'sensibility and propriety'; an objection to the realistic portrayal of the rape and forced marriage scenes. The criticism of the religious epilogue provides a glimmer of suspicion of American preaching at a time when utopian visions were beginning to ring hollow. Only the critic from a Liberal paper, the *Reynolds Newspaper*, offered any direct questioning of the historical accuracy: 'Mr. Cecil Chesterton's historical sketch of the period helps to an understanding of the pictures. I fancy it is a wee bit one-sided and the Ku Klux Klan is idealised.'[10]

The reception of the film during the Great War in Britain suggests that the interpretations encouraged by the advertising and the critics' comments attempted to highlight aspects of the film that de-emphasised or ignored the film's racist message in favour of those that coincided with the concerns of the British public at a time of national crisis. In this chapter I examine the release history of the film's first run, 1915–16, in terms of the discourses utilised by the advertisers, the critics, the exhibitors and the trade press. I want to explore why the film was accepted by the British cinema culture at the time through a number of different interpretive strategies: as an advance in the cinematic art, as a portrayal of the personal and familial consequences of war, as educational spectacle and as evidence of a shared Anglo-American historical trajectory. Each of these worked towards strengthening the national industry's argument for cinema's aesthetic and cultural legitimacy.

The Birth of a Nation played at the Scala and then the Drury Lane Theatre London from September 1915 until the spring of 1916. The film then played in the major cities throughout Britain. It was a full year in many cases before the film reached cities such as Southampton, Bristol or Portsmouth. The significance of that year cannot be overstated. By October 1916 British casualties had greatly increased and the effects of the disasters on the Somme were literally coming home.[11] This provides a background for considering the range of probable meanings available to reviewers and audiences at the time. A film that has war and its effect on the home and family as its main theme screened during this particular year raises a number of questions: how can the combination of the intentions and address of producers, critics and exhibitors be brought to bear on a film that is made for a US audience, dealing with issues of nationalism and historical memory? How were British audiences encouraged to interpret, or make sense of this film? What would they have recognised? In what way, if at all, did the exhibitors, news media and the advertisers treat the controversial nature of the film?

Tom G. Davies and the Western Import Company Ltd imported the film for the exclusive run at Drury Lane in London.[12] Sol Exclusives, a distribution company owned and run by Sol Levy of Birmingham handled its release in the regions. Levy bought the UK rights to the film and had in his employ a young Victor Saville and Michael Balcon. Saville stated in 1977:

> Instead of hiring it out to the trade in the usual way, he decided to exploit it himself, renting halls around the country which had been closed or temporarily abandoned during the war. Later I had the job of selling the epic around the cinemas. It cost Levy £10,000 and he grossed £100,000 out of it. A fabulous figure in those days.[13]

The accuracy of this account is questionable to the extent that most of the theatres that ran the film were not abandoned. For example, the Grand Theatre in Southampton, where the film was screened in October 1916, was a thriving venue for live theatre. The film's release in theatres with symphony orchestra accompaniment, rather than in the purpose-built cinemas, followed the exhibition practice of 'super-films' such as *Quo Vadis* and *Cabiria*. This type of 'roadshowing' differentiated the film, marking it out as a special event. Saville's job of selling the film as a 'second run' in cinemas occurred in the early part of 1917.

5.1 The Grand Theatre was the type of up-market theatre that screened *The Birth of a Nation* in its first run in Britain.

This was not the first time a feature-length film had been screened at the Grand, which normally produced popular plays advertised as coming direct from London. The Grand would occasionally screen films of 'particular interest' such as Kinemacolor newsreels and 'the race for the Derby showing the suffragette incident', and had screened *Cabiria*. The *Southampton and District Pictorial* of 25 October 1916 advertised the film as having 'A Soul Stirring Appeal to Every Briton'. The advertisement was drawn from the national advertising campaign for the film and was distinguished from the standard way the Grand advertised its coming attractions by being a quarter page in size as opposed to the usual brief mention given to dramatic productions in the Theatrical and Entertainment Announcements page. The standard black ball logo with the title of the film appeared on one side and on the other, under the 'soul stirring appeal', lay the following exhortations:

- See the Marvellous Battle Scenes
- See the Regeneration of a nation, as England will be reborn when the War is over.
- See the Development of a New Art -- an Epoch in Dramatic History
- A Vivid, Graphic Story of Anglo-Celt achievement which will make every Englishman, Woman and Child glow with pride, gasp with astonishment and thrill with marvellous realism!

The pronouncements above offer a way of addressing questions surrounding the reception of this film and can illuminate the negotiation between the intended meanings of Griffith, (by this I mean the production team represented by the name above the title), the meanings

5.2 The 'black ball' advertisement used in the US release and by Sol Levy in its first run in Britain. This is from the *Southampton District and Pictorial*, 25 October 1916.

134

directed by the advertising campaign and the attendant assumptions about the attractions of the film to an English audience.

'See the Development of a New Art—an Epoch in Dramatic History'

The Birth of a Nation was an 'authored' film with Griffith's 'name above the title'. It provided spectacle on a grand scale and utilised a specially arranged and composed score played by a forty piece orchestra. The theatrical trade journal *The Era* stated; 'It leaves no doubt as to the genius of Mr. Griffiths [sic], and the mere hugeness of this successful undertaking is almost stupefying'.[14] *The Biscope* gave the presentation of the film two pages where the writer, on a second viewing, praised the use of music that provided the vast spectacle with 'emotional power'. The article concluded: 'It is seldom if ever that the screening of a picture has been undertaken with such skill, care and intelligence, and the production as a whole constitutes a valuable object lesson on the "art of presentation"'.[15] The production had a tangible impact on trade debates about exhibition practices and the move to picture palaces in Britain. The identification of Griffith as author was a signifier of individual agency and artistic vision that influenced exhibition and advertising practices generally and was a successful attempt, in this case, to expand the constituency of cinema audiences.

Virtually all of the accounts and reviews I have researched foreground the artistic achievement of the film. The review in *The Times* after the premiere at the Scala connected the artistic merit of the film with the debate in the House of Commons over the chancellor of the exchequer's proposed duty on imported cinematograph films. The reviewer reported that Sir Alfred Maud 'caused some merriment in the House' when he asked, during question time, 'whether a committee of the cabinet was to assess the comparative values of last night's Scala production with those of a Charlie Chaplin film'. The reviewer also noted that 'it will be of some interest to the film industry to note the degree of popularity which may be obtained by a serious work, such as this of Mr. Griffith's, unrelieved by anything lighter than a love interest'.[16] By drawing attention to the serious nature of the film a reproval of the vulgarity of cinema is apparent in the distinction he draws between the Scala *production* and the Chaplin *film*. In the context of the debate on import duties Maud's sarcastic suggestion equates cultural value with economic worth and contrasts the exclusivity of a forty-piece orchestra in a large hall with the insignificant mass reproduction of a Chaplin comedy at the local 'bughouse'.

The Times' characterisation of the film industry reflected the ongoing debates among cinema exhibitors about the use of theatres to screen these 'super-films'. (*Cabiria* had been screened in the same way). There was significant concern among exhibitors that these film presentations would present heavy competition for picture houses that were not big enough to accommodate such ambitious productions. *The Bioscope* ran an article entitled 'The Super-Film', beginning with the heading 'A Protest' and reported a special meeting of Liverpool exhibitors who were concerned with the 'heavy competition engendered by . . . such big film attractions as *The Birth of a Nation*. The writer then proceeded to argue that the film represented the need for 'considerable readjustment of marketing and exhibition methods' and that it had 'raised the status of the film many grades higher in the opinion of the more wealthy and critical sections of the public . . . On strictly commercial grounds, it has definitely profited the industry by creating for the picture theatres a new and most desirable audience.'[17] In short, the article is a thinly veiled argument for the picture palace and the benefits of the prestige feature in broadening the 'class' of audience. '*The Birth of a Nation* is a picture spectacle too vast in itself, and involving too elaborate a presentation to be suited to the conditions of the ordinary present day picture theatre. . . . it will win increasing popularity for the amusement business among an increasingly large clientele'.[18]

In Bristol the case of the Colston Hall illuminates this debate. Colston Hall had been built by 'a number of public spirited men' in order to 'provide a place for meetings, concerts, musical entertainments and social gatherings' and to 'provide such healthy and instructive entertainments as would produce an income for the upkeep of the hall'. The hall was, however, in trouble financially as the programme of events had not been well attended. It had a cinematograph licence that allowed occasional screenings of films. *The Birth of a Nation* fitted the educational remit ideally, while the popularity of the film had presented an opportunity for some of the losses to be recovered, but a longer run was needed to maximise this effect. The run of the film had been lengthened and this had come to the attention of the Bristol licensing judges. In response the Colston Hall company directors made a representation to the justices that was reported in the *Bristol Observer*, 28 October 1916. They stated that in order to remain open the hall would have to be 'at liberty to let it for cinema shows'. The argument centred around an interpretation of what the term 'occasional' meant and was based on the stiff competition from cinemas that, they claimed, was having an adverse effect on the attendances at the hall. Opposing the directors of the hall was a solicitor representing the Cinematograph Exhibitors' Association as well as proprietors of the local cinemas, who were referred to as 'those responsible for the conduct of the picture houses in Bristol'.[19] The judgement of the justices was to allow the hall to continue its run. However, in their ruling they commented that the argument that the cinema trade had diminished attendances was perhaps exaggerated and that 'other things' apart from cinema competition were affecting attendances.

The judgement, as reported in the *Bristol Observer*, gave no indication as to what the other competition might be, but factors such as the entertainments tax, which had been in effect for a few months, would partly explain the fall in cinema and music hall attendance. There was also some truth in the complaint that competition from cinemas was having an effect on the hall. There were eight picture theatres advertised in the Bristol *Western Daily Press* on Tuesday 3 October 1916 (and four music halls), all located in close proximity. As a consequence of the open market system, exhibitors often showed the same films. As in Southampton and elsewhere this led to advertisements in the local press that would highlight any unique feature of the theatre itself. The Cheltenham Road Cinema in Bristol, for example, highlighted how pleasing it was 'to turn in from the moisture-laden atmosphere outside to enjoy a first class picture entertainment under pleasant and comfortable conditions'. As a way of differentiating the film from the average cinema fare the release of *The Birth of a Nation* was treated by the national and local newspapers as a special event and the vast majority provided special reviews of the film on the theatrical events page.

The national advertisement's inclusion of Griffith's pledge to present this film 'in only the highest class theatres and at prices charged for the best theatrical attractions' was an attempt to control the meaning not only of the film text but to present the produced film object as a rare commodity, a cultural event. The effect of screening the film in 'respectable' theatre halls in the regional towns and cities was to set the film outside the scramble for product (and audiences) that the open-market system produced. This had advantages for the distributor and producer. It was a form of exclusive, contract booking that, by controlling the number of screenings available in one area at a given time, allowed the film a much longer rental life. In the process this exclusivity, as emphasised in the advertisements, 'elevated' the experience beyond that of a night out at the cinema, for the higher price of a theatre ticket'.[20]

The promotion of the film as a milestone in the development of a new art provides a solution, in part, to the industry's dilemma of how to attract a 'better class' of clientele while not alienating their already existing audience. The advertisement articulates different appeals to different class groupings through an overriding attempt to underscore the national appeal. What is signalled by its attempt to redirect the meaning of the film is the connection between the transformation of cinema as an art form with the rebirth of England as a nation. Moreover, it hints at the renewal of social life necessary after the war. A discourse of uplift is evident in the combination of 'Art' and 'Dramatic History'. Drawing on a well-established tradition of restaging historical events, the advertisement emphasises the educative properties of Griffith's presentation of historically accurate scenes. The critic for the *Reynold's Newspaper* wrote:

> I found the scenes dealing with the Civil War and particularly the wonderful reconstruction of the assassination of Lincoln and the sad attempt to establish a tyranny in the South after that sad event the most attractive ... And for those who dislike the powder of instruction it is as good as if it were uninstructive.[21]

Other critics' accounts suggest that the medicinal 'powder of instruction' was sweetened by the grandiose spectacle. The *Pall Mall Gazette* wrote:

> There are no printed descriptions to dim the onlooker's impressions and set up barriers between events and the records of them. The events themselves are in progress under the eye. The truest principles of education call loudly for such directness of record, and every child of school age should be taken to see the vivid narrative of the American nation's birth at the Scala.[22]

The patina of exclusion, inherent in accentuating the 'high-class' nature of the production and exhibition, is offset then by the emphasis on the image, a story in pictures a child could understand. While the emphasis on art and dramatic history is evidence of the production of imagined, 'desirable' audiences by advertisers and exhibitors, the spectacle offers a much wider appeal through emphasising its educational value.

'See the Marvellous Battle Scenes!'

In the year prior to the release of the film there was a significant build-up to the film in the trade journals. The cost and size of the production were newsworthy items in themselves. *The Bioscope* indulged in the hoopla in an article entitled 'Some Facts about "The Clansman", D.W. Griffith's Biggest on Record'. The article reported: 'There are battle, murder and sudden death in the picture'. Griffith is depicted as a romantic cavalry figure (or cowboy) who 'directed many of the "combat" pictures from the back of a Wild West horse, and frequently he forgot himself and dived into the Kuklux *melees* to emerge almost without clothes and with many bruises'.[23]

The Bioscope employed a rhetoric that identifies generic qualities that exhibitors would recognise, notably the adventurous qualities of a western 'romance', which are readily transformed into a thrilling war drama complete with the dashing cavalry hero emerging scarred but victorious from a desperate struggle. The emphasis on being inside the battle—and its implications of identifying the camera's 'eye' with the director's vision—held a specific attraction for British exhibitors and audiences in the opening stages of the Great War.

The exhortation 'See the Marvellous Battle Scenes' is representative of the particular interest it was assumed British audiences had in the visualisation of war scenes. This assumption was held not only by the exhibition trade, who had been experiencing good business with newsreels depicting footage of the war, but also by the War Office, who had been supplying the official war footage of the British army through the Topical Film Company.[24] The date of the first screening of *The Birth of a Nation* in London pre-dates the release of *Britain Prepared* (December 1915) the first official war picture from Wellington House. This takes on significance for the first screening of *The Birth of a Nation* in that the 'marvellous battle scenes' would be read against a shortage of actual battle scenes from the front. Here the reception of the film across the year (September 1915–December 1916) in which the first-run theatrical presentation took place should be seen in the light of the rapidly changing representations of the conditions at the front. Through the official war pictures, and particularly *Battle of the Somme*, the shortage of filmed images of the British army at the front had been partially addressed by the time *The Birth of a Nation* had reached the provincial towns such as Southampton, Bristol or Coventry in the autumn months of 1916.

The official war pictures up until *Battle of the Somme* (August 1916) mainly consisted of images of soldiers marching, the display of war machinery, and the images of royalty and politicians visiting the front. In the last chapter we saw that the discernible shift in the approach to the use of war footage, from its treatment as spectacle in the style of the newsreel, for example, to a sense that narrative form or 'story interest' was essential in providing the footage with a cohesive 'plot'. These narrativised films proved to be more popular with a mass audience, but, until the release of *Battle of the Somme* in September 1916 there were regular complaints from the exhibition sector about the paucity of footage from the front. An article appeared in *The Bioscope* on 23 March 1916 entitled 'Peeps of the Hidden War; Official Pictures of Armegeddon', which drew attention to the public's perception of the war:

> It is a paradoxical fact that the ordinary civilian is practically shut off from any direct knowledge or experience of the greatest event in the world's history. The most tremendous war that has ever shaken the earth is being waged in virtual secrecy. Save for any brief news reports, the darkness of Armegeddon has been unrelieved by any graphic mental description of its dreadful yet heroic cause.[25]

The article draws attention to the spectacle of some of the recent Topical Budget films '. . . which would have aroused much attention even if they had been specially "staged" episodes of a spectacular play, and which naturally possess double fascination when one realises that they are glimpses of actual reality'.[26] The desire to see a 'graphic mental picture' reflects the frustration with the official films in the way that they differed so significantly from a narrative film style. The complaint that the spectator is unable to experience the battle arises out of the static shots of actuality footage, the long takes and the absence of any viewpoint from which to witness a heroic struggle as it is happening. D.W. Griffith's comment to Harry Carr of *Photoplay* that the front was visually disappointing refers in part to the problem of filming actual battles, for safety reasons if nothing else. 'Everyone is hidden away in ditches. As you look out over No-Man's Land, there is literally nothing that meets the eye but an aching desolation of nothingness.'[27] The Great War, as seen from the trenches, was 'cinematic' in terms of pyrotechnic spectacle, of 'looking up', but not conducive to narrativisation and the construction of an omniscient viewer who 'looks down'.

In his idiosyncratic but compelling book *War and Cinema*, Paul Virilio notes the uncanny coincidence of the filming of the battle scenes for *The Birth of a Nation* and the opening battles of the Great War. He characterises Griffith's style as shooting the scenes in long shot from on top of a hill, a 'vision' that 'belonged to the world of the Lumières' *Salon Indien*. It was a style in which Griffith looked 'from a stationary outside at objects moving before him: the camera reproduced the circumstances of ordinary vision, as a homogenous witness of the action'.[28] As must be necessary in a broadly conceived project such as Virilio's, certain details escape mention. While there are grand establishing shots for the siege at Petersburg sequence, Griffith's editing between opposing sides and the tracking shot of Colonel Cameron (actor Henry B. Walthall) are hardly static. Contemporary accounts of the battle scenes describe not only a mobile panorama of images but also a mobile viewing position; the *Pall Mall Gazette* commented:

> It is hard to know where to set the limits of pictorial illusion. Mr. Griffith's production is not stage acting: it is something far beyond the capacity of any directly acted production. He can find room on the Scala stage for the swiftly moving panorama of half a continent without sacrificing the illusion that the unending processions of scenes and people focused but a few yards away are real and tangible.[29]

The Bristol *Western Daily Press* praised the film 'as a work of great fascination for it depicts, in a series of remarkable pictures, the development of the United States from the days of slavery and the great war of the North v. the South', but went on to say, 'Two families, one in Pennsylvania and the other in Piedmont, S.C., between whose young folk great friendships had sprung up, now fight on the opposing sides, and it is surprising how well the thread of the story is maintained through that great conflict'.[30] By emphasising the techniques as 'staging', these accounts work from an aesthetic that marks out the boundaries of personal and epic as separate. This historical form of visual engagement foregrounds the *mise-en-scène* over the editing. An attempt to explain the fast changes in viewpoint is vaguely evident in the *Pall Mall Gazette*'s distinction between scenes and people but more prominent in the Bristol paper's comment on how well the 'thread of the story' is maintained. The *Reynold's Newspaper* is more specific in connecting the personal dimensions of the story with the spectacle of epic. 'On the technical side the photography is admirable, and there is a fairly interesting melodramatic story to give that personal touch of drama which big historical events must have on the stage or the screen'.[31] It is not surprising, however, that a theatrical trade journal, *The Era*, would be the most able to articulate the complexities of Griffith's narrative style: 'To stage a war of the magnitude of the Civil War of America and to bring home the horrible pathos of the affair by the dramatic possibilities of the mingling of two families throughout awful scenes of carnage and destruction is what Griffith has attempted'.[32]

The spectacle of battle as theatre was familiar to British audiences, from the panoramas of great military battles such as Waterloo to the military spectacles and the nautical plays that were popular in the late nineteenth century. 'Blood and thunder' melodramas depicted heroic battle sequences with identifiable 'Great Commanders' and 'Great Common Men' fighting against a usually unspecified evil, an enemy of the empire. By 1915 the cinema-going public was familiar with the depiction of battle sequences that worked to position the viewer through an omniscient narrator. Through narrative style, *mise-en-scène* and/or editing it became increasingly possible to identify with one or more participants in the battle, to see what they saw and through them experience the struggle.

For most British reviewers the distinctive qualities of the battle sequences that marked out *The Birth of a Nation* was their scale. As part of an argument for the film's educational properties the *Coventry Herald* cited the 'broad sweeps of landscape' and 'the fortunes of battle swinging as a pendulum' as evidence of realism that made the film 'a great advance upon the more familiar variety of cinematographic acting in which melodramatic actors strike heroic attitudes'.[33] Equating scale with realism, the article disavows the film's use of a character viewpoint in favour of qualities that square with what Daniel Pick has noted as an 'enduring theme across . . . nineteenth-century war literature . . . that war constitutes a transcendence of all petty calculations and self-serving motives'.[34] In this case the *Coventry Herald* activates an interpretive framework that highlights a selfless absorption into the struggle as the film's instructive quality where the 'thin strand of love interest' is only incidental 'to the working out of the greater drama in which individualities disappear in the clash of national forces and the fierce play of racial feeling'. The educational qualities lay in the film's distinction from other cinematic productions, which 'start from the assumption that they are to be exhibited before audiences composed of people incapable of serious thought'.[35]

The suppression of the personal viewpoint in the *Herald*'s review is striking, given the way the film constructs individualities. The depictions of battles in Griffith's earlier Biograph films of 1912 alternate the personal experience of the characters with panoramic overviews. The use of close-ups of the participants during the battle prefigure those in *The Birth of a Nation*. Griffith's previous films and the build-up to the release of this one helped to justify his name above the title as an assurance of an engaging spectacle. In *The Birth of a Nation* the battle scenes of the siege at Petersburg are remarkable in that they depict trench warfare of a kind that was not dissimilar to the warfare the soldiers at the front were experiencing. The connections that the advertisements and critics made between the film and those conditions gave less emphasis to the depictions of the front in favour of underscoring the experience of the nation and the selfless sacrifice of those who had 'given loved ones'.

Griffith's style of editing in this sequence makes the point. The siege begins with a set of shots that have established a general sense of the battlefield. The long shots of the whole battlefield set up the opposing forces by placing the Confederates on the left and the Northern army on the right. Once this opposition is established the camera cuts in to one side or the other and alternates between sides to relay either the spectacle of the struggle or the personal experience of Ben Cameron. The tracking shot of Cameron's charge is significant for two reasons. First, throughout the Petersburg sequence the movement has taken place in front of the camera. Here the camera runs with Cameron in his charge. The effect is to hold him in centre frame while expressing the dramatic moment through movement. The second significant element is the position of the camera. This is the first of only two instances in this whole sequence where the camera moves from its established axis to one from a high-angle position, suggesting divine omniscience. The other instance is the final punctuation of the scene when Cameron plants the Confederate flag in the barrel of the Union cannon. This low-angle shot from the Union position allows him a brief pose or attitude, (a similar image to that of Griffith emerging from the mêlée in *The Bioscope*'s report), statuesque in noble abandon. This visual emphasis on the heroic works to establish the bond between white men, North and South, around the central figure of Ben Cameron on the terms of what he represents, the white South.

The next four shots depict hand-to-hand fighting from the previously established viewpoint. There is a fade to the Cameron family in tableau. The father is reading from the Bible while the mother and her two daughters are praying. The function of this parallel edit is to reinforce the virtue and sacrifice of the Camerons when juxtaposed with the nobility of their last remaining son. Griffith's use of parallel editing connects the family spiritually. Tom Gunning has noted this stylistic use of editing as signalling the presence and power of the narrator, foregrounding the edit.[36] The meaning exists across the join. Michael Allen has characterised this cinematic construction of a metaphysical link between family members as the '. . . standard constructional use of the Doctrine of Sympathy in Griffith: characters gazing off-screen and "seeing" a space physically distant from their own which contains the object of their bond, whether lover, family member or friend'.[37] The image of a family praying while a son is heroically and desperately charging the enemy takes on a resonance for an English audience in wartime that certainly redirects the film's intended concerns with the rebonding of North and South in America in 1865. This redirection shows, in powerful, albeit melodramatic terms, how selfless sacrifice *feels*.[38]

The battle scenes offered 'peeps at the hidden war' from an omniscient vantage point, one that positioned the audience between and above the home and the battlefield. It was a viewpoint that was impossible and at the same time deeply desirable. It allowed interpretations such as that of the *Coventry Herald*, invoking wartime rhetoric of selfless sacrifice that, quite apart from the film's focus on individual experience, was hailed as instructive and educational.

See the Regeneration of a Nation, as England Will be Reborn when the War is Over

The force of *The Birth of a Nation*'s regeneration narrative becomes apparent in the second half of the film. While the first half combines stirring spectacles of the war with the personal stories of anguish and sacrifice, this is a prelude to the dissolution of the old South and a regeneration of the Aryan nation through the 'rise from the dead' of the spectres of the Ku Klux Klan. Here the narrative shifts into a register where the conflicts are apparently bound up with specifically American issues that might have seemed opaque to a British audience. Cecil Chesterton, in his 'Explanation' in the Scala programme, devotes half a page to the 'tyranny which went by the ironical name of "Reconstruction"'. He characterises the policies of Thaddeus Stevens as similar to those of Cromwell in Ireland, but with the 'additional horror that the instruments of his revenge were not even to be people of his own colour'. He makes an explicit connection with fears of miscegenation in the imperial imagination:

> ... the South defeated, disheartened and ruined, might have borne the yoke if they had been spared 'the inexpiable wrong, the unutterable shame' of Macaulay's poem. But not only the greed but the more awful animal passions of the negro were let loose on them and their women folk. *It was this last horror that produced the Ku Klux Klan.*[39]

Filtered through racist imperial discourse the 'Explanation' inscribes onto a British national narrative a regeneration trope that hinges on the construction and containment of a brutal other. Black sexuality as a marker of threat and dissipation is the key term in the return of the 'unjustly' oppressed and victimised white civilisation. Parallels with the nation's involvement in the war in Europe are drawn, featuring similar characterisations of a brutal enemy, the Germans. The 'rebirth' of the white South is explicitly joined with the regeneration of England in the terms of 'womanly sacrifice' and a righteous, crusading secret 'Invisible Empire of the South'.[40] The 'second war' to which Chesterton refers, then, is the one against a villainous other that bears the hallmarks of the Manichaean structures of popular, propagandistic, war rhetoric.

Chesterton's rhetorical devices are echoed in other interpretations that attempt to link the film with 'English' concerns. The sensitivity of two types of scenes was highlighted by *The Bioscope*'s main review of the film prior to its release in Britain:

> ... aspects of war are presented with equal power and vividness—the heart broken mother seeking for her son amid the human wreckage of a field hospital; the dreadful tension of searching the casualty lists for familiar names; the chaotic desolation of 'War's Peace'. (... it should be pointed out that some of the more poignant and terrible of these scenes are to be deleted before the film is exhibited to the public—a wise precaution in view of the many painful parallels for such episodes to be found just now in our own lives. Certain incidents dealing with the bestiality of the emancipated negroes are also to be modified. Their inclusion was thoroughly justified artistically, but they are doubtless unsuitable for general exhibition.)[41]

145

Both *The Bioscope* and Chesterton situate the threat of degeneration within racial terms that justify the actions of the Ku Klux Klan. *The Bioscope*'s identification of the family trauma and sacrifice and the sensitivity to the depiction of the bestiality of black 'oppressors' towards white women no doubt refers to grounds for censorship cited by the 1915 report of the British Board of Film Censors. Among these grounds were 'the exploitation of tragic incidents of the war' and 'the actual perpetration of criminal assaults on women'. The board's report a year earlier had referred to concern with scenes depicting outrages on women and themes relative to 'race suicide'. In spite of this the film had already been passed 'without cuts' for exhibition by the British Board of Film Censors with a 'U' on 5 August 1915, a month before *The Bioscope* article was published.[42] (Whether the film was actually cut for British release remains somewhat a mystery. The version that Griffith cut after the protests in the USA may have been the version shown at the Scala. However, films were often tailored for release in Britain during the war and therefore the possibility that it was cut in the way that *The Bioscope* indicates cannot be ruled out.) Couched in the terms of education and associated with the 'uplift' of art, *The Bioscope* provides a clue as to the terms on which the film's exhibition in Britain was allowed. The 'sensitivity' of the film was the propriety of the depictions of tragedy and the moral question of depicting sexual violence.

Newspaper accounts suggest that the moments in the film that feature the Ku Klux Klan are 'weird', yet there is no indication that the reviewers saw these scenes as confusing or disturbing. The account found in the *Southampton and District Pictorial* on 1 November stated:

> Probably the most thrilling scenes, however, are those in which the ghostly garbed ghouls of the Ku Klux Klan ride madly to the rescue of the women and children of the South. As the sorrows of the South, under the baneful Reconstruction Acts, began to be unbearable, the fiery cross of the Scottish Highlanders was again used as a call to arms. At first the Ku Klux Klan devoted their efforts to putting down disorder among the bad negroes. Generally all that was necessary was to play upon the credulity and superstition of that race. They would ride up to a negro's cabin in the dead of night, and one of the riders would call for a bucket of water, which he would drain to the bottom using a concealed leather bag. He would then say that was the first drink he had had since he was killed at the Battle of Shiloh. This is very effectively shown in *Birth of a Nation*.[43]

146

In this review the rebirth of the 'ghostly garbed' Ku Klux Klan was related for an English audience with both the rise of the war dead as heroes and the connection with the Scottish clan ritual. The ultimate regeneration comes with the last utopian scene of the film, which invokes a white, Christian, heavenly hereafter. The 'weird' is not a reference to the racist vigilante activity of the Klan, but to their otherworldly appearance.

Alongside the racist inflections of the review there are links to the regenerative powers of film as a medium. The animation of film, according to *The Bioscope*, was the appropriate medium for showing the 'life of the battlefield'. This was in contrast to still photography that was more suited to the reproduction of shattered buildings or the graves of the fallen.[44] Here the cinema's unique value lies in its ability to re-animate and this property had, since cinema's beginnings, held within it something of the quality of the supernatural. The equating of moving pictures with life and with the supernatural was born out in the official war films with their images of soldiers immortalised and reborn through the moving photograph. The publicity around the official films, holding out the possibility of seeing someone familiar also, as time passed, had the inevitable effect of depicting soldiers who had since died. Such ghostly images of dead soldiers and war victims consistently circulated through popular stories. For example, on the second page of the *Southern Daily Echo* on 4 September 1916 an article appeared entitled 'The Changed View of Death: Only an Episode'. The article begins: 'One of the most marked effects of the war is the alteration it is bringing about in the popular view of death. Before the war there seemed to be a growing tendency to regard death as the end of life: now we are coming to see in it merely an episode'. The story tells of a clergyman who calls on a widow who has just heard that her son has died on the front. Instead of finding the widow distraught she and her daughter are 'quite cheerful'. When asked why, the woman replied that her daughter had had a vivid dream in which had seen her brother 'and a lot of his brother officers engaged in merrymaking'. She said to him she thought he was dead to which he replied that they were simply 'waiting for new uniforms'. Like the soldiers depicted at the end of *Battle of the Somme* he was 'carrying on the advance'.[45]

Similar narratives of dissipation and regeneration were prevalent in a wide range of popular forms at this time. Melodramas and particularly dramas of oppression dealt with sacrifice and absolution. In the later part of the nineteenth century these narratives were often associated with the freeing of slaves by British heroes or, as in the case of a play called *My Poll and My Partner Joe*, slaves are made free at the end of the play by a wave of the Union Jack.[46] This dissipation/regeneration trope was also a central element in much of the enlistment propaganda. The pictures of civilians showed men and women transformed by enlistment and thus the war had joined together classes and the different inhabitants of the empire. Sir Gilbert Parker, in a pamphlet of 1915 entitled *Is England Apathetic?* stated that army discipline had relieved class tensions and even 'culturally' improved his own footman.[47] Advertising was another source of the application of transformative dynamics, imbuing the merchandise with magical properties of effecting changes. Dr Cassell's Tablets were aimed at the 'War Worn and Wounded'. Of course a great deal of advertising used war imagery such as 'Waverly Cigarettes; What the Navy Wants'. There were limits, however, to using the war as an advertising gimmick. This became the subject of some discussion in *Advertising Weekly*. A reader protested against the use of advertising circulars that 'at first glance seem to contain a telegram. . . . this idea serves only to create alarm at first and irritation later in the housewife who receives such a circular'.[48]

Similarly the regenerative effect of the cinema through realist depictions of the war became less effective in either attracting audiences or as an argument for cinema's social legitimacy. The animation of the ghostly images of soldiers became less and less tolerable as the war ground on. In January 1918 F. Graham, the proprietor of the Star Pictures cinema, wrote to E.H. Montague, the Selig Polyscope agent in London about the failure of their Civil War film *The Crisis* (1916):

> One must not forget that the seriousness of the affairs of today, and the news we are constantly reading in the press as to casualties etc., make it absolutely imperative that the entertainment at a Picture House should be of a bright and cheerful nature, so that the individual will be able to forget his worries and anxieties.[49]

Rather than become houses of the living dead, cinema's regenerative effect would lie increasingly in its function as entertainment.

'A Vivid, Graphic Story of Anglo-Celt Achievement which Will Make Every Englishman, Woman and Child Glow with Pride, Gasp with Astonishment and Thrill with Marvellous Realism!'

In *The Birth of a Nation* the development of the characters is played out across the geographic and ideological terrain of the American Civil War.

The characters emerge slowly through the Griffithian device of intercutting between the families, Washington, Piedmont and the battlefields. These are further interspersed with the historical depictions in 'facsimile' of scenes that include the assassination of Lincoln and the surrender at Appomatox. The progress through the trial of war depicted in this evocation of simultaneous action by parallel editing recalls Benedict Anderson's concept of 'simultaneity'. The linking of a set of geographically separate spaces and subjects under 'calendrical coincidence' is a central element in Anderson's concept of the 'Imagined Community' where 'the idea of a sociological organism moving calendrically through homogenous empty time is a precise analogue of the idea the nation . . .'. 'The nation' in Griffith's film is emerging from the forge of shared conflict and experience as a 'solid community moving steadily down (or up) history'.[50]

Central to the progression of this imagined community lies the resolution of the narrative disruption explicitly signalled at the film's beginning with the presence of African Americans. Ultimately this progression/resolution is offered at the end of the film, a *tableau vivant* depicting a white utopia. The project of the film's narrative is to keep racial categories distinct and there are parallels here for a British audience. The threat is to purity. The advertisement's focus on an 'Anglo-Celt achievement' is an attempt to not only make connections between Britain and America through the war but also to imagine a parallel existence between the two nations and in the process imply distinctions between British and German. By making connections with the 'Celtic', which has replaced the Germanic 'Saxon', a distinction is inferred, a preferred reading is announced. Referring to the 'Spirit of the Play', the *Coventry Herald*'s review stated:

> Beneath a surface of good acting and clever staging flows the spirit of liberty, pride of race, unselfish devotion to a cause. Those things gave the production a peculiar interest for an English audience in war-time, for many of the ideals which inspired the action of the play were, at bottom, the ideals for which we are fighting now.[51]

The equivalence of the film's subject matter with the audience's wartime experience raises questions as to the intelligibility of the film in its representation of African Americans. The 'redirections' pointed to by Chesterton, the publicity, and the majority of the press response utilise an imperial imagination to draw parallels with the ideological project of the film.

The film was accompanied by a score, written by Joseph Carl Breil, conducted at the Scala by Stephen R. Philpot with sound effects. By incorporating recognisable music, effects and performance traditions, the presentation of the film encouraged audience interpretations that reinforced the film's ideology from the established techniques of popular theatre. *The Bioscope* devoted a two-page article to the film's presentation suggesting that it could also be a 'new form of music drama'. The article mentioned the use of 'motives associated with particular characters or ideas' that 'recur whenever the subjects appear' and repeated at a slower tempo 'during a death scene of a semi-humorous [musical] phrase' introduced earlier. A 'mixed choir' had rendered 'Plantation songs from behind the screen during suitable scenes earlier in the picture'.[52] Each of these elements: the use of musical phrase for characters, the recurring motif in slower tempos and the use of 'Plantation songs' contribute to a representational lexicon familiar to audiences in England and, moreover, those performance traditions associated with the white representation of African-American culture and the African cultures of the colonies.

The depictions of blackness in the film centre around three representational traditions: the melodramatic villain, the devoted servant and the blackface minstrel. The trajectory of the representation of 'native' inhabitants of the empire in English popular culture in the nineteenth century shifts from the freedom for all who are touched by the Union Jack to a more beleaguered, defensive empire where 'Black natives were enemies to be coerced under the authority of the Great White Mother'.[53] By imagining a parallel relationship between subjects of the empire and emancipated slaves, the black soldiers threatening the cabin at the end of the film can take on added, or at least reconfigured, resonances for a British audience. Moreover, British propaganda in newspapers, posters and cartoons had depicted the Germans as beastly 'Huns'. The brutish behaviour, lasciviousness and bad manners of the mulatto Silas Lynch and the freed slave Gus depicted in *The Birth of a Nation* were reprised in the conduct of the German soldiers in Griffith's *Hearts of the World* (1918). Their threat to white virtue and innocence, which forces 'The Little Sister' to make the 'ultimate sacrifice', and the Ku Klux Klan to rescue Elsie Stoneman, lay at the heart of the popular imagery of 'little Belgium' and the German invasion.

The faithful servants of the Camerons need to be seen against the background of a crisis in domestic service and the rise in labour unrest in Britain during the war years and afterwards. On 27 April 1916 a

Kinematograph Weekly review of a film version of *Uncle Tom's Cabin* produced by the World Film Corporation of New York noted that :

> Old Wine, Old Friends and Old Books are Best.
>   In many ways this maxim holds good in Uncle Tom's Cabin for its main beauty lies in the devotion of old servants to old employers and the love of old associations and old traditions that overcomes every obstacle and leavens the sympathy that comes from unselfish love for faithful dependents.[54]

Here is an example of how nostalgia for a mythical past of benevolent masters and obedient servants is imagined through American scenes of the antebellum South. The 'Plantation' songs referred to in *The Bioscope*'s account of the music were the 'sentimental' part of the litany of blackface minstrel shows. Described as sung by a choir from behind the screen, it offers a visual (and aural) metaphor for the hiding of the vulgar, the vernacular, whitewashed through an orchestral treatment.[55]

The blackface minstrel figures that Griffith imposes on the black characters were familiar icons in the British music hall. Thomas Dartmouth Rice had performed his Jump Jim Crow in England in 1836. In the 1880s and 1890s British blackface minstrels such as G.H. Elliott and Eugene Stratton adapted this American tradition for a British audience. The songs they sang evoked a liberated land of '. . . smiling coal-black mammies, piccaninnies and faithful Lilies of Laguna, against a background of silvery moons . . . [which may have represented] . . . an idealised future for the British male immigrant to the colonies . . .'.[56] The support for this iconography was emphasised by the use of music associated with minstrelsy such as 'Turkey in the Straw', 'Home Sweet Home' and 'After the Ball' in the exhibition of the film, signalling the combination of racial stereotyping with nostalgia and longing, hallmarks of the blackface minstrel tradition. The review in the *Southern Daily Echo* bears this out: 'A word of praise must also be given to the orchestra, whose playing of the tunes of the period brings back ancient memories. . . . and then as if to drive home the "Anglo-Celt" connection he adds . . . Fancy listening once more to "In the Gloaming"'.[57]

'In the Gloaming' was used to represent the relationship between Phil Stoneman (Elmer Clifton) and Margaret Cameron (Miriam Cooper) throughout the film. The link between nostalgic longing, separated lovers, the hint of tragic sacrifice and a wartime audience's experience goes beyond the antebellum South, here standing in for pre-war peacetime. Much of the nostalgic music in the USA in the nineteenth century was influenced by Scottish folk music. English songwriters had been adapting Scottish folk melodies, rounding out the irregularities to conform to major keys in order to appeal to English middle classes; American songwriters in turn were adapting these modes by replacing the medieval Scottish castle with the Southern plantation.[58] The score to the film also produced one of the hits of 1915 'The Perfect Song'. Written by Breil and Clarence Lucas the song was a reworking of an old Italian melody by G. Bragas from 1867, called 'Angel's Serenade'. The song was the theme for Ben Cameron (Henry B. Walthal) and Elsie Stoneman (Lillian Gish).[59] The circularity of these traditions and references across the Atlantic are evidence of the complexity of meanings inherent in a British audience encountering a film made in the USA. It also shows how familiar they were with the cultural references in *The Birth of a Nation*.

'I Don't Want to Repeat the Experience'

The film's first special release lasted until December 1916. In many cases the film played a second run in the same theatrical format. In Southampton the Grand Theatre ran it a second time in January 1917. Finally the film had a third run in cinemas. In these exhibitions the advertising strategy and its implied address in its initial release was dispensed with and the film was often advertised simply as D.W. Griffith's 'mighty spectacle'. The production was considerably scaled down, with the forty-piece orchestra replaced by the regular musical accompaniment of the cinema, which could range from a lone piano to larger ensembles. It seems that the film put something of an endpoint onto the receptive possibilities of the Civil War production trend in Britain. By 1918 there is evidence from a number of exhibitors expressing audience dissatisfaction with other films with the same setting. In January 1918, Frank S. Manson of the Coatbridge Cinema in Glasgow wrote to cancel his booking of the Selig Polyscope Civil War epic *The Crisis* (1916) as the length 'was entirely against it and the story is similar to *The Birth of a Nation* and as I lost £80 on the running of this subject I do not want to repeat the experience'.[60] E. Hounsell was more direct: '. . . the public of this country will not have any more American Civil War stuff'.[61]

The poor audiences for *The Birth of a Nation* for exhibitors like Manson exemplified the concern that exhibitors had for the screening of super-films in theatres. As the film had been screened twice in one year this way, audiences were low for the screenings when the film finally became available to the cinemas. *The Birth of a Nation* intensified the super-film debate; while the industry welcomed the fact that the film had attracted a 'new and most desirable audience',[62] managers such as Manson were unable to capitalise on them. The super-films' theatrical runs had exhausted their market by the time they reached the cinemas. Perhaps more relevant in explaining the fact that the super-film became an important part of the cinema programme rather than a staple of the theatre is the relatively small number of films that were able to guarantee a return on the risk of roadshowing ventures. Sol Levy's venture with *The Birth of a Nation* had paid handsomely but *Intolerance* had been less successful. It may also be that the epic nature of these productions did not always lend themselves to the kind of marketing strategies that were so successful for *The Birth of a Nation*. These strategies, based as they were on connecting the depiction of a family undergoing the trials and anxieties of war, were themselves, by late 1917, out of touch with audience preferences.

The advertising and critical reception have provided some keys into the preferred reading of the film in Britain. This examination has opened up ways of thinking about the reception of non-British films at this period in terms of the interaction between the film text, an industry's sophisticated ability to redirect the address of the film for a British audience and the socio-historical context, which in this case was a significant period during the First World War. I have tried to pose some questions that may help illuminate the dynamics of audience reception through the examination of intention and address in the advertising and exhibition practices at the time. In this way we can recognise that the authorship (and authorisation) of even a super-film such as *The Birth of a Nation*, where the auteur (Griffith et al.) had exercised great effort to standardise its reception, is dependent upon a complex set of interactions between the film and, in this case, a 'differently intended' audience. At the same time these redirections demonstrate the ease with which the white supremacist discourse of Griffith's and Dixon's film was mapped onto, and paralleled, imperial projections of progress and nation and discourses of race and gender. In reading the address of *The Birth of a Nation* any evidence of resistance to these redirections still remains hidden. Perhaps their trace lies in the dwindling audiences for the cinema release and Frank Manson's remark 'I don't want to repeat the experience', but it is an indication that the references to wartime tragedy drew more attention than the white supremacist narrative of the film.

Civilization
A Super-film at the Palladium, 1917

Griffith's *The Birth of a Nation* was the kind of super-film that gave exhibitors cause for concern, yet in reality productions that lent themselves to the roadshow treatment that Sol Levy had been able to stage for Griffith's film were scarce. Ultimately the somewhat disappointing receipts of *Intolerance* gave entrepreneurs pause for thought and for the rest of the war there are few if any instances of the kind of major roadshow production that characterised these two films. Nevertheless, at the time the possibility that the theatres would become the showcase for prestige films leaving the cinemas to exhibit variety programmes of comedies and dramas seemed real. There had been an argument that only the larger theatres of the cities and towns were able to provide the appropriate facilities that these films required. Exhibitors were faced with the possibility of losing out on gaining first runs of prestige pictures to the theatres, which would have the effect of reducing their cinema halls to screening the shorter cheap dramas and comedies. They supported the kind of cultural currency these super-films gained for the industry but feared they would be relegated to a lower cultural status, a perception they had been trying to change since the beginning of the picture palace boom in 1910. As the exhibitors looked for a way to resolve their dilemma one strategy, proposed at the Cinematograph Exhibitors' Association's annual meeting in Birmingham in June 1917 was that the exhibitors in a town could cooperate and fund the screening in the theatre themselves. The chairman of the association, Mr J.P. Moore, introduced a resolution whereby 'the cooperation and combination of the exhibitors of various localities . . . should, between them, secure the rights for their districts of such superfilms as they considered would be a good business proposition. [This would be on] cooperative lines whereby each exhibitor took such a share as he thought good . . .'.[1] While the association resolved to act on this proposal, some of the proprietors of the larger cinemas pointed out that their establishments were actually better suited to showing these types of films than the theatres. In the end as the production companies on both sides of the Atlantic began to produce more feature-length films and the large financial outlay for theatrical presentation proved too great a risk, the voices of the managers of the larger cinemas were proved right and the competition with the theatres subsided.

The proprietors of the larger cinemas had more to lose in the super-film issue than the smaller houses, which depended on the shorter films for their continuous programme. In spite of the fact that all cinemas depended upon the variety format for profitability, the larger cinemas had begun to use the longer feature as a means of differentiating their halls in the highly competitive local markets. The eventual outcome was that the larger cinemas were able to secure the exclusive super-films for first runs, leaving the cheaper open-market films to the smaller cinemas. Rachael Low has generalised this phenomenon as the result of the smaller showman's 'competitive stupidity'. Yet this fails to take into account the exhibitors' own relationship with their audiences.[2] In Southampton George Elliot's approach to the working-class Northam Picturedrome differed from the tactics at the Carlton, where the target audience was mainly lower middle class. These strategies were addressed to specific audiences and not only reflected assumptions about audience taste preferences but were also techniques brought from the house management traditions of the music hall. Here the variety format was profitable and fulfilled his patrons' expectations. Arthur Pickup, at the 600-seat Gaiety, changed his strategy to attract the increasing numbers of women employed in and around Southampton as a result of the war. As we saw in chapter 2, Pickup established a reputation for showing films that appealed to a predominantly female audience by foregrounding society dramas in his advertising. These examples and the fact that in Southampton only one cinema closed during the war period and all of the others remained open at least until the mid-1920s—and in many cases much longer—suggests that audiences were attending regularly and, more importantly, that the cinemas were able to attract specific audiences. In this climate, the larger cinemas, which had established regular patrons, were competing with each other for 'floating' clientele, or the audiences who were not regular attendees. For cinemas in Southampton, like the Alexandra on the High Street with 1,000 seats, the super-films were an important part of their image as prestige cinemas, but they continued to run the majority of their programmes on a variety basis. The super-film received special attention in the Alexandra's advertising in the same way that the Gaiety emphasised society dramas. This was a way of giving the hall a distinctive appeal to a specific market while at the same time the attraction of the variety format was more general. Low's condemnation of the small showmen is based on a teleology where the feature-length fiction film finally, and in her view rightly, prevails. In fact exhibitors responded to the super-film by incorporating it as a means of differentiating their cinemas. The super-films like Thomas Ince's *Civilization* (1916) or Selig's *The Crisis* (1916) were special events rather than the norm. While the variety format underwent significant changes it remained remarkably resilient and did not fully give way to features until the 1960s.

It was against this background that the Palladium in Portswood was able to capitalise on its reputation as a cinema with a high-class programme and secure an exclusive booking of Thomas Ince's *Civilization*. This chapter takes the exhibition and reception of Ince's film as an example of the exhibition and house management strategies adopted by the proprietors Sydney Bacon and H.J. Hood. Hood and Bacon programmed 'high-class', often British features, and hosted civic events to establish a reputation as a socially respectable venue. Their reputation for this type of programming and presentation converged with that of the national advertising campaign for *Civilization*; the special editing for a British audience helped to redirect the film's original 'message'. I begin with a fictitious scenario of a woman's experience of viewing the film based on information and research into cinema-going at the Palladium at the time. The impressions made upon her are an amalgam of that research with assumptions based on the text as I have viewed it. I have only seen the version of the film that was released in the United States and I have inserted some of the changes that were made to the film for British audiences based on Kevin Brownlow's account in *The War, the West and the Wilderness*.[3] The idea behind this reconstruction is to outline a set of probable interpretations that can be construed from the text and the particular programming and house management strategies of a prestige cinema in Southampton. These strategies sought to attract audiences through screening quality films, often British, and through their emphasis on the cinema's educational value to the community.

The Premiere at the Palladium

It is Friday, 31 August 1917. Mabel, a young woman of eighteen, goes to the cinema with her new boyfriend, Walter, also eighteen. She lives with her parents in the suburb of Portswood, a little less than a mile north of Southampton town centre. She has a job as a shop assistant at Tyrell and Green's, a department store in Southampton. Walter works for the railway transporting the wounded from the docks to the medical trains and unloading them at Netley Hospital, the third-largest military hospital in Britain at the time. Walter's job brings him into direct contact with the broken bodies from the front and he is under little illusion about the brutal effects of modern war. The film they go to see is Thomas Ince's *Civilization*. The cinema is the Palladium, which is just within walking distance from her house. The picture has been advertised as costing more than $1,000,000 and involving 40,000 people and an array of military spectacle. Mabel's expectations of the evening are numerous. According to the advertisement in the *Southern Daily Echo* there are spectacles of horrific battle scenes and the re-enactment of the sinking of a liner by torpedo from a submarine. Apart from the experience of the film itself, there is also the opportunity to meet friends. Given the coded nature of courtship, the chance to be alone in the dark with her new beau is a source of anxiety as well as anticipation, and there are also the excitements of being out beyond the fetters of family and of forming part of an audience. On the whole, cinema offers Mabel her most accessible form of public entertainment. Her father, who owns a greengrocer's on Portswood High Street, not far from the Palladium, does not approve of her attending the music hall unaccompanied by himself. In any case, both the music hall and the theatre are too expensive to be anything other than a rare treat. Normally, Mabel goes to the cinema with her girlfriends, but this is a special event: both the première of a new super-film and the chance to 'court'. The programme has other attractions: the live music (she knew the pianist at school), the newsreel, and the comedy short; she has chosen the Palladium as much because of its location (it is close by and she regularly goes there) as because of the programme's content. That said, there has been a great deal of advertising for this film and her father had thought it would be a good film for her to see.

Walter comes to collect her at her house. As they approach the cinema there are posters advertising *Civilization* spelled the American way because the exhibitor had ordered his full-colour poster from the distributor the Transatlantic Film Company. Walter had booked their tickets the previous evening. As the couple enter the foyer they are greeted with a breeze from the ceiling fans and the pleasant smell of oranges, Walter buys them one each to eat during the performance. The cinema is filled with people. Some of them she knows and there is the anxious thrill of being seen with her boyfriend. There are a number of children at the film who contribute to the general atmosphere of noisiness. After buying their tickets, the couple take their seats towards the back and the programme begins. Mabel recognises a woman with her older children as one of the patrons of Tyrell and Green's and notes that she has never seen them at the cinema before. The small four-piece orchestra begins to play and then the lights dim. The newsreel is greeted with interest, particularly the information on the war news and the pictures of the American troops who have recently become involved. There are also the usual shots of the British army. The thought crosses her mind that her uncle Tom is 'somewhere in France' and, as usual, she looks to see if she can see him in the footage of soldiers marching past. There are some fairly boisterous lads two rows behind them who have already been told to quiet down by the usher during the comedy short.

The main feature begins and the music starts just after the image is shown. The opening titles are sombre and religious in tone and include a drawing of a church window with light streaming through. It reminds her of the kind of slide shows she had seen as a child at some church evenings. The opening scenes are of a peaceful rural setting and the farmers are dressed in a kind of peasant costume. The Emperor who declares war looks like the Kaiser. The hero, Count Ferdinand, is a friend and trusted aid to the Emperor, which is somewhat confusing. The hero's girlfriend Katheryn Haldeman joins a secret peace society that is symbolised by a Christian cross on her underclothes. She tries to persuade Ferdinand, the captain of a submarine, not to go on his mission and reveals her commitment to peace. He leaves, but when he receives an order to sink a liner that has women and children on it, he refuses. He then reveals the cross on his undershirt to his men, and sinks the submarine. As it goes down he has a vision of the chaos on the ship, the scramble for lifeboats while it is sinking and the loss of women and children. This vision reminds Mabel of the *Lusitania* and the general fear of German submarines. She also thinks of the sinking of the *Titanic*, on which her best friend's father worked and was lost. Earlier there have been scenes of soldiers fighting which are pretty gruesome and there are some very sad scenes of families having to give up their sons to rough and brutal soldiers in German uniforms. For Walter these scenes have little impact and seem more affected than real.

Ferdinand is rescued, but mortally injured. The Emperor's doctors are called in. While unconscious, he has a dream and is taken through a kind of hell. There are a great many tortured and naked men writhing and/or pushing boulders up hills. It looks like a scene from one of the pictures in Mabel's illustrated Bible. Christ appears and moves into Ferdinand's body. He awakens, resuscitated by the doctors, and proceeds to preach peace. This makes the Emperor angry, and Ferdinand is brought to trial and sentenced to death. A great crowd of women on the march for peace descends on the city and Ferdinand's girlfriend leads the petition for the release of the hero. The Empress Eugenie is moved by the call for peace and begs for Ferdinand to be spared, but it is too late, for he has died in prison. The Emperor visits the cell. Christ arises out of the hero's body and takes the Emperor (also in spirit form) by the hand. He is first taken to the battlefield and shown the horrors of war. There are more scenes of death and destruction in the city as he sees refugees moving with their belongings on their backs, women weeping over their husbands' dead bodies and lost children crying. Walter and Mabel had been discussing the war on their walk to the cinema. Walter was careful not to be explicit about the things that he sees everyday in his job but Mabel is not completely unaware of the condition of the wounded as she too has seen the medical trains coming from the docks. The silence of the trains is in marked contrast to the newspaper accounts of the wounded singing and cheering together on the trains. In fact both are aware that Walter is now of conscription age and that he may be at the front in a year's time. The scenes of the film therefore are taken by both to be dramatic rather than realistic.

The Emperor realises what he has brought upon his people and Christ shows him the book of judgement. He is horrified to learn that his page is 'stained with the blood of his people'. The Emperor is then returned to his world, where he declares peace. One scene at the end stands out. As the soldiers return home, there is a woman trying to console a grieving widow but she cannot contain her excitement as she sees her own husband returning alive. This scene reinforces the impression of dramatic licence for both Mabel and Walter. Mabel has friends who have relatives at the front and her uncle's return last December was quiet and solitary. Walter has seen relatives waiting at the station for their wounded son or brother or husband to arrive but this is the exception rather than the rule. Both have the overall experience of the war as a consistent and ominous background to their lives, marked by private anguish rather than public celebration.

The film ends and Mabel and Walter file out. The noise during the film was lower than normal but there was still a good deal of talking among the lads behind, particularly when the Emperor, thinly disguised as the Kaiser, was on the screen. Walter had whispered 'suffragette' during the peace-marching scene and Mabel had been reminded of a terse discussion she had had with her father about the right of women to vote; she wondered if Walter felt the same way. There had been a bit of sporadic irreverence during the Christ scenes as well as during the titles with the church windows. Overall the film was very impressive and Mabel is glad she has seen it. The film reminded them both of the war in ways which they found less entertaining and more 'educational', or to put it more bluntly, contrived. Nevertheless, both feel a duty to applaud outwardly the film's patriotic, albeit somewhat oblique, message. Inwardly Mabel wonders if she should raise the issue of women's suffrage with Walter, while Walter wonders whether he should relay some of his own experiences with the medical trains to compare with the overly dramatised scenes of the film. Both decide it was best to concentrate on other subjects altogether and they look forward to the Chaplin comedy that will be shown the following week.

High Class at the Palladium

The Palladium opened on 17 February 1913 and was one of the first purpose-built cinemas in the town. It was a combined business venture of H.J. Hood, a local entrepreneur, and Sydney Bacon, managing director of Sydney Bacon's Pictures Circuit, based in London. The Palladium was not part of this circuit, but Bacon's probable position in the partnership was to bring the conveniences and contacts that his circuit had developed to the Palladium to ensure that exclusives were acquired as first runs in the town.[4] Located in Portswood, adjacent to the affluent area of Highfield, the Palladium aimed to attract a regular clientele through specific programming, advertising and house management strategies that emphasised the cinema's 'high-class' quality of films, projection and decor and its educational value to the community. A year after it opened, the town's planning committee recognised the cinema as a public educational resource when it decided to build a branch library on the site next to it.[5]

The first move towards establishing a respectable reputation with the community was the opening of the cinema by the mayor, Mr Henry Bowyer, who described it as 'the prettiest Picture Palace south of London'. The decor was in the Wedgwood style, with blue and white walls, ornamental features and matching plush seats. The cinema held 650 seats: 150 balcony and 500 stalls. Seats cost 6d, 9d and 1/2, with a 3d charge for booking. Little touches of showmanship by the first house manager, a Mr Urqhuart, were even noted in the national trade press:

> ... the installation has now been completed of a patent multi-bladed electric fan, capable of changing the atmosphere of the hall nine times in an hour. One of the films to be screened at the Palladium is 'The Story of the Willow Pattern'. One of the tips which Mr. Urquhart has picked up during his travels in the East is that of perfuming the curtains and this practice is regularly pursued at the Palladium and helps to keep the hall fresh.[6]

These techniques were a form of address that anticipated a type of audience who would respond to the assurances of a comfortable and healthy environment, particularly during the difficult summer season.[7]

From its opening, the advertisements for the Palladium were prominently displayed on the front page of the *Southern Daily Echo*, usually in the centre. Rather than advertise in either the entertainment weekly *What's On in Southampton* or the *Southampton and District Pictorial*, the Palladium's exclusive use of the *Southern Daily Echo* indicates both its appeal to a specific regular suburban clientele and its attempt to impart a sense of the exclusive nature of the cinema. As the paper was a daily, the change of programme was advertised regularly and allowed for the kind of publicity build-up, or 'booming', that was required for the prestige features that were a mainstay in the Palladium's programming policy.

Although the advertising methods of the manager and directors indicate a specific clientele, the location of the Palladium at Portswood suggests that the appeal was not simply to the inhabitants of the immediate area. Located directly across from the tram depot, the cinema was accessible from all parts of the town. Its proximity to Highfield directly to the north was matched by the easy walking distance (about half a mile) to the working-class district of Northam, to the south, home to many of the local men who worked on the liners. The Palladium probably also attracted people from the nearby Basset and Shirley areas where stewards and other crew for the liners lived. This diversity of the cinema's catchment area was reflected in the stratification of its seats and prices, suggesting that it managed to attract both working-class and middle-class film-goers.[8] It also set up the conditions for the successful exhibition of super-films such as *Civilization*, because it was accessible to a wider range of audiences, and could therefore support the kind of lengthy runs (usually a week) that the distributors of these films demanded.

The Palladium distinguished its programme by offering features of 'high standards and distinct educational values'.[9] From its opening, it cultivated a reputation as a house for first-run prestige features. In January 1914, it ran *Antony and Cleopatra* for a week. Subsequent exhibitions of *Quo Vadis?* and Hepworth's *David Copperfield* indicated a distinct appeal to a reading public. *The Kinematograph Year Book* for that year could have been referring to the Palladium's programming strategy and its close proximity to the lending library when it noted the turn to this type of feature:

> A curious fact was made known at the beginning of the year, namely that the kinematograph fostered a taste for book reading. With the advent of 'Les Misérables', 'David Copperfield', 'Quo Vadis?', 'Antony and Cleopatra', 'Last Days of Pompeii', 'The Three Musketeers', 'The House of Temperley', and other films founded upon well known novels, the lucky publishers admitted that a tremendous demand had been created for their works. Librarians, too, experienced an extraordinary demand for certain works because films founded on them were being shown in their district. This seems to contradict the assertion so frequently made use of in press and pulpit that the picture theatre had destroyed the utility of public libraries.[10]

During the early months of the war the programme featured such a significant number of these literary adaptations that *The Bioscope* reported it as a good method of maintaining audiences during the uncertain climate of wartime:

> Portswood Palladium does not appear to have suffered on account of the war. On my last visit I found the hall filled and Mr. W.T. Bartlett, the manager, assured me that the attendances had been exceedingly well maintained. Book plays are great favourites with Palladium audiences. The picture dramatisations of Dickens' 'Old Curiosity Shop' and Jules Verne's 'Children of Captain Grant' formed the features for this week.[11]

The Palladium's reputation as a 'high-class' cinema was predicated on a combination of the type of films screened, the presentation and decor of the hall and the high-profile social events that were held there. Prior to the outbreak of war the cinema had played host to special events. During the war Bartlett built upon this policy by holding special screenings for soldiers and Belgian refugees.[12]

The Palladium's reputation for exclusive and educational entertainment explains why more controversial films such as Lois Weber's *Where are My Children?* (1915) were able to play only at the Palladium. *Where Are My Children?* opened on 2 December 1916 and was advertised as for adults only. This film concerned birth control and abortion and was sponsored by the National Council of Public Morals (NCPM). It was not intended for commercial release in Britain but for special educational screenings. Annette Kuhn has shown that the relationship between the NCPM and the industry around this film served to further the quite different interests of both. In 1916 the industry was eager to associate the cinema with social and moral education, and keen to acquire the endorsement of the NCPM to head off the threat of state censorship. The NCPM, in turn, was concerned with the use of cinema as an educational medium, and was also undertaking research for what would become the report of the Cinema Commission published in 1917. Cinemas such as the Palladium, with high profiles of 'educational and high class programmes' and an ostensibly more educated clientele, were the exception in a policy of screening *Where Are My Children?* in theatres and town halls associated with public lectures and educational events, rather than in commercial cinemas. This gives some indication of the profile that the Palladium enjoyed in the town.

This reputation had been gained by the management's consistent practice of catering to their local clientele. At the same time, however, the Palladium's easy access to the centre of the town suggests that the audience constituency was wider than the local area. The screening of *Where Are My Children?* indicates the flexibility enjoyed by the managers, who were able to appeal to specific audiences at given times. While they normally emphasised feature films, this was not the only means of maintaining their audiences: Chaplin films, for example, were introduced as a part of the programme during the summer of 1915 and these and other comedy films continued to be shown at the Palladium with some regularity throughout the war.

The way that the Palladium attempted to benefit from the Chaplin phenomenon offers an insight into the nature of the competitive environment of local cinema exhibition at the time, and reveals that 'uplift' was a convenient advertising tag as much as a committed policy. Chaplin films had been running in Southampton since the summer of 1914, with *Between Showers* (US release, 28 February 1914) appearing on 18 July at the Palace Music Hall as part of their Sunday evening 'first time screened' film programme.[13] Throughout the winter and spring of 1915 Chaplin's popularity had grown. The summer of that year is generally considered 'Chaplin's summer', when he achieved the international superstar status that he enjoyed for the next two decades. In January 1914 he had moved from the Keystone studios to Essanay, and such was the popularity of Chaplin films that, in September, Essanay sought to benefit by introducing an exclusive arrangement for exhibitors, including those in Britain. In order to obtain a Chaplin film cinemas were obliged also to rent three other Essanay subjects. This form of block booking ran counter to the open market system that was the standard means of acquiring films in Britain.[14] The Palladium had been fairly late in picking up on Chaplin, only screening re-run Keystones in March 1915 and then one or two per month from June. This was sporadic compared to other cinemas, large and small, which had been showing Chaplin Keystones since July 1914.[15] It was not until the early part of 1916 that the Palladium began showing Chaplin films with regularity and then, to avoid the controlling Essanay policy, they ran re-released Keystones under changed titles.[16] This can be understood as an attempt to maximise audiences by appealing to 'lower taste sensibilities' through slapstick, but it is more likely that Chaplin's name was proving a considerable draw generally and one that managers H. J. Hood and Sydney Bacon could not afford to ignore.

This is an important illustration of how the geography and demographics of medium to large towns and cities in Britain presented diverse problems and opportunities to local exhibitors. In the USA the outlying suburban areas were dependent upon a regular clientele and those theatres were more likely to support the feature.[17] The Palladium was able to mix its programme and cater to both regular patrons and a floating clientele. The increasing use of Chaplin films suggests that both types of audience were necessary for profitable business, particularly considering the large number of cinemas in the town. Such an appeal to a heterogeneous constituency, and its emphasis on 'uplifting' programming, made the Palladium a viable cinema for the exhibition of the super-films like *Intolerance*, *Civilization* or Selig's *The Garden of Allah* (1918); films that could only be obtained for the longer run of six days. Some exhibitors tried these super-films out with varying degrees of success. Mr D.

Stratton, the manager of the Palace in Runcorn, wrote to the Selig Company in April 1918 concerning his screening of *The Garden of Allah*: 'You forgot that all shows are not continuous and that seven reels while suiting city halls becomes a stumbling block to suburban halls. We outsiders must give a varied programme.'[18] The Palladium, on the other hand, was consistently able to run the super-films because of its mix of programming and its reputation for respectability. That reputation helped to build a particular set of expectations for its regular clientele, and these expectations in turn informed the reception of Ince's super-film in Britain.

'*Civilization*: What Every True Briton is Fighting For'

Thomas Ince's film *Civilization* had enjoyed a successful first run in the United States. The film had been premiered on 2 June 1916 at the Criterion Theatre in New York and had run for five months. The critical reception was enthusiastic. The picture generated acknowledgement from the Wilson administration for its message of peace and the spectacle of the battle scenes was highly praised. The film dealt with its subject matter in a way that gave space to contentious issues, such as the pacifist movement and the sinking of commercial liners by submarines, but then displaced them by setting them in a rural, distinctly Germanic, fictitious nation. The blame for the belligerence is placed on the Emperor; divine intervention in the embodiment of Christ implies forgiveness, the attitude necessary to the cessation of hostilities. In this way the call for peace was in line with Wilson's apparent proposal for 'taking the United States into the World War early in 1916 on the basis of a "clean peace" without offering any spoils to the Entente participants . . .'.[19] Most critics responded to the film's ambiguous allegory with positive reviews although one critic from *Photoplay*, articulating an isolationist's suspicion, wrote in August: 'What keeps this from being a master film? Absence of intimacy, not our people, not our war.'[20]

The British advertising campaign for the film began in earnest in the trade press in January 1917. Articles in *The Bioscope* and *Kinematograph Weekly* reflected the impact of the advertising campaign for *The Birth of a Nation*, emphasising spectacle and downplaying the pacifist message. *The Bioscope* featured an interview with the film's publicist, Raymond Bartlett. Asked about the changes made for the British market, Bartlett explained that 'it has been considerably modified. The full English title is

"Civilisation; What Every True Briton is Fighting For'".[21] Both journal articles focused on the 'Realistic Battle Scenes', with the *Kinematograph Weekly* stating that it was a 'Great American Sensation' that was 'no maudlin, sickly attempt to preach a moral, but a strong series of extraordinary scenes showing in all its vividness and reality the horror of war, including fierce fighting on land and sea'. There were also 'many domestic scenes and pictures of family life, . . . and other strong touches by the producer [to] relieve . . . the terrible scenes of warfare'.[22]

The film was screened for the trade at Marble Arch on 5 February. The critical reception of the trade show was enthusiastic, but not without some reservations. In an article subtitled 'The War through Neutral Spectacles', *The Bioscope* expressed concern for what they termed 'excessive sentimentality' for the Germans. Throughout this review it was assumed that the Teutonic world created by the film was in fact Germany and the Emperor was meant to represent the Kaiser. *The Kinematograph* reviewer also referred to the liner-sinking sequence as 'an attempt to realise the awful destruction of the "Lusitania"'.[23] *The Bioscope* found it necessary to comment on this scene in some detail:

> The sinking of the liner is an instance of the producer's anxiety to include every aspect of the war, for as it is only suggested as the outcome of the commander's imagination, the story provides a legitimate reason for its insertion. That it is a scene conjured up by the brain of a German officer, no doubt accounts for the state of wild panic, and which, we are proud to believe, is not in accordance with authenticated fact.[24]

The reviewer's nationalistic sensibilities consequently led him to deny that the scenes of panic presented in Ince's film were modelled on what actually happened on the Cunard liner *Lusitania* in May 1915. They could only exist in the tortured imagination of the German officer.

In many of the publicity efforts on the film's behalf, there were complexities and degrees of ambivalence. Part of the advertising campaign focused on patriotism. The original two-page fold-out advertisement for the film in the British trade press was modified by the added words 'What Every True Briton is Fighting For' (the 'z' in 'Civilization' remained). But the advertisement also contains a visual metaphor for pacifism: there is a depiction of the sun in the left-hand corner and, directly underneath, a torch of enlightenment with Ince's picture in the flame. Both are shining on the globe, on top of which a battle is taking place. This is not referred to in the text of the advertisement, where the only phrase that comes close to articulating pacifist sentiment describes *Civilization* as 'A Picture of modern warfare that thrills and appalls'.

6.1   Advertisement from *The Bioscope*, 8 February 1917.

The earlier, ambivalent advertising rhetoric was reproduced for the local premiere of the film at the Palladium on 25 August, but with some changes. The 'z' in the film's title had been replaced by the anglicising 's' but the tag line 'What Every True Briton is Fighting For' had been dropped. While the catchword in the majority of the advertisements was 'stupendous', which emphasised its super-film status, the large crowds and the amount of money it took to produce, the reference to the appalling nature of the images remained. The advertising campaign began a fortnight prior to the screening. A pre-review article entitled 'Super-film at the Palladium' stated that it was considered 'by many an expert in cinematography . . . cinema spectacle beyond compare. In it one is brought face to face with the grimmest reality of all ages, namely the last three years.'[25] The reference to the reality of the depiction of war had a resonance in Britain at this time, following as it did the screenings of

Battle of the Somme during the previous year and, earlier in 1917, of *The Battle of the Ancre and the Advance of the Tanks*. Both of these films played their first runs at the Palladium. The impact of these films and their intersection with the experience of loss in British lives had by this time become a significant aspect of adult cinema-goers' realm of experience.

At the beginning of the war there had been a flood of British fictional war films, but as casualty figures mounted such films were considered inappropriate. As early as April 1915 the Regent cinema, in the Southampton suburb of Shirley, advertised a film entitled *The Massacre of the 4th Cavalry* with the added phrase 'Nothing to offend the most sensitive'. Two-reel war films with a message fell from favour with audiences generally, but the war as a setting for adventure in serials such as *Pearl of the Army* (1916), and later comedies such as *The Better 'Ole* (1918) and Chaplin's *Shoulder Arms* (1918) fared better. Generally, films that displaced the war onto other historical periods or took place during an indeterminate war with Teutonic-looking enemies continued to enjoy popularity.

If the public was tiring of the official films there was still a good deal of mileage in the spectacle of war as it was expressed in the super-filmn, notably *The Birth of a Nation* and of course *Civilization*. On the night of 25 August 1917 it was standing-room only for the premiere of *Civilization* at the Palladium in Southampton. The review of the evening stated that it had attracted big crowds and that the film is 'undoubtedly one of the most astounding pictures of modern warfare which has been produced, showing as it does , all the phases of war'.[26] The review lists the types of warfare depicted and relates a brief summation of the film's story:

> It shows how a man of the enemy nation was chiefly instrumental in stopping a war which had almost wrecked civilisation, and of the cooperation of the women. Then it depicts, after the war was over, the home-coming of the men, and the great joy which was felt by all but those who had lost their nearest and dearest, and could not share in the general rejoicing.[27]

The review restates the tone of the national trade reviews by foregrounding the spectacle of the battle scenes and the counterbalance of the human story, the actions of one man helped by 'the women', the return of men to families and the grief of those who lost loved ones. The review also takes as read that the characters are German and that the peace message is that the recognition that war is destructive is a lesson for the Germans to learn. Finally there is a convergence of education and entertainment discourses in the final statement of the review: '*Civilisation* is a truly stupendous spectacle and one which brings home the horrors of war'. The Southampton reviewer's phrase that the film brings home the horrors of war places the interpretation at the convergence of the education/entertainment issue. 'Bringing the horrors of war home' had been a commonly used phrase by reviewers for the official war films. The fact that the film's publicity constructed it as a prestige production and focused on spectacle as 'stupendous and instructive' served to de-emphasise the potentially moralising tone (some of which had been removed in the version shown in Britain[28]) and particularly the sensitive issue of pacifism. Finally, the procedure of screening the super-films as special events and sometimes playing in theatres rather than cinemas indicates the status of the film and explains why the film was screened at the Palladium in the Portswood district of Southampton.

The film's depiction of war in all its phases, the sinking of the liner, the 'cooperation of the women' and the homecoming scenes all had a resonance for the Palladium audience to a greater or lesser extent within their wider horizon of expectation and experience. First and foremost is the reference to the sinking of the *Lusitania*. The ship was not based in Southampton but the re-enactment of the sinking held obvious significance for a Southampton audience. The *Titanic* had sunk five years earlier and the town was already in the process of erecting monuments to those who had lost their lives there. (125 children from the Northam primary school had lost a family member on the *Titanic*.) The sinking of merchant ships was a continuous threat to the community overall. There is evidence of a local discourse of memory and loss in the community in the structure and placement of the memorials to those lost on the *Titanic*. Each memorial is to a section of the ship's employed staff and each is located in a church or public grounds in the community where the dead had lived. On many of these memorials is the verse from Revelation 20:13 'And the sea gave up the dead which were in it'. The reference to resurrection is redolent of hope, the cleansing effects of Armageddon. Verse 20:12, just prior to this phrase has a direct relevance to the story told in *Civilization*. 'And I saw the dead great and small standing before the throne, and books were opened. Another book was opened which is the book of life. The dead were judged according to what they had done as recorded in the book.' These memorials provide an image of the coherent community in the face of loss. *Civilization*'s resurrection of

Count Ferdinand from death at sea, and the depiction of Christ showing the emperor the book of life restate these sentiments.

On 28 August 1917, three days after the premiere of *Civilization*, the *Echo* ran a letter from the Revd Frank Blandford, B.A., pastor of Bitterne Congregational Church. He was 'considerably impressed' by his visit to the Palladium. 'It is splendid', he writes,

> The picture is brilliantly conceived and brilliantly executed. Among its outstanding features . . . [are] the contrast between the method of autocracy and the method of democracy, a contrast which is frequently brought out. . . . The frequent emphasis on spiritual values, the suitable and pointed language of the narrative, the prominent part played by the 'Mothers of Men' in an anti-war crusade—these points and many others give a great teaching and inspiring power to a most splendid film.[29]

His reference to democratic process points to the Congregationalist method of self-determination and is probably a gentle swipe at the High Anglican and Catholic churches. However, the reference to 'Mothers of Men' is significant as it is connected to the anti-war message of the film. The anti-war message is not referred to as pacifist. The distinction between the two is an active interpretation of the film's profound ambiguity around this issue. The pacifist movement in the United States and in Britain had come under criticism from conservative pro-war groups and by government edict in both countries. Susan Zeiger has pointed out the way in which competing constructions of motherhood in the USA had equated the 'patriotic' mother with selfless sacrifice as a positive image, while the pacifist mother was condemned as 'feminist', selfish and exerting an overprotective and unhealthy control over her sons.[30] Sharon Ouditt has noted that the use of a maternalist discourse by suffragist pacifists in Britain caused difficulties in their attempt to 'catalyse large-scale political reorganisation . . . They used the image, though, as a literary and political device. World politics seen through the eyes of maternalism, is defamiliarised . . . leaving the way clear for a less barbaric, more egalitarian system to emerge'—one equivalent to the pacifist message of *Civilization*.[31]

The national attention received by British suffragist pacifists was generally derogatory in the press. However, members of the National Union of Women's Suffrage Societies (NUWSS), like Catherine Marshall and Helena Swanick, were involved in pacifist organisations such as the No-Conscription Fellowship and the Union of Democratic Control. Both organisations brought together suffragists and figures such as Ramsay MacDonald and Bertrand Russell. Since 1911 the NUWSS had been aware of the need to contact trade unions for support and had contacted the Independent Labour Party in Southampton. The NUWSS's relation to the unions in the local area was complicated by the organisation's own rift between those demanding the vote for women (or, at least, middle-class women with property) and the adultists, or advocates of universal suffrage. During the war, the position of the suffragists was still further complicated by the general support for the war and the work generated by the war effort. Southampton at this time was a focus for debates and disputes on conditions of service for women in jobs normally done by men. The scenes of women on the march in the film, when seen against this background, are potentially explosive. Yet their impact was no doubt mitigated by the way in which the cinema itself was identified as a site for entertainment. The screening of the film at the Palladium created specific expectations of the public space of this particular cinema; it functioned to prompt certain performative response codes and to reinforce accepted social codes of behaviour. The added understanding that the film was an American production provided a further distance from which the images of Germans learning to become peaceful could be read and interpreted.

Conclusion

Let us now return briefly to our fictitious cinema-goer and her boyfriend. Mabel had access to the local reception of the film both in the press and by word of mouth. She was able to go to the cinema weekly, if not more often, and her experience of the film *Civilization* was part of a much broader experience of cinema-going. This experience was characterised as a space where courting, for example, was sanctioned by both the prestige of the cinema and the educational character of the film. Her experience of working in the centre of Southampton in 1916–17 ensured that she witnessed the public impact of the war through the sight of the wounded and convalescing, while other effects, such as those resulting from her uncle's service, would have more individual resonances. For Walter this would have been more immediate, although patriotic propriety would probably have prevented explicit discussion of the condition of the wounded he was loading every day.[32] The personal context for Mabel's experience of viewing *Civilization* was therefore somewhat different to Walter's but with the subject matter of the film being both dutiful—in the sense that it purported to be an important moral message concerning the war—as well as a reminder of the true horrors of war, there was probably little reason to discuss experiences openly. The fact that all this was tied up with the ritual of dating intensified this effect. Two people's impressions illustrate one means of interpretation that contrasts with the Revd Blandford's, not only because of the obvious differences in their backgrounds and age, but also because of the different social forces governing public discourse in Blandford's case and the personal realm in the case of Mabel and Walter. Rather than argue for an infinite number of possible readings, I have tried to mark out the way in which the film and its advertising interacted with the prevailing conditions of reception within a particular local area to encourage specific public and private responses.

The strategies of the cinema exhibitor indicate the local complexities of film culture and impact on Mabel's and Walter's experience. Hood, Bacon and their managers worked to incorporate their cinema into the local suburban community with methods designed to highlight its benevolent social function. By making their programme a mix of short films and prestige features and super-films they were able simultaneously to extend their audience constituency and maintain a reputation for 'high-class' programmes that were educational and entertaining, hence Mabel's father could feel more comfortable both with the film and the venue. The role of US films, exemplified by the use of Chaplin films, was central to this, not only in terms of the number of films available compared to British, but also through the type of films on offer. The Palladium secured first runs of the Chaplin Mutuals and the First National 'million dollar Chaplins' from late 1917 until the end of the war and beyond. The fact that they showed very few Chaplin Essanays is arguably due to their rejection of the block-booking policy of Essanay so that they could maintain maximum flexibility in programming and therefore maintain their reputation in the local area. However, the move away from the sombre subject matter of war is evident in the Palladium's programming of more comedy and adventure serials in the last two years of the war. By speculating on the thoughts of the two fictitious characters, Mabel and Walter, I have tried to illustrate, rightly or wrongly, the nature of 'war-weariness'. Hood and Bacon were not unaware of this growing public attitude and it is clear that the Palladium, along with the general national

172

trend in programming in the later years of the war, attempted to position their venue accordingly.

The war amplified the shifting perception of cinema's social function from being a source of informative education to providing diverting, and regenerating, entertainment. Mabel and Walter would understandably be looking for a place of entertainment to set a tone of levity for their evening. The super-films such as the reconfigured *Civilization*—a ' great American sensation' in the words of *Kineweekly*—offered thrilling yet educational spectacle, where educational meant a convergence between the spectacle of war and concurrence with the dominant patriotic discourse. As we have seen, the Palladium was able to negotiate effectively between uplift and thrill in its programming, house management and advertising strategies so that both Chaplin and *Civilization* could be seen, with only slight latitude, as respectable and compatible with the war effort. Mabel and Walter could therefore be assured of a socially sanctioned date by attending the film at the Palladium, even though it may not have been their first choice of entertainment. The audience expectations encouraged by these strategies enhanced the interpretation of *Civilization* as significantly as the editorial changes imposed on the film nationally, and highlight the important role the exhibition sector played in the transnational reception and dominance of US cinema on British screens.

7

Chaplin
A Transatlantic Vernacular

I heard a girl say the other day after the Somme film, when her companion was about to go before the end, 'Oh stay Jack, there's a comic film coming next.'

Mr J.T. Legge, Director of Education Liverpool, 1917[1]

By and large the comic film escaped the reproach of the National Council of Public Morals' (NCPM) report of 1917, leaving the social or 'sex' melodramas and the crime film to occupy the attentions of regulating bodies both local and national. This fact raises the question of where and how the comic film, always on the programme, *did* fit into these debates. This chapter will use this question as a starting point to explore how exhibitors in Britain utilised comedy films to maintain and stabilise audiences but also as a response to ongoing public debates about the social function of cinema. In fact, exhibitors achieved this primarily through the rising popularity of Chaplin, but other examples such as Welsh comic Fred Evans as Pimple, or the English comedies of the Hepworth Company were also important. With all three of these examples the popularity of comedy depended upon already established comic performance traditions that often differed from those in the United States. While those differences are most obvious in the English and Welsh comedies of Hepworth and Evans respectively, this difference is perhaps most crucial in the case of Chaplin, an English performer with the Fred Karno Company, working in the US film industry.

'To Laugh and Even—Forget'

The transformational powers of the cinema, for good or ill, lay at the heart of the public debates and it was here that the regulatory dynamic between the industry and official and non-official bodies took place. At the national level the industry emphasised the positive social effects of the cinema: primarily that they provided a new, safe and instructive social space where before the options available to youth were 'hooliganism in the streets' and for adults, the public house.[2] In many respects this was the industry's strongest argument. Cinemas were a cheap form of entertainment available, through the general practice of the continuous programme, at accessible times throughout the day. The Saturday matinee, for example, occupied children while their mothers did the household chores. The counter-arguments of moral guardians and local governments also centred partly on the cinema's effects on social behaviour. The darkness of the cinema space gave ample opportunity for 'indecency'. Added to this were the physical effects, such as eyestrain and the effect on children's attention spans. The moral (or immoral) effect of the space together with the subject matter of the films was of primary concern and it was the 'sex films' and 'crook films' that drew the most attention.

Within these debates on effects, the potential for physical and moral 'damage' was countered by the industry's emphasis on the potential for social health and moral uplift. The comic film occupied a secondary position in these debates. Compared to the erotic nature of the society melodramas or 'sex films' and the violence of the burglary or 'crook films', comedy films were seen as the lesser threat. Often they were considered to be 'vulgar' but not 'indecent'. In the appendix of the NCPM report in 1917 there was written testimony from the chief constables of most of the major towns and cities in Britain. The majority of these singled out the burglary film as the greatest threat, along with the cinema's attraction as an amusement, as apparently some juvenile crime was committed to gain the price of admission. The comedy film was identified specifically only by the chief constable of Margate:

> I am of opinion that there are other classes of films besides those referred to in Mr. Ross's evidence which are harmful to the well-being of juveniles. I refer to the comedy films, more particularly to some of _____ and _____ films, which, to say the least are undoubtedly vulgar. I think pictures which show a man expectorating

175

on another and similar behaviour, as being outside the pale of decency and should be eliminated from public exhibitions.[3]

More common was the view of Guildford constable, William V. Nicholas, who felt the comedy film was at best 'frivolous' and ranked it with 'bald melodrama mostly with impossible situations, and combined with a romance which is very often an insult to one's intelligence'.[4] In the view of many, the comic film exemplified the positive aspects of the transformational power of the cinema. In Southampton the prevailing theme of George Elliot's advertising for the Northam Picturedrome and the Carlton emphasised the restive and recuperative powers of the cinema. In his emphasis on rest for the working man, Elliot was drawing on a widely held belief in the necessary and recuperative powers of leisure for the working classes evident in Lady Bell's study of workers and their families in 1907. She illustrates this by reporting that 'The resources provided for a man's leisure matter incomparably. It is during these that he may be ruined and dragged down, and not in the hours of work.'[5] Her concern extended to the leisure of women and she gives a lucid account of a music hall audience's transformation that is worth recounting at some length:

> The front row of the gallery generally consists of small children, little boys between seven and ten, eagerly following every detail of the entertainment. Each of them there must have paid 2d for his place— how he acquired it who can tell? probably by begging or playing pitch and toss in the street. There are workmen to be seen in the orchestra stalls; that means 1s a night. If a man takes his wife with him that means 2s: but there are many more men than women to be seen there. Women go oftener to the cheaper places: one may see a 'queue' of them waiting to go to the 2d. seats, often with their husbands accompanying them. Many of these women have their babies in their arms. There is no doubt that they come out looking pleased and brightened up. The kind of entertainment usually offered does not, to the critical onlooker, seem either particularly harmful or specially ennobling. The curious fact that, in almost any social circle, it makes people laugh convulsively to see anyone tumble down, is kept well in view and utilised to frequent effect.[6]

Her observation illustrates the prevailing discourse, expressed in sentiment, on the rejuvenating properties of leisure generally and slapstick or knockabout comedy in particular. She is careful to acknowledge the universal appeal of comedy and to place it somewhere between 'harmful' and 'ennobling'. This is recognisable in the secondary place comedy occupies in moral concerns about the cinema during the war.

In the same spirit the Revd A.J. Waldron wrote in to the *Picture Palace News*, January 1916, in support of Sunday opening: '. . . Sunday should always be a rest and meditation day'. There was a pragmatic reason; '. . . only 5% of the population (of London) go to church, . . . what about the 95% left?' Arguing for a healthy recreation that is 'free from anything that spells of white slavery' he recommends laughter and equates it with Christianity, 'Give people a chance to laugh and laugh purely, that is Christianity. When I think of the slums, the bare sordid horrible surroundings in which people live, I thank God that something is done on Sunday which gives them a chance to get out of their selves, to see colour, to imagine, to laugh to even—forget.'

By 1916 this emphasis on the word 'forget' had an added significance for people who had personal stakes in the war effort. As the war progressed, the emphasis on the nature of the recuperative powers of cinema and the comic film became more evident in the advertising discourse of the trades and fan magazines. In 1916 *Pictures and Picuregoer* encouraged fans to develop the 'cinema habit': 'The picture habit is the ideal panacea for the worries of life. It will not do your work or lessen your troubles; but it will assuredly brighten your existence, and take your minds from the worries of life.'[7] A *Bioscope* review of Charlie Chaplin's Mutual film, *The Cure* (1917) pronounced the film 'an excellent tonic for all forms of depression'.[8] In January of 1918 Percival Lee, manager of the Cinedrome in Torquay, wrote to the Selig Company about his audience's lukewarm reaction to their Civil War epic *The Crisis*: 'A nerve racked public are on the lookout for something a little less strenuous, a little more soothing and diverting'.[9] Bruce Bairnsfather, the creator of the popular cartoon Ol' Bill, produced a cartoon of a silhouette of Chaplin in derby, cane and baggy trousers with the caption, 'A Chaplain to the forces that would have been welcome'.

Bairnsfather's cartoon draws attention to the recuperative powers of cinema and humour for soldiers. The therapeutic qualities of entertainment in both the cinemas and the music halls provided the rationale for the benefit programmes. The wounded returning soldiers themselves were clear evidence of the physical price being paid, and within the wartime rhetoric, they represented a debt that could scarcely be repaid. Cinema managers offered a community service in this respect. David Robinson cites Langford Reed's account of an occurrence where a wounded soldier is 'cured' by a Chaplin film. The general manager of the United Picture Company of St Helens in Lancashire stated, 'Last week I was showing a "Charlie Chaplin", and a wounded soldier laughed so much he got up and walked to the end of the hall and quite forgot he had left his crutches behind'.[10] The war and its publicly visible effects on soldiers' bodies complicated the regulating discourses surrounding cinemas and the films they screened. The objections to the cinema's effect on young women and children did not apply to the returning wounded soldier or the soldier on leave and are conspicuously absent from the concerns expressed by the NCPM 1917 report.[11] Soldiers on leave looked to the entertainments at home as a means of reintegrating into their previous life.[12] Cinemas often allowed soldiers discounts on tickets in addition to providing special programmes for the wounded. The edifying properties of cinema were subsumed into a recuperative experience for soldiers, a harmless and necessary tonic to offset their experiences.

Behaviour that may have been counted as crime and larceny in young boys became a harmless prank when perpetrated by soldiers. The Winchester Picture Theatre reported that soldiers had stolen a Chaplin cut-out:

> A life-sized cardboard figure of this well-known actor was placed in the entrance hall, where it would appear impossible for anyone to steal it, as it could be seen from the street and also from the ticket office, this seems not to have prevented the abduction of Chas., for he disappeared suddenly from his post. We have reason to believe he was forcibly removed by one or more officers of His Most Gracious Majesty's Army. A little bird whispered that Chas. was interned for several days at their mess and after a nice holiday he was returned to his post at the Theatre by his hosts, with the following inscription attached to his breast, viz.:- "Many thanks for the company of Chas. Chaplin, who, during his short vacation, has been as usual a source of amusement to his abductors and others.[13]

During the summer of 1915 the 'Chaplin craze' emphasised this tonic effect of his image. *The Bioscope* reported:

> A detachment of the Highland light infantry, on the eve of their departure, captured a profile of Mr. Chaplin, and carried it off as a trophy. The idea, no doubt, is to plant him in front of the German trenches, and so incapacitate the enemy with helpless laughter that their capture will follow as a matter of course, the most effective form

of reprisal it would be possible to take; as even the German lack of humour could not resist the appeal of this talented comedian.[14]

The following week, as if to prove the effectiveness of the Highlanders' plan, *The Bioscope* ran a story about German prisoners of war carrying a Chaplin cut-out. 'No doubt the smiling features of the great comedian will help to while away many a long hour.'[15]

Comedy's position as a comparatively minor and secondary concern in the effects debates about cinema allowed exhibitors, and the industry in general, to make claims for its therapeutic and restorative properties. Undoubtedly its perceived 'harmlessness', when compared to 'erotic' or 'crime' films, enabled the comic form to speak to wartime anxieties, as entertainment, through the vernacular of existing comic traditions. Those traditions were employed by performers and recognised by audiences. The effects of the war, social and/or physical were part and parcel of the subjects of the comic sketches, songs and, of course, films. These did not need to take the war as their overt subject however. The comic subjects and characters that had been staples of cinema: 'the naughty boy', 'the inebriate', 'the philandering husband', 'the courting couple', 'the park sketch' or 'the suffragette' were able to incorporate and draw from the significant social changes brought about by mass mobilisation, conscription and/or the replacement of men by women in the workplace. In each of these cases the function of comedy was to order through disorder, to build on audience expectations and their understanding of comic traditions to make sense of the visibly changing world of everyday life.

Film comedy had been drawing on music hall sketch traditions since the beginning of cinema. As films, they presented at the same time, through their very materiality as a product of technological innovation, a vision of modernity. This is clearly evident in the fact that film comedy was a staple of the film programme throughout the war and that the most popular, or at least those most sought after by exhibitors were the anarchistic, fast moving comedies of Keystone and particularly Chaplin, films that did not directly address the war at all.[16] Also popular with audiences were the Pimple films of Fred Evans, which drew primarily from pantomime and the music hall sketch, building on British audiences' familiarity with the forms. Evans, along with his brother Joe, had already been incorporating the traditions of 'burlesquing' topical events of the day prior to the outbreak of the war. This proved an immensely successful formula and one that deftly translated to the gesture requirements of the 'mute' medium of film throughout the war. Chaplin's immense popularity during this period, however, affords a convenient and historically significant example of the role comedy played in the establishment of cinema culture in British everyday life. A close look at the circulation and reception of Chaplin's image here will account for the ways film comedy functioned both as a reliable form of attracting and maintaining audiences for exhibitors and as a means of social engagement for those audiences.

Charlie in Southampton

The circulation of Chaplin's image in Southampton provides a basis for understanding his reception in Britain. This begins before his move to the United States with Fred Karno's troupe. Chaplin made his first appearance in Southampton on 19 March 1906 at the Hippodrome music hall on Ogle Street in a sketch called *Repairs*. The sketch was a knockabout by the well-known music hall sketch writer Wal Pink in which Chaplin played a clumsy plumber's mate in a group of comically ineffective workmen.[17] The play was a moderate success but apparently not significant enough to sustain Chaplin, since he left the production two months later to join a touring sketch, *Casey's Court Circus*, 'a street urchin's idea of a circus'. He returned to Southampton with this touring show on 29 October, 1906, this time at the Palace Theatre which later featured the Sunday evening film programmes. He eventually joined the Fred Karno Company and, as has been well documented, on his second American tour signed a contract with Keystone in 1913.

At first, Chaplin's return to Britain on screen in 1914 was no more eventful than his appearance in *Repairs* or with *Casey's Court Circus*. But by early 1915 his films, as we have seen, were indispensable products for cinema managers such as George Elliot at the Carlton in establishing and maintaining an audience base for cinema at a time when the advent of the war could hardly have seemed more inconvenient. By November 1914, his appearance on the Sunday evening film programme of the Palace music hall warranted a mention of his name: 'Keystone's latest comic *A Busy Day* presenting Charles Chaplin is sure of a big reception'.[18] The trade press began to mention him by name in September 1914 and by the summer of 1915 the Chaplin craze had reached British audiences. In the middle of that summer Langford Reed wrote an article in *The Bioscope* estimating the number of daily performances of Chaplin films throughout 'the world'. His calculations were that 'every day he gladdens the heart of no fewer that 12,750,000 people!'[19] He was inspired to write this article while on a visit to Brighton where he noticed that of the twelve cinemas there, one-third of them were showing Chaplin films. His estimate for Britain was 4,500 appearances per night. The evidence of the number of Chaplin films shown in Southampton during this period supports this. It also raises the question of how Chaplin's films and his image circulated through magazines and stories in newspapers. It is clear that, even as early as November 1914, the first of the Keystone Chaplins had made a significant enough impression that the proportion of cinemas showing them, cited by Langford Reed, had already been reached. By the late spring of 1915 there were increasing numbers of Chaplin films featuring in almost every film theatre in the city.

The Chaplin films advertised in Southampton show that by the summer of 1915 there were still a number of Keystone Chaplins. These continued to be shown throughout the rest of the years of the war as Keystone continued to make them available for renters on the open market. This also allowed cinemas to advertise a Chaplin every week. These overlapped with the newer films he had begun making for Essanay so that nineteen out of the thirty programmes between July and September 1915 showed Essanay films. After September the number of Essanay films declined in proportion to five out of the thirty programmes listed between September and November. This was due to the new exclusives policy that Essanay introduced in 30 September where they rented their films to theatres direct. This was a form of block booking in that they required the theatre 'to take three reels of its films each week in order to get the Chaplins'.[20]

In the summer the newer films were shown by most of the cinemas in Southampton. The Palace on Sundays, the Palladium in Portswood, the Carlton, the Alexandra and the Atherley in Shirley all showed the Essanay Chaplins prior to 30 September. Following that the only two theatres to advertise the Essanay films were the Carlton and the Northam Picturedrome. The fact that these two cinemas were under the ownership of P.V. Bowyer suggests that this system of booking was advantageous to the extent that the managers could spread the risk of taking the other less popular Essanay films in order to secure up-to-date Chaplins. It also shows that Chaplin films were able to appeal across class boundaries. Chaplin was as secure a draw at the more upmarket Carlton as he was to the working-class audiences at the Northam Picturedrome. Nevertheless the larger prestigious cinemas such as the Palladium and the Alexandra reverted to showing Keystones, which they could still obtain from the Western Import Company on the open market. They continued to do this until the following summer.

From this snapshot of the release and exhibition pattern, the prevalence of Chaplin films on cinema theatre programmes clearly shows that cinema managers considered Chaplin films essential to an attractive and successful programme. From September 1914 to the end of the war, Chaplin films, on average, appear on one programme in the town per week. Between April 1915 and April 1916 these appearances were at times on every screen in the city. The Chaplin phenomenon played out its initial stages across the war years. From fast-moving and 'vulgar' slapstick shorts with Mack Sennett at Keystone to the refinement of his comedy and the incorporation of pathos at Essanay and Mutual and finally the move to features at First National, Chaplin's development was both unique and emblematic of the increasingly dominant Hollywood industry. Yet the manipulation of his image by exhibitors and publicists in Britain related specifically to the expectations of British audiences. Chaplin's background in music hall sketch comedy was referred to in advertisements and hence was seen as an attraction for local audiences. From the outset he was recognised as the professional performer whose characterisations extended beyond the role of the tramp. From the point of view of a British audience his status as an Englishman successful in the Hollywood system raised issues of national identity that differed from the perception of him by audiences in the United States. The subject matter of his films reflected audiences' own experiences and included the role of public spaces, such as parks and city streets, and the ongoing demographic and social transformations, particularly for women stepping into jobs formerly held by men who had now joined the military. These themes and settings are particularly relevant in that they address the official and unofficial regulating frameworks for social behaviour that characterised the discourse of respectability surrounding the social function of leisure and courting generally and the site of the cinema theatre specifically. Finally, this is the period in which Chaplin's reputation as a comic genius began to become established, a development that hinged on the increasing incorporation of pathos in his films. This move to pathos had a double effect: first it added a deeper dimension to the Charlie character, complementing the development of the feature that was—within contemporary industry debates in Britain as well as in Hollywood—the primary strategy for expanding the class base of audiences. Second, and more significantly, the incorporation of pathos with slapstick intensified the existing reflexive properties of Chaplin's comedy. It is to these aspects of Chaplin's reception in Britain that I now turn.

Performance Modes and Traditions

The Western Import Company held the distribution rights to all Keystone films and had been vigorously 'booming' them throughout the spring of 1914. One of the techniques they adopted was to convince cinema managers to book 'Keystone Nights'. These were bookings that featured a full evening of Keystone comedies. In its 25 June edition *The Bioscope* ran an article on the Queen's Picture Hall in Bolton and included a photograph of the audience on a Keystone Night that showed some of the 1,500 people 'who stayed till the close'.[21] A week later advertisements in *The Bioscope* claimed continued success. One featured a telegram from the Ramworth Electric Theatre in Bolton; the advertisement read: 'Keystone smashes all records—over three thousand paid for admission—hundreds turned away—pay box bombarded—traffic impeded writing'.[22]

In the week of the beginning of the war the 'Keystone Night' reappears in *The Bioscope* as a desirable technique for increasing business. This is not surprising in the wake of the general concern that the war would see business plummeting or perhaps even cause theatres to close. In keeping with the common advertising strategy of presenting films, and comedy films in particular, as a 'blues chaser', the Western Import advertisement for the new Keystone releases for September advertised the 'Keystone Quartette' of Mabel Normand, Mack Sennett, Charles Chaplin and Roscoe Arbuckle as '. . . going stronger than ever. Let them keep your audiences cheerful.' The 'All Keystone Night' was '. . . still the best money making scheme open to the exhibitor. It has in fact greater pulling powers now than ever. It gives your theatre that added attractiveness it needs in abnormal circumstances.'[23] Comedy films were significant in the growing image of the cinema as a place where everyday troubles and anxiety were alleviated at this time. Chaplin would become emblematic of this comic effect as his star image increased in popularity to the proportions of a social phenomenon. Film exhibitors and renters were quick to recognise this and used Chaplin films to stabilise profitable attendance figures. Chaplin's phenomenal rise to stardom became clear in June–August 1915, 'Chaplin's summer', but his star status in Britain had already had a significant boost in the summer of 1914, a boost that built upon his work in the halls.

'Charles' of the Halls

Chaplin's Keystone period dates from February to December 1914. Here he made thirty-five films, directed nineteen of those, and developed the initial 'tramp' character that he elaborated throughout his career.[24] The transition to the tramp character at this time has been the subject of speculation in virtually all Chaplin biographies. However, David Robinson makes the point: 'It is easy enough to find precedents for the costume in English music halls. Grotesquely ill-fitting clothes, tiny hats, distasteful moustaches and wiggle-waggle canes were the necessary impedimenta of the comedian.'[25] Rather than dwell on the transformation of these music hall antecedents into high cinematic art, a consideration of what elements of Chaplin's performance were recognisable for British audiences in the films made at Keystone during 1914 provides a key example of how comedy films were received during the war. British audiences' engagement with these films depended to a large extent on their familiarisation with both music hall sketch comedy, street comedy such as the Pierrot shows and the cinema comedy of Mack Sennett and British film comedians such as Fred Evans's character Pimple. It is clear that Chaplin's image as a performer in Britain was known well enough for the advertisers to stress it. As with Fred Evans, the traditions of the comic sketch and pantomime offered familiar forms for audiences to respond to, and with Chaplin, those traditions are combined with both the developing and already established representational strategies of the Hollywood cinema.

Charles Maland points out that Chaplin's arrival at Keystone was at the moment that the film industry was 'groping toward the star system'.[26] In his account of Chaplin's reception and rise to fame in the USA in the years at Keystone, Essanay, and Mutual, 1914–16, Maland focuses on the vulgarity of the broad slapstick of the Keystone style in order to detail the significant shift, in the eyes of the 'cultural elite' in the USA, to a recognised 'creative genius' who had transcended his vulgar comic roots. Maland shows that it was not until August 1914 that Chaplin's name was beginning to be mentioned in fan magazines such as *Motion Picture Magazine* in the USA and it was not until 1916—helped significantly by an article in *Harper's* by the well-respected theatre actress Minnie Maddern Fiske—that he began to be seen as 'comic genius' and 'extraordinary artist'.[27] In Britain, however, these early months of Chaplin's film work were characterised by attempts by the Western Import Company to build on his already fairly well-established reputation among music hall patrons. As early as June 1914 the advertisements in the trade press for Keystone films drew the copy from the US publicity and mentioned him by name: 'Are you prepared for the Chaplin Boom? ... then book the rest before its too late'. Taking the cue, exhibitors began to make references to his appearances in Fred Karno's sketch *Mumming Birds*. In July the Royal Cinema Stockton advertised *Making a Living* as 'featuring Charles Chaplin of Mumming Birds fame'.[28] What is notable in these advertisements, and in this one in particular, is the professionalisation of the music hall performer implied in the reference to 'Charles', rather than Charlie.

'Charlie', a signifier of the burgeoning star system's effect of fusing, or conflating, the character with the real life of the performer had yet to appear. According to Maland, in the USA Chaplin's persona developed in three stages: initial recognition as 'character type', through repeated appearances in the tramp costume; the attachment of the name 'Charlie' to the character; and finally, the separation of character and performer, Charles as the genius behind the pathetic tramp figure. In the summer of 1914 his main quality was a virtuoso comic performer of a range of characters. In his first film for Keystone, *Making a Living*, Chaplin plays a recognisable English music hall character, a down-at-heel and unscrupulous fop with morning coat and drooping moustache, who would have been seen differently by British and American audiences. Chaplin here is performing a character familiar to English audiences from the music hall stage and acting within a setting of the fast-paced comedy of the Keystone style.

Charles Musser has provided an enlightening example of 're-situating Chaplin's films' of this period 'within the historical conditions from which they arose'. He argues that Chaplin biographers and critics have succeeded in smoothing out the radical potential in the early Chaplin character. He suggests that Chaplin's tramp figure needs to be seen as a figure whose anarchic disruptions of the workplace appealed to working-class audiences by playing off their experiences in the workplace and resonating with 'spectators' fantasies'. Central to his argument is the idea that, in order to reassert this radical potential, account needs to be taken of the relationship of the social counterpart of the tramp with Chaplin's characterisation. While he recognises the tradition of the tramp in nineteenth-century theatre, English music hall, vaudeville and popular forms such as newspaper comics, Musser focuses on the tramp as a reference to social realities and draws attention to evidence that Chaplin modelled his character to some extent on the American tramp, 'a figure few people in the United States were able to avoid in the course of their daily lives'.[29] By contrast, the reception of Chaplin in Britain was dependent upon the performance tradition of the tramp as a character in English music hall, theatre and earlier forms of film. This makes it possible to account for Chaplin's ability to appeal across class boundaries in his performance of the tramp through his attention to detail, his use of by-play, in short, his virtuosity. His deftness with objects was an attraction and was an important element in his ability to disrupt not only the workplace but also, although they often converge, the regulating mechanisms of public leisure spaces and private domestic spheres. The performance traditions that Chaplin and his British audiences drew upon, with references to social realities, were the currency of the comic song, the comic sketch and specifically Karno's sketches. Their interdependency provided the basis for the specific pleasures that a British audience found in Chaplin's comic performance.

British audiences' familiarity with the business and costume of Chaplin's character in his second film *Kid's Auto Races* lay in the costume of the sketch comedian of music hall. Sketch veteran Fred Kitchen often complained that Chaplin had taken the tramp costume from him. Kitchen was appearing at the Palace in Southampton in April 1916 and *What's On* included a picture of him in costume. In the picture he is wearing oversized turned out boots, baggy trousers, a long overcoat and a top hat. His make-up included heavy eyebrows and what appears to be a white powder base on his face. Alongside the photograph was an article reprinted from *The Umpire*, Sunday 19 September, 1915, in which he complained that he couldn't take up an offer to go to America because Chaplin had copied his costume and act. He remembers having worked with Chaplin:

> I remember just after I had produced 'G.P.O.', Mr. Karno sent down to me a young fellow and asked me what I could do with him. . . . I was not overstruck with him, so he returned to Mr. Karno, and played in several of his sketches. Subsequently he went to America and took to film work and soon became famous. But as the films show, it is Chaplin with Fred Kitchen's feet, boots, trousers, coat, hat and even tie, while almost the whole of his bye-play [sic] is business created by myself . . .[30]

Remarkably, the Chaplin costume he describes in September 1915 is not the one of the tramp but, apart from the shoes, more the character of the 'fop' that Chaplin played in *Making a Living*. He combines the costume with the 'by-play' to indict Chaplin as plagiarist. His brief complaint demonstrates the ubiquity of the costume of the music hall sketch comedian and the flexible nature of Chaplin's image in Britain at the time. Chaplin's 'tramp' character was not fully formed in 1914 and audiences could expect him to appear in a range of different guises, such as his drag performance in *The Busy Day*. An early advert for Keystones in *The Bioscope* in 17 September 1914 is topped by a bust drawing of 'Chas. Chaplin' in the costume with upturned collar and tie to which Kitchen refers. In Britain his identity as a member of Karno's troupe created certain expectations and recognitions in audiences that allowed his films to have a broad appeal. (Karno's *Mumming Birds* came to Southampton no less than three times during the war.) As Chaplin appeared in more Keystones in the summer of 1914 his ability to play a range of characters was part of his public image. On 1 August *Pictures and the Picturegoer* ran a full-page photomontage. At the centre Chaplin is depicted seated on a table in an immaculate suit, with an expensive-looking cane; this image is surrounded by four superimposed busts of him in various roles. Three are identifiable as the characters in Sennett films: the English fop in *Making a Living* with monocle, droopy moustache and top hat, the tramp character soaking wet from the comic climax of *A Film Johnny* (1914), another tramp character with an aggressive grimace, and finally a photograph that looks to have been taken from his days with Karno in the character of 'the inebriate' from *Mumming Birds*. The blurb beneath the photograph emphasises Chaplin's status as a versatile comic actor who seeks verisimilitude in his portrayal of characters:

> It was Mr. Charles Chaplin's inimitable acting in Karno's 'Mumming Birds' which first attracted the attention of Mack Sennett, the great Keystone head. Without uttering a word, Mr. Chaplin played the part of 'a drunken swell.' Getting the business over so cleverly by pantomime that Mr. Sennett made him a proposition on the spot. Several other motion picture companies also put in their bids, but Keystone came out ahead, and Mr. Chaplin is now starring in Keystone Comedies. He admires Americans, and is a devoted reader of fiction dealing with American life. One of his chief amusements and sources of character study is sitting in cafes or railway stations watching the crowds. Here he comes upon any number of new types which he delights in working up for the screen. He is already a popular comedian.[31]

7.1 'Film Faces by a Famous Funny Fellow', Chaplin in *Pictures and the Picturegoer*, 1 August 1914.

Creative with the truth (there is no record of other film companies bidding for Chaplin against Sennett and Keystone) the blurb emphasises the work of the actor as striving for accuracy and stresses the diversity of his range. Chaplin's Englishness is implicit in the reference to his admiration for Americans; throughout his career Chaplin was discussed in Britain as an Englishman in America. Articles and images in British magazines such as *Pictures and the Picturegoer* helped to set that in motion and it is important to note that it is his craft and ability to develop a number of comic personalities that characterised his reputation at this early stage of his reception in Britain.

The virtuosity of the English performer in America and the contrast between the theatricality of the tramp and the actuality of the crowd and events in *Kid's Auto Races* on these terms had, for a British audience, no more comic impact than Chaplin in drag in *A Busy Day* (US release, 7 May 1914). *A Busy Day* features Mack Swain and Chaplin as a married couple with Chaplin in the role of the wife and in music hall drag costume. It is one of the improvised films typical of Sennett's method at this time. Like *Kid's Auto Races*, it takes place at a public function, in this case a military parade, and features the antics of Swain, Chaplin and Phyllis Allen as 'the other woman'. According to Chaplin, the methods of directors such as Henry Lehrman (*Kid's Auto Races*) and George Nichols were based on speed, whether it was a chase or physical comedy, and the use of simple film continuity techniques, like screen direction. Further, Chaplin refers to the editors at Keystone as 'the butchers in the cutting room'. In these early films much of his by-play apparently ended up on the cutting-room floor or not allowed by either director. He gives an account of a strategy he adopted in the early Sennett period to counteract this: 'Familiar with their method of cutting films, I would contrive business and gags just for entering and exiting from a scene, knowing they would have difficulty cutting them out'.[32] Yet both films allow considerable time for business in the scenes where Chaplin, as tramp or in drag, performs for the camera.

The set-ups in a film like *A Busy Day* are only vaguely maintained through narrative coherence. The driving force behind the gags in *A Busy Day* is the flirtatious relationship of Swain and Phyllis Allen. Chaplin's dame character pursues them as they try to sneak off and in the process interrupts the filming of a military parade, thus attracting the ire of the director and a policeman. These films rely on business or by-play for their comic effect while the costume and the performance combine to present recognisable types. The longest takes in the film are the shots of the gags, for example, at the beginning of the film where the character and the relationship between the husband and wife are set up through the actors' bits of business. The comic performance of Chaplin in drag is that of the music hall dame, distinctly vulgar and aggressive.

One of the first films Chaplin directed illustrates the contrast between his style and the speed of the Keystone style. *Twenty Minutes of Love* (US release, 20 April 1914) takes place in a park. The first eight shots are enough to indicate how the comic sketch tradition is integrated by mixing short shot-reverse-shot combinations of eyeline matches that set up spatial relations through 180 degree continuity editing and then much longer shots in terms of time to allow the comic business to play out:[33]

> *Shot 1:* (7 secs) Chaplin walks towards the camera to medium close-up (mcu) and looks right.
> *Shot 2:* (2 secs) In medium shot (ms) a couple on a park bench kiss.
> *Shot 3:* (10 secs) (mcu) Chaplin mugs and mimes disgust, interest, and desire.
> *Shot 4:* (2 secs) (ms) Couple still kissing
> *Shot 5:* (11 secs) (mcu) Chaplin goes through a number of facial and bodily gestures and at one point hugs and kisses a tree as he looks at the kissing couple.
> *Shot 6:* (2 secs) (ms) Couple still kissing.
> *Shot 7:* (4 secs) (mcu) Chaplin grimaces and walks off screen right.
> *Shot 8:* (1 min. 15 secs) (ms) Chaplin enters from the left of frame which contains the couple kissing. He stands over them, looks very closely at their faces as they kiss, fans himself and finally taps the girl on the shoulder. They both throw their hands up in horror, as they were unaware of being watched. He sits down next to her, laughs and puts his hand on her hand, which is in her lap. Chaplin turns his head and the couple switch places. The man glares at him and gets so close to him that the handlebar moustache tickles Chaplin's ear. Chaplin realises his hand is now on the man's thigh. The man gestures threats at Chaplin and then turns to kiss his girlfriend. Chaplin taps him on the shoulder and whispers in his ear. The man shoves him off the bench. Chaplin sits back on the bench with his back against the man. They push and shove and just as the man gives a strenuous push Chaplin gets up and the man falls off the bench. While he is on the ground Chaplin sits next to the girl and tries to 'make love' to her. She pushes him away. Getting up from the ground the man threatens fisticuffs. Chaplin smiles, tips his hat and as he walks away he kicks the man twice, the second time knocking his hat off.

The first seven shots set up Chaplin's look with an average shot length of 5.42 seconds. This is contrasted with shot eight, that is a full 1 minute and 15 seconds, giving the space for the kind of by-play that characterised the sketch format.

In his autobiography Chaplin recalls that soon after arriving at Keystone he had wanted to direct his own pictures but for his tenth film *Mabel at the Wheel* was assigned to Mabel Normand:

This nettled me, for, charming as Mabel was, I doubted her competence as a director; so the first day there came the inevitable blow-up. We were on location in the suburbs of Los Angeles and in one scene Mabel wanted me to stand with a hose and water down the road so the villain's car would skid over it. I suggested standing on the hose so that the water can't come out and when I look down at the nozzle I unconsciously step off the hose and the water squirts in my face. But she shut me up quickly: 'We have no time! We have no time! Do what you are told!'[34]

Chaplin's insistence on his by-play within a fast-moving physical comedy style contrasts of his way of working with Sennett's, and also illustrates the different requirements of cinema technique. In *A Busy Day* and *Kid's Auto Races* the attempts by the directors to get Chaplin out of the way of the camera re-enact the frustration of both, and of course provide a solution. For the comic dependent on by-play the long take of the actuality becomes the ideal space to interrupt because it allows the space for the bits of comic business that is denied not only in the Keystone style of fast editing across spaces, but in the general trend in fiction filmmaking at the time. At the level of a developing cinematic style, as well as character and performance, Chaplin was a foreign interloper.

The three elements that were central to the development and reception of Chaplin's star persona during the Keystone period and that can be construed as speaking to a British audience are: first, his dependence on the traditions of performance from the music hall; second, the tendency, as was the case in British music hall, to emphasise the performer's virtuosity rather than subsuming the performer into the personality of the character (although this would change as Chaplin's development of the tramp proceeded);[35] and finally the reflexive nature of the films themselves. In spite of its secondary status within public debates about the cinema, the comedy film was increasingly being seen as a metonym for cinema's social function as an acceptable, and even desirable, leisure space. With his rising popularity, Chaplin was becoming a synonym for that role. At the level of social debate, cinema's general acceptance was partly due to the place of comedy already existing within the music hall tradition. Certainly it was a history of contestation, but one that produced modes of performance and reception that had been deemed by and large to conform to codes of respectability.

Yet the reflexive nature of slapstick comedy worked also at the level of the content of the films. The performances of Chaplin in films such as *A*

Busy Day, *Twenty Minutes of Love* and *Kid's Auto Races* were recognisable to British audiences but so were the situations: the husband with the roving eye, the pursuit of love in a public space, or conflicts with police officers or irate film directors. Slapstick's ability to utilise everyday settings as prime sites for disruption is central to Charles Musser's argument that Chaplin films, particularly those of Charlie in the workplace, held a radical potential for US audiences.[36] However, the workplace was not the only site for anarchy in Chaplin films; it is at least as important to consider his use of public spaces such as parks, the street and even the cinema, alongside the rapidly shifting cultural terrain of the British homefront. While the setting of the workplace prompted laughter through the disruption of the regime of the clock or the regulating mechanics of shopfloor hierarchies, public spaces offered recognisable situations and behaviour that were the subject of the same public debates and regulations as the leisure spaces of the dance hall and the cinema theatre.

The Park, the Street and the Cinema

The 'park film' constitutes a sub-genre of the comedy film. It had been a part of film comedy tradition on both sides of the Atlantic since the earliest period of cinema and was a mainstay of the Keystone style.[37] David Robinson recounts the role this sub-genre played in Chaplin's failed contract renewal negotiations with Sennett in August 1914. Sennett warned that Ford Sterling, Keystone's most popular star until Chaplin, was regretting his departure from Keystone. Chaplin replied famously, 'all *he* needed to make a comedy was a park, a policeman and a pretty girl.'[38] That formula perfectly outlines the ingredients for a set-up where attempts at formal and informal, official and unofficial regulation of sexuality and social behaviour are resisted and, in the comic frame, disrupted. Chaplin's early park films feature Charlie as a sexually aggressive pest rather than an infantile clown. The public space—offering opportunities for the comic and the pretty girl to 'misbehave' while avoiding the regulating gaze of the policeman or irate husband or boyfriend—held significant comic potential for audiences for whom these environments were part of everyday life. The park films Chaplin made for both Keystone and Essanay celebrate the leisure space, the respite from the rigours of work and the anxieties that the war brought about; they construct those spaces as anarchistic and full of unexpected delight. They not only build on the social realities of the existence of transgressive gentleman tramps but also celebrate the disruption of those spaces and their attendant social codes of behaviour.

The playing out of *Twenty Minutes of Love* in the park resonates with dating practices in British cities and town. A long walk on the Common in Southampton was a chance to be alone. As we have seen earlier, the Common was promoted in *Kelly's Directory* as a place that offered 'sequestered nooks where young love may babble its dreams undisturbed'. In addition to the Common Southampton also had three parks within easy walk of the town centre, convenient places for picnics and sport. As heterosocial spaces the parks, or the Common, echo the public/private nature of the cinema as an appealing place to court. Always the site of some anxiety, these spaces were the subject of considerable concern as the demographic shifts brought on by the war saw more women entering the workplace, more cross-class contact, the separation of families and the increase of soldiers in cities and towns. By September 1914 the Common had become the last staging post for troops off to the front. John Oates Lord described the Common as being 'like a huge field of mushrooms, dotted with thousands of tents . . .'.[39] The park, like the cinema, was a contested space and potential site of 'indecency' because, again like the cinema, it offered a kind of privacy in a public setting. What constituted indecency in the way the cinema was talked about included 'petting' between young adults, anxieties about covert prostitution, assaults on women and fears of molestation of children by adults. Jeffrey Weeks has pointed out that in Britain the period 1914–39 saw the organisation of sexuality '. . . as clearly a product both of inheritance of a series of moral codes and practices, and of exposure to the felt needs of the time. The result was a complexly changing situation which makes any simple schematisation virtually impossible.'[40] The 1917 NCPM Cinema Commission report bears out Weeks's observation that '. . . purity, familialism, public decency remained the social norms which the apparatus of formal regulation sought to uphold. The areas of tension occurred not with the desired aim but over the boundaries between public and private spheres.'[41] After her testimony to the commission Mrs Basil L.Q. Henriques, secretary of the Oxford and St George (Jewish) Girls' Club, was asked by the Cinema Commission if she had noticed any acts of impropriety in the cinema. She said she had. When asked if people 'passing up and down the gangway' could see it she responded 'Well, I looked closely for it'. When questioned on the nature of this impropriety she said that she had 'several times seen couples in regard to whom one would have no doubt as to what is going to happen'.[42] These references to indecency hinge on the behaviour, or performance, of the couple in public, behaviour that 'implies' more intimate practices in private. Similar accounts appear in the London Public Morality Council report on the sexual activities of couples in open spaces, particularly parks and military encampments. Weeks points out that these accounts 'convey an irresistible picture of respectable ladies pursuing their moral passion to the point of prying' and being unable to distinguish at times acts that were only an offence when committed in public.[43] The weekly journal *The John Bull*, edited by Horatio Bottomley, often ran stories of these encounters. A story entitled 'Peeping Polls' recounted an incident where a 'pretty maid' had met a 'young man' while walking on the common in Wimbledon. '. . . They sat down upon a seat, provided by a thoughtful Council for the purposes of being sat upon, and they engaged in a quiet and affable chat . . .'. They were then interrupted by 'the rays of an electric torch' held by two 'sternly silent policewomen' who told them to 'sit up straight'. The paper thought it 'rude and impertinent' of them to 'make sudden searches in the hope of discovering impropriety'.[44] The following month the same paper ran a story 'Kissing—A Crime' which told of a couple having to spend the evening in the Warminster jail when arrested by a policeman for 'a vigorous exchange of kisses' after an evening stroll. This case went to court ,where it was thrown out. The paper decreed that '. . . such conduct implies no moral turpitude' nor should it 'form the pretext for criminal proceedings'.[45] The satirical tone adopted by *The John Bull* concurs with the comic park films'—and particularly Charlie's—mistrust of policemen and the prevalence of surveillance in public leisure spaces, like parks and the darkness of the cinema. When Chaplin acted out comic rendezvous with equally flirtatious young women in the park he was acting out scenarios that were consistently the subject of discussion, particularly in popular magazines and the press.

The 'social norms of public decency' dominated popular magazines and were the primary subjects of fictional stories and advice columns. *The Family Journal* ran a regular column entitled 'Cupid's Corner; Weekly Chat with Sweethearts and Wives' by 'Y.Z.' advising its readership on the limits of propriety. On 2 September 1916 the subject was 'Walks with Wounded Soldiers'. Recognising the increased visibility of wounded and returning soldiers in the public space, the article cautioned against becoming over-familiar with them.

> Hero worship is a beautiful thing . . . some people are inclined to
> carry [it] a little too far . . . Young girls in particular are apt to think

they are bound in honour to comply with every wish their hero thinks fit to express . . . They should remember that they owe it to the brave lads "over the water" to do nothing which could be possibly construed —nothing which could be made to reflect on their honour.[46]

In the Chaplin park films these restrictions were completely disregarded and offered the audience a humorous, yet relevant, diversion.

Such social regulation through the popular press was also a topic of humour and the Chaplin cartoons and stories in the fan magazines were no exception. In *Pictures and the Picturegoer* the story of 'Charlie's New Job', his first film for Essanay, ran in May 1915. The story recounts the film's narrative of Charlie seeking employment with a film company. Sitting in the outer office of the 'Lodestar Motion Picture Company' he sees a woman: 'Then romance warmed the cockles of his heart and his importunate landlady was forgotten as his eyes fell upon the dainty girl who occupied the chair next to him. Their eyes met and lingered, drifted apart, came together again. Charlie gulped hard, and the fair unknown smiled. It was the glad eye with a vengeance.'[47] Six months later the magazine's resident cartoonist Frank R. Grey drew a series of cartoons depicting the comic scenes in *Work* (21 June 1915). One of the gags shows Charlie looking at the maid of the house (played in the film by Edna Purviance) and hitting his boss over the head with a plank. The caption is 'the glad eye'. In the same cartoon another vignette depicted Charlie standing, paintbrush in hand, looking at Edna with the caption 'more glad eye'.

The glad eye is a central motif in the Keystones generally and the Chaplin Keystones in particular. In the film *Those Love Pangs* (October 1914) Charlie and Chester Conklin are 'rival mashers'. The film begins at the breakfast table in their boarding house. When the young landlady enters the adjoining room Charlie and Chester compete with each other in vying for her affections. This relationship with the landlady seems to build on the ruse of gaining the landlady's good graces in order to escape paying the rent.[48] Following the comic business where Chester and Charlie alternately jab each other in the backside with a fork Charlie points to his watch and they go outside. As they pass what looks to be a theatre Charlie appears to act faint and points to his throat. Chester gives him some money for a drink. As Charlie is about to enter the theatre, a well-dressed woman, played by Vivian Edwards, walks by, first looking at him up and down and then catching his eye before walking away. He immediately does an about face and follows her down the street.

7.2 Frank Grey cartoon of Chaplin's Essanay film *Work* (1915), from *Pictures and the Picturegoer*, 8 January 1916. Note the reference to 'the glad eye' in the top left and bottom left corners.

Next there is a scene with Cecile Arnold and Chester in the park; the shot alternations are revealing:

> *Shot 1:* (ms) Chester in park scratching his head.
> *Shot 2:* (mcu) Cecile sees Chester and clearly says 'Hi Chester' and
> signals to him to come to her.

196

Shot 3: (ms) Chester looks directly at the camera and shrugs and then turns to look over to her (screen left).

Shot 4: (mcu) Cecile continuing to gesture and giving him 'the glad eye'.

Shot 5: (ms) Chester leaving frame to go to her.

Shot 6: (medium long shot or plan américain) of Vivian at street corner; Charlie enters frame.

The following scene goes back to Charlie and Vivian, engaging in flirtatious behaviour while standing on the street corner; there is some comic business with a watch, and her boyfriend interrupts them. Charlie disappears into the park.

Back in the park, Cecile initiates the flirtation with Chester. Chester, addressing the camera in an appeal to the audience, shrugs and goes ahead. In this scene and the scene with Charlie and Vivian at the theatre the women instigate the 'glad eye'. However, rather than display reticence or shyness as Chester does, Charlie eagerly responds. Chester displays a further kind of innocence later, when he tells Cecile that he has no money. Charlie possesses no such inhibitions. He is aggressive and frustrated when placed in the enforced position of the voyeur. In both instances he is the outsider, just as in *Twenty Minutes of Love*, and this allows him to disrupt the official bodies of surveillance and regulation, such as the policeman, and the social norms of courting and dating in the public sphere.

This sexual aggressiveness is central as it is in many of the Keystone films, where the comic world consists of aggressive males, flirtatious young women and various 'regulating' characters: policemen, invalid relatives and alternately 'promiscuous and self-righteous' husbands and wives, boyfriends and girlfriends. The 'love pangs' Charlie feels are the frustration brought on by his observation of kissing and canoodling in the park by Chester and Cecile and later Vivian and her boyfriend, Edgar Kennedy. Cecile and Chester, 'carrying on' behind a tree, are aware that Charlie is watching and seem to be enjoying it. A few frames later Charlie is sitting forlorn on a park bench. Chester and Cecile enter the frame and Chester seems to protest nobly to Cecile that he has no money. In response Cecile places her foot on the bench next to Charlie. Charlie stares at her leg as she lifts her skirt to retrieve her purse from the top of her shoe. He looks at the purse and her leg and his eyes pass back and forth between them. Cecile gives her purse to Chester, which Charlie subsequently takes from him after he has knocked him out. Later, when

197

Charlie finally manages to rid himself of the two suitors, he follows the women into the cinema where he sits down between them. Since he has both arms around them he explains how he got rid of his rivals using his feet and legs to mime his story. The film ends with his rivals finding him in the cinema, his eyes blissfully closed. Sensing a fight, the women leave and Chester and Edgar take their place. After blindly stroking their beards Charlie realises his predicament and tries to get away. The cinema erupts in chaos as a huge fight ensues and Chester and Edgar throw him through the cinema screen.

This film depicts the different kinds of behaviour associated with different public spaces, the street, the park and the cinema. The glad eye that Vivian and Charlie exchange on the street initiates the action; the parade of settings in the film trace the boundaries of propriety within public spaces and social behaviour as Charlie transgresses them to comic effect. From boarding house to street to park, the play of looks fits the way that looking in the public sphere has been shown to have operated within London urban environments. This has been demonstrated by, among others, Judith Walkowitz and Erika Rappaport, who both note that there were a number of dangers and limitations associated with women walking alone in the city.[49] Rappaport highlights the 'physical inconveniences and dangers' that were constraints to bourgeois women's access to the city in her account of the transformation of public life in the West End of London from the 1880s to 1914. Walkowitz points to the way that during the latter part of the nineteenth century the presence of bourgeois women in the West End of London created certain conflicts; '. . . the presence of perambulating prostitutes, window shopping ladies, "girls in business" and idle male civil servants in one public area provoked territorial tensions and hostile social acts on the part of men towards women.'[50] Much of this sexual harassment of women was the result of blurred social signifiers 'written on the body of women'. The 'vices and virtues of femininity' were expected to be reflected in the clothing and appearance of women but often 'prostitutes dressed in "meretricious finery", could and did pass as respectable, while virtuous ladies wandering through the streets, "window gazing at their leisure", often found themselves accosted as streetwalkers'.[51] Charlie's transgression as an outsider is one who is unable, and unwilling, to read these codes. Chaplin here is enacting the street behaviour of the 'male pests' prevalent in the London's West End and shopping district during the late Victorian and Edwardian periods. Marshalling a great deal of evidence from personal accounts and popular journals of this period, Walkowitz has found that these 'pests' were not 'tradesmen or errand boys who could be ignored' but 'gentlemen . . . [who] crowded the streets of the West End, released from their desks by the short working hours of Victorian officialdom'.[52] This is complicated by the initiation of the flirtation by the women who are actually performing the role of 'new women', engaging in activities of the *flâneuse*. Walkowitz's sources do not, however, recount the kind of flirtatious behaviour of Cecile and Vivian. She quotes C.S. Peel 'then a dress editor for *Hearth and Home,* [who] recalled: '. . . Although I was quietly dressed, I hoped I looked what I was, a respectable young woman . . .'.[53] Vivian and Cecile are well dressed and clearly 'new women', Cecile's 'forward' behaviour with Chester, and the fact that she has money, shows that she has means. Charlie's play of looks between her leg and her purse takes on an added significance in that the display is for Charlie and underscores a conflict between the woman's body as commodity and the woman as consumer. Not only is he forced, through his exclusion, to be the voyeur, but he is not allowed the voyeur's pleasure of secret viewing. On the contrary, he is the object of both Cecile's and Vivian's performance. Charlie is anachronistic in his behaviour and is finally punished for it by being thrown into the cinema screen, the window of modernity.[54]

This qualifies Charles Musser's point that the Chaplin tramp figure became fixed in time and increasingly anachronistic, a development that made him 'susceptible to romanticisation by Chaplin, middle-class commentators and his audience'.[55] In Musser's formulation the increasingly nostalgic image of the nineteenth century 'knight of the road' de-emphasised the Chaplin tramp's relationship with his 'real life' social counterpart and thus ameliorated the radical potential of the tramp's responses to the inequities and the vagaries of the workplace. Yet by 1915 in Southampton and other urban centres the radical demographic shifts and the entry of working-class as well as middle-class women into the workplace had resulted in increased disposable income. This provided the potential for more frequent access to the public spaces of leisure and amusement such as parks and the cinema. In this sense there are other elements to the Chaplin comedies that would appeal to these audiences beyond those that reflect the workplace. The anachronism of Chaplin's 'pest' behaviour in *Those Love Pangs* is not the anachronism of the tramp but a celebration of the relatively new ability of women to partake of these public spaces. Such reflections resonated emphatically in Southampton and Britain. Oral history accounts by Southampton women support this. One woman who worked on the trams—which began employing women in September 1915—at the time that the 'Chaplinitis' was beginning to be felt in Southampton, remembered her wages: 'We earned £1.00 (per week), or thirty shillings (£1.50) and then it went up'. Another said, 'We earned good money. We thought we were millionaires.' This of course created opportunities for going out that had not existed before the war; 'On Saturdays we didn't get to bed after the night shift. We went home and got dressed up and went to town and looked around the shops and went dancing. Then we rushed back just in time to clock on for the six o'clock shift.' Another talked of the special events that were on offer: 'I was dancing mad, every night of the week if I could'. While another claimed; 'We used to pay 6d some nights and 9d if it was a gala night. The Pier was a favourite place.'[56] The Pier regularly held dances on the weekend evenings throughout the war.

Elizabeth Roberts has pointed to the importance of dances in the working-class cultures of Barrow and Preston. Public dances were held throughout the war but were strictly controlled. One Mrs Mulholland had a brother who organised dances and 'was most strict, terrible, they had to dance so far apart. He wouldn't let them dance cheek to cheek. He'd separate them if they were too close, and say, "That is enough," and they knew.' She recounted that there were the new dances of the Boston Two-Step, the Military Two-Step and the King's Waltz (she pointed out that the Charleston was later). Roberts notes that there was anxiety about uncontrolled sexual behaviour and that the tight regulations on dancing were the reason that the working-class girls were allowed to attend them.[57] Prior to the war, Southampton, as many other towns, had the tradition of promenading, another socially regulated outlet for courting. With the shifting dynamics taking place in the city these traditions were truncated as the Common—now filled with billeted troops—left the parks, the pier, and the cinema as the best places to meet the opposite sex. Most often the season for promenading was the summer with the longer days, extended further with the creation of daylight savings time during the war. This allowed at specific times 'groups of young men and women' to parade 'up and down hoping to catch someone's eye'.[58] This restricted access to courting behaviour created its own kind of desires that the park films of Chaplin addressed. So while the tramp figure does in many films disrupt the workspace it is just as common to see that disruption of social codes in spaces of leisure, codes that the audience recognised and participated in.

It is the 'reflexive potential' of these films that helps to account for their popularity in Britain. Miriam Hansen has recently suggested that

Hollywood films of the classical period 'offered something like the first global vernacular' and, when considered within the various contexts of their reception, constituted a '. . . provincial response to modernisation and a vernacular for different, yet also comparable experiences . . .'.[59] Although Chaplin films pre-date this cut-off point of classicism (1917) it is clear that through their immense popularity and their reflexive nature they traded in something approximating this 'global vernacular'. Crucially, they took on a resonance of national specificity at a time when the mass effort of mobilisation was articulating positive representations of the 'public'. The discourse of national emergency primarily ennobled soldiers and the new occupations for women in the war effort, however much it generated anxieties around social propriety. Images of that mobilisation and its effects were the centrepiece of the official war films, while special programmes for recruiting, for refugees and for wounded soldiers all provided a highly visible and 'positive' social function for the cinema theatre. Comedy films, and Chaplin films particularly, played a role in circulating this image of a new, modern public. As his comedy developed at Essanay, and later at Mutual, and as his popularity increased, that role became more prominent as a highly visible support for the incorporation of cinema-going as a socially recognised part of commercial entertainment. In tandem with the newsreels of the front, the official war films and the move to prestige features such as Griffith's *The Birth of a Nation*, Chaplin's pictures maintained their popularity and, like those other films, worked to expand the class base of cinema audiences.

Pathos and Prestige

As we have seen, the circulation of Chaplin films reached a peak in the summer of 1915. His popularity in Britain was noted in the national press as well as the trade journals and fan magazines. In August *The Times* ran an article entitled 'Notes from a Neutral' written by an anonymous US observer who noticed a 'phlegmatic attitude' to the war in Britain, particularly from the middle classes, which was evidence of a general lack of understanding of the events and the action at the front. The writer boldly suggested that the English middle classes had less of an understanding of the war than their German equivalent. Instead there was an almost incomprehensible preference for entertainment rather than information.

The chief popular indoor amusement in England—as well as Germany and the rest of the world—is the cinematograph theatre. Out of curiosity I went to one of the largest you have. There was not one film shown to give any idea of the work of the British Army or the British Navy. The whole audience looked forward to the antics of one Charlie Chaplin. [He went on to say that the only evidence of the war going on was that] . . . some of your generals were thrown on the screen but they received relatively small applause [while] Chaplin received a positive ovation.[60]

The article resonates with the attitudes and 'cultural values' of the 'Genteel Tradition' in the USA that emphasised the educational or 'uplift' value of the arts and saw the cinema as both problematic because of its mass popularity and potentially useful in enlightening the masses. These sentiments paralleled the debates about the cinema in Britain, which were intensified by the war. While in the USA the Genteel Tradition was part of a conservative response to the rise of a new professional middle class in the late nineteenth century, in Britain these debates centred on the concerns about the degeneration of the nation, concerns that were a formative principle of the NCPM, for example.[61] Knowledge of the progress of the war, its history and an awareness of the gravity of the struggle were all yardsticks by which to measure and ensure the level of commitment and morale of the nation. The fact that those debates centred around the war in the public imagination has relevance here since the antagonistic element for the US 'observer' is Chaplin, who acts as the icon of cinema as a vulgar, and irresponsible, entertainment. By doing this the commentator associates cultural 'respectability' with, and attaches value to, a determined 'war mentality', a quality he finds lacking in a laughing British audience.

The concern for the attitudes of the British middle class can perhaps be easily dismissed as the American commentator's misreading of a British audience. It does impose a notion of 'suitable behaviour' on a people at war that may have existed in the early days of the war but had given way to a more practical acceptance of the role that leisure forms had to play in the nation's morale. But the report is notable for its depiction of the enthusiasm of a large prestige city cinema. Taken at face value the audience he describes is a mixture of classes. Written at the end of the summer of 1915 when the Chaplin craze was reaching its zenith, the article suggests that Chaplin was already appealing to a heterogeneous audience.

The circulation of the Chaplin films in Southampton supports this. In September 1915, after the Essanay Company decided to release on an exclusive basis the Chaplins it had been renting on the open market all summer, the number of houses showing Essanays drastically reduced. Only the Carlton and the Northam Picturedrome screened the Essanays, while the rest of the theatres from the neighbourhood Woolston Picture Palace to the large High Street cinemas were showing Keystone Chaplins. This is largely due to the fact that Keystone re-released their Chaplin films to compete with Essanay during the summer of 1915.[62] While the Carlton and the Northam Picturedrome capitalised on the Essanays throughout the autumn of 1915, the Keystones continued to circulate throughout the whole year of 1916 amongst all of the cinemas and appeared sporadically throughout the rest of the war years. By the beginning of 1916 the Essanays began to appear at the High Street cinemas such as the Alexandra and the Gaiety, which often ran them and the Keystones on alternate weeks. In October 1917 the first Mutuals appeared at the Palladium in the well-to-do area of Portswood and at the Atherley in Shirley in an exclusive arrangement similar to that of the Carlton and Northam Picturedrome with the Essanays. These two cinemas shared the first-run exclusives of these films until the beginning of 1918, when there was a wider distribution of the Mutuals throughout the rest of the cinemas in the town coinciding with Mutual's nationwide re-release of its Chaplin films.

The map of Chaplin's reception in Southampton, then, is one of an overlapping circulation. The rough and vulgar comedies of the Keystone Chaplins were almost always available to be seen in competition with the Essanays and the Mutuals. Chaplin's longer length films—*A Dog's Life* (US release April 1918; UK release July 1918) and *Shoulder Arms* (US release 20 October 1918; UK release December 1918) both for First National, the 'Million Dollar' Chaplins—were played as features on the programmes at the Palladium and the Atherley and consequently were not in direct competition. The exclusive distribution of the Chaplin films provided the rationale for their appearances at selected theatres rather than any clear evidence of class specificity, particularly in the case of the Essanays after September 1915. In that case the two cinemas that captured the exclusives aimed their programme and advertising at very different markets: the Picturedrome appealed to the constituency of the neighbourhood, which was predominantly working class, while the Carlton, situated within an area dominated by retail shops, professional and business offices, strove to draw a more affluent audience. Similarly the Mutuals received their first screenings at the Palladium in prosperous Portswood and at the Atherley in Shirley, the centre of which was mainly a working-class area. In both cases these cinemas continued to run Chaplin Mutuals on an almost exclusive basis until December 1918, with only the King's Cinema in Kingsland Square (a market centre with a high concentration of retail businesses) occasionally gaining access to the Mutuals after December 1917. Finally, in the summer of 1918 the first of the First National Chaplins, *A Dog's Life*, received the treatment of prestige features generally and was shown in the Alexandra, the Palladium and the Atherley in the week of 13 July 1918.

This cross-class appeal of Chaplin films and their simultaneous or overlapping circulation from the summer of 1915 to the end of the war helps to place a different emphasis on the trajectory of his reception. Rather than endorsing the 'struggle to maturity' characterised by Walter Kerr or even the diachronic reception of Chaplin's image in the USA from vulgar clown to genius, as ably argued by Charles Maland, the local context offers a kind of kaleidoscopic shape to Chaplin's reception. The move to pathos and romance that Maland regards as the crucial elements in winning over the 'genteel moralists of America' is not as clear in the local circulation of his films. It is possible to sketch out roughly the level of popularity of each Chaplin film by noting the number of times they were screened. Although exhibitors were not always able to acquire the films that were most popular with their audiences, and in spite of the exclusive practices of Essanay, Mutual and First National, there is enough repetition in titles on advertised programmes to be reasonably certain that some films were specifically sought after by exhibitors. Taking into account that a significant number of Chaplin films were simply advertised as 'Chaplins', those that appeared on advertised programmes the most throughout the war were *In the Park* (eight times), *Champion Charlie*, *The Tramp*, *Charlie's Elopement* and *By The Sea* (seven times) and *One AM* (six times). Of these only one, *The Tramp*, can be regarded as containing romance and pathos. Of the Mutuals, which are seen as the most 'serious', *The Vagabond* appears three times, and *Police*, *Easy Street* and *The Immigrant* only once. Yet the exclusive booking practices of the Mutuals would tend to reduce the number of times those films appeared on programmes, while the re-release patterns of Keystone and later Essanay would privilege the number of times they were screened. This pattern reflects Chaplin's popularity across these years but it does not signal a preference for the films with romance and pathos, although in the last year of the war there is a greater proportion of Mutuals generally, since they were re-released after Chaplin's departure in late 1917. In fact, one of the most frequently shown Chaplin films, at five times, was the unauthorised *Chase Me Charlie* (1917), which was edited from clips from the Essanay period by English publicist Langford Reed. Nevertheless, the frequency of films such as *The Tramp* and *The Vagabond*, and the fact that they were shown in both prestige and neighbourhood cinemas suggests there is a significant enough representation of films with moments of pathos to consider its impact on the reception of Chaplin films as a whole.

As Chaplin developed his tramp character as outsider in the Mutual films he began to explore the potential for pathos. Films like *The Vagabond* (10 July 1916), *Easy Street* (22 January 1917), and *The Immigrant* (17 June 1917), with their emphasis on the social realities of poverty and homelessness, provided a backdrop for a poignant type of humour that was crucial to the development of Charles Chaplin 'genius artist' in contemporary popular, and later critical, discourse. Yet the Essanay films such as *The Tramp* (11 April 1915) and *The Bank* (16 August 1915) are the first to give this indication. As both of these centre the pathos around the rejection of Charlie by Edna, the inability of Charlie to understand the codes of courtship begins to be overshadowed by his immutable position as outside Edna's social circle, and consequently, beyond her realm of desire. In *The Tramp* his heroic actions in protecting the farm from the robber tramps earn him a permanent place of work, a dubious reward for Charlie. After being wounded by the farmer's own shotgun he is nursed back to health by Edna, a recuperation that includes smoking cigars and drinking. He only realises that Edna feels a piteous gratitude rather than love when her boyfriend arrives. In *The Bank* Charlie is the cleaner and during the course of 'cleaning/ destroying' the bank president's office he leaves a note and a meagre bunch of flowers for Edna, the president's daughter. She discovers these and, reading the note, she says 'fool' (it is possible to read her lips) and tears the note up. Charlie hears this from the other room and after a set of pathetic gestures to camera eventually makes his way back to his mop, sits down and sleeps. He wakes to the screams of Edna as she and her suitor, the bank manager, are being taken to the vault by bank robbers and, after much slapstick, rescues Edna (her suitor proves to be a coward) and foils the bank robbers. His heroic efforts are, however, in the end, only a dream and as he is holding Edna in his arms and stroking her hair he awakes only to be stroking a wet mop. In both cases Charlie has no real hope of social integration. Yet his desire is really for Edna rather than for a place in the social order.

Charles Musser cites the ending of *The Tramp* to support his argument that the romanticisation of the life on the road is the central cross-class appeal of the Chaplin figure and the core of his radical populist potential:

> ... he is representative of American individualism, an important factor in accounting for Chaplin's popularity among middle-class audiences and many intellectuals. Since the work ethic and individualism are normally linked in American culture, the rejection of degrading work and advocacy of individualism produced a comic opposition and a radical populism.[63]

Yet 'Charlie' as the character of Charles Chaplin, the English performer in America, offers a way of considering his reception in Britain that incorporates the romance of the 'knight of the road' with the Englishman abroad or, moreover, the immigrant as seen from the old country. The incorporation of work, individualism and the exploitative potential of the new world was not alien to the popular imagination in Britain. This held true, not only for the middle classes, but also for the 'imperial imagination' of the working classes. Emigration from Britain had reached significant proportions prior to the outbreak of the war. Between the years of 1911 and 1913 emigration to non-European destinations totalled almost one million. Jay Winter has compiled this data and offers a tentative profile of 'the "typical" migrant in Edwardian Britain . . . if there was such a person he was male, unmarried and between the ages of 18 and 30'.[64] The year that Chaplin came to the USA was 1913, he was twenty-three years old.

'A Dash of Poetry': English Tramps in America

While many examples of tramps exist in British theatre and music hall, one striking antecedent attests to the pervasiveness of the myth of an English tramp in America. It comes from the memoirs of young Welsh poet William Henry Davies, who spent a number of years on the road travelling the United States. His *Autobiography of a Super-Tramp* (1908) was an account of these travels. He made two extended visits to the USA and lost his leg in a venture in the Klondike. The relationship of this setting with Chaplin's *Gold Rush* is probably coincidental but then so may be the fact that in 1905 George Bernard Shaw received Davies' first volume of poems in an envelope with the postscript 'The Farm House, Kennington', which Shaw described as 'a dosshouse, or hostelry where single men can have a night's lodging for, at most, sixpence'. Kennington is the area of London where Chaplin spent his youth, often in similar circumstances. In his preface to the book Shaw praised the realism of Davies' low-key writing style as 'unexciting in matter and unvarnished in manner ... It is of a very curious quality. Were not the author an approved poet of remarkable sensibility and delicateness I should put down the extraordinary quietness of his narrative to a monstrous callousness.'[65] The tramp life that Davies undertook was attractive to Shaw and it recounts the kind of exploits in which Charlie finds himself in many of his films. As Shaw records, he 'begs, steals and drinks' and often finds himself in the casual wards and in police courts.

Moreover, Shaw articulates the kind of 'cultural elevation' of Davies' existence that critics, beginning with Minnie Madern Fiske, performed for Chaplin's career from 1916 onwards.[66] Within Davies' dual identity as a poet and a tramp lay a precursor for Chaplin's romantic tramp and an implied national identity. Here Shaw outlines what could be a template for the attraction of the Chaplin persona for British audiences:

> Another effect of this book on me is to make me realise what a slave of convention I have been all my life. When I think of the way I worked tamely for my living during all those years when Mr. Davies, a free knight of the highway, lived like a pet bird on tit-bits, I feel I have been duped out of my natural liberty. Why I had not the luck, at the outset of my career to meet that tramp who came to Mr. Davies, like Evangelist to Christian, on the first day of his American pilgrim's progress, and saved him on the very brink of looking for a job, by bidding him to take no thought for the morrow; to ask and it should be given him; to knock and it should be opened to him; and to free himself from the middle class assumption that only through taking a ticket can one take a train. Let every youth into whose hands this book falls ponder its lesson well, and, when next his parents and guardians attempt to drive him into some inhuman imprisonment and drudgery under the pretext that he should earn his own living, think of the hospitable countrysides of America, with their farmhouses overflowing with milk and honey for the tramp, and their offers of adoption for every day labourer with a dash of poetry in him.[67]

Chaplin's own experience in coming to America with Karno, and being lured away from the touring company by the promise of more money in films, seems to answer Shaw's call. Undoubtedly Shaw considers the 'dash of poetry' an essential ingredient and one that can easily apply to Chaplin's virtuosity as a performer, his ability to perform characters, the balletic motion of his by-play and his development of the tramp figure's 'pathetic' potential. For Shaw the reality of the tramp's life and Davies' ability to be 'quite at home in tramp wards' is what distinguishes him from, and endears him to, other poets. Yet he is also elevating the reality of a tramp's existence to that of a sublime performance, a level that can liberate and exalt the performer (every youth). That emphasis on performance, with the setting of 'the countrysides of America, with their farmhouses overflowing with milk and honey', anticipates the attraction not so much of the tramp but of the *British* poet/performer in America. Chaplin's persona as the virtuoso performer behind the tramp sits easily within this romantic tradition. Much later, in 1931 in his published correspondence with the actress Ellen Terry, Shaw wrote of the actor Henry Irving:

> He was utterly unlike anyone else: he could give importance and a noble melancholy to any sort of drivel that was put into his mouth; and it is this melancholy, bound up with an impish humour, which forced the spectator to single him out as a leading figure with an inevitability that I never saw again in any other actor until it rose from Irving's grave in the person of a nameless cinema actor who afterwards became famous as Charlie Chaplin. Here I felt is something that leaves the old stage and its superstitions and staleness completely behind, and inaugurates a new epoch in the theatre.[68]

This passage comes at the end of a fairly extended lament about the stinginess of London theatre landlords that drove great actors like Henry Irving and Barry Sullivan to the provinces and to America in order to make their fortunes. In finding his metier and fortune in the United States, Chaplin, for high-culture critics such as Shaw, carried this tradition on while simultaneously inaugurating a new epoch. In 1931 Chaplin had just released *City Lights*, at least fifteen years after the Essanay and Mutual periods. Seeing a film and performance that seamlessly integrates the melancholy with humour no doubt influenced Shaw. Nevertheless his words are instructive as they articulate the terms of Chaplin's popularity with cultural critics as they were taking shape during the war years.

'Wistfulness' and a Universal Appeal

Chaplin was well acquainted with playing to cross-class audiences in England. His and Fred Karno's roots of development were in the comic sketch that was developed at the turn of the century for the 'new audiences' of variety and the 'educated family middle class'.[69] Performances and sketch material were designed to appeal at a number of levels. Stan Laurel recalls Karno's particular emphasis on sentiment in the knockabout comedies, which Karno called 'wistful':

> 'Wistful' for him meant putting in that serious touch once in a while. . . . I seem to recall: you would have to look really sorry, for a few seconds after hitting someone on the head. Karno would say, 'Wistful, please, wistful.' It was only a bit of a look, but somehow it made the whole thing funnier. The audience didn't expect that serious look. Karno really knew how to sharpen comedy in that way.[70]

This unexpected display of emotion had the effect of deepening the character, necessary to extend the appeal of the act. Investing motivation and character depth bypassed criticisms of the knockabout as simply childish. The more sophisticated comedy was that which encouraged thought. Max Beerbohm described and endorsed this higher form of humour in an article he wrote for the distinctly middle-class *Pall Mall Magazine* in 1902:

> Precisely because you [the reader] and I have sensitive intelligences, we cannot postulate certainly anything about each other. The higher an animal be in grade, the more numerous and recondite are the points in which its organism differs from its peers. The lower the grade, the more numerous and obvious the points of likeness. (Of course, this classification is made without reference to social 'classes'. The public is recruited from the upper, the middle and the lower class. That the recruits come mostly from the lower class is because the lower class is still the least well educated. That they come in as high proportion from the middle class as from the less well-educated upper class, is because the 'young Barbarians' reared in a more gracious environment often acquire a grace of mind which serves as well as would mental keenness.) Whereas in the highest grade, to which you and I belong, the act that a thing affects one man of the lowest grade in a particular way is likely to affect all the rest similarly. The public's sense of humour may be regarded roughly as one collective sense.

Referring to the intelligent humour appreciated by himself and the reader he goes on:

> A joke that has not a serious background, or some serious connection, means nothing to him. Nothing to him the crude jape of the professional jester. Nothing to him, the jangle of bells in the aged [sic] cap or the thud of the swung bladder. Nothing, the joke that hits him violently in the eye, or pricks him with a sharp point. The jokes that he loves are those quiet jokes which have no apparent point—the jokes which never can surrender their secret, and so can never pall. His humour is an indistinguishable part of his soul, and the things that stir it are indistinguishable from the world around him. But for the primitive, untutored public, humour is a harshly definite affair. The public can achieve no delicate process of discernment in humour. Unless a joke hits it in the eye, drawing forth a shower of illuminative sparks, all is darkness for the public. Unless a joke be labelled "Comic, come why don't you laugh?" the public is quite silent. Violence and obviousness are thus essential factors.[71]

He side-steps the attachment of class specificity and establishes a consensus with his reader by suggesting that the sensitivity to a higher order of humour is based not on social class or heredity but on education and an acquired 'grace of mind'. If the majority of the unsophisticated are of the 'lower classes' it is because they don't have access to education. The ideal joke for the sensitive educated man (for he gives no indication that he includes women) is the one which provokes an 'inward' rather than 'outward' laughter. Although Beerbohm's article is written with a degree of light-heartedness he pays a great deal of attention to the development of his thesis that the 'higher order' laughter is unpredictable while the lower order is provoked by formula and vulgar overstatement. Seen in this light Chaplin's introduction of love interest and its hopelessness because of his social status provides—in *The Bank* for example—the film's slapstick with an unexpected 'serious background', a development of the Karno 'wistfulness' that begins to position his comic development towards this more refined sentiment or pathos by deepening his character.

This introduction of sentiment, derived as it was from the comic sketch formula of bringing together elements that would appeal to a wider public, occurred at the time when discussions about the future of comedy were beginning to take place throughout the industry. In January 1918 Robert S. Duncan, MA, wrote an article entitled 'The Future of Screen Comedy' in *The Bioscope*. The subheadings of his piece were

'Where Comedy is Failing'; 'What Is Wanted'; and 'Trust the Audience'. Chaplin's position within this article is implicitly, but distinctly, identified with the 'gradually failing' form. The references to the Keystone film *Dough and Dynamite* (26 October 1914) and two of his Mutual films *The Floorwalker* (15 May 1916) and *The Cure* (16 April 1917) are not accidental; the cinema-goer was made to undergo the same type of humour, predictable and generic:

> He [sic] is expected to roar with laughter night after night when one gentleman with unerring aim obscures the sight of another with a handful of dough, [*Dough and Dynamite*] or to chuckle with glee when the same pair find tar an equally suitable decoration. He becomes convinced that the fount of all humour is situated either on a staircase [*The Floorwalker*] or at a revolving door [*The Cure*], and that the funniest thing in the world is a backward step into a tub of water. Wholesale breakage and complete demolition are calculated to provide him with mirth; the comic policeman and the eccentric waiter should, between them, broaden his grin. So they do—to-night and, yes, perhaps tomorrow evening too. But the time will come when they and others of their kind will fail to raise even a smile.[72]

He observed that the sophistication of the dramatic films was making obvious the 'artistic gap' with film comedy; film audiences were 'worthy of a less primitive appeal to their sense of humour'. There were now 'scenario writers who . . . conceive comedies whose humour is derived from cleverness and the skilful handling of plot and situation rather than from boisterous action . . . [and these] were oases of real humour in a desert of alleged comedy'. As for the audience, it was the job of 'progressive' cinema to 'take its patrons with it'.[73] Chaplin's comedy by implication is clearly outside the kind of integrated comedy Duncan is outlining. It stands outside Duncan's parameters of narrative, not only in terms of the laughter provoked by the slapstick but also in the emotive response provoked by the pathos. In both cases the sensory experience is excessive to an integrated comedy.

Beerbohm's and Duncan's insistence on a simple dichotomy of inward/ outward forms of laughter were qualified by other critical positions that sought to give the sensory pleasures of slapstick and the visual gag more consideration. In May 1918 *The Kinematograph and Lantern Weekly* ran an article entitled 'The Science of Laughter, Comedy and the Critics; Is Slapstick Doomed?' by 'E.M.', which argued that the recent critical debate on the future of screen comedy had 'failed to discriminate between the various branches of comedy'. The comparisons that were consistently made between the 'epigrammatic comedy' of Sidney Drew[74] and Chaplin did not recognise that both were 'perfectly satisfactory representatives of perfectly legitimate yet totally different branches of an extremely difficult art, that of keeping the public amused'. The main thrust of the argument was that the comic forms were no better or worse than the ability of the artist and the job of the critic was to try to 'solve the riddle of why in the hand of one man a lump of clay remains a lump of clay and in the hands of another becomes a living work of plastic beauty'. Perceptively recognising that the debates about comedy centred around Chaplin and slapstick E.M. points to Chaplin's genius in 'working out the common denominator of mirth':

> His humour is that of the universal type that appeals to all classes irrespective of age, nationality or sex. The small boy will yell when Chaplin slips on a banana skin—and indeed the small boy is not unique in this respect—whilst men of letters marvel at the man's amazing sureness of characterisation, his sense of artistic balance, his achievement of big results with the greatest economy of means. His work has all the virtuosity of the supreme artist in caricature, the few swift telling strokes, exaggerated but intensely human, 'getting there' every time.[75]

The key to Chaplin's universal appeal is his virtuosity and his 'intensely human' treatment. E.M. goes on to cite the 'quarter episode' in *The Immigrant* (17 June 1917) and the alarm clock scene in *The Pawnshop* (2 October 1916) as examples of how Chaplin's artistry has transcended the old stunts and 'bewhiskered gags'. For this critic, Chaplin's artistry lay in his incorporation of situations over which hang the relentless threats of modern life. The 'quarter episode' in *The Immigrant* works its comedy from the unsettling situation of not having enough money to pay a restaurant bill, while the alarm clock sequence in *The Pawnshop* comes after Charlie has been threatened with the sack. The attachment of these inequities and the recognition of the reflexive quality of these films anticipate the role Chaplin plays in the work of social critics such as Henri Lefebvre, among others, throughout the twentieth century.[76]

E.M. finds value in Chaplin's comedy through his virtuosity and uses the endorsement of 'men of letters' as evidence of Chaplin's singularity, his uniqueness. He ends the article in a prediction that slapstick will 'die a natural death'. Chaplin had learned from the school of slapstick and 'found himself' in the process. He had 'taught the cinema-goer to demand something more subtle'. E.M. then closes with a swipe at the American press criticisms of Chaplin as merely vulgar and, stressing Chaplin's nationality, states: 'I sometimes think that in this respect that it is Chaplin who in the corresponding Transatlantic vernacular can with the greatest justice say, *"Nous avons change tout cela."*'

Duncan's critique, on the other hand, reproduced the Hollywood industry's trade press discussions on the need for the refinement of humour. This debate echoed those that produced the music hall comedy sketch, where the aim was to broaden the appeal to a more mixed public for the variety theatres twenty years before.[77] Yet these calls for refinement were set against the background of the popularity of the slapstick comedy of Sennett's Keystones and of course Chaplin's work there and at Essanay and Mutual.[78] E.M. felt it was futile to ignore their appeal when 'the benighted individual in the next plush seat is weeping ecstatic tears . . .'.[79] An indication of the role that performance and virtuosity played in these debates lies in an article penned by Sennett that appeared in *The Bioscope* six months earlier than Duncan's article and a year earlier than E.M.'s. He emphasised the importance of naturalistic acting: 'The actor who seems to be trying to be funny massacres all the laughs. . . . The real laughs pursue the actor who seems to be making frantic but futile struggles not to be funny'.[80] Sennett's emphasis on the actor's craft and naturalism reveals the multifaceted nature of these debates. By appealing to virtuosity and naturalistic acting in the *performance* of the gags Sennett counters the call for narrative integration and he articulates, and advocates, the wider sensory, visceral appeal of these comedies.[81]

The use of sentiment worked to deepen the character's psychological make-up *and* provoke a sensory response across the range of his films. Chaplin's character, built as it was across a number of films, constructed its comedy around the tramp's status as outsider. The addition of this double action of deepening character and prompting visceral, emotive responses—linked as it was to Chaplin's artistry—laid the groundwork not only for Chaplin's critical reception but also for a growing cultural respectability for cinema generally. The emphasis on sensory response had a further effect in that it provided support for the industry's argument for the social function of cinema as a transformative experience.

The use of pathos intensified the reflexive nature of the comedy, having specific resonances for a British audience during wartime. As we have seen, that reflexive property worked in conjunction with the particular social upheavals brought about by the war as effectively in relation to leisure as it did in relation to the workplace. Chaplin's respectability as an artist centred on public discourse on his virtuosity and his use of pathos at a time when many critics, such as Duncan, were advocating a move to a more sophisticated comedy of manners. The unexpected psychological depth of the clown intensified through pathos presented a resolution to the growing demands for more sophisticated comedies that Duncan articulated, a resolution that was not solved by the incorporation of plot and situation but by the sensory appeal to the emotions. In *The Bank*'s final gag Charlie is dreaming he is holding Edna but wakes up stroking the wet strands of his mop. Charlie's unexpected psychological depth is built upon in this structure so that through the dream the audience is given access to his desire to be the hero. When he awakens nothing has changed, there is no chance for love with Edna, who is probably going to marry the bank manager, while Charlie will either continue to disrupt the place or, more likely, move on. It was this reflexive potential provided through pathos that Chaplin would develop for the rest of his career.

Conclusion

The role that comedy played in the industry's move to respectability through the contention that cinema was a palliative for the pressures and anxieties of everyday life seems paradoxical, particularly given the increasing human cost of the war. This is epitomised perhaps nowhere more acutely than in Chaplin's choice of the trenches as a setting for his feature *Shoulder Arms* (1918). What pleasures could be gained from a Chaplin film that drew attention to the terrors and violence of an existence that held a profound potential for personal loss for the majority of cinema-goers? In a comment that parallels the dream structure Chaplin used in both *The Bank* and *Shoulder Arms* Henri Lefebvre paraphrased the industry's conception of the cinema's transformational properties when in 1954 he argued that in Chaplin films:

> Suffering itself is denied, and this denial is put on display . . . On leaving the darkness of the cinema, we rediscover the same world as before, it closes around us again. And yet the comic event has taken place, and we feel decontaminated, returned to normality, purified somehow . . .[82]

Walter Benjamin famously noted that the function of American cinema was '. . .where sentimentality is restored to health and liberated American style, just as people whom nothing moves or touches any longer are taught to cry again in the cinema'.[83] A film such as *The Vagabond*, where Charlie rescues Edna from Gypsies who had kidnapped her when she was a child, made reference to the terrors of loss and anonymity. The loss or safety of a loved one was of paramount concern during the war years, a time when the impact of modernisation was literally imposing itself on the human body at the front and on the bodies of those at home. And yet, as Benjamin's observation suggests, it was the very direct engagement with melancholy in films that offered a moment's respite. He envisioned, in Miriam Hansen's words, 'a regeneration of affect' through the cinema.

The cinema's power of regeneration was a central point on which the industry and regulatory bodies would be able to find common ground albeit, at times, on different terms. The educational properties of the medium suited the regulatory bodies while the recuperative property of the cinema as a leisure form was stressed by the industry. The filmic depiction of events at the front formed the basis around which the cinema would gain a certain amount of respectability, although the example of *Shoulder Arms* demonstrates that ultimately it would retain its status as a form of entertainment rather than education. It is this cinematic engagement with the 'war weariness' in homefront imagination in 1918 that is the subject of the next chapter. Yet, rather than leave behind the regenerative and the reflexive properties of the film comedy, and of Chaplin's particular impact on cinema culture, it is important to recognise that these qualities helped to shape the 'horizon of expectation' of British cinema audiences as the war reached its final year.

8

1918

Anguished Voices and Comic Slackers

In January 1918, two months after the premier of *Civilization* in Southampton, the *Kinematograph Year Book* reported that the exclusive subject of five reels or longer was both destroying the variety programme and was more likely to cause eye-strain. The London and Home Counties Exhibitors' Association declared that '. . . a variety programme is the essence of the kinematograph business . . .'. They requested a meeting with manufacturers and renters to '. . . urge upon manufacturers the limitation of the length of the feature films to 4,000 or 5,000 feet at the outside, and that all films should be offered at option of exhibitors for three or six days as they may require'.[1] The London exhibitors combined two arguments, both of which were aimed at the production companies. The first was the concern that the super-film was a threat to the variety format. This was a thinly veiled attack on the restrictions that had become evident with the change from the open market system to the exclusive system of booking films. The exclusive system offered benefits to the exhibitor by ensuring that the films they were showing would not be run at the same time by their competitors. Normally acquiring a first run was the most desirable option, but in the case of some of the more popular subjects like Chaplin and Mary Pickford this was less of an issue. However, the super-film or films of five reels or longer hindered the kind of risk-spreading afforded by the variety format. Further, the variety format was central to audiences' expectations and many exhibitors voiced concern that unless a full programme was offered there was a feeling that they hadn't got their money's worth.

The second part of their argument invoked the running debate about the physical effects of the cinema. The National Council of Public Morals (NCPM) Cinema Commission report had been published in July 1917 and was widely reported in the trade press as an endorsement of the industry. In the summation of their findings the commission also reported particular concerns about the cinema's potential physical damage:

> The continuous display of films extending over some hours is extremely injurious, especially to the young and those with defective eyesight. Hence we recommend that frequent intervals of music song, or other form of entertainment, should be encouraged to relieve the constant strain on the eyes.[2]

The commission took these dangers seriously but also emphasised that the exhibition end of the trade had taken steps to improve conditions in their theatres. In claiming that longer films may cause eye-strain the London exhibitors were attempting to validate their argument by using the language of the report and mobilising the debate concerning the cinema's properties. By aligning themselves with the NCPM report they were trying to put pressure on the production companies and the renters. In many ways this attitude is explained by the fact that it was the small entrepreneur who directly suffered if the local councils exercised its right either to censor a film or to deny or revoke their licence.

The two points to their argument: the disruption of the variety format and the concern about the physical effect of the cinema, usefully illustrate the multifaceted character of the debates about the social function of cinema generally and the degree to which the cinema had become an accepted part of the fabric of British social life. Exhibitors presenting their case from this accepted position were pitched against the trends in the industry that were advantageous to the producers, such as exclusive booking and the longer feature or super-film. However, their opposition took the shape of an appeal against the physical effect of the cinema because the super-film had, as we have seen, been the high-profile example of the cinema's potential, in the words of the NCPM report, 'for the cultivation of moral and aesthetic appreciation'.[3] Desired by all in the industry, these educative qualities of the cinema had been aided significantly not only by fiction films such as *Quo Vadis?*, *The Birth of a Nation* and *Civilization*, but by the official feature-length war films. The NCPM report's section on the educational aspects of the cinema for the young stated: 'The child, after seeing such films as the *Battle of the Somme* and *The Battle of the Ancre* would naturally be able to form a far more intelligent conception of the nature of warfare than would be possible by means of reading or class instruction.'[4] The war films and other practices of practical patriotism had helped gain for exhibitors a social acceptance not previously enjoyed; the resulting large audiences for most films had been profitable.

The official acceptance of the educational properties of the cinema was highlighted by the *Kinematograph Year Book*, which noted the invitation by the 'Kinema Committee of the Department of Information' to the Trade Council to '... assist in the Government propaganda work by means of the screen ...'.[5] The most high-profile of the resulting combination of the commercial film production with the government was D.W. Griffith's *Hearts of the World*. The background for the reception of the film was based partly on the assumption by both Griffith and the War Office that the fiction feature was the best means by which to maintain audiences who had been showing a declining interest in the non-fiction format. Griffith's choice as director for this feature, partly financed by the War Office, reflects the concern to export the war message. Griffith made a film that was aimed at keeping morale up in the USA. However, the film's qualified reception in Britain suggests that significant shifts had taken place in audience expectations concerning the depiction of the war on screen since the release of *Battle of the Somme* in September 1916. The reception of *Hearts of the World* in Britain highlights these shifts and illustrates the limited appeal of the cinema as a venue for public enlightenment.

The London Exhibitors' reference to eye-strain was a rare reference by the industry to a negative effect of the cinema. More often the emphasis was on its rejuvenating powers. In the section entitled 'The School and the Cinema' the NCPM report concluded that 'In the public cinema performance healthy amusement and recreation should be the main function'.[6] As we saw in the previous chapter, in debates about the social and moral acceptability of cinema, comedy was seen as an innocuous, albeit vulgar, form of film. The NCPM report endorsed this view, pointing out that 'Its moral standard, moreover, compares very favourably with that of the theatrical and music-hall farces'. Referring directly to Charles Chaplin the report stated; 'The great success of this type of film is to a large extent due to the popularity of a famous film comedian.' Chaplin's effect on schoolboys was a cause for some concern and the report found that 'The complaint of some teachers, however, that boys imitate the actions of the film artist, and that their ideal of humour becomes that of the low comedian, is probably well founded'.[7] Comedy, and Chaplin in particular, exemplified the conflicting positions in public discussions concerning the cinema's affective properties. Where eye-strain provoked a physical response that caused concern, comedy provoked the physical response of laughter and was widely seen as literally a physical release from the burden of the anxiety of life during wartime. The fact that the NCPM equated the comedy of Chaplin with that of theatrical and music hall farce shows that Chaplin's comedy, at least, had acquired the kind of acceptance that those forms had enjoyed. Nevertheless the NCPM's caveat that the schoolboy's ideal of humour' exemplified that of the 'low comedian' shows a lack of confidence in the ability of the young to appreciate the finer points of his comedy.

These issues of the restorative powers of film comedy and their attendant concerns were at play most forcefully in Chaplin's 1918 film *Shoulder Arms*. If *Hearts of the World* depicted the front through melodrama and traded on the educative qualities of the epic and historical reconstruction, *Shoulder Arms* did so through the comic frame. Provoking different kinds of expectations, *Shoulder Arms* attracted large audiences. This final chapter explores the depictions of the front through the reception of Chaplin's film and links these to existing traditions of treating the war with humour. A comparison of the reception of this film with that of *Hearts of the World* illustrates the dynamics at play in the final year of the war, which ultimately resulted in positioning the social function of cinema as a form of recreation and restoration rather than education and enlightenment.

'A Limit to Human Endurance'

> People go to the pictures to get away from the war, not because their patriotism is open to doubt, but because there is a limit to human endurance, and he who is condemned to carry a daily burden must of needs for a moment lay it aside and rest.
>
> *Pictures and the Picturegoer*, 13 July 1918.

There were a number of reasons for the journalist of *Pictures and the Picturegoer* to call attention to the 'daily burden' experienced by most people during the last year of the war. The influenza epidemic was in full swing, Zeppelin and then Gotha bomber raids on British cities and towns were increasing in their frequency and the German spring offensive had been a serious setback. The progress of the war seemed to have come to a halt and most felt that 1918 would be another grim year of a static front, mounting casualties, rising shortages and continued uncertainty. Those in the exhibition trade had been dealing with the effects of the entertainments tax and a gradual but chronic reduction in attendances. Predictions about the effects of the tax remained divided but the Cinema Exhibitors' Association continued to argue for a reprieve, primarily by citing the importance of the film industry to the war effort.

Concerned with maintaining audiences, the trade urged exhibitors to 'Let the junk be relegated to oblivion, give the public the latest pictures from the seat of the war and a good sprinkling of the best features and exclusives, and dry rot will be absent from the box office'.[8] The form for the latest war pictures had settled on the short newsreel format of which the Pictorial News (Official) had, by 1918, become the most popular.[9] By this time the feature official war film had lost the impact, and popularity, it had achieved with *Battle of the Somme* and *The Battle of the Ancre and the Advance of the Tanks* eighteen months earlier. By 1918 the feature-length film offering a version of the progress of the war had all but ceased and the exclusives and feature fiction films were generally considered the main attraction of the programme.[10]

The Bioscope's advice indicates the level to which the exclusive and the fictional feature had become endorsed by the trade. Further, the short war films were favoured primarily for their information about war news rather than the war rhetoric of the feature official war films. Yet even fiction films like *Civilization*, dealing in war rhetoric and didacticism, were less popular with audiences in the last year of the war. Sensitivity to audience preference for 'sensational' entertainment was evident in written accounts in the form of letters from exhibitors to the Selig Company about their Civil War film *The Crisis* that was doing the rounds throughout the winter and spring of 1918. The manager of the Popular Cinema Company in Llanelly wrote that:

> The film is a good one and well acted and had I shown it two or three years ago should have had packed houses. But today any war picture is at a premium the more so when most of the scenes are sad as in the *Crisis*. It wants a touch of comedy introduced but personally although I liked it I don't think any house will make a success of it in present day surroundings.[11]

This evidence of a popular conception of a society under extraordinary pressure agrees with modern historian Jay Winter's findings on the changes in health conditions across the four years of the war. Important paradoxes occurred in relation to civilian health during this time. The war economy had produced a fall in mortality rates generally. Infant mortality rates had significantly declined, as did those due to certain infectious diseases. Instances of diseases such as kidney failure and cirrhosis of the liver were lower, with the latter probably due to restrictions on alcohol consumption. In short, the overall health of civilians improved during the war years, albeit with some important anomalies. Of these the most significant Winter found was the increase in mortality due to respiratory infections. He suggests that this may have occurred because of the large-scale shift in populations from rural and suburban areas to '. . . urban centres of war production and their concentration in munitions factories',[12] aggravated by a general deterioration in housing conditions. The less quantifiable qualities in this statistic are the emotional or psychological conditions that accompanied these developments within the unique situation of wartime. Winter notes: 'The stress of overwork and anxiety over the fate of family and friends in the army may also have undermined the resistance of those (especially among the elderly) suffering from this and other diseases'.[13] Although elderly people were a minority of the cinema audience, the rise in mortality from respiratory ailments such as tuberculosis and influenza was necessarily accompanied by a rise in their incidence among all age groups. There is ample evidence that cinema managers often faced the unpredictable occurrence of the flu as a business hazard, which also lends some weight to the concern by health officials for proper ventilation of cinema theatres. The manager of the Palladium at Lichfield suffered losses on the weeks that he had booked the Selig film *The Garden of Allah*. He found he was a '. . . victim of circumstance for the last fortnight owing to the influenza. The Palladium has been out of bounds to all gentlemen in Khaki.'[14] Such examples of the stresses of wartime had become commonplace by 1918 and were a fixture in the public vocabulary concerning the war.

The War's Master Narrative

The prevalence of such views of a 'daily burden' shows that the war's continuation and effects were an overriding concern that significantly shaped people's everyday existence and thereby also shaped the way exhibitors were gauging their audiences' taste preferences. The concern for morale evident in the ways in which the war and its effects were discussed and debated in the trade press suggests a broader narrative adhered to by exhibitors and audiences: the open-ended story of the war itself. As we have seen in the film *Battle of the Somme* the British army's

221

progress was portrayed through movement and the parades of men and military machinery across the screen. A sense of progress towards the end of the war is signalled in the structure of all of the feature war films and it formed the central plank in their rhetoric. Yet the war's effects and the ensuing years of stasis at the front undermined these films' overall message. As these films declined in popularity by late 1917 it was their assurance of progress that rang hollow. Still, within the public rhetoric of newspapers, newsreels as well as fiction films the commitment to an over-arching narrative of victory remained resolute. However many setbacks there were, the conception of the progress of the war in the homefront imagination as expressed in the newspapers and the newsreels depended upon an agreed structure of the narrative, that the war was an 'Armageddon' and that it would end in victory for the Allies. This agreed structure in public accounts concerning the progress of the war provided the basis for the reception of war films and fiction films depicting the effects and/or the experience of war, negative, positive or indifferent, during the last year of the war.

Perpetual War or Inevitable Victory?

As we have seen, the ease with which parallels between the American Civil War and the Great War were possible was one of the appeals of Griffith's *The Birth of a Nation* for the entrepreneur Sol Levy, who toured the film around the country for its initial run in Britain. Arguably this was also a resonant quality of the film for British audiences. Griffith's editing across spaces between the home and the battlefield, culminating in the wounding of the Little Colonel illustrates Benedict Anderson's concept of 'calendrical coincidence'. Editing in this instance, like the newspaper, provides the 'technical means for re-presenting the kind of imagined community that is the nation'.[15] Anderson argues that the imagined modern nation-state is predicated upon a conception of simultaneity, or 'meanwhile', which binds members of a community or nation together. The newspaper with its arrangement of current stories is a visual expression of events occurring simultaneously: 'An American will never meet, or even know the names of more than a handful of his [sic] 240,000-odd [sic] fellow Americans. He has no idea of what they are up to at any one time. But he has complete confidence in their steady, anonymous, simultaneous activity.'[16] Anderson sees this concept of a modern simultaneity as a secular idea that has taken the place of what he refers to as the medieval 'simultaneity-along-time' where events are preordained by Divine Providence. He illustrates his point by quoting Auerbach's *Mimesis*:

> ... the here and now is (not) a mere link in an earthly chain of events, it is simultaneously something which has always been, and will be fulfilled in the future; and strictly in the eyes of God it is something eternal, something omnitemporal, something already consummated in the realm of fragmentary earthly event.[17]

In direct opposition to this sacred structuring of temporality is the modern conception of simultaneity that, for Anderson, is marked by 'temporal coincidence, and measured by clock and calendar'.[18]

A full discussion of the concepts Anderson employs in his argument for the conceptual origins of the nation-state is not appropriate here but his use of these contrasting ideas of simultaneity provide a basis for laying out the parameters of the homefront imagination as expressed through cinema culture during the last year of the war. His conception of an imagined community given coherence through shared narrative forms such as newspapers, novels, magazines and cinema is the basis of what I have been calling the 'homefront imagination'. It is through these texts that a narrative of the progress of the war was conveyed. Anderson's construction of the dichotomy medieval-religious/modern-secular in this case generates two primary levels of interpretation in the 'overarching' war narrative. This can be illustrated by Robert Graves's comment on the paradox of contemporary attitudes: 'We held two irreconcilable beliefs: that the war would never end and that we would win it'.[19] The first, that the war would never end, can be read to express Anderson's modern conception of simultaneity in which the nation, and history, proceeds linear fashion across 'homogeneous, empty time'.[20] Anderson's use of this secular notion of time is prompted by Walter Benjamin's phrase 'History is the subject of a structure whose site is not homogenous, empty time, but time filled by the presence of the now'.[21] The war's status as 'history' at the time was central to public discourse. That the war would never end illustrates a perpetual state of conflict and suggests an amnesis, or disavowal, in regard to the past, or more succinctly a purgatory of an eternal present. In Graves's ironic phrase it is meant to be difficult to ascertain which is the most disdainful, the perpetuity of the war or the equally ridiculous conviction of a victory that would give the catastrophe meaning. The never-ending war is a dark vision of modernity where the past is destroyed never to return. This landscape of the future where history has come to a stop is the converse of Benjamin's notion of history as the subject of a structure 'filled by the presence of the now'. Benjamin's next sentence elucidates the concept. 'Thus, to Robespierre ancient Rome was a past charged with the time of the now which he blasted out of the continuum of history.' In this second level of interpretation there is a predestination of the order defined by Auerbach implicit in the second part of Graves's statement, 'that we would win it', which can be found in other references to the war such as the 'struggle for Civilisation' or 'the present Crisis' prevalent at the time. In both of these terms there is the adherence to a pre-ordained outcome, a triumph of good over evil, 'something already consummated'. The advertisements for *The Birth of a Nation*, then, were a depiction of 'history' as a pre-ordained structure, which ensured victory, albeit through sacrifice. This was the plot structure of the public narrative of the war ('that we would win it'), which was given force by the private anxiety that the war, like mass production, would become a permanent fixture of existence.

The War's Plot

It is evident in the various forms of media and public discourse that a narrative of the war was implicit, and that it had an agreed, or hoped for, plot structure. A brief summary of the plot of this narrative prior to the end of the war can be expressed with one sentence: peace *was* disrupted by the German invasion of Belgium and France and following terrible trials and personal anguish the war *would* come to an end with a victory for the Allies. By establishing this type of plot as central to a shared horizon of expectation among audiences it is possible to apply a strategy of analysis that assumes first that such an overarching narrative structure performs the function of interpreting the events of the war. Consequently, the official film *The British Advance* made in 1918 could be so called in spite of the fact that it was depicting episodes in the British retreat during the German advance in the spring offensive of 1918.[22] Secondly the existence of such an overarching narrative and its attendant sets of expectations is apparent in the advertisements and reviews for films that use it as a means of prompting audience expectations and interpretations. This method of reorganising and processing the events of the war for a reading and viewing public as the events are reported and represented in public forms acts as a 'master plot' shared by producers and consumers alike. The ending is an inevitable victory sometime in the future. Moreover, it is marked by its emphasis on an ending that is characterised by restoration and renewal, in itself contradictory. D.W. Griffith's *Hearts of the World*, made in 1918 with support and partial finance by the British government, illustrates the interpretive guidelines of this 'master-plot'.

Hearts of the World

Previewed for the industry on 23 June 1918 at the Palace Theatre in London, Griffith's *Hearts of the World* was reviewed by the trade papers *Kinematograph Weekly* and *The Bioscope* as well as the *The Times* and the *Evening News*. *The Bioscope* reviewer called it 'in some respects disappointing' and yet predicted that 'there can be no doubt at all concerning its qualities as a popular success'. While the reviewer did not question Griffith's abilities as a filmmaker and modern historian as he replaced 'studio properties . . . for the real machinery of actual battle', it was also '. . . inevitable that he should have been unable to adopt the impersonal standpoint of the artist towards a theme so intensely personal and real and close-at-hand as that of to-day's world tragedy' as he had done in *The Birth of a Nation* and *Intolerance*. The reviewer outlined the type of expectation afforded to a Griffith film at this time where artistry equals the ability to depict the 'Armageddon with an intimacy, a vividness, and a breadth of survey never before achieved'. This was afforded by a structure similar to *The Birth of a Nation*, which set up the story of two families and then followed their lives as they were swept up in the conflict. Here, however, the sensitive nature of these depictions of a nation at war were made evident in the critic's remark that he had 'brought up to date and invested [them] with personal and topical significance'. Unlike the distance achieved by *The Birth of a Nation*, these depictions of actual experiences had positioned Griffith outside the realms of the objective historian/artist that for these critics were the qualities of his genius.[23]

The publicity for the film in both the USA and Britain, though, chose to highlight Griffith's special abilities as objective historian. The programme distributed at the initial roadshow screenings in the USA and in Britain included an endorsement from Dr Francis Trevelyan Miller of the 'Board of Historians at present engaged in compiling the Standard Contemporary History of the Great War'. Miller wrote:

> While we are at work analyzing the official documents from the
> belligerent governments and battle fronts for our cumbersome
> volumes on the Great War, you reveal the world tragedy in two and a
> half hours with Hearts of the World. ... I have come to the
> conclusion that hereafter history must be divided into four epochs:
> Ancient, Medieval, Modern - and the Motion Picture ... of which
> you are the FIRST of the great Cinema historians.[24]

The Bioscope critic's suggestion that its intimacy and attention to the
effects of war on individuals at the time was a weakness highlights the
themes that characterised the film's reception: the special qualities of
Griffith to bring the broad expanse of the war to bear on individuals and
his failure to describe fully, for a British audience, its effects. Further,
there is a hint even in the most generous of reviews by E. Codd in *Pictures
and the Picturegoer* that this had been the problem with so many American
war films:

> To a certain extent, one can understand this unconvincing quality in
> the war plays that America has hitherto provided for our war-worn
> millions. We, who are so close to the mighty struggle, whose daily
> thoughts and prayers are fearfully turned to some dear member of our
> little circle fighting our battles out there, who daily see in our streets
> war's pitiful human wreckage, are doubly sensitive to the least touch
> of insincerity in what we see on the screen. After four years of bitter
> experience we know that this war is not going to be won by heroic
> posings, grandiloquent speeches and the waving of little flags, nor by
> underestimating the intelligence and fighting powers of the universal
> enemy. Now that the great heart of America is beating with the same
> hopes and fears as our own, she will understand what she has not
> understood before, that sincerity must be the very keynote of any film
> product dealing with this terrific sacred theme, if it is ever to reach
> the hearts that have felt it in all its bitter reality.[25]

Although this is Codd's preamble for a review that praises Griffith it
details the expectations created by an American film about the war for a
British audience. In a less enthusiastic review for the *Kinematograph
Weekly* written a week later Codd found the film's battle scenes
monotonous and the overall effect of the film one of imbalance.[26] His
audience for *Kinematograph Weekly* was primarily the exhibitors, those
who had been complaining that their audiences were not responding to
war films. The message to these exhibitors outlines his pragmatic

response to the film in terms of whether it would gain an audience. Alternatively, the review for *Pictures and the Picturegoer* works towards the magazine's object of contributing to the promotion of cinema culture. The story of the film's production—the shooting of the scenes on the front—had been running sporadically for the previous year. Seen in conjunction with the *Kinematograph Weekly* review the articulation of what makes American-made war films unpopular with British audiences implied that *Hearts of the World* had failed in the project of depicting their personal experience of the war.

British Hearts

All evidence suggests that *Hearts of the World* was a moderate success in Britain. The profits on the film for the War Office Cinematograph Committee, which held the rights for the film in the British Empire, were £30,000, roughly one-third of the British profits for *The Birth of Nation*.[27] Further, the release pattern that began as a roadshow in the manner of *Birth* and *Intolerance* quickly went to distribution in cinemas. The run at the Palace in London was followed by a short engagement at Drury Lane and then it went to major cities. Beginning on 18 November the Scala Super-Cinema in Liverpool put the film on with the full orchestral and sound effects accompaniment. The film did not play in Southampton until 1920, where it had a three-day run at the King's Cinema in Kingsland Square, just adjacent to the High Street. The film's release pattern stretched from the exclusive run in London during the summer and early autumn of 1918 to its roadshow release in other towns in Britain up to and after the Armistice. While this demonstrates statistically the comparatively lacklustre performance of the film generally; the warm but reserved reviews suggest that there were textual elements of the film that, for British critics and audiences, worked against it.[28]

The conflict for British exhibitors lay, on the one hand, in the fact that the attraction was Griffith's artistic depiction of the war's effect on everyday life, and on the other hand that such a depiction might keep audiences away. This was complicated by the film's address to an American audience that had not experienced the war first hand. (Unfortunately there are no surviving versions of the film that had been edited for British audiences.) The synopsis of the film in the programme booklet ended with an appeal:

The things that occur may not have happened in quite the sequence as told here but all these incidents have really happened in that land where nothing seems impossible, where all the world is in Gethsemane and the earth is a forest of crosses on which hang the atoms of broken humanity. In the night outside our house anguished voices cry out. Whatever the darkness holds, we must take the lantern and go out into it.

This was reproduced in the booklet for the screenings at the Liverpool Scala on 18 November and was part of the nationwide publicity for the film. The call to patriotic endeavour clearly lines up with the public expression of morale and the exhibitors' practical patriotism, but the qualified praise of the press and the depiction of distressing scenes give a stronger insight into the reasons for the film's muted success in Britain. It seems that the representation of the realities of enduring total war proved less attractive when depicted through the emotional realism of the Griffithian melodrama. In the rest of this chapter I will explore the reasons why Charles Chaplin had much greater success with his film *Shoulder Arms* by representing the horror and devastation at the front through comedy.

'Imagine Charlie at the Front': *Shoulder Arms* (1918)

Hearts of the World had an exclusive release across the country from late October 1918 but many of the cities, including Southampton, which had screened previous Griffith super-films didn't play it until much later. These later versions were heavily edited with much of the cruelty of the Germans, particularly toward the 'the Girl' played by Lillian Gish, edited out.[29] *Shoulder Arms*, Charles Chaplin's feature-length comedy parodying the trenches, was released nationwide in December 1918 and enjoyed huge success throughout the following months of early 1919. In Southampton the film opened with week-long runs at the Palladium and at the Alexandra on the High Street. Runs at the Southampton Picture Palace followed this and the film ran consistently at most of the local cinemas throughout the next few months. In contrast with *Hearts of the World*, *Shoulder Arms* proved to be popular with a war-weary audience. The publicity and the film itself was able to build upon an already widely circulating association of Charlie with the war in the public consciousness, and a well-established preference for the representation of the front through comedy generally.

Do you know Charlie Chaplin?

Of course you do! But can you imagine him as a Tommy in the trenches with an egg whisk and a mouse trap, and a coffee pot and a cheese grater? Imagine your hardest and then some! You'll never do it. Neither will your patrons. Let them see it. Book at once.

Western Import Co. Ltd,
Eight Provincial Branches.

8.1 From *The Bioscope*, 26 September 1918.

Imagining Charlie as a Tommy

The Western Imports Company, which handled the release of the First National Chaplin films in Britain, announced the release of *Shoulder Arms* in the 26 September 1918 issue of *The Bioscope*:

> Do you know Charlie Chaplin?
> Of course you do! But can you imagine him as a Tommy in the trenches with an egg whisk and a mousetrap, and a coffee pot and a cheese grater? Imagine your hardest and then some! You will never do it. Neither will your patrons. Let them see it. Book at once.[30]

Notice Chaplin is presented as a British soldier here. Yet this was not the first time that Chaplin had been imagined as a Tommy at the front. His character Charlie had been the subject of public speculation since his rise to fame in 1915. In July of that year *Punch* ran a cartoon depicting a 'Near-sighted Old Lady (a keen Recruiter)' passing a Chaplin cut-out in front of a cinema and remarking 'Now look at that young fellow. A couple of months in the Army would make a new man out of him!'

Near-sighted Old Lady (a keen Recruiter). "NOW LOOK AT THAT YOUNG FELLOW. A COUPLE OF MONTHS IN THE ARMY WOULD MAKE A NEW MAN OF HIM !"

8.2 Frank Reynolds's cartoon appeared in *Punch*, 28 July 1915. It anticipated Lord Northcliffe's attack on Chaplin as a 'slacker', launched in 1917.

A more curious example of imagining Charlie involved in the British war effort was *The Film Renter*'s review of a film called *Charlie and the Zepp* in December 1916. Subtitled 'An Original and Topical Chaplin Comedy', this film was probably produced by a Chaplin imitator, as there is no record of Chaplin having made such a film. Yet in some important aspects the scenario that is recounted in *The Film Renter* anticipates that of *Shoulder Arms*.

> In the opening scenes Charlie is seen wandering at large within the danger zone. With his headful of stories of Zeppelin scares, he dozes off, and then follows a series of amazing adventures. Fleeing from the

approaching Zepps, Charlie rescues a panic-stricken girl, gets his precious trousers ignited in the rear, calls up the police, attacks the Zeppelin crew, and by his antics keeps the onlooker in laughter from start to finish.[31]

Shoulder Arms has two sequences that are similar: in the second section there is Charlie wanders behind the lines camouflaged as a tree and there is also the overall dream structure of the film as Charlie dozes off and dreams of rescuing the girl and seeing off the enemy. The dream structure was probably inspired by Chaplin's Essanay film *The Bank* (1915). The ease with which the scenarios of Chaplin are attached to the topical issue of the front illustrates the wide circulation of his image in entertainment culture in Britain. The two examples here broadly draw out the opposing positions that characterised the way that Chaplin was discussed in public forums and debates. The *Punch* cartoon parodies the nearsighted woman and keen recruiter but manages to play off suggestions that Chaplin may be shirking his duty to his country. *Charlie and the Zepp*, on the other hand depicts the Chaplin character as an outsider who comically engages the enemy but within his own dreams. The implication of 'slacking', or avoiding service, in the *Punch* cartoon is countered by the depiction of the antics of Charlie bringing comic chaos to the sober topic of bombing raids. Here he literally brings comic relief to the embattled homefront. Providing laughter for the homefront later formed the centrepiece of Chaplin's defence against accusations of 'slacking'.

The Meaning of a Slacker

The *Punch* cartoon anticipates a critique of Chaplin that has become known as 'the slacker controversy'. Lord Northcliffe launched a sustained attack on Chaplin in an editorial in *The Weekly Dispatch* in 1917. In it he accused Chaplin of avoiding his duty to serve at the front, choosing instead to amass a fortune in Hollywood. At the time Chaplin countered by publicising his contributions to the British war effort and then, when the USA entered the war, he put his full support behind the war bond campaign. This exchange took place within both local and national press and yet, in spite of reports of some cinemas refusing to show Chaplin films, the controversy seemed to have little or no effect on their popularity.

The debate on Chaplin's fitness for duty was an indication of the extent to which the image of 'Charlie' had permeated the popular imagination.

Between 1916 and 1918 his popularity continued unabated through the circulation of Charlie across a remarkable range of commercial products, from films to dolls to comic books. As these commercial artefacts centred on Chaplin's character 'Charlie' rather than the performer/artist Charles Chaplin so did the differing voices in the slacker debate. This issue had been raised in an earlier article that pre-dated the Northcliffe editorial. The *Daily Mail* in March 1916 had pointed out that the contract Chaplin had signed with Mutual had stipulated that he was not to return to Britain until the war ended. This was followed by a discussion through letters to the editor calling for a boycott of his films and criticised Chaplin's high salary '. . . for playing the fool while his compatriots play the man in Khaki for a mere weekly pittance of shillings'.[32] The populist paper *The John Bull* in April 1916 picked up on the issue but came to his defence:

> Much discussion about Charlie Chaplin has led to much confusion of thought and not a little romance. One journal describes his engagement to a 19 year old girl, another says he has a wife and four children in England, while several others advocate a boycott of Chaplin pictures, because he does not come home to fight. To which we add our information . . . to the effect that Charlie, and all British members of his company who are of military age have attested before the British vice-consul. So evidently he's not quite as bad as he is pictured.[33]

The reference to 'Charlie' blurs the distinction between the character and the performer and this seems to be consistent with the tendency in the wider entertainment industry's dialogic relationship between the construction and manipulation of star personas and their circulation in street culture. The Chaplin phenomenon belonged to more than cinema culture and had been incorporated into the well-established tradition of 'up-to-dateness'. As we have seen, his cut-outs could be seen at the front of theatres from the summer of 1915. He was a regular feature in bylines in both the trades and fan magazines, which reported his public appearances as well as his private affairs. When the USA entered the war in 1917 newsreels depicted Chaplin's work for the war effort, particularly his savings bond drive that culminated in a huge public appearance in New York where, famously, he was hoisted on to Douglas Fairbanks's shoulders. More important for the reception of *Shoulder Arms* is the way in which Charlie featured in popular street culture. For example, Charlie's name replaced Lottie Collins's in the children's skipping song 'Ta-ra-ra-boom-de-ay':

> Charlie Chaplin [Lottie Collins] had no sense
> He bought a fiddle for eighteen pence
> And all the tunes that he could play
> Was ta-ra-ra-boom-de-ay[34]

The placement of Charlie into this nonsensical rhyme highlights his general popularity and his association with comic chaos and blunder. This became more pointed in soldiers' songs. The most enduring of these was 'Charlie Chaplin' sung to the tune of 'Pretty Red Wing':

> The moon shines bright on Charlie Chaplin
>   His boots are cracking
>   for want of black'ning
> And his khaki trousers they want mending
>   Before we send him
>   To the Dardanelles
> The moon shines down on Charlie Chaplin
>   He's going barmy
>   To join the army
> And his old bags they want a-mending
>   Before we send him
>   To the Dardanelles[35]

The song refers to the slacker issue but it does so through highlighting Chaplin's costume, his tramp status, in a way that allows his character to be both the object of ridicule and at the same time stand in for the experience of the soldier. Other songs were less explicit about the slacker issue and used Chaplin as an up-to-date reference such as in the saucy song 'A Little Bit of Fluff' which became popular when the War Office enacted a ban on moustaches (sung to the tune of 'Tipperary'):

> It took a long time to get it hairy,
>   'Twas a long time to grow;
> Took a long time to get it hairy
>   For the toothbrush hairs to show.
> Goodbye, Charlie Chaplin
>   Farewell, tufts of hair;
> 'Twas a long, long time to get it hairy
>   But now my lip's quite bare.[36]

The function of Charlie Chaplin in the rhyming scheme adds to the air of comic intent and defiance. Rather than simply representing Chaplin as an object of ridicule as a result of the slacker controversy, his association with chaos as both outsider and everyman made his image a convenient one to associate with military blunder and futility. For example, he figured in the regimental song 'Fred Karno's Army' which was sung to the tune of 'The Church's One Foundation':

> We are Fred Karno's Army
> A jolly fine lot are we
> Fred Karno is our Captain
> Charlie Chaplin our O.C.
> And when we get to Berlin
> The Kaiser he will say:
> Hoch! Hoch! Mein Gott!
> What a jolly fine lot
> Are the 2-4th R.E. T.[37]

The use of stars' names was part of the music hall publicity tradition and from that standpoint the goal was to be included in a song or chant that ostensibly came from the public. Inclusion in satirical troop songs was a sign of a successful artiste.[38] The tone of these was to treat adversity and dire circumstances with dismissive and bawdy humour and Chaplin's persona as 'King of Mirth', rather than genius, reigned. In the satirical trench newspapers such as *The Wipers Times* his name stands in for the cinema and, as an emblem of bungling, fits with the satirical tone of the papers. On the second page of the *New Church Times* (incorporated with *The Wipers Times*) for Monday 22 May 1916 was a mock bill for the Neuve Eglise Hippodrome: 'This week at 6.30 and 8, Charlie Taplin In That Stirring Drama Entitled The Rusty Dud or All Is Not Dead That's Dirty'.[39] The kind of comic chaos that reigned in Chaplin films, as well as in much film and music hall knockabout, often ended in explosions. Here the image of Charlie finding a bomb and tapping it to see if it was a dud was an easy transistion from the play with explosives in *Dough and Dynamite* (1914) or the collapsing house at the end of *Work* (1915). It was also clearly relevant to soldiers. J.G. Fuller, in his study of troop morale, has pointed out that the 'whole conflict was like a giant Chaplin gag . . .'. He quotes D. Black's memoirs:

> The great comic of those days was Charlie Chaplin. Some critic has said that the basis of Chaplin's humour was the sudden collapse of a great and overwhelming cardboard dignity. We all knew that the gulf between the ranks, though necessary, was arbitrary and in a sense a

sham. The collapse of that cardboard dignity may have been a reason for our mirth.[40]

For Black the structures of rank, which largely reflected class in the civilian social world, gave Chaplin's comedy a forceful relevance for the troops. This perspective on Chaplin tends to isolate him from other modes of engagement with popular forms and personalities. Fuller associates Chaplin with the cinema and notes that, while the cinema was a popular medium for troops, projectors and facilities were often too difficult to obtain and it was easier for the soldiers to put on their own review. Yet Chaplin imitators often figured in these impromptu reviews. The circulation of Charlie's image through the cinema had succeeded in crossing the boundaries into other forms and become part of the popular imagination, both with soldiers and with the homefront, in the same way that well-known entities from the music hall, such as Fred Karno or Ally Sloper, had. By incorporating the war as a contemporary topic this type of circulation continued a method that had been central in the dissemination of entertainment culture for the better part of thirty years. These phenomena suggest that cinema, and Chaplin, were part of a larger and dialogic entertainment culture. Chaplin's image expanded beyond that of cinema to the extent that his association with the cinema was as much a part of his modern and up-to-date image as he was an emblem for the cinema.

There was a clear preference for the 'Charlie' image in the public imagination over the discussions about Chaplin's increasing wealth or his personal life generally. Instead, the primary preoccupation concerned his body. In April 1916 the entertainment paper *What's On in Southampton* reprinted part of an interview with American vaudeville comedian Raymond Hitchcock from *The Globe* earlier that month. Hitchcock had:

> . . . something to say with reference to the ridiculous attacks on Charlie Chaplin that have been common in the 'facing-both-ways' Press lately. 'He and I worked together for the Keystone people in California for many months . . . he's so delicate, he couldn't last one day in the trenches. No Army doctor would pass Charlie if he offered him ten thousand dollars to do it. He weighs less than 120 lbs., can't take anything stronger than water, and has to take the most elaborate care of himself in every way. Hear me tell you that I honestly believe, if Charlie were a strong man he would do what my friend Vernon Castle has done.[41]

Hitchcock's plea for Charlie highlights his unsuitability through appealing to what was known about Chaplin's bodily constitution through his films and to some extent knowledges that were circulating about his private life. It was fairly well known that Chaplin was not a drinker and that he was a hard worker but the general tone of the interview is to conflate the character Charlie with the artist Charles. A year later the Northcliffe editorial attempted to do the reverse: 'Charles Chaplin, although slightly built, is very firm on his feet, as is evidenced by his screen acrobatics. The way he is able to mount stairs suggests the alacrity with which he would go over the top when the whistle blew . . .'.[42] No doubt referring to the moving staircase sequence in *The Floorwalker*, this emphasis on Chaplin's performing body, while referring to 'Charles' rather than 'Charlie', attempts to separate the comic frame from the more serious reality of wartime while maintaining an equivalence between Charlie the character, the comic performing body, and Charles the man, the body for conscription.

Chaplin's own response of contributing to charitable causes also held on to the separation of Charlie the character from Charles the artist and, in this case, the philanthropist. In the end his best response was that he could contribute more to the war effort as a morale booster through continuing his work. In fact this separation of the artist from the character, which is exonerated by the real work behind the clown, exposed the work ethic that lay behind the slacker accusation. Charlie in most of his films was taken for a slacker, a shirker of work. The tramp is the most obvious manifestation of this, but the drunken swell or dude characters were also gold bricks and layabouts. The introduction of pathos, or wistfulness, in the tramp deepened the character and encouraged an empathetic engagement through his outsider status and impoverished condition. This combination of anti-authoritarian behaviour with the deeper level of characterisation was imported fully formed in *Shoulder Arms* by placing Charlie in the regime of the military and the frightening and horrific world of the front.

Charlie and Old Bill

The identification of soldiers with workers doing a necessary job at the front was a centrepiece of patriotic rhetoric. The Northcliffe accusation, and the use of the term 'slacker', bears this out. Chaplin's character, nationality and popularity made him a high-profile target for these.

Although not so highly publicised, similar concerns had been raised by military officials about the cartoons of Bruce Bairnsfather and their widespread popularity with the soldiers at the front, people on the homefront and the Allies, including the United States. The depiction of the British soldier as Old Bill did not align with the kind of heroic representation the War Office was committed to. Although Bairnsfather was later allowed to produce his cartoons as the main part of his military responsibility, this was a pragmatic decision by the War Office in response to the popularity of his work. On 21 December 1916, the *Literary Supplement* reviewed his first written account of his experiences, *Bullets and Billets*, published by Grant Richards: '. . . we regret unfeignedly that when the Empire laughs we must remain dumb . . . It is not with Captain Bairnsfather's humour that we quarrel, for his situations are invariably amusing. . . . It is because he standardises—almost idealises—a degraded type of face.'[43] Because of his service record, Bairnsfather himself was immune to the accusations of 'slacker' that were directed at Chaplin, but the 'vulgarity' of the faces and dress of his characters drew the kind of criticism from these quarters that Chaplin had experienced since his early days at Keystone. As with Chaplin, however, it was the function of morale that provided the official acceptance. Bairnsfather was particularly identified as representative of that unique British national characteristic, a sense of humour. After the war Wyndham Lewis wrote that

> Old Bill was the real hero of the World War, on the English side, much more than any V.C. A V.C. is after all a fellow who does something heroic; almost unEnglish. It is taking things a bit too seriously to get the V.C. The really popular fellow is the humorous 'Old Bill' a la Bairnsfather. And it really was 'Old Bill' who won the war—with all that expression 'won the war' implied.[44]

Bairnsfather had been at the front during the first six months of the war and had been invalided out with shell shock. His time in recovery had been spent developing his drawing skills and depicting the front through a resigned and dry humour that highlighted the plight of the trench soldier. Afterwards, Bairnsfather was put in charge of 200 soldiers from the Royal Warwickshires who had been at the front and were recuperating at the regiment's depot on the Isle of Wight. It was from these veterans that Bairnsfather found inspiration for the characters Old Bill, Bert and Alf that would appear in his cartoons: 'I love those old work-evading, tricky, self-contained slackers—old soldiers'.[45] Slacking here was a way of pointing out the absurdity of military hierarchies and endless tasks, which matched the work sketches that were a music hall and cinema staple. Bairnsfather's use of the term slacker applied to Old Bill indicates the contested meaning that the term represented. On the one hand the 'slacker' meant a shirker of duty and cowardice, while on the other it was also a term for the anti-heroics of 'Old Bill' and his friends and of course Chaplin as the tramp in his earlier films such as *Work*, *The Bank*, and in *Shoulder Arms*.

'The "Real War" At Last!': The Front through the Comic Frame

The cinematic depiction of the conditions at the front had always had a certain requirement of humour, even in the actuality films of the Topical Budget or the Pathé or Gaumont newsreels. The Gaiety in Southampton advertised regular screenings of the latest war pictures as 'depicting many humorous incidents'. Whether through this attempt at maintaining a light-hearted tone to actuality footage or through the humorous nature of propaganda shorts and cartoons, comedy proved a resilient frame for representing the front throughout the war. In April 1916 *The John Bull* ran a story entitled 'The Laughter that Runs with Death' in which 'A. Private' recounted slapstick stories of events in the trenches. He told of a crowded trench as rifle grenades began to come in: 'Just as they got near to me the whistle went and they began to run down the trench, some this way, some that, falling into each other . . . My Heavens but they were funny'. He then recounted an incident that could have been a Chaplin gag. He tells of his friend caught in no-man's-land when a barrage of shells began to burst round him.

> . . . he kept making little darts, now to the right, now to the left, as he imagined the minenwerfer was going to drop. He had the wind up like blazes . . . After the explosion he emerged (from his cover) and stared about as I imagine chickens do when they toddle out of their shells and he got up again and waited for the next.[46]

The depiction of the front through humour gave expression to the chaos, physical violence and terror where the melodramatic depictions of heroics such as *Hearts of the World* still clung to a sense of divine agency and purpose. By contrast, the random destruction of the shells, the sky filled with lead and the woeful inadequacy of the dugouts were the central elements of the cartoons of Bairnsfather and to the comic effect of *Shoulder Arms*. In *Shoulder Arms* the air above the trench is so lethal Charlie opens a beer bottle by simply holding it above the parapet, or strikes a match to light his cigarette by the same method. Chaplin's and Bairnsfather's depiction of the front come close to Griffith's own description of it as 'Gethsemane' in the publicity for *Hearts of the World*.

The gags that Chaplin employed could have been easily placed in Bairnsfather's cartoons. The most explicit link between the two follows the trench sequence in *Shoulder Arms* where Chaplin is disguised as a tree in order to observe enemy lines. In 1926 Chaplin was sued by the writers of the film *The Rookie*, which used the same gag, claiming that Chaplin had stolen the idea from them. Earlier than either film, in 1916, Bairnsfather had published a cartoon in his collection *Fragments from France* depicting a soldier disguised as a tree who has been seen and shells are raining down on him. His movements suggest those of Chaplin and, in turn, those of the hapless soldier in 'Private A's' account of darting back and forth. Chaplin engaged Bairnsfather as a witness to demonstrate that '. . . all the involved ideas instead of being original inventions were really observations and as such were common property . . . anyone might have thought of, say, a man disguised as a tree, because during the war men were occasionally disguised as trees'.[47] Although Chaplin never fully acknowledged Bairnsfather's influence on *Shoulder Arms* the circumstantial links lie not only in the specific gags but in the overall depiction of the brutal conditions of the trenches.

Giving voice to this claim, Max Pemberton of *The Weekly Dispatch* reviewed the theatrical version of Bairnsfather's cartoons, *The Better 'Ole* as 'A real war play at last . . .'.[48] The play was named after Bairnsfather's most famous cartoon which depicted two soldiers in a foxhole with a terrifying amount of shells bursting all around them and the caption 'Well if you knows of a better 'ole, go to it'. Written by Bairnsfather and Arthur Elliott, it opened at the Oxford Music Hall in 1917. Pemberton's review lauded the realism of the play:

> Nightly you may see Guardsmen laughing and little milliners' assistants weeping and then hear the cheer of the men in khaki *who know*. Mother and son, the son who fought, sit side by side and hold hands. And he tells her proudly, 'It was just like that out there.' Yes, it was and is just like that out there, and no surer tribute could be paid.[49]

The gendering of the response in Pemberton's review constructs a world where jolly soldiers laugh because 'they know' and women and mothers weep because they can't know. Through this gendered topography Pemberton builds a consensus of feeling by reproducing the public language of patriotic support and acknowledging the existence of private anxieties. Pemberton chose to represent those anxieties as feminine, assuaged by the assurances of the men and the humour with which the trenches were treated. The placing, and gendering, of humour and sentiment side-by-side in this way suggests a symbiotic relationship where the responses and quips of the soldiers provide the humour and the backdrop and the setting of the trench invoked pathos. This combination of the comic chaos and wistfulness of pathos was by this time Chaplin's stock in trade.

George Pearson recalled seeing the stage production and was '. . . stirred by the waves of laughter from that British audience seeking solace for a while from the wartime gloom . . . a sublimation of world tragedy in the derisive cockney humour of "if you knows of a better 'ole go to it" . . . .'.[50] In January 1918 Pearson adapted the play as the first film for the newly formed Welsh, Pearson and Company. Pearson was not completely convinced of its potential as a film at first as the contrast between the humour and the pathos in the stage production had caused him some concern. He had told his partner Thomas Welsh he welcomed making '. . . a film [which] might strengthen the nation's will to carry on to the bitter end, and would certainly bring a little laughter to many a worried family, but film reproduction of the war-front was vastly different from the simple decor of the music-hall stage'.[51] Pearson, like Pemberton, saw the necessity for a certain reverence in depicting the front which, given the realistic quality of film photography, may have overwhelmed the humour.

The Bioscope review of the film also applauded the realism of the Pearson production and predicted the success of the film based on the responses of the audience. Unlike Pemberton's endorsement of the complementary elements of sentiment and humour in the play, *The Bioscope* reviewer saw that the film's weakness lay in its sentiment, 'Which sometimes seems a little artificial because of its surroundings'. Referring to the contrasting sardonic humour with the drudgery and terror of trench life, *The Bioscope* found Pearson's use of a poet soldier to lecture Old Bill and his pals, and the audience, on the causes of the war somewhat unbelievable. '. . . One wonders that such irrepressible subjects such as Bert and Alf listen with such evident interest and lack of flippant comment. For it is the flippancy of the British soldier which enables him to play the hero under conditions which the thoughtful man at home can hardly contemplate without a shudder.'[52] Chaplin's *Shoulder Arms* and Bairnsfather's cartoons both downplay the pathos of the trench setting by foregrounding the implacable nature of their characters. Old Bill, Bert and Alf have seen everything and meet the adversity of their situation with a pugnacious resignation. Apparently much of this humour made it into the Pearson film, such as the title 'Don't put your feet in the water we have to sleep in'.[53] The appeal of both Charlie and Old Bill lay in their opposition to the heroic figures of the propaganda posters, with the stasis of the trench set contrasted with the charging horse of the cavalry or the action in the battle scenes of *Hearts of the World*.

The Trench View

The depiction of the trenches in both the Bairnsfather cartoons and Chaplin's film are for the most part laid out from the position of inside the trench or from the point of view of a comrade sheltering in another dugout. Following the opening gag of Chaplin at drill the trench scene begins with the title 'Over There'. Chaplin, with his back to the camera, is the tramp as doughboy loaded down with a huge pack stamped with the number '13' and various kitchen utensils hanging from his person. He walks down the trench with the camera tracking behind him, passing signs pointing to 'Broadway' and 'Rotten Row' and through the smoke of an explosion. As the scene develops the camera never leaves this position of inside the trench. The trenches in *Hearts of the World* were mainly shot from above, a favourite shot of Griffith's, which offered a panoramic shot of the field of battle. By contrast, in Chaplin's and Bairnsfather's depictions of what Paul Fussell has called the 'troglodyte world', the unearthly landscape of no-man's-land is unknowable. When Charlie goes over the top the camera doesn't follow him. It remains in the trench until he returns having captured thirteen German prisoners. Even in the later escapades Charlie is behind the enemy lines first as a tree and then in disguise as a German officer, but the contested area of no-man's-land remains unrepresented. George Pearson remembers his own reasoning behind the lack of representation of the actual site of conflict in his film as one of dramatic impact through pathos:

> I . . . pondered long over the final scene to the film, for it needed the utter simplicity of an unmistakable message. I hoped I had found it in

a scene of a country lane that rose to its brow outlined against a clear English sky. Far away, nearing that brow, the three Tommies, their seven days' leave ended, were tramping away to some distant port of embarkation, silhouetted for a moment, then lost to sight as they crossed over the top, with never a glance back, surely the simple message 'Carry On' . . . and nothing more.[54]

Bairnfather's cartoon 'What it really feels like' shows a frightened Tommy with hair standing on end surrounded by imagined heads of German soldiers looking down on him. Or consider the cartoon 'That 16mm sensation'. It depicts the condition that provoked the kind of breakdowns that Bairnsfather himself suffered by showing the same Tommy, both legs shackled to balls and chains, trying to crawl away from a shell that is bearing down on him. In *Shoulder Arms* Chaplin too approximates this kind of helpless feeling that was a feature of life in the trenches. Prior to going over the top Charlie is told to 'Make himself at home' and a barrage begins. As each shell bursts closer and closer to him he looks directly into the camera and begins to shake and then he pulls out his lucky charm which is actually his number, 13. It was this quality of helplessness and resistance in the face of the cosmic terror of the front that prompted *The Bioscope* to use similar terms in praising both Pearson's *The Better 'Ole* and Chaplin's *Shoulder Arms*. The column's praise for Charles Rock's performance was for '. . . his facial play and the general bearing [which] make Old Bill a very human type'.[55] For *Shoulder Arms* *The Bioscope* speculated '. . . perhaps his secret is that he is so essentially human'.[56]

Terror, Innervation and the Transforming Quality of Cinema

If both Charlie and Old Bill represent human frailty in the face of mechanical obliteration, the impact of the terror on their bodies provoked quite different responses. Old Bill's laconic demeanour hides the wiles of a good-natured slacker and the 'flippant comment' conceals the hero. The overriding impression of Old Bill is stasis, an almost catatonic state developed in the trenches in resistance to the absurdities of military excess and regimen and as a means of negotiating the terrors of technology. Chaplin, on the other hand, is infused with energy. He brings to the trenches an ability to take whatever comes with comic ingenuity and aggression, qualities acquired in the modern world of work and leisure. His dream of the homefront in the split screen is not of a family or a sweetheart but of first a panoramic view of the bustling metropolis with traffic and skyscrapers and then a fade to a bartender mixing a drink. Charlie's fondness for the alienating city and the effects of alcohol are reflected in the kind of gifts he receives from home. In the only moment of overt pathos in the film he is left out of the mail call. Then a bit later the posting officer comes to him and hands him the package containing stale biscuits and Limburger cheese with the title 'This must be for you'. Charlie is singled out for his lowly status, a package of cast-off goods, probably some anonymous donation to the war effort. Old Bill, Alf and Bert dream of the comforts of home or those available behind the lines such as warmth, hot food and the company of girlfriends or French girls.

The cartoons of Old Bill reinforce this sense of stasis and acceptance in their form of the still image. The situations that are reconstructed in the stage play and in the film are dependent on dialogue and staging rather than movement. Chaplin's comedy, however, is wholly movement, hysterical and frenetic. Old Bill's preservation of unnecessary movement contrasts with Chaplin's constant movement. It is possible to see in this comparison between catatonia and involuntary tics the extreme range of symptoms exhibited by soldiers with war trauma.

I do not raise this to suggest a concrete link to shell shock as an intended reference in Chaplin or Bairnsfather, or to work through a more plausible connection with the widely discussed issue of war neuroses and malingering that had been going on since at least 1915. Rather, I want to raise this in connection with an interpretation of Chaplin that was made a number of years later in the work of Walter Benjamin, and elaborated on more recently by Miriam Hansen, in order to illustrate a theoretical basis for considering the transformational property of comedy. Hansen has noted that in Chaplin Benjamin found an 'allegory' for what he called mimetic innervation. Hansen defines the concept of a mimetic faculty as 'the capacity to relate to the external world through patterns of similitude, affinity, reciprocity, and interplay . . . the mimetic is . . . a form of practice that transcends the traditional subject–object dichotomy and its technologically exacerbated splittings of experience and agency . . .'.[57] Benjamin used the example of children at play who mimic not only persons and social types but also objects such as trains, planes etc. This type of mimetic innervation

> . . . entails dynamics that move in opposite, yet complementary directions: 1) a decentering and extension of the human sensorium beyond the limits of the individual body/subject into the world that

243

stimulates and attracts perception; and 2) an introjection, ingestion, or incorporation of the device, be it an external rhythm, a familiar madeleine, or an alien(ating) apparatus.[58]

In *Shoulder Arms*, after being passed over by the post the first time, Charlie reads a letter over the shoulder of another soldier and mimes the same emotions. Chaplin had done this type of gag before, most notably 'catching' the hiccups from another passenger in *The Immigrant*. This illustrates the first dynamic and Hansen suggests this 'excentric' perception could be 'at work as well in the dispersed subjectivity of the cinema experience'.[59] Relating Chaplin's performance to the processes of spectator identification or empathetic engagement sets up the second dynamic that is 'incorporative' where the apparatus replaces the 'inner impulses and the bodily centre'. The clown is a representative figure along with the child. The performance of Chaplin provides a liberating expression of modernity's destructive effects. As the bombs fall near him he gets nervous and jumps with each explosion, in another scene when his dugout floods he incorporates a gramophone horn as a breathing device and of course he 'becomes' a tree which is really a part of the technological apparatus of the war. At one point, upon waking up, he reaches into the water and scratches the sergeant's foot, not realising it is not his own. The performance of Chaplin is designed to provoke laughter, a physical response that requires an incorporation of the cinematic apparatus.

In trying to explain the reception of *Shoulder Arms* and the depiction of the front through the comic film frame, it may be useful to attach Hansen's reading of Benjamin's notion of mimetic innervation as a form of 'psychic inoculation ... because they effect a "premature and therapeutic detonation" of mass psychoses, of sadistic fantasies and masochistic delusions in the audience by allowing them to erupt in the collective laughter'.[60] For a British audience Chaplin's innervated performing body, his tics, his expressions of fear, hint at the punishment the war had brought forcefully to bear on the human body and mind. Chaplin's body in *Shoulder Arms* offered a means of incorporating that punishment and reversing its destructive effects so that they were rendered as rejuvenating. Chaplin as a British performer brings to the screen also a modern energy associated with America, either explicitly as the property of the new ally, or implicitly as the centre of the newly emerging modern world. Old Bill provides a more static and verbal response, but also through the kind of resistance through humour and wit that became another type of comic renewal. In both cases this was a kind of renewal that looked forward to a chaotic and frenetic future where *Hearts of the World* was only able to envision a return to the traditions and social order of the past.

I am not arguing that these two comic examples of psychic inoculation were somehow resistant to dominant ideological forces. In fact it is impossible to avoid recognising their complicity with the war effort. I want to point out, though, that it was these comic representations of the front and their comic, rejuvenating effect that the exhibition industry endorsed, following the preferences of their audiences, for they were the basis for securing the social function of cinema as a legitimate space of leisure in its capacity as a space for reinvigoration. A week after the end of the war the Western Import Company played on the recuperative powers of Chaplin's comedy in an advertisement that announced that the release of *Shoulder Arms* '. . . has come at the right time. People can laugh at it now without feeling guilty.'[61] The comic treatment of the front had succeeded in momentarily alleviating the anxieties of a war-weary audience where the emotional realism of *Hearts of the World* had failed.

Conclusion

Shoulder Arms' popularity with audiences across the spectrum of cinemas from the smaller houses to the picture palaces stands as an emblem for the lasting effect the war had on British cinema culture. The depiction of the front through the incorporation of comic devices drawn from the music hall sketch and the Bairnsfather cartoons contrasted with the sombre realism of *Battle of the Somme* and the melodramatic fantasy of *Hearts of the World*. Both of these films were intended to be educational and uplifting while *Shoulder Arms'* comic frame testified to the 1917 National Council of Public Morals (NCPM) report's observation that: '. . . the cinema is to be regarded as a means of amusement and recreation . . .'.[1] The report had identified this as a 'value', stating 'We are convinced that the picture house means so much happiness not only to children but even to adults living and working under adverse condition, that any attempt at suppression would be a grievous social loss . . .'.[2] The reference to adverse conditions was primarily meant to be those of the poor and the working classes:

> We must recognise that the picture house fulfills a useful and needful function amid social conditions which press very hard not only on the very poor, but even on the bulk of the working classes. So unsatisfactory is housing both in town and country, that there are few homes in which the leisure hours can be spent in quiet comfort and enjoyment.[3]

Exhibitors, and the industry generally, saw this as an endorsement of their own arguments for the social function of cinema. However, as reports from the trade press and letters from exhibitors have revealed, there was the increasing feeling that adverse conditions were directly related to the effects of the war. The view that the function of the cinema space was to be a site of refuge from the house or street expanded to become a vision of the cinema as a relief from the anxieties felt across regions and class due to the war. Exhibitors had long been expressing their audience's preference for fiction films over educational and propaganda films. The traditions of house management with the goal of providing 'good fellowship', and a rejuvenating form of leisure inherited from the music hall and variety theatre generally, drove the exhibitors' own perceptions of cinema's place within the community. In turn, these kinds of presentation techniques and traditions had helped to shape audience expectations. The NCPM report recognised this in its conclusion that 'The atmosphere in which such [educational] films are introduced is highly antagonistic to their favourable reception and to their educational value'.[4]

The report's conclusions about the primary social function of the cinema lends depth to Rachael Low's assessment that 'The picture show . . . was established as part of the economic and social structure of the country by the end of the war in 1918'.[5] In this book I have tried to explore the dynamics of that shift towards social acceptance. This journey across the four years of the war from the perspective of exhibition practices, the reception of specific films and film personalities, and the discursive background against which they were set qualifies Low's assertion. Rather than see the exhibitor as a shortsighted petit bourgeois entrepreneur less interested in the development of cinema as an art than as a means of profit—thereby opening the floodgates for the domination of British screens by US films—I have attempted to draw attention to the vagaries and uncertainties facing the local cinema manager during the time of world war. The British exhibitors' response to the outbreak of war and to its continuation across four years pre-dates the practices of US exhibitors' practical patriotism by at least three years.[6] British exhibitors' practices were predicated on ensuring the 'up-to-dateness' of their establishment in line with trends in the wider entertainment culture at the time. Yet these practices themselves shifted from the overt patriotism of special events and the Roll of Honour films to the more subtle argument of the transforming and rejuvenating properties of the cinema for a war-weary audience. As we have seen, the Roll of Honour films and the feature-length official war films offered an apparently popular form of practical patriotism that gave way to a conviction that the role of the cinema was to entertain.

Considering the history of British cinema culture during the First World War from the perspective of reception has afforded more than the rather simple assessment that the war afforded the cinema the opportunity of incorporation into the fabric of British social life. The detailed focus on the local space of Southampton has shown how cinema managers responded to the intense competition that was markedly different from that experienced by US exhibitors at the time. Their attempts to appeal to both regular clientele and the floating audience were varied. It is clear that the open market and the transition to exclusives was used by managers to shape their programmes to their intended audience. This has afforded a more accurate and detailed picture than the homogeneous concept of the exhibitor in Rachael Low's account.

By exploring the promotional strategies of local cinema managers it has been possible to outline their convergence with those of the production companies, both US and British. The Palladium's consistent exhibition of Hepworth's literary adaptations made up the kind of programming the proprietors Hood and Bacon wished to promote as part of their reputation as an educational as well as an entertainment venue. *The Birth of a Nation*'s exhibition in Southampton illustrated the way that a national campaign, which worked to redirect interpretations of the film to make it more relevant to a British audience, was intended for a higher-paying audience that did not normally attend the cinema. The consistent promotion of society melodramas in its advertising has suggested that the Gaiety attempted to appeal to the increasing number of women who were taking up employment in the city. The Chaplin films' circulation, and re-circulation, across local cinemas during the whole of the war has illuminated the extent of the use of his films by exhibitors to attract audiences. Reports in the trade press about the local scene in Southampton and other areas such as Preston and Leeds have lent support to determining the way that the Roll of Honour films were publicly received.

The attention to reception, exhibition and the use the local cinema culture of Southampton as a comparative basis in accounting for wider national trends and developments has extended this study beyond the tracking of screening histories and the notation of promotion and exhibition strategies. Advertising strategies, along with the reviews, the fan magazines and the film texts themselves where available, have made up the evidence-base to determine modes of address. The changes made to the British version of *Civilization*, the redirections of *The Birth of a Nation* and the advertisement of Charlie as a Tommy in *Shoulder Arms* provide an insight into the mechanics of transnational reception and point to wider discourses of national identity generally. To be more specific, they have been markers for the public debates and the circulation of imagery that constituted cinema's participation in the homefront imagination. Through a study of reception that has tried to outline probable interpretations it has been possible to suggest that there were public and private levels of response to specific types of films that dealt directly with the war. The performative public response to the Roll of Honour films, the scenes of battle in the official war films and those fictional depictions of the tragic consequences of war in films such as *The Crisis*, *The Birth of a Nation* or *Hearts of the World* was accompanied by more private responses that, for reasons of social propriety and support for the war, were not allowed public expression. Evidence of this exists in personal accounts of specific films like *Battle of the Somme* and in the comparatively lacklustre business for films such as *Hearts of the World* towards the end of the war.

Yet the reception of films such as *Battle of the Somme* and the Roll of Honour films reveals many anomalies and a wide range of attitudes and positions. Crucially, those films also represent the beginnings of the memorialising process of the dead and in that way they provide an important insight into cinema's role in the developing cultural memory of the Great War.

By outlining these probable interpretations it has been possible to examine them more specifically. I have been selective in choosing comedy and melodrama to illustrate the dynamic interplay between texts and interpretation. In both cases I have chosen films that held a clear reflexive potential for British audiences. Chaplin's park films highlight the films' specific reflexivity for British audiences who were familiar with the social function of parks. Melodramatic tropes of reception have helped to account for the public/private nature of the response to the Roll of Honour films and the official war films. I have been able to outline a melodramatic mode of reception by suggesting that narrative tropes such as recognition, fears of anonymity and the tendency towards Manichaean structuring of good and evil existed across a range of fiction and actuality films and their intertexts. Familiarity with these tropes shaped audience's expectations and acted as a template for interpretation.

By selecting Chaplin's star persona, Griffith's super-films and the official war films, I have necessarily left out significant aspects of cinema culture during this period. Nevertheless, I hope I have drawn attention to the kind of work that is needed for a more complete history. The society melodramas favoured by Arthur Pickup at the Gaiety deserve more attention. The differences that are evident in the British-made films of these types, like Florence Turner's *Alone in London* (UK, 1917), compared to films such as Cecil B. DeMille's *The Cheat* (US, 1916), will further enhance the transnational reception history of cinema in this period and provide a more complete understanding of the role that this type of film played in the domination of British screens by US films. While I chose to concentrate on Chaplin, work on Mary Pickford—whose films were at least as popular as Chaplin's—may deepen our understanding of the significance of women audiences in the shaping of cinema culture during and after the war.

The focus on Southampton has allowed insight into the way the local cinema culture functioned, but similar work on other areas will deepen our understanding of the role that regulating forces played in the establishment cinema as a socially accepted leisure form. The Southampton Council was fairly liberal when compared to that of Liverpool or Middlesex, where strict positions on Sunday opening and on censorship are evidence of the diversity of local cinema cultures. While many of the comparative examples I have used have come from English towns, I have also included the local cinema cultures of Wales, Northern Ireland and Scotland where appropriate. Nevertheless these areas need further investigation. I have also not included the local areas of Ireland prior to 1916. This deserves a much more comprehensive study than I have been able to include here. The nature of practical patriotism there during this period would obviously differ from that in England, Scotland or Wales.

A history that takes as its starting point a local space will necessarily elide a number of important areas, issues and dynamics that are relevant and necessary for a complete history. I have tried to use the 'bottom-up' approach to gain insight into the detail that is missed in broad national histories. In that way I hope I have revealed something of the nature of George Emlyn Williams's memory of the space that cinema held in his imagination:

> It occupied the foreground of my life, vibrant and near, while fuzzy in the background was the Quay [his neighbourhood] moreover, while the phantoms were all the more real for being mute, reality was sterile with sound . . . And when I moped along the High Street to collect the margarine from the Maypole, all the faces were grey compared to the shadows I had watched; they looked like prisoners of war.[7]

Williams's memory here poetically endorses the arguments for the social function of cinema here as a transformative experience. Further, he is articulating the experience of a young boy. As in the quotation at the opening of this book, apart from the references to the people he encountered on the street as prisoners of war, in his recollections there is almost no sense of the war that was clearly affecting everyday life. That omission neatly illustrates the problem of writing a history of watershed moments. The individual experiences, the local details, often highlight the continuities rather than the changes. Paradoxically Fred Goodwin's concern for the effect the war was having on audiences underscores his understanding of his historical moment as a break in the fabric of history. In this book I have aimed to hold together the contrapuntal themes of watersheds and continuities of the history of cinema culture during the Great War in Britain. The war presented challenges to the industry, which responded by drawing on existing traditions. The reception of films concerning the war changed from enthusiastic support and curiosity to a preference for the short newsreel report of the front as part of the variety programme. The industry pragmatically played up the way that the cinema's value was beginning to be established as rejuvenating entertainment. These developments were a combination of the disruption of war and of 'business as usual'.

Finally, Williams's omission of the war in his memory provokes the cultural memory of the Great War as a tragedy of history. For the modern reader it is enough simply to know that his memories are concerned with the period 1916–20. While this has not been the main object of the book, the shifts in the reception of the official war films suggest how the remembrance of the war through the cinema had begun with the screening of the first images from the front. The Roll of Honour films and *Battle of the Somme* now stand as emblems of that memory of the war in the early twenty-first century. By recognising the way that the war shaped reception in Britain it is hoped that this project has had its own reflexive dimension concerning the contemporary memory of the war and the role of cinema in its construction.

Notes

Introduction

1 Emlyn Williams, *George, An Early Autobiography* (London: Hamish Hamilton, 1961), p. 162.
2 Mr F.R. Goodwin, (Chairman of the Cinematograph Exhibitors' Association (London Branch) in National Council of Public Morals (NCPM), *The Cinema: Its Present Position and Future Possibilities, Being the Report of Chief Evidence taken by the Cinema Commission of Inquiry Instituted by the National Council of Public Morals* (London: Williams and Norgate, 1917; New York: Arno Press and the New York Times, 1970), p. 1.
3 I am using the 'Great War' throughout this book rather than the more well-known 'First World War' or 'World War I' as that is how the war was generally referred to in the war years and in the interwar period.
4 F.R. Goodwin, in NCPM, *The Cinema: Its Present Position*, p. 6.
5 Andrew Higson, 'The Concept of a National Cinema', *Screen*, vol. 30, no. 4 (Autumn 1989), p. 45.
6 'Practical patriotism' is a term I have borrowed from Leslie Midkiff DeBauche who identifies the concept of combining 'allegiance to country and business' as a central tenet in the US film industry's practices during the last eighteen months of the First World War. While not widely used as a term at the time in Britain it serves as a convenient phrase for my purposes here. However, it is worth noting that British house management strategies of staging patriotic programmes and events had been a part of entertainment culture in Britain throughout the nineteenth century. When managers adopted these techniques they were acting on their own experience rather than taking their cue from US how-to manuals. Leslie Midkiff DeBauche, *Reel Patriotism: The Movies and World War I* (Madison: University of Wisconsin Press, 1997), p. xvi.
7 Janet Staiger, *Interpreting Films: Studies in the Historical Reception of American Cinema* (Princeton: Princeton University Press, 1992).
8 Higson, 'The Concept of a National Cinema'.
9 Staiger, *Interpreting Films*, p. 9.
10 Yuri Tsivian, *Early Cinema in Russia and its Cultural Reception*, trans. Alan Bodger (London: Routledge, 1994), p. 5.
11 *East Lynne* by Mrs Henry Wood was first published in 1861 in serial form and then was produced as a stage play throughout the rest of the nineteenth century. The novel was, in 1910, one of the five most-borrowed books from

Southampton Library. In 1915 a film of the story was made by the William Fox Company, starring Theda Bara; it was screened at the Standard Cinema on 2, 3 and 4 August 1917 in Southampton. (See Mrs Henry Wood, *East Lynne*, ed. Norman Page and with an introduction by Kamal Al-Solaylee (London: Everyman, 1994).) The novel *Trilby* by George du Maurier was published in serial form from January to July 1894 and then was produced as a play by Paul Potter in October of the same year. The London Film Company's 1914 version of the story starred Sir Herbert Tree, reprising his role in the Potter play, and was directed by Harold Shaw. This was screened at cinemas in Southampton in the same year. (See George du Maurier, *Trilby*, ed. and with accompanying text by Leonee Ormond (London: Everyman, 1992); and also Paul Potter's play *Trilby*, in *Trilby and Other Plays: Four Plays for Victorian Star Actors* ed. with an introduction by George Taylor (Oxford and New York: Oxford University Press, 1996).)

12   William Uricchio and Roberta E. Pearson, *Reframing Culture: The Case of the Vitagraph Quality Films* (Princeton: Princeton University Press, 1993), p. 10. Following Stanley Fish, Urrichio and Pearson identify these forces in part as 'interpretive communities'. By this they mean 'groups whose members share common standards for creating meaning'. They go on to outline that there are 'authorised interpretive communities' that hold significant influence over public policy, official and sometimes non-official.

13   Annette Kuhn, *Cinema Censorship and Sexuality, 1900–1925* (London: Routledge, 1988), pp. 122–23. Kuhn describes this as '. . . the regulation of films and their contents wherever prohibitions as to the character of films shown in public cinemas were written into cinema licensing conditions.'

14   Urrichio and Pearson, *Reframing Culture*, p. 10. Urrichio and Pearson describe these unofficial bodies as significantly involved in the 'contemporary production and circulation of . . . intertexts . . . [and which] selected, valorised and circulated certain expressive forms rather than others'.

15   Ibid., p. 6.

16   Michael Hammond, '"Cultivating Pimple": Performance Traditions and the Comedy of Fred and Joe Evans', in Alan Burton and Laraine Porter, eds, *Pimple, Pranks and Pratfalls: British Film Comedy Before 1930* (Trowbridge: Flicks Books, 2000), pp. 58–68.

17   Gregory A. Waller, *Mainstreet Amusements: Movies and Commercial Entertainment in a Southern City, 1896–1930* (Washington and London: Smithsonian Institution Press, 1995), p. 259.

18   Miriam Hansen, *Babel and Babylon: Spectatorship and American Silent Cinema* (Cambridge: Harvard University Press, 1991), p. 64.

Chapter 1

1   Nicholas Hiley suggests that the cinema boom nationwide began in earnest in 1910, Southampton generally follows along these lines with the greatest increase in purpose-built cinemas ocurring between 1912 and 1914. Nicholas Hiley, 'Cinema Building in Britain from 1909 to 1914', in Andrew Higson, ed.,

Young and Innocent?: The Cinema in Britain 1896–1930 (Exeter: University of Exeter Press, 2002), pp. 11–127.

2 'Easter Monday in Town', *What's On in Southampton*, week ending 5 April 1914 (note: this paper has no page numbers).

3 Copy for *What's On* was often supplied by the managers of entertainment establishments themselves and in articles such as this one the establishments mentioned were those that bought advertising space in the paper. The use of newspapers by cinema exhibitors is clearly spelled out on p. 843 of the 22 February 1914 edition of *The Bioscope* by Mr T. Butt, manager of the New Savoy cinema in Glasgow: '. . . most editors are usually willing enough to give you advance paragraphs, and do not forget . . . these advance notices or paragraphs are worth far more than the actual advertisement for which you pay'. In other words, managers were allowed column space to write their own copy if they paid for advertising space.

4 Gordon Sewell, 'Southampton in the Twentieth Century', in J.B. Morgan and Philip Peberdy, eds, *Collected Essays on Southampton* (Southampton: Entertainments and Publicity Committee of the County Borough of Southampton), p. 99.

5 Edwin Welch, *Southampton Maps from Elizabethan Times* (Southampton: City of Southampton), p. 30. Population figures cited are from this source.

6 This play was later made into a film in 1917 by the American film company Paragon and directed by Maurice Tourneur. A comprehensive account of the play's transition to screen can be found in Lea Jacobs and Ben Brewster, *Theatre to Cinema* (Oxford: Oxford University Press, 1997), pp. 201–10.

7 'Easter Monday in Town', *What's On in Southampton*, week ending 5 April 1914.

8 'Southampton Shows', *The Bioscope*, 2 July 1914, p. 9. As part of its practice of reports from the regions *The Bioscope* ran 'Southampton Shows', a regular feature that appeared bi-weekly until 1916. The standard structure of the column gave a paragraph on each cinema, reporting on styles and practices, changes in management and/or ownership, relations with councils, and examples of programmes.

9 'Picturedrome, Northam', *What's On in Southampton*, week ending 2 January 1915.

10 'Screen Gossip', *Pictures and the Picturegoer*, 14 March 1914, p. 93.

11 Works Committee, 'Minutes of the Proceedings of the Council and Committees from 9th Nov. 1913 to 9th Nov. 1914', Southampton City Council Archives, 1914, p. 110.

12 'What's On Notes', *What's On in Southampton*, week ending 30 May 1914.

13 'The Carlton', *What's On in Southampton*, week ending 30 May 1914.

14 'Southampton Shows', *The Bioscope*, 16 July 1914, p. 253.

15 Allen Eyles and Keith Skone, *London's West End Cinemas* (Sutton: Keystone Publications, 1991), p. 43.

16 'Report on the Regions', *The Bioscope*, 13 August 1914, p. 643.

17 Nicholas Hiley, 'The British Cinema Auditorium', in Karel Dibbets and Bert Hogenkamp, eds, *Film and the First World War* (Amsterdam: Amsterdam University Press, 1995), pp. 160–70.

18 Adrian Rance, *Southampton: An Illustrated History* (Southampton: Milestone Publications in Association with the City of Southampton, 1986), pp. 138–39.

19 The number of cinemas is based on those listed in the Southampton City Council Minutes from 1914 to 1918. The population figures are from the 1911 census and were found in A. Temple Patterson, *A History of Southampton 1700–1914* (Southampton: Southampton University Press, 1975), p. 115.

20 Kristin Thompson, *Exporting Entertainment* (London: BFI, 1985), p. 29.

21 John D. Tibbett, managing director of the Trans-Atlantic Film Company, which was a major film importer and distributor based in Britain, gave this explanation of the 'exclusive' to the Cinema Commission of Inquiry in 1917, carried out by the National Council of Public Morals: 'The exclusive picture is the property of one man who has the sole rights for Great Britain'. Making it clear that the exclusive was generally reserved for the feature 'quality' picture, he explained the advantages of this system for the exhibitor: 'For instance, take three very popular picture houses in the same vicinity at Hammersmith; a good open market picture is shown; they all book it showing it at the same time. Naturally, none of the picture houses make money, but if this had been an exclusive picture, it would have been booked in one of these houses, which would have had a chance to make some money.' National Council of Public Morals (NCPM), *The Cinema: Its Present Position and Future Possibilities, Being the Report of and Chief Evidence Taken by the Cinema Commission of Inquiry Instituted by the National Council of Public Morals* (London: Williams and Norgate, 1917; New York: Arno Press and The New York Times, 1970), p. 61.

22 Thompson, *Exporting Entertainment*.

23 This particular quote comes from the 14 November issue of *What's On in Southampton* but the phrase FIRST TIME SCREENED in capital letters appears consistently throughout the years 1914–16.

24 Thompson, *Exporting Entertainment*, p. 36.

25 Ibid.

26 Miriam Hansen, *Babel and Babylon, Spectatorship in American Silent Film* (Cambridge, MA: Harvard University Press, 1991), p. 92.

27 Ibid., p. 17.

28 In the majority of areas, cinemas were prohibited from opening on Sundays. This would further reduce the competition for films on this day.

29 G.S. Mellor, *The Northern Music Hall* (Newcastle: Frank Graham, 1970), pp. 185–88.

30 Peter Bailey, 'Introduction: Making Sense of Music Hall', in Peter Bailey, ed., *Music Hall: The Business of Pleasure* (Milton Keynes: Open University Press, 1986), pp. xii–xiii.

31 'Theatres and War', *What's On in Southampton*, week ending 29 August 1914.

32 'Sunday Evening at the Palace', *What's On in Southampton*, week ending 22 August 1914.

33 'Sunday Evening at the Palace', *What's On in Southampton*, week ending 29 August 1914.

34 'Talks to Managers: No. 3 "Dressing the Window"', *The Bioscope*, 10 June 1915, p. 1099.

35 Works Committee, 'Minutes of the Proceedings of the Council and Committees from 9th Nov. 1913 to 9th Nov. 1914', Southampton City Council Archives, 24 March 1914, item 8 (iii), p. 508.

36 'Southampton Shows', *The Bioscope*, 16 April 1914. p. 295.

37 'Picturedrome, Northam', *What's On in Southampton*, week ending 28 November 1914.

38 'Picturedrome, Northam', *What's On in Southampton*, week ending 23 January 1915.

39 Emlyn Williams, *George: An Early Autobiography* (London: Hamish Hamilton, 1961), p. 158.

40 'Picturedrome, Northam', *What's On in Southampton*, week ending 9 January 1915.

41 'Sunday Evening at the Palace' *What's On in Southampton*, week ending 15 August 1914.

42 'Northam Picturedrome', *What's On In Southampton*, week ending 13 February 1915.

43 'Letter from A.S. Strom, Balsall Heath Picturedrome, Balsall Heath Road, Birmingham, September 9, 1914', Selig Collection, Academy of Motion Picture Arts and Sciences, Folder 490.

44 'The Film Serial: A Remarkable Development', *The Bioscope*, 7 January 1915, p. 3.

45 Ibid.

46 Hiley, 'The British Cinema Auditorium', p. 160.

47 'Southampton Common', *Southampton Annual, 1902* (Southampton: The Pictorial Printing and Publishing Company, 1902), p. 39.

48 Works Committee, 'Minutes of the Proceedings of the Council and Committees from the 9th Nov. 1913 to 9th Nov. 1914', Southampton City Council Archive, 2 March 1914, Chief Constable's Report.

49 NCPM, *The Cinema, Its Present Position*, p. xxvii.

50 'The Carlton', *What's On in Southampton*, week ending 19 December 1914.

51 Peter Bailey, 'A Community of Friends', in Bailey, *Music Hall*, p. 41.

52 *What's On in Southampton*, week ending 26 June 1915.

53 Ibid.

54 Bailey, 'A Community of Friends', p. 35.

55 'Winchester Picture House and the Troops', *The Bioscope*, 26 November 1914, p. 901.

56 *What's On in Southampton*, week ending 26 June 1915.

57 *What's On in Southampton*, week ending 3 July 1915.

58 *What's On in Southampton*, week ending 17 July 1915.

59 'The Carlton', *What's On in Southampton*, week ending, 24 July 1915.

60 'The Carlton', *What's On in Southampton*, week ending, 7 August 1915.

61 Rachael Low, *The History of the British Film 1914–1918* (London: Allen and Unwin, 1950), p. 41.

62 'Entertainment to the Sick and Wounded', *What's On in Southampton*, week ending 23 October 1915.

63 'The Carlton', *What's On in Southampton*, week ending 2 October 1915.

64　David Williams gives an example of a sacred concert and picture entertainment at the Evington Cinema in Leicester where a feature *The White Lady* (Thanhouser, 1916) was accompanied on the bill by several sacred and patriotic songs. *Cinema in Leicester, 1896–1931* (Loughborough: Heart of Albion Press, 1993), pp. 125–26.

65　'The Carlton', *What's On in Southampton*, week ending 18 November 1916.

Chapter 2

1　'Sunderland and Wearside', *The Bioscope*, 13 August 1914, p. 643.

2　Peter Bailey, 'Musical Comedy and the Rhetoric of the Girl', in Peter Bailey, ed., *Popular Culture and Performance in the Victorian City* (Cambridge: Cambridge University Press, 1998), pp. 175–93; D. Forbes Winslow, *Daly's: The Biography of a Theatre* (London, W.H. Allen and Co, 1944).

3　'Southampton Shows', *The Bioscope*, 22 October 1914, p. 370.

4　'Southampton's Fine New Hall', *The Bioscope*, 1 October 1914, p. 68.

5　'Gaiety Picture Theatre', *What's On in Southampton*, week ending 2 October 1914.

6　'Southampton's Fine New Hall', p. 68.

7　Ibid.

8　Antonia Lant, 'The Curse of the Pharoah, or How Cinema Contracted Egyptomania', in Matthew Bernstein and Gaylyn Studlar, eds, *Visions of the East: Orientalism in Film* (London: I.B.Tauris, 1997), p. 90.

9　Miriam Hansen's insights into the Babylonian scenes in *Intolerance* suggest that they go beyond that of the educational or didactic pretence and act as a 'stalking horse' for erotically charged images. The 'oriental' theme also recalls 'a more archaic stage of consumer fetishism, exemplified by the tradition of the World Expositions that flourished during the middle and late nineteenth century . . .'. Referring to Walter Benjamin's concept of distraction she states: 'Visitors entered this phantasmagoria for the purpose of distraction, rehearsing modes of collective reception that were to become the domain of the entertainment industry, which in turn distracted receptivity by raising its consumers to the level of the commodity'. Miriam Hansen, *Babel and Babylon: Spectatorship in American Silent Film* (Cambridge, MA, and London: Harvard University press, 1991), p. 237.

10　Lant, 'The Curse of the Pharoah', p. 90.

11　Bailey, 'Musical Comedy', p. 183.

12　Kathryn H. Fuller, *At the Picture Show: Small-Town Audiences and the Creation of Movie Fan Culture* (Washington: Smithsonian Institution Press, 1996), p. 112.

13　For a full discussion of the association of the London West End theatres with the staging of consumption through musical comedy see Erika Diane Rappaport, *Shopping for Pleasure: Women in the Making of London's West End* (Princeton: Princeton University Press, 2000), pp. 178–214.

14　'Gaiety Picture Theatre', *What's On in Southampton*, week ending 2 October 1914.

15 Lucy Bland, *Banishing the Beast: English Feminism and Sexual Morality, 1885–1914* (London: Penguin, 1995), p. 298.

16 Southampton's status as an official emigrant station had been established in 1846 and had been extended as a main site of debarkation for the government emigrant ships which left for Australia beginning in 1853. The port's status as an emigrant depot was a significant aspect of local arguments for Southampton's suitability as a troop embarkation point for the Crimean War. Adrian Rance, *Southampton, an Illustrated History* (Southampton: Milestone Publications, 1986), p. 120.

17 Bland, *Banishing the Beast*, p. 301.

18 F.J. Monkhouse, *A Survey of Southampton and its Region* (Southampton: University of Southampton Press, 1964), p. 242.

19 Watch Committee, 'Minutes of the Proceedings of the Council and Committees from 9th Nov. 1913 to 9th Nov. 1914', Southampton City Council Archives, 2 March 1914, p. 280.

20 A significant body of work has been undertaken around this area. See: Robert C. Allen, 'Traffic in Souls', *Sight and Sound*, vol. 44, no. 1 (1974–75), pp. 50–52; Ben Brewster, 'Traffic in Souls: An Experiment in Feature Length Narrative Construction', *Cinema Journal*, vol. 31, no. 1 (Fall 199), pp. 137–47; Shelly Stamp Lindsey, '*Traffic in Souls* and the White Slavery Scare', *Persistence of Vision*, vol. 9 (1991), pp. 99–102, and 'Is any Girl Safe? Female Spectators at the White Slave Films', *Screen*, vol. 37, no. 1 (Spring 1996), pp. 1–15; Kay Sloan, *The Loud Silents: Origins of the Social Problem Film* (Urbana and Chicago: University of Chicago Press, 1988), pp. 80–86; Kevin Brownlow, *Behind the Mask of Innocence: Sex, Violence, Prejudice, Crime: Films of Social Conscience in the Silent Era* (New York: Alfred Knopf, 1990); Richard Maltby, 'The Social Evil, The Moral Order, and the Melodramatic Imagination, 1890–1915', in Jacky Bratton, Jim Cook and Christine Gledhill, eds, *Melodrama: Stage Picture, Screen* (London: BFI, 1994), pp. 214–40.

21 National Council of Public Morals (NCPM), *The Cinema: Its Present Position and Future Possibilities, Being the Report of and Chief Evidence Taken by the Cinema Commission of Inquiry Instituted by the National Council of Public Morals* (London: Williams and Norgate, 1917; New York: Arno Press and The New York Times, 1970), p. 60.

22 Lindsey, 'Is any Girl Safe?', p. 2.

23 'Southampton Shows', *The Bioscope*, 22 October 1914, p. 370.

24 Michel Foucault 'The Repressive Hypothesis: from The History of Sexuality, Volume I', in Paul Rabinow, ed., *The Foucault Reader* (London: Penguin, 1984), p. 312.

25 'Southampton Shows', *The Bioscope*, 22 October 1914, p. 370.

26 'The Gaiety', *What's On in Southampton*, week ending 31 October 1914.

27 NCPM, *The Cinema: Its Present Position*, p. 134–35.

28 Sir Arthur Quiller-Couch, 'Trilby', in *Adventures in Criticism* (London: Cambridge University Press, 1924), pp. 193–97, p. 194. The essays in this collection are all articles that had been previously published in *The Speaker*.

29 NCPM, *The Cinema: Its Present Position*, p. 140.

30 Evidence of the conditions of the kind of work women encountered in the munitions factories in and around Southampton can be found in two sources: 'Til the Boys Come Home', in Southampton Museum's Oral History Project, Special Collection, Southampton City Council Archives (no date); and Peggy Hamilton, *Three Years or the Duration: Memoirs of a Munitions Worker* (London: Peter Owen, 1978).

31 'Eastleigh Variety Theatre', *What's On in Southampton*, week ending 3 April 1915.

32 'The Grand', *What's On in Southampton*, week ending 29 May 1915.

33 'The Gaiety', *What's On in Southampton*, week ending 5 December 1914.

34 'The Gaiety', *What's On in Southampton*, week ending 12 December 1914.

35 'The Gaiety', *What's On in Southampton*, week ending 1 May 1914.

36 'The Gaiety', *What's On in Southampton*, week ending 31 July 1914.

37 'The Gaiety', *What's On in Southampton*, week ending 14 August 1914.

38 Works Committee, 'Minutes of the Proceedings of the Council and Committees', Southampton City Council Archives, 28 September, 1916, item 27.

39 The advertisements for these films in The *Southampton Times* read as follows: 'Monday/Tuesday/Wednesday Lillian Braithwaite in The World's Desire. Vibrating with heartstirring emotion and pathos. The wife's dream is fulfilled but the doctor dare not tell her the truth. His decision and it consequences are the subject of this brilliant and intensely human drama. Thursday/Friday/Saturday Her Nameless Child: Powerful drama of a brave young wife who kept her marriage a secret—and her child nameless—to save her brother's honour. Throbbing with dramatic moments this grand film play shows Elisabeth Risdon in yet another brilliant success.'

40 NCPM, *The Cinema: Its Present Position*, p. 18.

41 Epes Winthrop Sargent, *Picture Theatre Advertising* (New York: The Moving Picture World, Chalmers Publishing Company, 1915), pp. 8–9.

42 'The Amazing Mr. Fellman', *The Bioscope*, 22 April 1915, p. 311. Both this article and that by Epes Winthrop Sargent imply that the actual images on the posters may not have been necessarily from the film. This was a common practice with poster art companies often providing the same images for both plays and films.

43 Emlyn Williams, *George, An Early Autobiography* (London: Hamish Hamilton, 1961), pp. 161–62.

44 Annette Kuhn, *Cinema, Censorship and Sexuality, 1909–1925* (London: Routledge, 1988), p. 120.

45 'The Amazing Mr. Fellman'.

46 NCPM, *The Cinema: Its Present Position*, p. xlvi.

Chapter 3

1 'Southampton Shows', *The Bioscope*, 10 September 1914, p. 999.

2 'The Bioscope Parliament', *The Bioscope*, 3 September 1914, p. 873.

3 'Patriotism Imperative: The Cinema Theatre Must Help to Win the War', *The Bioscope*, 3 October 1918, p. 4.

4 Ibid.

5 These topical local films were a staple of film production and exhibition throughout the country from the mid 1890s. At the time of writing the recently discovered Mitchell and Kenyon films, the majority of which are 'local topicals', demonstrate both the popularity of these films at the time and the importance that this relationship between local audiences and the cinema holds in film history. See Vanessa Toulmin, Simon Popple and Patrick Russell, eds, *The Lost World of Mitchell and Kenyon: Edwardian Britain on Film* (London: BFI, 2004).

6 'Southampton Shows', *The Bioscope*, 18 June 1914, p. 1203.

7 Six examples of these films survive in the archives. Four in the Imperial War Museum are from the towns of Milnrow and Newhey, now part of Greater Manchester, Braintree in Essex and Chapel St. (possibly the coastal town of Chapel St. Leonards in Lincolnshire). The National Film and Television Archive holds Roll of Honour films from Westhoughton, also in Manchester, and from Preston a series of these films made by Will Onda, owner of the Prince's Theatre but also directing manager of the Will Onda regional film renters.

8 Leslie Midkiff DeBauche, *Reel Patriotism: The Movies and World War I* (Madison: University of Wisconsin Press, 1997), p. xvi.

9 *Durham County Advertiser*, 28 January 1916. I am grateful to David Williams for pointing this reference out to me.

10 The homefront imagination is a term I use to describe the relationship between the public images of the front and the reception of those images in Britain.

11 Tom Gunning, 'From the Kaleidoscope to the X-Ray: Urban Spectatorship, Poe Benjamin and *Traffic in Souls* (1913)', in *Wide Angle*, Vol. 19, no. 4 (October 1997), pp. 25–61. Travelling exhibitors often took films of the local area and its inhabitants and, in the evening, screened them to those same inhabitants, audiences who wished to see themselves, their friends and their locality. This was carried out on a Europe-wide scale by the Lumières in the late 1890s and 1900s. Discussing the Lumières' street scenes, Tom Gunning has suggested that these films take on the role of the Baudelarian *flâneur*, and he likens the cinema images of the city to the kaleidoscope: 'Instead of an evanescent and immediate experience, the transfer to film allowed the city streets to become another sort of spectacle, one mediated by the apparatus' (p. 35). Following this the familiar local space of any size town or village takes on this quality of mediated, and uncanny, spectacle.

12 Timothy Neal, Vanessa Toulmin and Rebecca Vick, 'Mitchell and Kenyon: A Successful, Pioneering and Travelled Partnership of Production', in Toulmin, Popple and Russell, *The Lost World of Mitchell and Kenyon*, pp. 6–12.

13 Ine Van Dooren and Peter Kramer, 'The Politics of Direct Address', in Karel Dibbets and Bert Hogenkamp, eds, *Film and the First World War*, (Amsterdam: University of Amsterdam Press, 1995), p. 105.

14 Richard Ohmann, *Selling Culture: Magazines, Markets and Class at the Turn of the Century* (London: Verso, 1996), pp. 244–45.

15 Rt Hon. Sir Herbert E. Maxwell, MP, 'Victoria the Well Beloved', *Pall Mall Magazine*, vol. 23 (January–April 1901), p. 414.

16 'Topics of the Hour', *Southern Daily Echo*, 8 July 1916, p. 2.

17 'Topics of the Hour', *Southern Daily Echo*, 31 August 1916, p. 2.

18 'Preston's Pictures', *The Bioscope*, 15 April 1915, p. 237.

19 Ibid.

20 Memorial films were not unfamiliar to cinema audiences at the time. Films of the assassination and funeral of McKinley famously ended with the static tableau shot of a woman in a classical gown lying at the foot of a monument upon which were projected the 'martyred presidents' Lincoln, Garfield and McKinley. The funerals of Victoria and Edward VII were popular films during the previous decade. After the death of Lord Kitchener in 1916 commemorative slides were similarly popular.

21 *Durham County Advertiser*, 28 January 1916. I surmise that these were slides based on other contemporary accounts of slides of Kitchner being 'projected'. Slides were particularly regularly reported at the Palladium in Southampton.

22 J. Morton Hutcheson, 'Music in the Cinema', *The Bioscope*, 17 August 1916, pp. 627–28. See also Hutcheson, 'Music in the Cinema', *The Bioscope*, 3 May 1917, p. 449.

23 His recommendation for the attack sequence of *Battle of the Somme* was the 'Light Cavalry' overture. It is hard now to understand how this piece fits Hutcheson's requirements of gravity without thinking of its use as a parody of military march music. I can only think of a modernday equivalent: apparently, during the week leading up to Princess Diana's funeral, programmes broadcast on the BBC were 'toned down' to avoid being incongruous with the feelings of a grieving nation.

24 Miriam Hansen, *Babel and Babylon: Spectatorship in American Silent Cinema* (Cambridge, MA: Harvard University Press, 1991), pp. 7–8.

25 Ibid., p. 13.

26 'Pathé Types', advertisement for Pathé Newsreels, *Pictures and the Picturegoer*, 28 October 1915, p. 95.

27 'Pathé Types', advertisement for Pathé Newsreels, *Pictures and the Picturegoer*, 4 November 1915, p. 115.

28 Yuri Tsivian, *Early Cinema in Russia and its Cultural Reception*, trans. Alan Bodger (London: Routledge, 1994), pp. 3–4.

29 'Queer Folks in Theatre Audience', *Bristol Observer*, 29 January 1916, p. 6.

30 Richard Sennett, *The Fall of Public Man* (London: Faber and Faber, 1977), p. 153.

31 Jennifer Green-Lewis, *Framing the Victorians: Photography and the Culture of Realism* (Ithaca, NY, and London: Cornell University Press, 1996), pp. 160–61.

32 Ibid., p. 161.

33 Sir Oliver Lodge, *Raymond or Life and Death: With Examples of the Evidence of the Survival of Memory an Affection After Death* (New York: George H. Doran and Company), 1916. pp. 113–14.

34 Ibid., pp. vii–viii.

35 Tsivian, *Early Cinema in Russia*, p. 5.

36 O.V. Vyotskaya, 'Moi Vospominia' [My Memoirs], unpublished manuscript, Institute of Russian Literature, MSS Division, no. 41, p. 42, quoted in Tsivian, *Early Cinema in Russia*, p. 4.

37 Tom Gunning, 'The Cinema of Attractions: Early Film, Its Spectator and the Avant-Garde', in Thomas Elsaesser with Adam Barker, eds, *Early Cinema: Space Frame Narrative* (London: BFI, 1990), pp. 52–62.

38 Terry Castle, 'Phantasmagoria: Spectral Technology and the Metaphorics of Modern Reverie', *Critical Inquiry*, vol. 15, no. 1 (Autumn 1988), p. 27.

39 Joanna Bourke, *Dismembering the Male: Men's Bodies, Britain and The Great War* (London: Reaktion Books 1996), p. 220.

40 Adrian Gregory, *The Silence of Memory: Armistice Day 1919–1946* (Oxford and Providence: Berg Publishers, 1994), p. 22.

41 Lou Taylor has suggested that this is '. . . perhaps an attempt to rationalise and cope with the deaths—a way of making the sacrifice and loss more bearable, and demonstrating that the deaths had not been in vain nor the lives of the loved ones wasted'. She also suggests that these restricting forms of mourning were associated with the kind of repressive rituals of Victorian society generally and they were discarded by women as a result of the '. . . freedoms won during the 1914–18 war'. Lou Taylor, *Mourning Dress: A Costume and Social History* (London: George Allen and Unwin, 1983), pp. 268–70.

42 Raymond Williams, *The Politics of Modernism: Against the New Conformists* (London: Verso, 1989), pp. 37–48.

43 Dominic Hibbard *Wilfred Owen, War Poems and Others* (London: Chatto and Windus, 1973) p. 63. Samuel Hynes attributes this comment to mean the paintings of the Somme battlefield that were displayed in London in 1917. However, I would like to suggest that it is entirely possible that he is referring to the film since it was being circulated to the troops at this time and that 'pictures' was the common term for the cinema at this time. In either case the point to emphasise here is not only the disparity between homefront imagination and those at the front but the private communication of it to those at home. Samuel Hynes, *A War Imagined: The First World War and English Culture* (London: Bodley Head, 1990).

44 Vanessa Schwartz, 'Cinematic Spectatorship before The Apparatus: The Public Taste for Reality in *Fin de Siècle* Paris', in Leo Charney and Vanessa Schwartz, eds, *Cinema and the Invention of Modern Life* (Los Angeles: University of California Press, 1995), p. 229.

45 George du Maurier, *Trilby* (London: Everyman, 1994), p. 86.

46 'These Were Picked Up Where Our Soldiers Fell', *Daily Sketch*, 15 September 1914, p. 1.

Chapter 4

1 Aristotle, *Poetics*, trans. Ingram Bywater, *On the Art of Poetry* (Oxford: Clarendon Press, 1920), pp. 52–53.

2 From Wilfred Owen, 'Preface' to a volume intended to include only his war poems, in Dominic Hibberd, ed, *Wilfred Owen: War Poems and Others* (London, Chatto and Windus, 1973), p. 137.

3   'The Topical "War" Drama', *The Bioscope*, 21 January 1915, p. 205.
4   S.D. Badsey, 'Battle of the Somme: British War Propaganda', *Historical Journal of Film, Radio and Television*, vol. 3 (1983), pp. 91–115.
5   Modris Ecksteins, *Rites of Spring: The Great War and the Birth of the Modern Age* (London: Bantam, 1989), p. 318.
6   Ibid.
7   Nicholas Reeves, 'Cinema, Spectatorship and Propaganda: "Battle of the Somme" (1916) and its Contemporary Audience', *Historical Journal of Film Radio and Television*, vol. 17, no.1 (1997), p. 23.
8   For a full discussion of the changes in the relationship between the War Office and the film industry see Nicholas Hiley, 'Making War: The British News Media and Government Control, 1914–16', PhD thesis, Open University, 1985; the relationship in terms of the issue of exhibition of the official films is detailed in sections 3 and 4. See also Nicholas Reeves, *Official Film Propaganda During the First World War* (London: Croom Helm, 1986). This is an invaluable source of information on the production contexts of these films.
9   Miriam Hansen, *Babel and Babylon: Spectatorship in Early Silent Film* (Cambridge, MA: Harvard University Press, 1991), p. 95.
10 Miriam Hansen, 'Whose Public Sphere?', in Thomas Elsaesser with Adam Barker, eds, *Early Cinema: Space, Frame, Narrative* (London: BFI, 1990), p. 231.
11 Ibid., p. 233.
12 Nicholas Hiley, 'The British Cinema Auditorium', in Karel Dibbets and Bert Hogenkamp, eds, *Film and the First World War* (Amsterdam: Amsterdam University Press, 1995) p.166.
13 Quoted in Hiley, 'Making War', p. 400.
14 Reeves, *Official Film Propaganda*, p. 49.
15 Hiley, 'Making War', p. 366.
16 Ibid.
17 Ibid., p. 382.
18 John Springhall, ' "Up Guards and At Them!" British Imperialism and Popular Art, 1880–1914', in John MacKenzie, ed., *Imperialism and Popular Culture* (Manchester: Manchester University Press, 1986), pp. 49–72.
19 T.D., 'The Real Film Hero', *Pictures and the Picuregoer*, week ending 27 January 1917, p. 376.
20 *Yorkshire Evening Press*, 17 October 1916, p. 1.
21 Quoted in Richard Schickel, *D.W. Griffith and the Birth of Film* (London: Pavilion Books, 1984), p. 353.
22 Reeves, *Official Film Propaganda*, p. 157.
23 To my knowledge there is no evidence that the faked scenes were shot after Urban had seen the initial rushes.
24 Hiley, 'Making War', pp. 437 and 469.
25 An example of this is a story that ran in the *Southern Daily Echo* on Monday, 10 July 1916 entitled 'Battle of the Somme. The Preliminary Phases—Terrific Bombardment by British Guns.—Dazed German Prisoners'. The structure of the article reproduces the structure of the battle; the preliminary phases, the 'effect on the enemy', the 'chaos of sound', 'the attack' and ending with a section titled 'British Heroism'.

26 Urban to Brade, 1 March 1918, Science Museum/Urban Papers 1:URB 4/3, cited in Hiley, 'Making War', p. 453.

27 *Southern Daily Echo*, 14 September 1916, p. 1.

28 'Dramatic Scene at Southampton Docks: The Outward and Inward Bound, A Profound Moment', *Southern Daily Echo*, 7 July 1916, p. 4. As the main port where the wounded of the Somme returned, newspaper coverage of this in the local press was extensive.

29 National Council of Public Morals (NCPM), *The Cinema: Its Present Position and Future Possibilities, Being the Report of Chief Evidence taken by the Cinema Commission of Inquiry Instituted by the National Council of Public Morals* (London: Williams and Norgate, 1917; New York: Arno Press and the New York Times, 1970), p. 132.

30 *Sir Douglas Haig's Great Push: The Battle of the Somme* (London: Hutchinson and Co., 1916), part 1, pp. 24–29. The series of photographs taken from the shot of 'hidden batteries' is depicted in the magazine as shells bursting over a German trench. The film clearly depicts it as hidden batteries, a fact that is borne out by the movement of a horse across the screen in the background, lending a perspective to the image that the photographic reproduction of the magazine does not allow.

31 Ibid., p.24.

32 NCPM, *The Cinema, Its Present Position*, p. 137.

33 Ibid., p. lxv.

34 Ibid., p. lxiv.

35 Ibid., p. llx.

36 Ibid.

37 *Kinematograph and Lantern Weekly*, 7 September 1916, p. 121.

38 *Kinematograph and Lantern Weekly*, 14 September 1916, p. 91.

39 Tom Gunning, 'The World as Object Lesson: Cinema Audiences, Visual Culture and the St. Louis World's Fair, 1904', *Film History*, vol. 6, no. 4 (1995), p. 444.

40 Ibid., pp. 423–24.

41 *Southern Daily Echo*, 2 September 1916. There are numerous such accounts and it was undoubtedly one of the primary attractions of the official war films. The music columnist for *The Bioscope*, J. Morton Hutcheson, wrote of the film *The Battle of the Ancre and the Advance of the Tanks* (1917): 'Everyone has an interest in this war, and will naturally flock to see what father, husband, brother, sweetheart, relative, or friend is going through for us at home. I myself "spotted" an old friend of touring days at one of the clearing stations and have been able to "dig" him out after many years', 'Music in the Cinema', *The Bioscope*, 25 January 1917, p. 368.

42 'Film That Will Make History', *Kinematograph and Lantern Weekly*, 10 August 1916, p. 7.

43 Giuliana Bruno, *Streetwalking on a Ruined Map: Cultural Theory and the City Films of Elvira Notari* (Princeton: Princeton University Press, 1993), p. 172.

44 C.T. Atkinson, *The Royal Hampshire Regiment, Volume Two, 1914–1918*, printed for the regiment by Robert Maclehose & Co. Ltd. (Glasgow: Glasgow University Press, 1952).

45 Hiley, 'The British Cinema Auditorium', p. 168.

46 Adrian Gregory, *The Silence of Memory: Armistice Day 1919–1946*, (Oxford and Providence: Berg Publishers, 1994), p. 20.

47 Ibid.

48 Ibid.

49 Ibid., p. 22.

50 Ibid., p. 23. See also Elizabeth Kubler Ross, *On Death and Dying* (London: Tavistock, 1970), Geoffrey Gorer, *Death Grief and Mourning in Contemporary Britain* (London: Cresset, 1965). Gregory also cites David Cannadine, 'War and Death, Grief and Mourning in Modern Britain', in Joachim Whaley, ed., *Mirrors of Mortality: Studies in the Social History of Death* (London: Europe, 1981), pp. 187–252.

51 'Somme: Impressions of the Great Battle Picture', *The Film Renter*, 16 September 1916.

52 See Reeves, 'Cinema, Spectatorship and Propaganda', pp. 9–21. In this section of his article Reeves provides a number of examples of published responses to the film.

53 Peter Brooks, *The Melodramatic Imagination: Balzac, Henry James, Melodrama and the Mode of Excess* (New Haven, CT: Yale University Press, 1976, new edn 1995).

54 Mary Ann Doane, 'Melodrama, Temporality, Recognition: American and Russian Silent Cinema', *East West Film Journal*, vol. 4, no. 2 (June 1990), pp. 106–28. Franco Moretti, *Signs Taken For Wonders: Essays In the Sociology of Literary Forms* (London: New Left Books, 1988).

55 'Orbatus to the Editor', *The Times*, 5 September 1916, p. 6. Quoted in Reeves, 'Cinema, Spectatorship and Propaganda', p. 18.

56 Quoted in Marie Seton, 'War', *Sight and Sound*, vol 6, no. 24 (Winter 1937–38), pp. 183–84.

57 Ibid., p. 184

58 Reeves, 'Cinema, Spectatorship and Propaganda', p. 18.

59 A report in the 'Scottish Section' of *The Bioscope*, 15 February 1917, p. 737, stated that *The Battle of Ancre and the Advance of the Tanks* had '. . . not been a success on their first run. It may be that so many houses, city and urban were showing them, and it may be that the public were fed up with war pictures, but the fact remains . . . it failed to draw.'

60 Geoffrey Klingsporn, 'Icon of Real War: A Harvest of Death and American War Photography', *The Velvet Light Trap*, no. 45 (Spring, 2000), pp. 4–19, p. 17.

61 Geoffrey H. Malins, *How I Filmed the War*, ed. Low Warren (London: Herbert Jenkins, 1920), pp. 303–4.

62 Ibid., p. 8.

63 'H. Hensley Henson, 'Letter to the Editor', *The Times*, 1 September 1916, p. 7.

64 Daniel Pick, *War Machine: The Rationalisation of Slaughter in the Modern Age* (New Haven, CT, and London: Yale University Press, 1993), pp. 165–66.

65 *Russell's Handbook of Southampton* (Southampton: Russell and Co., 1925), p. 58.

66 *Southern Daily Echo*, 2 September 1916, p. 1.

67 Hiley, 'The British Cinema Auditorium', p. 167.

68 This phrase was printed on advertisements for the film throughout Britain.

Chapter 5

1 Percy Nash, 'Some Thoughts on Film Producing', *Kinematograph Year Book, Film Diary and Directory*, 1916, p. 451.

2 Ibid.

3 D.W. Griffith, 'The Birth of a Nation', *Kinematograph Year Book, Film Diary and Directory*, 1916, p. 450.

4 Ibid., p. 449.

5 Stefan Collini, *Public Moralists: Political Thought and Intellectual Life in Britain, 1850–1930*, (Oxford: Clarendon Press, 1991) pp. 78–79. Collini has drawn attention to this 'culture of altruism' in late Victorian intellectual culture which raised '. . . the question of how to stimulate the imaginative sympathy necessary to provide 'enduring motives to noble action . . .'.

6 Cecil Chesterton, 'An Explanation', Scala film theatre programme for the premiere of *The Birth of A Nation* in London, 27 September 1915, p. 2.

7 *Pall Mall Gazette*, 27 September 1915, p. 8.

8 David W. Blight, 'W.E.B. Du Bois and the Struggle for American Historical Memory', in Genevieve Fabre and Robert O'Mealley, eds, *History and Memory in African-American Culture* (New York and Oxford: Oxford University Press, 1994), pp. 45–71.

9 'The Birth of a Nation', *The Era*, 29 September 1915, p. 7.

10 'Stageland and Thereabouts', *Reynold's Newspaper*, 3 October 1915, p. 8.

11 Public Record Office WO95/1495· Southampton, in Hampshire, was the main port used for the transportation of wounded and the 1st Hampshire Regiment had suffered officer casualties of almost one hundred per cent. J.M. Winter, *The Great War and the British People*, (London: MacMillan, 1985), p. 81. Winter has shown that war-related male mortality figures for the year 1915 were 68,000. The figure for the year 1916 was 123,000. Although the increase from 1914 to 1915 was from 27,000–68,000 the 1915–16 figures show the largest increase in numbers of war-related deaths throughout the war.

12 'Magnificent Presentation of a Great Picture. The Birth of a Nation at the Scala', *The Bioscope*, 30 September 1915, pp. 1515–16.

13 Zoë Josephs, ed., *Birmingham Jewry, Volume II*, (Birmingham: The Birmingham Jewish History Research Group, 1984), p. 106.

14 'The Birth of a Nation', *The Era*, 29 September 1915, p. 7.

15 'Magnificent Presentation of a Picture. The Birth of a Nation at the Scala', *The Bioscope*, 30 September 1915, pp. 1515–16.

16 *The Times*, 28 September 1915, p. 5b.

17 'The Super Film', *The Bioscope*, 4 May 1916, p. 6.

18 Ibid.

19 'Colston Hall and Cinema Shows: A Definite Issue Involved, Decision of the Licensing Justices', *Bristol Observer*, 28 October 1916, p. 4.

20 At the Grand Theatre in Southampton the prices ranged from 3/3 for the circle to 7d in the Gallery. The highest price paid in fixed-site cinemas in 1916 was 1s. The average price was 3d. Tickets for the theatrical screening, then, were at least more than twice the price of a normal night at the local cinema.

21 'Stageland and Thereabouts', *Reynold's Newspaper*, 3 October 1915, p. 3.

22 *Pall Mall Gazette*, 27 September 1915, p. 8.
23 'Some Facts About "The Clansman": D.W. Griffith's Biggest on Record', *The Bioscope*, 10 December 1914. Samuel Hynes points to a similar image of war as the 'ultimate field sport' in the cavalry textbook *Our Cavalry* by Major General M.F. Rimmington, published in 1912: 'The addiction to manly, and especially to rough and dangerous, field sports must be regarded as an immense asset towards efficiency for war. . . . We particularly want the hunting breed of man, because he goes into danger for the love of it', quoted in Samuel Hynes, *The Soldiers' Tale: Bearing Witness to Modern War* (London: Pimlico, 1998), p. 33.
24 The ban on cameramen at the front lasted effectively until October 1915 when the War Office made an agreement with Cinematograph Trade Topical Committee. This resulted in the creation of the British Topical Committee for War Films, which produced a series of six short films that were unsuccessful. These differed little from the type of footage seen in the newsreels from Gaumont Graphic and Pathé Gazette, showing the parade of soldiers marching and military hardware but nothing that approximated the type of action being reported in the press. *Britain Prepared* was the product of Wellington House under the direction of Charles Masterman, who later in June 1916 produced *Battle of the Somme*. See Luke McKernan, *Topical Budget: The Great British News Film* (London: BFI, 1992, pp. 11–12 and pp. 36–37.
25 'Peeps at the Hidden War: Official Picture of Armegeddon', *The Bioscope*, 23 March 1916, p. 1235.
26 *The Bioscope*, 23 March 1916, p. 1235.
27 Kevin Brownlow, *The War, the West and the Wilderness* (London: Secker and Warburg, 1979), p. 149.
28 Paul Virilio, *War and Cinema: The Logistics of Perception*, trans. by Patrick Camiller (London: Verso, 1989), p. 12.
29 *Pall Mall Gazette*, 27 September 1915, p. 8.
30 '"The Birth of a Nation" Remarkable Production at Colston Hall', *Western Daily Press*, 3 October 1916, p. 7.
31 'Stageland and Thereabouts', *Reynold's Newspaper*, 3 October 1915, p. 3.
32 'The Birth of a Nation', *The Era*, 29 September 1915, p. 7.
33 'History by Cinema. The Possibilities of a new Educational Force. "The Birth of a Nation" Exhibited at Coventry', *Coventry Herald*, 23 and 24 June 1916, p. 6.
34 Daniel Pick, *War Machine: The Rationalisation of Slaughter in the Modern Age*, (New Haven, CT, and London: Yale University Press, 1993), p. 15.
35 'History by Cinema. The Possibilities of a new Educational Force. "The Birth of a Nation" Exhibited at Coventry', *Coventry Herald*, 23 and 24 June 1916, p. 6.
36 Tom Gunning, *D.W. Griffith and the Origins of American Film Narrative: The Early Years at Biograph* (Urbana: University of Illinois Press, 1991).
37 Michael Allen, *Family Secrets: The Feature Films of D.W. Griffith*, (London: BFI, 1999), pp. 54–55.
38 This was not lost on the advertisers, who were trying to direct specific meanings through relating the wartime experience to the film. One of the black ball advertisements, which ran in the *Coventry Herald* on 16 and 17 June 1916 and

in the Southampton *Southern Daily Echo* on 25 October 1916, stated : 'Every woman who has given a loved one to fight his country's battles will feel the appeal of this heart-searching and historic story . . . Magnificent in its vastness, it is yet splendid in its ever-recurring touches of Romance, Mother Love, and Womanly sacrifice'.

39 Chesterton, 'An Explanation'.

40 Ibid.

41 '"The Birth of a Nation" An American Odyssey', *The Bioscope*, 9 September 1915.

42 James C. Robertson, *The British Board of Film Censors: Film Censorship in Britain, 1896–1950*, (London: Croom Helm, 1985), p. 11. What is striking is that *The Bioscope* believed that the film would gain a release in the cinemas. This suggests that Sol Levy had yet to make the deal for the rights to the film at the time the article went to press.

43 Three things arise out of this review. First, the use of the Ku Klux Klan seemed to generate, in the local and national press, no overtly negative reactions. Second, the authorial presence is recognised in terms of the effective presentation of the story. Most intriguing, however, is the fact that in the copy that I have been working with, which is the Kevin Brownlow restored version, this scene appears but there is no title to explain it. (It may be that the journalist was drawing on Thomas Dixon's novel *The Clansman* or a version of the play and was simply elucidating the scene for readers. It could also point to the existence of footage or a title that is now missing. In any case this points to the value of connecting the traces of spectatorship through the use of local reviews with the restoration imperatives of the archive.)

44 "Peeps at the Hidden War: Official Picture of Armegeddon', *The Bioscope*, 23 March 1916, p. 1235.

45 'Carrying on the Advance' is the last intertitle in the film.

46 P. Sommerfield, 'Patriotism and Empire', in John MacKenzie, ed., *Imperialism and Popular Culture* (Manchester, Manchester University Press, 1986), pp. 17–48, p. 32.

47 P. Buitenhuis, *The Great War of Words* (Vancouver: University of British Columbia Press, 1987), p. 30.

48 'We Hear—', *Advertising Weekly*, 2 January 1915, p. 288.

49 'Letter from F. Graham, Star Pictures, 180 Devonshire Street, Sheffield, 18 January 1918', Selig Collection, Academy of Motion Picture Arts and Sciences, folder 48.

50 Benedict Anderson, *Imagined Communities* (London: Verso, 1983), pp. 24–25. His metaphor and example for this is the daily newspaper.

51 'History by Cinema. The Possibilities of a new Educational Force. "The Birth of a Nation" Exhibited at Coventry', *Coventry Herald*, 23 and 24 June 1916, p. 6.

52 'Magnificent Presentation of a Great Picture. "The Birth of a Nation" at the Scala', *The Bioscope*, 30 September 1915, p. 1515.

53 Sommerfield, 'Patriotism and Empire', p. 34.

54 'Uncle Tom's Cabin, Pictured by World's Film Corporation of New York', *Kinematograph and Lantern Weekly*, 27 April 1916.

55 For a lucid account of the shifting role blackface minstrelsy performed in the expression of vernacular tradition in Hollywood cinema see Peter Stanfield, '"An Octoroon in the Kindling": American Vernacular and Blackface Minstrelsy in 1930s Hollywood', *Journal of American Studies*, vol 31, no. 3 (1998), pp. 407–38.

56 Sommerfield, 'Patriotism and Empire', p. 35.

57 *Southern Daily Echo*, 31 October 1916. The song 'In the Gloaming', by Meta Orrid and Annie F. Harrison, is English in origin and was introduced into the USA in 1877. Gloaming is an English word for twilight. The song is an example of the nostalgic songs that were popular in the mid-nineteenth century. Using the voice of a dead lover the lyrics recall a golden past cut short by tragedy: 'Though I passed away in silence,/Left you lonely set you free, for my heart was crushed with longing,/What had been could never be,/It was best to leave you thus my dear, best for you and best for me'.

58 L. Glazer and S. Key, 'Carry Me Back: Nostalgia for the Old South in Nineteenth Century Popular Culture', *Journal of American Studies*, vol. 30, no. 1 (April 1996), pp. 1–24.

59 In an odd reversal of the 'minstrelsy-to-legitimacy' trajectory *The Perfect Song* became the signature tune for the *Amos 'n' Andy* radio show in the USA in the 1930s and 1940s.

60 'Letter from Frank S. Manson', Selig Collection, Academy of Motion Picture Arts and Sciences, folder 48.

61 'Letter from E. Hounsell', Selig Collection, Academy of Motion Picture Arts and Sciences, folder 48.

62 'The Super-Film', *The Bioscope*, 4 May 1916, p. 6.

Chapter 6

1 'The C.E.A. Parliament: Last Week's Session at Birmingham', *The Bioscope*, 14 June 1917, pp. 1047–48.

2 Rachael Low, *The History of the British Film, 1914–1918* (London: George Allen and Unwin, 1950), p. 24. Low suggests that the increasing attendances at the cinema during the war was capitalised on by the larger halls '. . . which could best bear the rising costs of exhibition. It was not an absolute lack of patronage which ruined many a small man, but his own competitive stupidity'.

3 Kevin Brownlow, *The War the West and the Wilderness* (London: Secker & Warburg, 1979), pp. 69–77.

4 Sydney Bacon's Picture Circuit is listed in the *Kinematograph Year Book, Film Diary and Directory* for 1914 and 1915. The circuit consisted of five cinemas: the Electra Palace in London, the Olympia in Newcastle, the Public Hall and Her Majesty's Theatre, both in Carlisle, and the Public Hall in Kent. The Palladium does not appear as a part of the circuit, which suggests that Bacon was a silent partner.

5 Sir Sidney Kimber, *Thirty-Eight Years of Public Life, 1910–1948* (Southampton: privately published, 1949), pp. 20–21.

6 'The Southampton Shows', *The Bioscope*, 4 June 1914, p. 1054.

7 The summer season in Britain was difficult for exhibitors because of the warm weather and the competition from summer fairs and other outside activities.

8 Nicholas Hiley, 'The British Cinema Auditorium', in Karel Dibbets and Bert Hogenkamp, eds, *Film and the First World War* (Amsterdam: Amsterdam University Press, 1995), pp. 160–68.

9 'Cinema Notes', *Southern Daily Echo*, 15 January 1914, p. 4.

10 'A Retrospect of the Year', *Kinematograph Year Book, Film Diary and Directory*, 1915, p. 19.

11 'Southampton Shows', *The Bioscope*, 8 October 1914, p. 166.

12 'Southampton Shows', *The Bioscope*, 13 August 1914, p. 643.

13 The Palace had been able to secure exclusive 'first time screened' films for Sunday evening performances, probably because it was a part of the MacNaughton's music hall circuit. Films were booked for the circuit as a whole through well-established relationships with renters. It was also common practice for exhibitors to work through the same renter and therefore share programmes. As the Alexandra, the larger High Street cinema located a short distance from the Palace, screened Keystones regularly at this time, it is possible that such an arrangement was made between the two.

14 Kristin Thompson, *Exporting Entertainment: American in the World Film Market 1907–1934* (London: BFI, 1985), p. 82.

15 As an indicator of the kind of market saturation for Chaplin films in Southampton between 1914 and 1918, I have found only a two-week period between mid-March and early April 1916 when it was not possible to see a Chaplin film at one of the cinemas. The general tendency was that most cinemas showed at least one Chaplin programme per month and some, like the Carlton, advertised 'A Chaplin on every programme.'

16 In fact the Palladium ran very few Essanay Chaplins, but did secure an exclusive run of the Mutual Chaplins in 1917. Interestingly, this coincides with Chaplin's increasing control over his films and his development of the mixture of pathos and humour that would characterise his later work, and is arguably the focal point of the elevation of Chaplin to the status of artist in the critical discourse of the period.

17 Richard Koszarski, *An Evening's Entertainment: The Age of the Silent Feature Picture, 1915–1928* (Berkeley: University of California Press, 1990), p. 163. Koszarski quotes Horace Plimpton, Edison's production manager, arguing that 'the theatres in residential sections are more likely to do better with long films because families are able, or more apt, to make an evening's entertainment out of their visit, whereas those catering to more transient trade are better off with more and shorter subjects' ('How Long Should Films Be?', *New York Dramatic Mirror*, 24 February 1915, p. 22). According to Koszarski, US picture palaces eventually adopted a policy of showing features and shorts on a variety programme (p. 164). The Palladium showed significant foresight by adopting such a policy by 1914. Nevertheless, in Britain, as Stratton's letter shows, while the solution was eventually the same, the sets of problems for exhibitors differed significantly from those in the USA as outlined by Plimpton.

18 'Letter from D. Stratton', Selig Collection, Academy of Motion Picture Arts and Sciences, folder 55.

19 Charles A. Beard, 'A Frenchman in America', *The New Republic*, vol. 51, no. 653 (8 June 1927), pp. 75–76. Beard's reference is to the House–Grey Memorandum of February 1916, through which Wilson made a 'probable' commitment to a US entry into the war if the Germans declined to attend a peace conference he proposed to call.
20 *Photoplay Journal*, August 1916, p. 135. I would like to thank Kevin Brownlow for his generosity in sharing his notes. Of course any factual errors or misinterpretations are entirely my own.
21 'Civilisation. Great Spectacular Film to be seen in England. Interview with Mr. R.K. Bartlett', *The Bioscope*, 25 January 1917, p. 307.
22 'Thomas H. Ince's "Civilisation", Coming Great American Sensation that is Said to Eclipse Anything Before Shown', *Kinematograph and Lantern Weekly*, 25 January 1917, p. 32.
23 'Civilisation: A Stupendous Production', *Kinematograph and Lantern Weekly*, 8 February 1917, p. 25.
24 'A Great Spectacular Triumph. Civilisation—The Supreme Art of Thomas H. Ince—The War Through Neutral Spectacles', *The Bioscope*, 8 February 1917, pp. 544–45.
25 'Civilisation: Super-film at the Palladium', *Southern Daily Echo*, 25 August 1917, p. 2.
26 'The Palladium', *Southern Daily Echo*, 28 August 1917, p. 2.
27 Ibid.
28 The account of the changes to the film for the British market are as follows: 'Away went the introductory title subtitle: "Can we call ourselves civilized when we shut our eyes against the command of the Prince of Peace—Love the Neighbor as thyself?" Luther Rolfe was spared any change of name—his own sounded German enough—but he was transformed into a Socialist'. The King was changed to Emperor. 'The similarity of the fictitious country Wredpryd to Germany caused this British version to run into trouble. How could Christ,— hardly ever shown on the screen in England—appear to British audiences in the guise of a German officer? The emphasis was hurriedly altered; Count Ferdinand's body returned to earth merely animated by the spirit of Christ'. Additional recruiting scenes were also shot 'To ensure the film's acceptance in Britain . . .', Brownlow, *The War, the West and the Wilderness*, p. 77.
29 'Topics of the Hour', *Southern Daily Echo*, 28 August 1917, p. 3.
30 Susan Zeiger, 'She Didn't Raise her Boy to be a Slacker: Motherhood, Conscription, and the Culture of the First World War', *Feminist Studies*, vol. 2, (Spring 1996), pp. 6–39.
31 Sharon Ouditt, *Fighting Forces, Writing Women, Identity and Ideology in the First World War* (London: Routledge, 1994), pp. 139–40.
32 The Red Cross and the military made considerable efforts to hide the convalescing soldiers from public display. However, the enormous number of casualties meant that on average two full trains per day were loaded at Southampton Docks and were taken to Netley Hospital, so it was possible either through direct witness or by word of mouth to get a sense of the severity of the situation. For a detailed account of the embarkation of the wounded from

Southampton to Netley Hospital see Philip Hoare, *Spike Island: The Memory of a Military Hospital* (London: Fourth Estate, 2001), pp. 175—95.

Chapter 7

1 National Council of Public Morals (NCPM), *The Cinema: Its Present Position and Future Possibilities, Being the Report of Chief Evidence taken by the Cinema Commission of Inquiry Instituted by the National Council of Public Morals* (London: Williams and Norgate, 1917; New York: Arno Press and the New York Times, 1970), p. 39. This is Legge's response to a question by the Cinema Commission about children's ability to become 'absorbed in the cinema'.

2 Nicholas Hiley, 'The British Cinema Auditorium', in . Karel Dibbets and Bert Hogenkamp, eds, *Film and the First World War* (Amsterdam: Amsterdam University Press, 1995), p. 161.

3 NCPM, *The Cinema: Its Present Position*, p. 360. Unfortunately the names of the comedians or film companies were left out of the published report. However the comic gag of 'expectorating' appeared as a cartoon in *Pictures and the Picturegoer* as part of the series 'Scenes We are Sick of'. This depicted Chaplin spitting his drink out onto a large man in bowler hat and checked suit underneath a sign that says 'Gentlemen are requested not to spit'. This series seems to be part of a general tendency by 1918 to present this type of comedy as old fashioned in the ever changing and progressing film industry. Crucially the point to the cartoon is that it is the audience who are tiring of this type of gag.

4 NCPM, *The Cinema: Its Present Position*, pp. 352–353.

5 Lady Florence Bell, *At the Works: A Study of a Manufacturing Town* (1907; London: Virago, 1985), p. 131.

6 Ibid., pp. 134–35.

7 'Exit Worry—Enter Picture', *Pictures and Picturegoer*, week ending 27 March 1916, p. 538.

8 'A Remedy For All Depression', *The Bioscope*, 21 June 1917, p. 1219. The film *The Cure* was released in the USA by Mutual on 16 April 1917 and had had its trade show by June. The Mutuals were handled by the J.D. Walker Company in Britain.

9 'Letter from Percival Lee', Selig Collection, Academy of Motion Picture Arts and Sciences, Folder 49.

10 David Robinson, *Chaplin: His Life and Art*, (1985; New York: Da Capo Press, 1994), p. 147. Langford Reed was Chaplin's publicist in Britain.

11 As the war progressed soldiers were given latitude when off the line at the front and at home on leave. Army policy at the front had been to allow entertainments such as concert parties, where the men would put on their own shows, drawing primarily from music hall and pantomime. While at the divisional level these live entertainments were relatively mild those at the brigade or battalion level were often very 'hot and strong'. J.G. Fuller has shown that these entertainments 'reinforced the soldier's habit of attempting to defuse the horrors of their situation through humour.' J.G. Fuller, *Troop Morale and*

Popular Culture in the British and Dominion Armies 1914–1918 (Oxford: Clarendon Press, 1990), p. 110.

12 Fuller notes that the 'domestic music hall remained overwhelmingly popular as a resort for soldiers on leave', Fuller, *Troop Morale*, p. 124

13 'Winchester Note', *What's On in Southampton*, week ending 10 July 1915.

14 'Trade Topics', *The Bioscope*, 8 July 1915, p. 125.

15 'Trade Topics', *The Bioscope*, 15 July 1915, p. 254.

16 I am persuaded by Henry Jenkins' reasons for using the term *anarchistic* rather than *anarchic* as it '. . . first, preserves a sense of process in the texts, a movement from order to disorder, while anarchic comedy might suggest a constant state of anarchy; second anarchistic comedy foregrounds the active central role of the clowns as bringers of anarchy'. I recognise that he is concerned to qualify his term in this way in the service of his argument for a consideration of the dynamic relationship between the formal and ideological dictates of the classical Hollywood style and the vaudeville aesthetic in early sound comedies, but the term is useful for this study in establishing that this comic form, which was prevalent and exceedingly popular at the critical moment of the formation of the Hollywood style, also exemplifies negotiations with the formal and ideological dictates for clarity and comprehension as they were perceived by British producers, distributors and exhibitors.

17 Robinson, *Chaplin*, p. 64.

18 'Sunday Evening At the Palace', *What's On in Southampton*, week ending 14 November 1914.

19 Langford Reed, 'Chaplin's Wonderful "Feat"', *The Bioscope*, 29 July 1915, p. 524.

20 Kristin Thompson, *Exporting Entertainment: America in the World Film Market, 1909–1934* (London: BFI, 1985), pp. 82–83. Thompson has shown that this was a turning point in the history of US film distribution in Britain where the open market system began to be replaced by this exclusive system: 'Over the next five years, that system [the open market] turned completely around, so that theatres contracted sometimes for one or two years in advance, for films which had not been previewed, or even made. Britain went from being one of the most flexible, open markets in the world to one of the most rigid, closed ones. The system perpetuated the American firm's advantage, since it kept the theatres tied to their larger outputs, eliminating open playdates into which other countries' films might slip.'

21 'Keystone Night at Bolton: A Record House', *The Bioscope*, 25 June 1914, p. 1353.

22 Keystone advertisement, *The Bioscope*, 30 July 1914, pp. xviii and xix.

23 'The Keystone Comedy Quartette', *The Bioscope Supplement*, 20 August 1914, pp. xx–xxi. Although these were the first advertisements to appear in the trade press mentioning Chaplin by name the actual British release dates are unclear. In the *Bioscope Supplement* of 4 June 1914 the Western Import Company published the release dates of the films. *Making a Living* appears in the advertisement as being released on 18 June 1914. The delay between US and British release dates varied considerably but generally it was anywhere from three to six months. The US release date for *Making a Living* is given by David

Robinson as 2 February 1914 (see Robinson, *Chaplin*, p. 700). All of the US release dates for his films are from this source. By June 1914, Chaplin had already made twenty films for Keystone and the possibility that other films such as *Kid's Auto Races* (7 February 1914) or *Tango Tangles* (9 March 1914) had been released in Britain prior to 18 June cannot be discounted. However, close examination of both *The Bioscope* and *What's On in Southampton* suggest that if they had been released prior to that date there was no attempt to 'boom' Chaplin. The fact that none of the sixteen cinemas in Southampton named any Chaplin films on their programme before June is a fair indication that his first appearance on British screens was with *Making a Living*.

24 Robinson, *Chaplin*, pp. 700–10.

25 Ibid., p. 114.

26 Charles Maland, *Chaplin and American Culture: The Evolution of a Star Image* (Princeton: Princeton University Press, 1989), p. 4.

27 Ibid., p. 26.

28 'Teeside Topics', *The Bioscope*, 23 July 1914, p. 378.

29 Charles Musser, 'Work, Ideology and Chaplin's Tramp', *Radical History Review*, vol. 41 (1988), pp. 36–66.

30 'Reprinted from the "Umpire"', *What's On in Southampton*, week ending 22 April 1916. p. 1.

31 This last photograph could possibly be from the same session as the 1910 photograph of Chaplin and 'the inebriate' in Karno's *Mumming Birds* sketch that David Robinson has included in *Chaplin* (the first set of photographs in the book).

32 Charles Chaplin, *My Autobiography*, (London: Bodley Head, 1964; London: Penguin Books, 1966), p. 149.

33 Chaplin films exist in a number of different versions and it is extremely difficult to assign authority to a particular one. I am using a version that has French titles and appears on *The Chaplin Collection*, Madacy Music Group Inc. 1993.

34 Chaplin, *My Autobiography*, p. 149. David Robinson in *Chaplin: His Life and Art* offers a perspective on Chaplin's recollection of this incident and suggests that this bit of business was 'the oldest joke in cinema' and that Mabel probably knew this. See pp. 120–21.

35 For an illuminating discussion of the development of the Keystone style during this period see Douglas Riblet's 'The Keystone Film Company', in Kristine Brunovska Karnick and Henry Jenkins, eds, *Classical Hollywood Comedy* (London: Routledge, 1995), pp. 168–89. See also Peter Kramer 'Vitagraph, Slapstick and Early Cinema', *Screen*, vol. 29, no. 2 (Spring 1988), pp. 190–210 on Keystone's emphasis on comic action in relation to the general shift in comedy film production toward characterisation and the development of star personas in the late 1910s and 1920s.

36 Musser, 'Work, Ideology and Chaplin's Tramp', also Eileen Bowser 'Subverting the Conventions: Slapstick as Genre', in Eileen Bowser, ed., *The Slapstick Symposium* (Brussels: Federation Internationale des Archives du Film, 1988), pp. 13–16.

37 See Gerry Turvey, 'Weary Willie and Tired Tim Go into Pictures: The Comic Films of the British and Colonial Kinematograph Company', and Frank Gray

'George Albert Smith's Comedies of 1897', both in Alan Burton and Laraine Porter, eds, *Pimple Pranks and Pratfalls: British Comedy Before 1930* (Trowbridge: Flicks Books, 2000), pp. 69–75 and pp. 17–23.

38 Robinson, *Chaplin*, p. 131.

39 Jon Oates Lord, 'The Visitor', *What's On in Southampton*, 19 September 1914, p. 3.

40 Jeffrey Weeks, *Sex, Politics and Society: The Regulation of Sexuality since 1800* (2nd edn, London and New York: Longman, 1981), p. 199.

41 Ibid., p. 214.

42 NCPM, *The Cinema: Its Present Position*, pp. 240–41.

43 Weeks, *Politics and Society*, cites both the Association for Moral and Social Hygiene, Committee of Enquiry into Sexual Morality, London 1918 and the files in the Public Record Office: HO 45/10526/141896: 'Indecency on Hampstead Heath', 1906–1919. p. 228.

44 'Peeping Polls', *The John Bull*, 5 February 1916, p. 6.

45 'Kissing—A Crime', *The John Bull*, 3 June 1916, p. 7.

46 'Cupid's Corner; Weekly Chat with Sweethearts and Wives: Walks With Wounded Soldiers', *The Family Journal*, 2 September 1916.

47 Michael Deane, 'Charlie's New Job', *Pictures and the Picturegoer*, 13 May 1915, p. 103.

48 This relationship is at the centre of an earlier Keystone film *The Star Boarder* (released 4 April 1914, directed by George Nichols and screenplay by Craig Hutchinson).

49 Judith Walkowitz, *City of Dreadful Delight: Narratives of Sexual Danger in Late-Victorian London* (London: Virago Press, 1992); and Erika Diane Rappaport, *Shopping for Pleasure: Women in the Making of London's West End* (Princeton: Princeton University Press, 2000).

50 Walkowitz, *City of Dreadful Delight*, p. 50.

51 Ibid.

52 Ibid., p. 51.

53 Ibid.

54 As a counter to my reading Glenn Mitchell has noted that there is an implication that the two women played by Cecile Arnold and Vivian Edwards are prostitutes. '. . . When Charlie decides to follow the brunette [Edwards] instead of buying a drink, he examines his money as if to decide which commodity to purchase. Similarly, one might query Chester's status with Cecile Arnold (herself sporting a stereotypical "streetwalker" kiss-curl) when she gives him a sum of money retrieved from her shoe. Such references appear in several non-Chaplin Keystones of the period, and must have been quite shocking to contemporary audiences.' Such a reading I believe could certainly be possible for British audiences at the time but would remain implied rather than explicit. Glenn Mitchell, *The Chaplin Encyclopedia* (London: B.T. Batsford, 1997) p. 257.

55 Musser, 'Work, Ideology and Chaplin's Tramp', p. 45.

56 From 'Til the Boys Come Home', Southampton Museum's Oral History Project, Special Collection, Southampton City Council Archives, no date given.

57 Elizabeth Roberts, *A Woman's Place: An Oral History of Working Class Women 1890–1940* (London: Basil Blackwell, 1984), p. 71.

58 Ibid., p. 71.

59 Miriam Hansen, 'The Mass Production of the Senses: Classical Cinema as Vernacular Modernism', in Christine Gledhill and Linda Williams, eds, *Reinventing Film Studies* (London: Arnold, 2000), p. 343.

60 'Notes By a Neutral', *The Times*, 28 August 1915, p. 5, col. b.

61 The existence of such parallels in the USA and Britain are striking in even a cursory glance at the histories of reform and social regulation on both sides of the Atlantic. Charles Maland has shown that the genteel tradition was central to Chaplin's reception in the USA while Annette Kuhn has traced the regulating practices of quasi-official bodies such as the NCPM in Britain. See Maland, *Chaplin and American Culture*, pp. 14–20, and Kuhn's *Cinema, Censorship and Sexuality 1909–1925* (London: Routledge, 1987), pp. 28–48. The writing on this issue is much wider, however; a few examples are: Lawrence Levine, *Highbrow/Lowbrow: The Emergence of Cultural Hierarchy in America* (Cambridge, MA: Harvard University Press, 1988); Stow Persons, *The Decline of American Gentility* (New York: Scribner's, 1973); Daniel Pick, *Faces of Degeneration: A European Disorder* (London: Yale University Press, 1989).

62 Riblet, 'The Keystone Film Company', p. 186.

63 Musser, 'Work, Ideology and Chaplin's Tramp', p. 48.

64 Jay Winter, *The Great War and the British People* (London: MacMillan Education, 1985), p. 267.

65 George Bernard Shaw, 'Preface to W.H. Davies', *The Autobiography of a Super-tramp*' in *Prefaces by George Bernard Shaw* (London: Odhams Press, 1938), p. 798.

66 Maland, *Chaplin and American Culture*.

67 Shaw, 'Preface to W.H. Davies', pp. 798–99.

68 Shaw, 'Ellen Terry and Bernard Shaw: A Correspondence', in *Prefaces by George Bernard Shaw*, p. 789.

69 Lois Rutherford, 'Harmless Nonsense: The Comic Sketch and the Development of Music Hall Entertainment', in J.S. Bratton, ed., *Music Hall: Performance and Style* (Milton Keynes: Open University Press, 1986), p. 142.

70 This is from an interview Laurel did with John McCabe and is quoted in Robinson, *Chaplin*, p. 86.

71 Max Beerbohm, 'The Laughter of the Public', *Pall Mall Magazine*, vol. 26 (January–April 1902), p. 423.

72 Robert S. Duncan, 'The Future of Screen Comedy', *The Bioscope*, 17 January 1918, p. 9. I have inserted the particular Chaplin films he was referring to in brackets.

73 Ibid.

74 See Henry Jenkins, *What Made Pistachio Nuts: Early Sound Comedy and the Vaudeville Aesthetic* (New York: Columbia University Press, 1992). Jenkins's discussion of the appeal of the Sidney Drew comedies helps to provide a link between the more thoughtful humour advocated by Duncan with its dependence on sentimentality. Jenkins uses Epes Winthrop Sargent's numerous articles in the Hollywood-based *Motion Picture World* to trace industry discourse

on the future of humour in order to provide backstory for the introduction of the vaudeville aesthetic in the early sound comedies. In this account the Sidney Drew comedies provide the template for Sargent's call for 'thoughtful humour'. 'Drew's insistence on the subordination of gags to plot, the linkage of comic plots to real-world situations, and the need for a higher degree of audience identification made him the ideal champion of Sargent's comic aesthetic'. (p. 54) Sidney Drew's background in legitimate theatre further accounts for his insistence on naturalistic acting. Jenkins has pointed out that this emphasis 'allowed for a broader range of emotional experiences than could be offered by the more gag-centred comedies' (p. 56). Paradoxically this is the same appeal that Sennett makes but with the important difference that it is naturalistic *performance* that makes the gag more effective rather than the narrative more believable.

75 E.M., 'The Science of Laughter; Comedy and the Critics: Is Slapstick Doomed?', *The Kinematograph and Lantern Weekly*, 16 May 1918, p. 57.

76 For example Lefebvre notes that in Chaplin films '. . . the critique of everyday life takes the form of a living dialectical pair: on the one hand, "modern times" (with everything they entail: bourgeoisie, capitalism, techniques and technicity) and on the other, the Tramp. The relation between them is not a simple one. In a fiction truer than reality as it is immediately given, they go on producing and destroying one another ceaselessly. In this way the comic produces the tragic, the tragic destroys the comical and vice versa, . . . It is in the spectator personally that the Charlie Chaplin constantly manages to unite these two ever-present and conflicting aspects, the tragic and the comical; laughter always manages to break through; and like the laughter of Rabelais, Swift and Molière (i.e. the laughter of their readers and audiences) it denies, destroys, liberates. Suffering itself is denied , and this denial is put on display. In this fictitious negation we reach the limits of art.' Henri Lefebvre, *The Critique of Everyday Life*, Vol. 1, trans. John Moore (London: Verso, 1991), p. 13.

77 Rutherford, 'Harmless Nonsense',p. 151.

78 Jenkins, *What Made Pistachio Nuts*, p. 49.

79 E.M., 'The Science of Laughter'.

80 Mack Sennett, 'Over-Acting Fatal in Comedy Work; Being Natural the Surest Way to get Desired Results', *The Bioscope*, 7 June 1917, p. 989.

81 Ibid.

82 Lefebvre, *The Critique of Everyday Life*, p. 13.

83 Walter Benjamin, 'One Way Street', trans. Edmund Jephcott, in Marcus Bullock and Michael W. Jennings, eds, *Selected Writings: 1913–1926* (Cambridge, MA: Harvard University Press, 1996), p. 476.

Chapter 8

1 'A Retrospect of Nineteen Hundred and Seventeen: A Few Recollections and Reflections', *Kinematograph Year Book, Film Diary and Directory*, 1918, p. 29.

2 National Council of Public Morals (NCPM), *The Cinema: Its Present Position and Future Possibilities, Being the Report of Chief Evidence taken by the Cinema*

Commission of Inquiry Instituted by the National Council of Public Morals (London: Williams and Norgate, 1917; New York: Arno Press and the New York Times, 1970), p. lxxix.

3 Ibid., p. lxvii.
4 Ibid., p. lxi.
5 'A Retrospect of Nineteen Hundred and Seventeen', p. 21.
6 NCPM, *The Cinema: Its Present Position*, p. lxiii.
7 Ibid., p. lxii.
8 'Exhibitors and their Trials', *The Bioscope*, 13 June 1918, p. 54.
9 Luke McKernan, *Topical Budget; The Great British News Film* (London: BFI, 1992). McKernan notes that rental increases of Pictorial News (Official) was partly due to an increasing number of cinemas accepting the newsreel and the effective distribution of the films by Jury's Imperial Pictures.
10 Nicholas Reeves, *Official British Film Propaganda During the First World War* (London: Croom Helm, 1985), pp. 180–84. Reeves points out that the production of feature official war films did not cease and three films *The British Offensive*, *The Life of an RAF Officer in France* and *Britain's Future Air Fighters* (1918) were produced in the last year of the war.
11 'Letter from the Manager of the Popular Cinema Company in Llanelly Wales, 3 March 1918', Selig Collection, Academy of Motion Picture Arts and Sciences, Folder 48.
12 J.M. Winter, *The Great War and the British People* (London: MacMillan Education, 1986), p. 139.
13 Ibid.
14 'Letter from the Manager of the The Paladium, Lichfield, 13 July 1918', Selig Collection, Academy of Motion Picture Arts and Sciences, Folder 48.
15 Benedict Anderson, *Imagined Communities Reflections on the Origins and Spread of Nationalism* (London: Verso, 1992), p. 23.
16 Ibid., p. 26.
17 Erich Auerbach, *Mimesis: The Representation of Reality in Western Literature*, trans. Willard Trask (Garden City, NJ: Doubleday Anchor, 1957), quoted in Anderson, *Imagined Communities*, p. 24.
18 Anderson, *Imagined Communities*, p. 24.
19 Robert Graves, *Undertones of War* (1928), quoted in Paul Fussell, *The Great War and Modern Memory* (London: Oxford University Press, 1975), p. 73.
20 Anderson, *Imagined Communities*, p. 24.
21 Walter Benjamin, *Illuminations* (London: Fontana Press 1992) p. 253.
22 Reeves, *Official British Film Propaganda*, p. 181. There is little evidence that this film was ever released, a fact that is undoubtedly connected to the overwhelming evidence of cinema audiences' dissatisfaction with war pictures as feature attractions.
23 'Hearts of the World: Griffith's Great War Picture, An Unparalleled Spectacle', *The Bioscope*, 27 June 1918, p. 9.
24 From the souvenir programme sold for 3d at Scala Super Cinema in Liverpool, dated 18November 1918. From the Anderson Collection, BFI.
25 E. Codd, 'The War Film and D.W. Griffith', *Pictures and the Picturegoer*, 13–20 July 1918, pp. 55–56.

26 E. Codd, *Kinematograph Weekly*, 25 July 1918.
27 Reeves, *Official British Film Propaganda*, p. 122. Reeves calculates these from WOCC papers. This total is as of August 1919. The total for *Birth of a Nation* is an estimate based on an interview with Victor Saville in Zoë Josephs, ed., *Birmingham Jewry, Volume II* (Birmingham: The Birmingham Jewish History Research Group, 1984), p. 106, see chapter 7.
28 Lillian Gish later remembered that the film had been released just at the end of the war and '. . . enjoyed great success until the Armistice when people lost interest in war films'. She was referring to the American success of the film, which was significantly greater than that of Britain, Lillian Gish, with Anne Pinchot, *The Movies Mr. Griffith and Me* (London: Columbus Books, 1988), p. 201.
29 Ibid., p. 201. Gish commented that Griffith had regretted making the film so brutal in this way: 'I don't believe that Mr. Griffith ever forgave himself for making Hearts of the World. "War is the villain," he repeated, "not any particular people."'
30 Advertisement for *Shoulder Arms*, *The Bioscope*, 26 September 1918, pp. 62–63.
31 'Charlie and the Zepp: An Original and Topical Chaplin Comedy', *The Film Renter*, 23 December 1916, p. 2.
32 'Charlie Chaplin: Why See Films of a Briton Too Rich to Fight?', *Daily Mail*, 23 March 1916, p. 3.
33 'Concerning Charlie', *The John Bull*, 8 April 1916, p. 3.
34 Andrew James Horrall, 'Music Hall, Transportation and Sport: Up To Dateness in London Popular Culture 1890–1914', unpublished PhD thesis, Faculty of History, University of Cambridge, October 1997, p. 34.
35 This version can be found in *Songs that Won the War*, collected and edited by S. Louis Girard (London: Lane Publications, 1930), p. 96.
36 F.T. Nettleingham, 2nd Lieutenant R.F.C., ed., *Tommy's Tunes* (London: Eskine MacDonald, 1917), p. 23.
37 Ibid., p.42.
38 Horrall, 'Music Hall, Transportation and Sport', p. 34.
39 Lieutenant-Colonel F.J. Roberts, M.C., *The Wipers Times* (London: Eveleigh, Nash and Grayson, 1930).
40 J.G. Fuller, *Troop Morale and Popular Culture in the British and Dominion Armies, 1914–1918* (Oxford: Clarendon Press, 1991), p. 112.
41 'Chaplin Defended', *What's On in Southampton*, week ending 8 April 1916, p. 6. Vernon Castle was one half of the famous husband and wife dancing partnership Vernon and Irene Castle. Castle was English by birth and at the time was serving in the British army at the front as a pilot.
42 From *The Weekly Despatch*, June 1917, quoted in David Robinson, *Chaplin: His Life and Art* (London: Da Capo Press, 1995), p. 185. David Robinson has suggested that Northcliffe was seeking a kind of retribution for the successful halt of publication of an unauthorised biography by Rose Wilder Lane, *Charlie Chaplin's Own Story*.
43 Quoted in Tonie and Valmie Holt, *In Search of the Better 'Ole: The Life, the Works and the Collectables of Bruce Bairnsfather* (Portsmouth: Milestone Publications, 1985), p. 55.

44 P.W. Lewis, *Blasting and Bombardiering* (1967), pp. 37–38. Quoted in Fuller, *Troop Morale*, p. 147.

45 Quoted in Holt, *In Search of the Better 'Ole*, p. 41.

46 'The Laughter That Runs With Death, by A. Private', *The John Bull*, 19 April 1916, p. 7.

47 Holt, *In Search of the Better 'Ole*, p. 110.

48 Quoted in ibid., p. 41.

49 Quoted in ibid., pp. 60–61.

50 George Pearson, *Flashback: The Autobiography of a British Filmmaker* (London: George Allen and Unwin. 1957), p. 70.

51 Ibid., p. 71.

52 'Criticisms of the Films; *The Better 'Ole*', *The Bioscope*, 25 April 1918, p. 27.

53 Ibid.

54 Pearson, *Flashback*, p. 73.

55 *The Bioscope*, 25 April 1918, p. 27.

56 *The Bioscope*, 21 November 1918, p. 29.

57 Miriam Bratu Hansen, 'Benjamin and Cinema Not a One Way Street', *Critical Inquiry*, vol. 25 (Winter 1999), p. 329.

58 Ibid.

59 Ibid., p. 332.

60 Ibid., p. 340.

61 Advertisement for *Shoulder Arms*, *Kinematograph Weekly*, 21 November 1918, p. 33.

Conclusion

1 National Council of Public Morals (NCPM), *The Cinema: Its Present Position and Future Possibilities, Being the Report of Chief Evidence taken by the Cinema Commission of Inquiry Instituted by the National Council of Public Morals* (London: Williams and Norgate, 1917; New York: Arno Press and the New York Times, 1970), p. lix.

2 Ibid., p. xliv.

3 Ibid., p. xlv.

4 Ibid., p. lix.

5 Rachael Low *The History of the British Film: 1918–1929* (London: George Allen and Unwin, 1971), p. 46.

6 Leslie Midkiff DeBauche, *Reel Patriotism: The Movies and World War I* (Madison: University of Wisconsin Press, 1997), p. xvi.

7 George Emlyn Williams, *George, An Early Autobiography* (London: Hamish Hamilton, 1961), pp. 158–59.

Bibliography

Collections

The James Anderson Collection, Special Collections, British Film Institute, London

William F. Jury Collection, Special Collections, British Film Institute, London

The Southampton Council Minutes from 1914–18, 'Proceedings of the Council and Committees', Special Collection, Southampton City Council Archives

Southampton Museum's Oral History Project, Special Collection, Southampton City Council Archives

Selig Collection, Margaret Herrick Library, Academy of Motion Picture Arts and Sciences, Beverly Hills, California

Journals

Trade Journals
The Bioscope
The Era
The Film Renter
Kinematograph and Lantern Weekly
Kinematograph Year Book
Photoplay Journal
The Picture Palace News, 1913–15
Pictures and the Picture Goer

Newspapers
Bristol Observer
Coventry Herald
Daily Sketch

The John Bull
Lancashire Daily Post
Pall Mall Gazette
Reynold's Newspaper
Southampton Times
Southern Daily Echo
Southern District and Pictorial
The Times
What's On in Southampton
Yorkshire Evening Press

Magazines
Punch
The Pall Mall Magazine
Sir Douglas Haig's Great Push: The Battle of the Somme

Reports

The National Council of Public Morals, *The Cinema: Its Present Position and Future Possibilities, Being the Report of Chief Evidence taken by the Cinema Commission of Inquiry Instituted by the National Council of Public Morals* (London: Williams and Norgate, 1917; New York: Arno Press and the New York Times, 1970)

Pamphlets and Programmes

Programme for *The Birth of a Nation*, Scala Theatre, London, 25 September 1915 (from the Anderson Collection, BFI)
Programme booklet for preview screening of *Hearts of the World*, Palace Theatre, London, 23 June 1918 (from the Anderson Collection, BFI)
Russell's Handbook of Southampton (Southampton: Russell and Co., 1925)
Souvenir programme for *Hearts of the World*, Scala Super Cinema in Liverpool dated 18 November 1918 (from the Anderson Collection, BFI)

Books and Articles

Allen, Michael, *Family Secrets: The Feature Films of D.W. Griffith* (London: BFI, 1999)

Allen, Robert C., 'From Exhibition to Reception: Reflections on the Audience in Film History', *Screen*, vol. 31, no. 4 (Winter 1990), pp. 347–56

——, 'Traffic in Souls', *Sight and Sound*, vol. 44, no. 1 (1974–75), pp. 50–52

——, and Douglas Gomery, *Film History: Theory and Practice* (New York: Alfred A. Knopf, 1985)

Anderson, Benedict, *Imagined Communities: Reflections on the Origin and Spread of Nationalism* (London: Verso, 1992)

Aristotle, *Poetics*, trans. Ingram Bywater, in *On the Art of Poetry* (Oxford: Clarendon Press, 1920), pp. 52–53

Atkinson, C.T., *The Royal Hampshire Regiment, Volume Two, 1914–1918* (printed for the regiment by Robert Maclehose & Co. Ltd.; Glasgow: Glasgow University Press, 1952)

Austin, Bruce A., *The Film Audience: An International Bibliography of Research* (Metuchen, NJ: The Scarecrow Press, 1983)

Badsey, Stephen, 'Battle of the Somme: British War Propaganda', *Historical Journal of Film, Radio and Television*, vol. 3 (1983), pp. 99–115

Bailey, Peter, ed., *Music Hall: The Business of Pleasure* (Milton Keynes: Open University Press, 1986)

——, 'Musical Comedy and the Rhetoric of the Girl', in Peter Bailey, ed., *Popular Culture and Performance in the Victorian City* (Cambridge: Cambridge University Press, 1998), pp. 175–93.

——, *Popular Culture and Performance in the Victorian City* (Cambridge: Cambridge University Press, 1998)

Beard, Charles A., 'A Frenchman in America' *The New Republic*, vol. 51, no. 653 (8 June 1927), pp. 75–76

Beerbohm, Max, 'The Laughter of the Public', *Pall Mall Magazine*, vol. 26 (January–April 1902), p. 423

Bell, Lady Florence, *At the Works: A Study of a Manufacturing Town* (1907; London: Virago, 1985)

Benjamin, Walter, *Illuminations* (London: Fontana Press 1992)

——'One Way Street', trans. Edmund Jephcott, in Marcus Bullock and Michael W. Jennings, eds, *Selected Writings: 1913–1926* (Cambridge, MA: Harvard University Press, 1996), pp. 444–88

Berry, David, and Simon Horrocks, *David Lloyd George: The Movie Mystery* (Cardiff: University of Wales Press, 1998)

Bland, Lucy, *Banishing the Beast: English Feminism and Sexual Morality 1885–1914* (London: Penguin, 1995)

Blight, David W., 'W.E.B. Du Bois and the Struggle for American Historical Memory', in Genevieve Fabre and Robert O'Mealley, eds, *History and Memory in African-American Culture* (New York and Oxford: Oxford University Press, 1994), pp. 45–71

Bordwell, David, Janet Staiger and Kristin Thompson, *The Classical Hollywood Cinema: Film Style and Mode of Production to 1960* (New York: Columbia University Press, 1985)

Bouissac, Paul, *Circus and Culture: A Semiotic Approach* (Bloomington: Indiana University Press, 1976)

Bourdieu, Pierre, *Distinction: A Social Critique of the Judgement of Taste* (Cambridge, MA: Harvard University Press, 1984)

——, *In Other Words* (Cambridge: Polity Press 1990)

——, *The Field of Cultural Production: Essays on Art and Literature* (Cambridge: Polity Press, 1993)

Bourke, Joanna, *Working Class Cultures in Britain, 1890–1960: Gender, Class and Ethnicity* (London: Routledge, 1994)

——, *Dismembering the Male: Men's Bodies, Britain and the Great War* (London: Reaktion Books, 1996)

Bowser, Eileen, 'Subverting the Conventions: Slapstick as Genre', in Eileen Bowser, ed., *The Slapstick Symposium*, May 1985, The Museum of Modern Art, New York (Brussels: Federation Internationale des Archives du Film, 1988), pp. 13–16

Bratton, J.S., *Music Hall: Performance and Style* (Milton Keynes: Open University Press, 1986)

Brittain, Vera, *Testament of Youth* (London: Virago, 1999)

Brooks, Peter, *The Melodramatic Imagination* (New York: Columbia University Press, 1984)

Brownlow, Kevin, *The War the West and the Wilderness* (London: Secker & Warburg, 1979)

——, *Behind the Mask of Innocence* (London: Jonathan Cape, 1990)

Bruno, Giuliana, *Streetwalking on a Ruined Map: Cultural Theory and the City Films of Elvira Notari* (Princeton: Princeton University Press, 1993)

Buitenhuis, Peter, *The Great War of Words: British, American and Canadian Propaganda and Fiction* (Vancouver: University of British Columbia Press, 1987)

Burrows, Jon, *Legitimate Cinema: Theatre Stars in Silent British Films, 1908–1918* (Exeter: University of Exeter Press, 2003)

Cannadine, David, 'War and Death, Grief and Mourning in Modern Britain', in Joachim Whaley, ed., *Mirrors of Mortality: Studies in the Social History of Death* (London: Europe, 1981), pp. 187–252

Carbine, Mary, 'The Finest Outside the Loop: Motion Picture Exhibition in Chicago's Black Metropolis, 1905–1928', *Camera Obscura*, vol. 23 (May 1990), pp. 9–41

Castle, Terry, 'Phantasmagoria: Spectral Technology and the Metaphorics of Modern Reverie', *Critical Inquiry*, vol. 15, no. 1 (Autumn 1988) pp. 26–61

Cave, Terence, *Recognitions: A Study in Poetics* (Oxford: Clarendon Press, 1988)

Crump, Jeremy, 'Provincial Music Hall: Promoters and Public in Leicester, 1863–1929', in Peter Bailey, ed., *Music Hall: The Business of Pleasure* (Milton Keynes: Open University Press, 1986), pp. 53–72.

Davidoff, Leonore, Megan Doolittle, Janet Fink and Katherine Holde, *The Family Story: Blood, Contract and Intimacy, 1830–1960* (New York: Longman, 1999)

DeBauche, Leslie Midkiff, *Reel Patriotism: The Movies and World War I* (Madison: University of Wisconsin Press, 1997)

Dibbets, Karel, and Hogenkamp, Bert, eds, *Film and the First World War* (Amsterdam: Amsterdam University Press, 1995)

Doane, Mary Ann, 'Melodrama, Temporality, Recognition: American and Russian Silent Cinema', *East West Film Journal*, vol. 4, no. 2 (June 1990), pp. 106–28

Ecksteins, Modris, *Rites of Spring: The Great War and the Birth of the Modern Age* (London: Bantam, 1989)

Eyles, Allen, and Keith Skone, *London's West End Cinemas* (Sutton: Keystone Publications, 1991)

Fiske, John, *Reading the Popular* (London: Unwin Hyman, 1989)

Foucault, Michel, 'The Repressive Hypothesis: from The History of Sexuality, Volume I', in Paul Rabinow , ed., *The Foucault Reader* (London: Penguin, 1984). pp. 12–145

Fuller, Kathryn J., *At the Picture Show: Small Town Audiences and the Creation of Movie Fan Culture* (Washington and London: Smithsonian Institution Press, 1996)

Fuller, J.G., *Troop Morale and Popular Culture in the British and Dominion Armies 1914–1918* (Oxford: Clarendon Press, 1990)

Fussell, Paul, *The Great War And Modern Memory* (London: Oxford University Press, 1975)

Girard, S. Louis, ed., *Songs that Won the War* (London: Lane Publications, 1930)

Gish, Lillian, with Anne Pinchot, *The Movies Mr. Griffith and Me* (London: Columbus Books, 1988)

Glazer, L., and S. Key, 'Carry Me Back: Nostalgia for the Old South in Nineteenth Century Popular Culture' *Journal of American Studies*, vol. 30, no. 1 (April 1996), pp. 1–24

Gomery, Douglas, *Shared Pleasures: A History of Movie Presentation in the United States* (Madison: University of Wisconsin Press, 1992)

Gorer, Geoffrey, *Death Grief and Mourning in Contemporary Britain* (London: Cresset, 1965)

Gray, Frank, 'George Albert Smith's Comedies of 1897' in Alan Burton and Laraine Porter, eds, *Pimple Pranks and Pratfalls: British Comedy Before 1930* (Trowbridge: Flicks Books, 2000), pp. 17–23

Gregory, Adrian, *The Silence of Memory: Armistice Day 1919–1946* (Oxford/Providence: Berg Publishers, 1994)

Green-Lewis, Jennifer, *Framing the Victorians: Photography and the Culture of Realism* (Ithaca, NY, and London: Cornell University Press, 1996)

Gunning, Tom, *D.W. Griffith and the Origins of the American Film Narrative: The Early Years at Biograph* (Urbana: University of Illinois Press, 1991)

——, 'The World as Object Lesson: Cinema Audiences, Visual Culture and the St. Louis World's Fair, 1904', *Film History*, vol. 6, no. 4 (1995), pp. 420–50

——, 'From the Kaleidoscope to the X-Ray: Urban Spectatorship, Poe Benjamin and *Traffic in Souls* (1913)', *Wide Angle*, vol. 19, no. 4 (October 1997), pp. 25–61

Hamilton, Peggy, *Three Years Or The Duration: The Memoirs of a Munitions Worker* (London: Peter Owen, 1978)

Hansen, Miriam, 'Whose Public Sphere?', in Thomas Elsaesser with Adam Barker, eds, *Early Cinema: Space, Frame, Narrative* (London: BFI, 1990), pp. 228–46

——, *Babel and Babylon; Spectatorship in American Silent Film* (Cambridge, MA: Harvard University Press, 1991)

——, 'Benjamin and Cinema Not a One Way Street', *Critical Inquiry*, vol. 25, Winter 1999, pp. 306–44

——, 'The Mass Production of the Senses: Classical Cinema as Vernacular Modernism', in Christine Gledhill and Linda Williams, eds, *Reinventing Film Studies* (London: Arnold, 2000), pp. 332–50

Hepworth, Cecil, *Came the Dawn: Memories of a Film Pioneer* (London: Phoenix House, 1951)

Hibberd, Dominic, *Wilfred Owen, War Poems and Others* (London: Chatto and Windus, 1973)

Higson, Andrew, 'The Concept of National Cinema', *Screen*, vol. 30, no. 4 (Autumn 1989), pp. 36–47

——*Waving the Flag: Constructing a National Cinema in Britain* (Oxford: Clarendon Press, 1995)

Hiley, Nicholas, 'The British Cinema Auditorium', in Karel Dibbets and Bert Hogenkamp, eds, *Film and the First World War* (Amsterdam: Amsterdam University Press, 1995), pp. 160–70

Hoher, Dagmar, 'The Composition of Music Hall Audiences, 1850–1900', in Peter Bailey, ed., *Music Hall: The Business of Pleasure* (Milton Keynes: Open University Press, 1986), pp. 73–93

Holt, Tonie, and Valmai, *In Search of the Better 'Ole: The Life, the Works and the Collectables of Bruce Bairnsfather* (Portsmouth: Milestone Publications, 1985)

Hynes, Samuel, *The Soldier's Tale: Bearing Witness to Modern War* (London: Pimlico, 1998)

Jauss, Hans Robert, 'Literary History as a Challenge to Literary Theory', in *Toward an Aesthetic of Reception* , trans. Timothy Bahti (Brighton: Harvester Press, 1982) pp. 20–22

Jenkins, Henry, *What Made Pistachio Nuts: Early Sound Comedy and the Vaudeville Aesthetic* (New York: Columbia University Press, 1992)

Jones, Gareth Stedman, *Studies in English Working Class History 1832–1982* (Cambridge: Cambridge University Press, 1983)

Josephs, Zoë, ed., *Birmingham Jewry, Volume II* (Birmingham: The Birmingham Jewish History Research Group, 1984)

Karnick, Kristine Brunovska, and Henry Jenkins, *Classical Hollywood Comedy* (London: Routledge, 1995)

Klinger, Barbara, 'Digressions at the Cinema: Reception and Mass Culture', *Cinema Journal*, vol. 28, no. 4 (Summer 1989), pp. 3–19

——, *Melodrama and Meaning: History, Culture, and the Films of Douglas Sirk* (Bloomington and Indianapolis: Indiana University Press, 1994)

——, 'Film History Terminable and Interminable: Recovering the Past in Reception Studies', *Screen*, vol. 38, no. 2 (Summer 1997), pp. 107–29

Klingsporn, Geoffrey, 'Icon of Real War: A Harvest of Death and American War Photography', *The Velvet Light Trap*, no. 45 (Spring 2000), pp. 4–19

Koszarski, Richard, *An Evening's Entertainment: The Age of the Silent Feature Picture, 1915–1928* (Berkeley: University of California Press, 1990)

Kramer, Peter, 'The Making of a Comic Star: Buster Keaton and the Saphead', in Kristine Brunovska Karnick and Henry Jenkins, eds, *Classical Hollywood Comedy*, (London: Routledge, 1995), pp. 190–210

Kubler Ross, Elizabeth, *On Death and Dying* (London: Tavistock, 1970)

Kuhn, Annette, *Cinema, Censorship and Sexuality, 1909–1925* (London: Routledge, 1988)

Lant, Antonia, 'The Curse of the Pharoah, or How Cinema Contracted Egyptomania', in Matthew Bernstein and Gaylyn Studlar, eds, *Visions of the East: Orientalism in Film* (London: I.B. Tauris, 1997), pp. 69–98

Lefebvre, Henri, *The Critique of Everyday Life, Volume One*, trans. John Moore (London: Verso, 1991)

Levine, Lawrence, *Highbrow/Lowbrow: The Emergence of Cultural Hierarchy in America* (Cambridge, MA: Harvard University Press, 1988)

Leybourne, Keith, 'The Guild of Help and the Community Response to Poverty 1904–c.1914', in Keith Leybourne, ed., *Social Conditions, Status and Community 1860–c.1920*, (Stroud: Sutton Mill Publishing, 1997) pp. 9–28

——, ed., *Social Conditions, Status and Community 1860–c.1920*, (Stroud: Sutton Mill Publishing, 1997)

Lindsey, Shelly Stamp, '*Traffic in Souls* and the White Slavery Scare', *Persistence of Vision*, no. 9 (1991), pp. 99–102,

——, 'Is any Girl Safe? Female Spectators at the White Slave Films', *Screen*, vol. 37, no. 1 (Spring 1996), pp. 1–15

Lodge, Sir Oliver J., *Raymond or Life and Death: With Examples of Evidence for Survival of Memory and Affection after Death* (New York: George H. Doran Company, 1916)

Low, Rachael, *The History of the British Film 1914–1918* (London: George Allen and Unwin, 1950)

——, *The History of the British Film, 1918–1929* (London: George Allen and Unwin, 1971)

Lowe, R., 'The Ministry of Labour, 1916–1919: A Still, Small Voice?', in Kathleen Burk, ed., *The War and the State* (London: Allen and Unwin, 1982), pp. 157–81

MacKenzie, John M., *Propaganda and Empire; The Manipulation of British Public Opinion 1880–1960* (Manchester: Manchester University Press, 1984)

——, *Imperialism and Popular Culture* (Manchester: Manchester University Press, 1986)

McKernan, Luke, *Topical Budget: The Great British News Film* (London: BFI, 1992)

Maland, Charles J., *Chaplin and American Culture; The Evolution of a Star Image* (Princeton: Princeton University Press)

Malins, Geoffrey, *How I Filmed the War*, ed. by Low Warren (London: Herbert Jenkins, 1920)

Maltby, Richard, 'The Social Evil, The Moral Order, and the Melodramatic Imagination, 1890–1915', in Jacky Bratton, Jim Cook and Christine Gledhill, eds, *Melodrama: Stage Picture, Screen* (London: BFI, 1994), pp. 214–40

du Maurier, George, *Trilby*, ed. and with accompanying text by Leonee Ormond (London: Everyman, 1992)

Mellor, G.J., *The Northern Music Hall: A Century of Popular Entertainment* (Gateshead: Howe Brothers, 1970)

Merritt, Russell, 'Dixon, Griffith, and the Southern Legend', *Cinema Journal*, vol. 12, no. 1 (Fall 1972), pp. 26–45

——, 'The Making of Hearts of the World', *Quarterly Review of Film Studies* (Winter 1981), pp. 45–65

Metz, Christian, *Psychoanalysis and Cinema: The Imaginary Signifier*, trans. Michael Taylor (New York: Oxford University Press, 1982)

Monkhouse, F.J. ed., *A Survey of Southampton and Its Region* (Southampton: Southampton University Press, 1964)

Montgomery, John, *Comedy Films: 1894–1954* (London: George Allen and Unwin, 1954)

Moretti, Franco, *Signs Taken for Wonders: Essays in the Sociology of Literary Forms.* (London: New Left Books, 1988)

Musser, Charles, 'Work, Ideology and Chaplin's Tramp' *Radical History Review*, vol. 41 (1988), pp. 36–66

Nettleingham, F.T., ed., *Tommy's Tunes* (London: Eskine MacDonald, 1917)

Ohmann, Richard, *Selling Culture: Magazines, Markets, and Class at the Turn of the Century* (London and New York: Verso, 1996)

Ouditt, Sharon, *Fighting Forces, Writing Women, Identity and Ideology in the First World War* (London: Routledge, 1994)

Patterson, A. Temple, *A History of Southampton 1700–1914* (Southampton: Southampton at the University Press, 1975)

Pearson, George, *Flashback: The Autobiography of a British Filmmaker* (London: George Allen and Unwin, 1957)

Persons, Stow, *The Decline of American Gentility* (New York: Scribner's, 1973)

Petro, Patrice, *Joyless Streets: Women and Melodramatic Representation in Weimar Germany* (Guildford: Princeton University Press, 1989).

Pick, Daniel, *Faces of Degeneration: A European Disorder* (London: Yale University Press, 1989)

——, *War Machine: The Rationalisation of Slaughter in the Modern Age* (New Haven, CT, and London: Yale University Press, 1993)

Potter, Paul, *Trilby* (the play), in *Trilby and Other Plays: Four Plays for Victorian Star Actors* ed. with an introduction by George Taylor (Oxford and New York: Oxford University Press, 1996)

Quiller-Couch, Sir Arthur, 'Trilby', in Arthur Quiller-Couch, *Adventures in Criticism* (London: Cambridge University Press, 1924), pp. 193–97

Raitt, Suzanne, and Trudi Tate, *Women's Fiction and the Great War* (Oxford: Clarendon Press, 1997)

Rance, Adrian, *Southampton, An Illustrated History* (Southampton: Milestone Publications, 1986)

Rappaport, Erika Diane, *Shopping for Pleasure: Women in the Making of London's West End* (Princeton: Princeton University Press, 2000)

Reed, Langford, *The Chronicles of Charlie Chaplin: The 'Official' Chaplin Book Based on the Essanay-Chaplin Photoplays* (London, New York, Toronto, Melbourne: Cassell, 1916)

Reeves, Nicholas, *Official Film Propaganda During the First World War* (London: Croom Helm, 1986)

——, 'Cinema, Spectatorship and Propaganda', *Historical Journal of Radio, Film and Television*, vol. 17, no. 1 (1997), pp. 5–28

Riblet, Doug, 'The Keystone Film Company and the Historiography of Slapstick', in Kristine Brunovska Karnick and Henry Jenkins, eds, *Classical Hollywood Comedy* (London: Routledge, 1995), pp. 168–89

Roberts, Elizabeth, *A Woman's Place: An Oral History of Working Class Women 1890–1940* (London: Basil Blackwell, 1984)

Roberts, Lieut.-Col. F.J., *The Wipers Times* (London: Eveleigh Nash and Grayson, 1930)

Robertson, James C., *The British Board of Film Censors: Film Censorship in Britain, 1896–1950* (London: Croom Helm, 1985)

Robinson, David, *Chaplin: His Life and Art* (London: Da Capo Press, 1995)

——, *Chaplin, The Mirror of Opinion* (London: Secker and Warburg, 1984)

Rutherford, Lois, 'Harmless Nonsense: The Comic Sketch and the Development of Music Hall Entertainment', in J.S. Bratton, ed., *Music Hall: Performance and Style* (Milton Keynes: Open University Press, 1986), pp. 130–45

Sargent, Epes Winthrop, *Picture Theatre Advertising* (New York: The Moving Picture World, Chalmers Publishing Company, 1915)

Schickel, Richard, *D.W. Griffith and the Birth of Film* (London: Pavilion Books, 1984)

Scott, Derek, *The Singing Bourgeois: Songs of the Victorian Drawing Room and Parlour* (Milton Keynes: Open University Press, 1989)

Scott, Harold, *The Early Doors: Origins of the Music Hall* (London: Ivor Nicholson and Watson, 1946)

Sennett, Richard, *The Fall of Public Man* (Cambridge: Cambridge University Press, 1973)

Seton, Marie, 'War', *Sight and Sound*, vol. 6, no. 24 (Winter 1937–38), pp. 183–84

Shaw, George Bernard, 'Ellen Terry and Bernard Shaw: A Correspondence', in *Prefaces by George Bernard Shaw* (London: Odhams Press, 1938), pp. 780–95.

——, 'Preface to W.H. Davies' *The Autobiography of a Super-tramp*', in *Prefaces by George Bernard Shaw* (London: Odhams Press, 1938), pp. 796–99

Singer, Ben, 'Female Power in the Serial Queen Melodrama: The Etiology of an Anomaly', in Richard Abel, ed., *Silent Film* (London: Athlone, 1992), pp. 163–93

Sloan, Kay, *The Loud Silents: Origins of the Social Problem Film* (Urbana and Chicago: University of Chicago Press, 1988)

Sommerfield, Penny, 'Patriotism and Empire', in John MacKenzie, ed., *Imperialism an Popular Culture* (Manchester: Manchester University Press, 1986), pp. 17–48

Springhall, John, '"Up Guards and At Them!" British Imperialism and Popular Art, 1880–1914', in John MacKenzie, ed., *Imperialism and Popular Culture* (Manchester: Manchester University Press, 1986), pp. 49–72

Stacey, Jackie, *Star Gazing: Hollywood Cinema and Female Spectatorship* (London and New York: Routledge, 1994)

Staiger, Janet, *Interpreting Films: Studies in the Historical Reception of American Cinema* (Princeton, Princeton University Press, 1993)

——, 'Taboos and Totems: The Cultural Meanings of Silence of the Lambs', in Jim Collins, Hilary Radner and Ava Preacher Collins, eds, *Film Theory Goes to the Movies* (London: Routledge, 1993), pp. 142–54

——, *Bad Women: Regulating Sexuality in Early American Cinema* (Minneapolis: University of Minnesota Press, 1995) pp. 163–64

Stanfield, Peter, '"An Octoroon in the Kindling": American Vernacular and Blackface Minstrelsy in 1930s Hollywood', *Journal of American Studies* vol. 31, no. 3 (1998), pp. 407–38

Taylor, Lou, *Mourning Dress: A Costume and Social History* (London: George Allen and Unwin, 1983)

Thompson, F.M.L., *The Rise of Respectable Society: A Social History of Victorian Britain 1830–1900* (London: Fontana Press, 1988)

Thompson, Kristin, *Exporting Entertainment: America in the World Film Market, 1909–1934* (London: BFI, 1985)

Tranter, Neil, *Sport, Economy and Society in Britain: 1750–1914* (Cambridge: Cambridge University Press, 1998)

Tsivian, Yuri, *Early Cinema in Russia and its Cultural Reception*, trans. Alan Bodger (London: Routledge, 1994)

Turvey, Gerry, 'Weary Willie and Tired Tim Go into Pictures: The Comic Films of the British and Colonial Kinematograph Company', in Alan Burton and Laraine Porter, eds, *Pimple Pranks and Pratfalls: British Comedy Before 1930* (Trowbridge: Flicks Books, 2000), pp. 59–75

Uricchio, William, and Roberta E. Pearson, *Reframing Culture: The Case of the Vitagraph Quality Films* (Princeton: Princeton University Press, 1993)

Van Dooren, Ine, and Peter Kramer, 'The Politics of Direct Address', in Karel Dibbets and Bert Hogenkamp, eds, *Film and the First World War* (Amsterdam: University of Amsterdam Press, 1995), pp. 97–107

Vasey, Ruth, *The World According to Hollywood, 1918–1939* (Madison: University of Wisconsin Press, 1996)

Waller, Gregory A., *Mainstreet Amusements: Movies and Commercial Entertainment in a Southern City, 1896–1930* (Washington and London: Smithsonian Institution Press, 1995)

Weeks, Jeffrey, *Sex, Politics and Society: The Regulation of Sexuality since 1800* (New York: Longman, 1981)

Whaley, Joachim, ed., *Mirrors of Mortality: Studies in the Social History of Death* (London: Europe, 1981)

White, Bill, Jemima, Sheila and Hyslop, Donald, *Dream Palaces: Going to the Pictures in Southampton* (Southampton: Southampton City Council, 1996)

Williams, David R., *Cinema in Leicester: 1896–1931* (Loughborough: Heart of Albion Press, 1993)

Williams, Emlyn, *George, An Early Autobiography* (London: Hamish Hamilton, 1961)

Williams, Raymond, *The Politics of Modernism:Against the New Conformists* (London: Verso, 1989)

Winslow, D. Forbes, *Daly's: The Biography of a Theatre* (London, W.H. Allen, 1944).

Winter, Jay, *The Great War and the British People* (London: MacMillan Education, 1985)

——, *Sites of Memory, Sites of Mourning: The Great War in European Cultural History* (Cambridge: Cambridge University Press, 1995)

Wood, Mrs Henry, *East Lynne*, ed. by Norman Page and with an introduction by Kamal Al-Solaylee (London: Everyman, 1994)

Zeiger, Susan, 'She Didn't Raise her Boy to be a Slacker: Motherhood, Conscription, and the Culture of the First World War', *Feminist Studies*, vol. 2 (Spring 1996), pp. 6–39

Unpublished Theses

Burrows, Jonathan, '"The Whole English Stage To Be Seen For Sixpence": Theatre Stars in British Cinema, 1908–1918', unpublished PhD thesis, University of East Anglia, 2000

Hiley, Nicholas, 'Making War: The British News Media and Government Control, 1914–16', unpublished PhD thesis, Open University, 1985

Horrall, Andrew, 'Music Hall, Transportation and Sport: Up to Dateness in London Popular Culture 1890–1914', unpublished PhD thesis, Faculty of History, University of Cambridge, 1997

Filmography

The Adventures of Kathlyn (Serial) (US, Selig Polyscope Co., d. Francis J. Gordon, 1913)

Alone in London (UK, Ideal, d. Harold Shaw, 1915)

Battle of the Ancre and the Advance of the Tanks (UK, War Office Cinematograph Committee, 1917)

Battle of the Somme (UK, War Office Cinematograph Committee, 1916)

The Better 'Ole (UK, Welsh, Pearson and Co., d. George Pearson, 1918)

The Birth of a Nation (US, Epoch Production Co., d. D.W. Griffith, 1915)

Britain Prepared (UK, War Office Cinematograph Committee, 1915)

Broken in the Wars (UK, Hepworth Mfg. Co., d. Cecil Hepworth, 1918)

Bulldog Grit (UK, Burlingham Drama, d. Ethyle Batley, 1917)

Civilization (US, Triangle Productions, d. Reginald Barker and Thomas Ince, 1916)

A Feud in the Kentucky Hills (US, Biograph, d. D.W. Griffith, 1912)

Hearts of the World (US/UK, Famous, Players-Lasky, prod. D.W. Griffith, War Office Cinematograph Committee, d. D.W. Griffith, 1918)

Her Greatest Performance (UK, Ideal, d. Fred Paul, 1916)

History of the War: Ypres (UK, Pathé, 1917)

The Informer (US, Biograph, d. D.W. Griffith, 1912)

Intolerance (US, Triangle Productions and Wark Producing Corp. d. D.W. Griffith, 1916)

The Lure of Drink (UK, Barker, d. A.E. Coleby, 1915)

The Man Who Came Back (UK, Regent, 1915)

The Massacre (US, Biograph, d. D.W. Griffith, 1912)

The Mystic Glove (UK, Bamforth, d. unknown, 1914)

The Mysteries of London (UK, Colonial Pictures, d. A.E. Coleby, 1915)

Recruits (UK, 1915) NFTVA lists this under the title *Recruiting for the 5th Essex*

Trilby (UK, London Film Co., d. Harold Shaw, 1914)

Tubby's Rest Cure (UK, Hepworth Mfg. Co., d. Frank Wilson, 1916)

Tubby's Typewriter (UK, Hepworth Mfg. Co., d. Frank Wilson, 1916)

War Neurosis: Netley, 1917, Seale Hayne Military Hospital, 1918 (UK, d. unknown, 1918)

What's the Use of Grumblin'? (UK, Ministry of Information, d. unknown, 1918)

Whitewashing the Ceiling (UK, Cricks and Martins, d. Will Evans 1912)

Chaplin Films

Making a Living (US, Keystone, d. Henry Lehrman, 1914)

Kid's Auto Races (US, Keystone, d. Henry Lehrman, 1914)

A Film Johnny (US, Keystone, d. George Nichols, 1914)

A Busy Day (US, Keystone, d. Charles Chaplin, 1914)

Dough and Dynamite (US, Keystone, d. Charles Chaplin, 1914)

Twenty Minutes of Love (US, Keystone, d. Charles Chaplin, 1914)

Those Love Pangs (US, Keystone, d. Charles Chaplin, 1914)

In The Park (US, Essanay, d. Charles Chaplin, 1915)

Champion Charlie (US, Essanay, d. Charles Chaplin, 1915)

The Tramp (US, Essanay, d. Charles Chaplin, 1915)

Charlie's Elopement (US, Essanay, d. Charles Chaplin, 1915)

By the Sea (US, Essanay, d. Charles Chaplin, 1915)

The Bank (US, Essanay, d. Charles Chaplin, 1915)

One A.M. (US, Mutual, d. Charles Chaplin, 1916)

The Vagabond (US, Mutual, d. Charles Chaplin, 1916)

Police (US, Mutual, d. Charles Chaplin, 1916)

Easy Street (US, Mutual, d. Charles Chaplin, 1916)

The Immigrant (US, Mutual, d. Charles Chaplin, 1916)

Chase Me Charlie (US, Mutual, d. Charles Chaplin, 1917)

The Floorwalker (US, Mutual, d. Charles Chaplin, 1916)

The Cure (US, Mutual, d. Charles Chaplin, 1916)

The Pawnshop (US, Mutual, d. Charles Chaplin, 1916)

A Dog's Life (US, First National, d. Charles Chaplin, 1918)

The Bond (US, First National, d. Charles Chaplin, 1918)

Shoulder Arms (US, First National, d. Charles Chaplin, 1918)

Pimple Films

Pimple's Wonderful Gramophone (UK, Phoenix, d. Fred and Joe Evans, 1913)

Pimple's Motorbike (UK, Phoenix, d. Fred and Joe Evans, 1913)

Pimple's Battle of Waterloo (UK, Phoenix, d. Fred and Joe Evans, 1913)

Pimple's Charge of the Light Brigade (UK, Phoenix Films, d. Fred and Joe Evans, 1914)

Pimple Enlists (UK, Phoenix, d. Fred and Joe Evans, 1914)

Pimple's Trilby (UK, Phoenix, d. Fred and Joe Evans, 1914)

Pimple; Special Constable (UK, Phoenix, d. Fred and Joe Evans, 1915)

Pimple Has One (UK, Phoenix, d. Fred and Joe Evans, 1915)

Pimple in the Whip (UK, Ideal, d. Fred and Joe Evans, 1917)

Roll of Honour Films (held at the NFTVA, London)

West Houghton Roll of Honour Films (UK, unknown, 1915)

First Section: 4th Loyal North Lancashires Roll of Honour Film (Will Onda's Pictures, 1915)

Preston and District Roll of Honour (UK, Will Onda's Pictures, 1915)

Index